NOTHING EVER HAPPENS TO THE BRAVE

OTHER   BOOKS   BY

CARL   ROLLYSON

Marilyn Monroe: A Life of the Actress

Lillian Hellman: Her Legend and Her Legacy

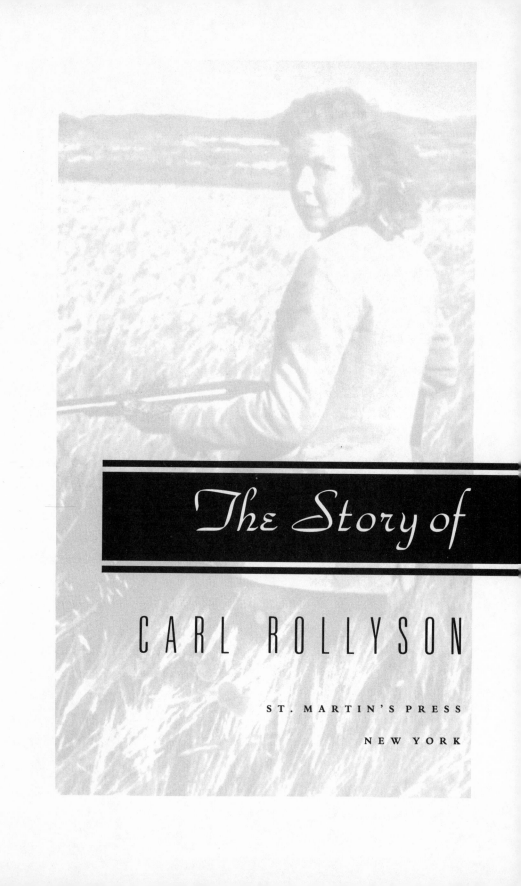

The Story of

CARL ROLLYSON

ST. MARTIN'S PRESS

NEW YORK

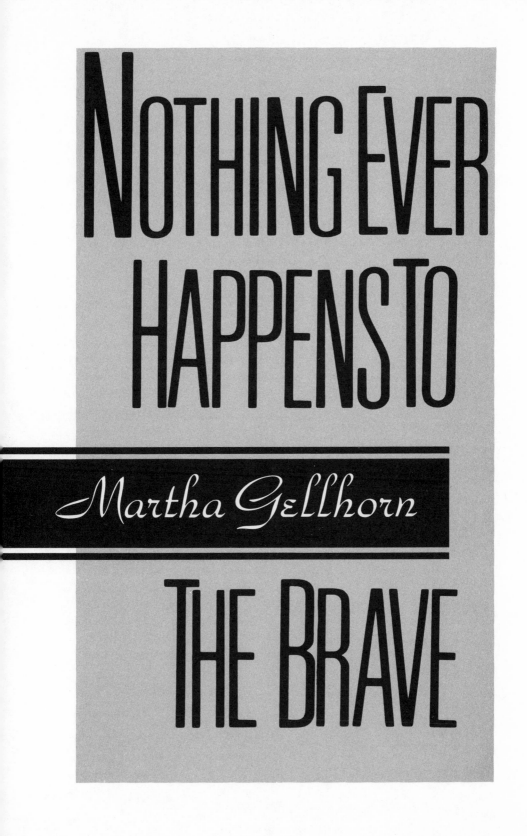

NOTHING EVER HAPPENS TO

Martha Gellhorn

THE BRAVE

EDITOR: TONI LOPOPOLO

DESIGN BY BARBARA M. BACHMAN

Library of Congress Cataloging-in-Publication Data

Rollyson, Carl E. (Carl Edmund)
     Nothing ever happens to the brave : the story of Martha
          Gellhorn / Carl Rollyson.
          p.   cm.
     ISBN 0-312-05125-5
     1. Gellhorn, Martha, 1908-   —Biography.   2. Hemingway,
     Ernest, 1899-1961—Biography—Marriage.   3. Novelists,
American—20th century—Biography.   4. Journalists—United
States—Biography.
     I. Title.
PS3513.E46Z84   1990
070.4'333'092—dc20
     [B]   90-37291
                                                              CIP

FIRST EDITION: NOVEMBER 1990

10 9 8 7 6 5 4 3 2 1

TO LISA

"We really are the same one and we musn't
misunderstand on purpose."
"We won't."
"But people do. They love each other and they
misunderstand on purpose and they fight and then suddenly
they aren't the same one."
"We won't fight."
"We musn't. Because there's only us two and in the
world there's all the rest of them. If anything comes
between us we're gone and then they have us."
"They won't get us," I said. "Because you're too brave.
Nothing ever happens to the brave."

—ERNEST HEMINGWAY
A Farewell to Arms

Contents

PROLOGUE

August 8, 1989: It was getting on toward sunset, the sky turning into darker hues of blue merging into vivid pockets of light, the green countryside subsiding into shadows. I was beginning to doubt that I would be able to take the photograph of Catscradle that appears in this book. I had never been to Wales and had only the vaguest address to go by. Ron and Beryl Gadd, who have lived in Wales all of their lives, were driving my wife and me through Chepstow, where we hoped to find Martha Gellhorn's cottage. In Chepstow, Ron pulled over to the side of the road, and Beryl began asking people whether they had heard of Catscradle, which was supposed to be in New Church West. No one recognized it, but Beryl persisted— on one occasion getting out of the car to ask for directions at a home with a fiercely barking dog. I watched her from the comfort of my backseat, deciding not to test the dog's intentions. After some confused consultation of a map at the Gwent Constabulary and a discussion with a friendly constable, we set off on the road to Shirenewton, which we were assured would take us to New Church West. On the way—certain that we had gone too far—we stopped at a pub. This time (thinking it was safe) I got out, curious to see the interior. No one had heard of Catscradle, but we were on the road to New Church West all right, and they did have places with names such as Catscradle—"the Rampant Cat and such." Another stop: We approached a home with what sounded like a very large dog barking loudly behind a door. I stood behind Beryl as she knocked. After several seconds, a friendly woman appeared, and I finally found my tongue. "Does Martha Gellhorn live around here?" Her reply startled me, for I had not expected her first words to so exactly recall the way people react when they recognize the name: "The wife of the famous writer?"

Now it seemed just possible that I would come face-to-face with Martha Gellhorn. I had written her after I had started my biography, sent her my biography of Marilyn Monroe and a piece on William and Estelle Faulkner, and reminded her that she had replied to a letter about Lillian

Hellman I had sent her a year earlier. She responded with praise for my article on the Faulkners. I wrote well, but she did not believe writing about the personal lives of artists illuminated their art, and she did not think anyone's personal life was anybody else's business. As for her, she detested the idea of biography and planned to outlive as many of her biographers as possible, for she knew they would do a perfectly dreadful job on her life. Her answer to me was the same answer she gave to everyone: NO BIOGRAPHY. I was not to take it personally. I liked the letter very much and did not take it personally. I had just read all of her work, written a book proposal, and could not stop myself, at that point, from writing more about her. I drafted a reply to Gellhorn's letter, marshaling arguments in favor of the kind of biography I thought she would like, and then I never sent the letter, for I realized that the point was not to please her but simply to write my book. As David Roberts, Jean Stafford's biographer, says: "The truest biography is not likely to please its subject."

To say that Gellhorn is not pleased is to put it mildly. She almost never grants interviews, but in the April 1988 issue of *Vogue* she took the trouble to chat with Victoria Glendinning, who informs us that Gellhorn is "doing her damndest to make sure there will never, ever, be a biography of Martha Gellhorn." Gellhorn went on to say that there is an "academic kook" (me) who is attempting a biography anyway:

I'm writing around asking anyone he might approach to tell him to sod off. I hate modern biographies of writers who are not public figures and not fair game. The only thing biographers are interested in are your love affairs and your eccentricities. A writer should be read, not written about. I wish to retain my lifelong obscurity.

This from a woman whose glamorous photo has appeared on the cover of *The Saturday Review* and on numerous book jackets, who lived a spotlighted period with Ernest Hemingway, including a filmed appearance in a Hedda Hopper documentary. *Collier's* magazine went out of its way to advertise and to feature Gellhorn as their blond and beautiful war correspondent; Eleanor Roosevelt made Gellhorn the focus of several of her "My Day" nationally syndicated newspaper columns; and Gellhorn herself has fictionalized and dramatized her experience, including her "eyewitness" account of a lynching that (she confessed to Mrs. Roosevelt) she made up. In the *Vogue* interview, Gellhorn spoke simultaneously about her "lifelong obscurity" and her status as "an historic monument." How many obscure figures get an interview published in *Vogue*?

If I had any doubts about pursuing a biography of Gellhorn, they were laid to rest when I received a letter from Bill Buford, editor of *Granta,* a curious choice to serve as Gellhorn's emissary. He is legendary for the high-handed way he treats his authors, as Gellhorn herself suggested in a recent issue of *Vanity Fair:*

"He did something absolutely terrible to me, and everyone thought I'd never forgive him. He simply stole something from my book, *The View from the Ground,* which was being published in America. He claims he asked me. But when I do business, I expect a letter or something. He just pinched a part of the book and put it in the magazine. I seriously thought of killing him, but I was too busy." So she sued? "Don't be ridiculous! I called him a monster, a creep, and told everyone I'd never speak to him again. Then came the big bouquet of flowers and the abject letter of apology, full of lies of course. And I was back talking to him within three weeks."

Writing on Gellhorn's behalf, Buford expressed his dismay that I was going ahead with my biography. Didn't I know that there was an authorized biography in the works? This was news, especially since it did not square with anything Gellhorn has said about her loathing of biographies. None of the people I had interviewed had heard of an authorized biographer, and I was troubled only by the suspicion that Gellhorn might be behaving like Lillian Hellman—wanting a handpicked man or woman to write the official, uncontested version of her life. At any rate, the very suggestion that someone else might be doing a biography spurred me on.

Yet on the road to Catscradle (after I had finished a draft of the biography), I was gripped by a sense of unreality. Would I have to go home and tell my editor that I had not been able to find Gellhorn's cottage? One last stop—because we were sure that we had somehow gone past it. No, a neighbor told Beryl, Catscradle was just ahead. The neighbor did not think anyone was at home; the car had been gone all day.

A hundred feet ahead, we found the tidy white cottage, serene in its white-railed enclosure, sitting upon flat, greenish tan ground. It was precisely the kind of quiet, modest hideaway I would expect Gellhorn to have. I started taking photographs from the road. "Aren't you going to go in?" Ron asked.

"I don't think there's anyone home," I almost gasped, expecting any moment that a car would pull up and Gellhorn would ask me what I was doing on her property.

As we approached the cottage, my wife had been giving me glances that put the question: What are you going to do? What will you say?

Ron opened the gate, and I walked in. It was just like writing her biography. Once I had begun, I could not stop. I took close-ups and shots from various angles. It was getting dark and many of the photographs, I knew, would give only a dim view of the surroundings. I imagine that every biographer, sooner or later, has this feeling of being at once so near and yet so far away from his or her subject. As we drove away, I took a photograph of the road sign pointing to Kilgwrrwg, the place name Gellhorn had put at the end of her book *The View from the Ground*.

So I have never met Martha Gellhorn. I have had to work from the outside in, so to speak, fashioning a character the way Olivier said he did—finding the right tone of voice, the clothing, the makeup—all the externals that give evidence of personality. I visited the John Burroughs School, which had such an important influence on Gellhorn, walked its hallways, sat in its classrooms, and spoke with Gellhorn's classmates. I made several visits to St. Louis, the city that shaped her early life. Gellhorn has always denied its important place in her life; she has always wanted to be from somewhere else. She gives St. Louis only a sentence in her *Vogue* interview, so naturally I was curious as to why she disparages her hometown. This, I take it, is the difference between autobiography and biography. The biographer looks for, in Leon Edel's words, "the figure under the carpet, the evidence in the reverse of the tapestry, the life-myth of a given mask."

Gellhorn is a highly theatrical personality, and she has worn many masks: "more or less Junior League . . . with a touch of exquisite Paris clothes and 'esprit' thrown in"; the intrepid reporter covering virtually every major conflict from the Spanish Civil War to Vietnam; the expatriate and polished novelist of manners, at home in both European and American settings, commenting wryly on the complex state of modern marriage; the social activist fighting government bureaucracy and cheering on dissenters; the hilarious travel writer who sets off looking for paradise and finds herself trapped in "horror journeys"; the sexy, feisty Ernest Hemingway heroine—the only wife who ever walked out on him.

Much to Gellhorn's chagrin, it is always Hemingway we return to when we recognize her. This is not simply because her marriage to him was the most celebrated part of her life. Gellhorn hates Hemingway, yet she has modeled herself after his early characters. Her favorite book is *A Farewell to Arms,* the story of a courageous couple confronting the world. Having read Hemingway in high school, having played the game of love with him, sometimes pursuing him, sometimes letting herself be pursued, she was aghast at their marriage, when she had to play helpmate to "Papa" and become "the wife." She wanted her life to be the Hemingway fiction she had read. She has never escaped the bitterness of his fall from grace.

I began this book after reading several biographies of Hemingway, none of which captured Gellhorn's comic and prickly character. I wondered about the subordinate place she had had to take in books about him. What would she look like in a book devoted to herself? This is a seductive question for a biographer, one that I could not let alone.

Like all great biographical subjects, mine is a mass of contradictions. Like other larger-than-life figures, she combines opposing principles. Behind her masks, however, there is a life-myth—a surprising one: No one, I daresay, would link Huckleberry Finn and Martha Gellhorn in the same thought. What has this Bryn Mawr–educated, exquisitely dressed woman—still beautiful in her eighties—to do with that unkempt, uneducated boy who loved to sleep in a barrel? They share no less than a profound argument with civilization. Gellhorn left the comforts of St. Louis and a doctor's family, the privileges of Bryn Mawr, and the security of marriage to constantly launch out on her own, to light out for the territory. Underneath her now perfectly modulated British accent lurks the wayward child, subversive of authority, not really comfortable anywhere, spoiling for a new adventure.

Part One

... TO BELONG TO THE BIG WORLD.

St. Louis

1 8 6 0 – 1 9 2 3

n 1908, the year Martha Gellhorn was born, her native city was undergoing a campaign of moral and civic renewal. The impetus for much of this improvement came after more than a decade of discussion and planning for the St. Louis World's Fair of 1904. That year, Martha's mother, Edna, became involved in one of her first major projects: cleaning up the city's water supply in preparation for the fair's Louisiana Purchase Exposition. St. Louis wanted to celebrate a century of growth and to commemorate President Jefferson's acquisition of a new territory that stimulated the settlement of land and the development of a new civilization.

In fact, the city had been seriously damaged by the Civil War. It took more than a generation to recover its position as a major trading center, and by the turn of the century it faced stiff competition from Chicago, which had surpassed St. Louis in population, industrial output, and trade. The World's Fair, then, was a bid to recoup some of the economic strength St. Louis had lost, to regenerate the glory of its myth as the gateway to the West, and to deliver on promises of progress that had never been fulfilled.

Martha Gellhorn grew up in this atmosphere of agitation for a better life. Her mother was a suffragette who believed in big demonstrations, in getting things done with a certain flair. It was not enough to be in favor of good causes; you had to dramatize your point and make people pay attention. There was the time, for example, when Edna was raising funds for a new hospital. She hit upon the idea of parading eight elephants through town to attract the public to a concession booth selling peanuts she had begged from merchants. She certainly caught the community's interest, especially when the herd got separated and the event turned into a "big game hunt."

As a small child, Martha was included in her mother's public activities, in large meetings and parades for women's suffrage. Martha rode on floats festooned with slogans championing the cause and pointing to her as "the spirit of the future."

For the Democratic Convention held at St. Louis in June 1916, Edna helped to organize seven thousand women decked out in yellow parasols and sashes proclaiming VOTES FOR WOMEN. They lined both sides of what became known as "The Golden Lane," the streets that led to the convention center. Although the men along the route made fun of the women, Edna had made her point. As she told a reporter in 1963, "we had a tableau." Different groups of women were dressed in white, gray, and black (the black ones dragging chains)—representing states that had suffrage, partial suffrage, or no suffrage for women. In the front row, representing future voters, were two little girls, one of whom was Martha Gellhorn.

Martha's family had deep roots in St. Louis's tradition of community service and reform. She was named after her maternal grandmother, Martha Ellis, whose family descended from English settlers. Martha Ellis's father, Turner Morehead Ellis, was born in Kentucky in 1808, and had become a commission merchant (traveling salesman). Born on May 25, 1850, in Jackson, Mississippi, Martha Ellis lost her mother when she was only five, and was cared for on a nearby plantation by her aunt and uncle and a "personal attendant." She had no white playmates, and all her early education took place on the plantation and in a private school— except for the times when she accompanied her father in "memorable excursions on river boats" to St. Louis, where he decided to settle in 1860.

Enrolled in a St. Louis public school during the Civil War, Martha Ellis reacted sharply to the divided loyalties expressed by her fellow students. In her first act of public protest, she marched back and forth outside of a federal prison, defiantly displaying a Confederate flag. While still a child, she found herself in the heady milieu of a frontier capital and border state full of the remnants of its founding French families, Southern sympathizers, and reform-minded immigrants, especially German liberals who had fled Europe after the failed democratic revolutions of 1848.

Although Martha Ellis grew up as the child of a lost cause, she quickly absorbed the elements of the progressive atmosphere surrounding her and rejected the status quo. Her family was part of a nineteenth-century genteel society that she steadily and shrewdly undermined. She began by becoming a teacher—virtually an unheard-of act for a woman of her social prominence. If you were from a good family, you did not work. Exceptions were made for poor women, but even then the preferred option was passivity. It was better to pine away in poverty than to push your way into the cruel, hard world. As a newspaper account of her life put it, Martha Ellis was "one of the first of social standing to earn her own living." She did it gradually: Taking care not to embarrass her family, she found her first position in a small country school, teaching English language and customs to Russian refugees. After two years at schools in Florissant and Bellefontaine, Missouri, she became principal of Howard College—the female auxiliary of Central Methodist College—before returning to St. Louis to teach in the public schools. Assigned to a school in north St. Louis, she had the taxing experience of teaching ninety-three six-year-old children, none of whom could speak or understand English. Her diction and platform presence were impressive. Like her daughter and granddaughter, she had a gift for words that could spur people to action.

In 1876, Martha Ellis married Washington Emil Fischel, a native of St. Louis whose family had come from Prague. As the most important internist in St. Louis, Dr. Fischel soon established himself as a distinguished physician who was known for his liberal political and ethical convictions. A professor in clinical medicine at Washington University, he was the "founder and president of the medical staff of the Barnard Free Skin and Cancer Hospital." He was esteemed for his devotion to patients "rich and poor." Dr. Fischel died in 1914, before his granddaughter's sixth birthday; but he was always alive in her grandmother's mind. Martha Gellhorn remembered that her grandmother called him "Wash" and spoke of him as if he were still alive and simply out of town. She wanted her granddaughter to know what a good doctor he had been and how fond people were of him. They had had confidence in his judgment, and had enjoyed his humor and good temper. Martha came away with the impression of a grandfather who was eternally youthful and who brought fun to everything he did.

Martha Ellis profoundly believed in self-culture and conscience. In her day, there were no social workers, so she had to go about inventing her own "home-making classes" for the poor. She visited schools, picking out the students who seemed "most neglected." From the teachers, she got the names and addresses of parents. More often than not, she would find a student's mother lying about in a "dirty house." Would it be all right if the child came to the settlement house on Saturday? she would ask the mother, who was usually grateful to be relieved of family responsibilities. Then Martha Ellis would invite her female friends to help teach these children and to treat them as they would their own offspring. In borrowed facilities (a room over a bakery), she set up a cook stove, kitchen equipment, and bedroom and living room furniture, so that children could be instructed in how to prepare and serve meals and how to make an attractive, well-planned home. Eventually, these classes became the basis of the home-economics curriculum in the St. Louis public schools.

For both Martha Ellis and her daughter, Edna, every good deed radiated from the home. Reviewing her life in 1938, just months before she died, Martha Ellis told a reporter for the St. Louis *Globe-Democrat* that "she never undertook public work which would require considerable time away from her family without first consulting her husband and children." She also revolutionized what could be accomplished at home, for example establishing in the early 1880s the Shelley Club, thirty-two women devoted to analyzing every aspect of the poet's life and work. This meant addressing Shelley's atheism and radical political views and incurring severe criticism in St. Louis, where it was thought such subjects were not "fit for discussion in polite society." Undaunted by this disapproval, she organized the Wednesday Club, a group of one hundred women who began by discussing cultural and literary topics but soon became involved in various welfare projects.

Before she married, Martha Ellis was present at the meetings of the earliest suffragettes. She believed in "equal pay for equal work," but in her own words, she "deferred to my husband in not flaunting my views on the subject. Dr. Fischel admitted the principle of the thing, but he feared results that might lead to the lessening of home ties." Edna became her mother's pride when she took up the battle for women's rights, while remaining firmly devoted to her St. Louis home. As Martha Ellis put it, "My light shines through my daughter."

In 1939, Martha Gellhorn wrote a memorial tribute to her grandmother. She recalled the epitaph Martha Ellis had put on the gravestone of her dearly beloved husband: *Ich Dien*—I serve. That was her grandmother's credo, Gellhorn explained: You should help others, especially if you are safe and secure, and well sheltered and educated. There is no question that Martha Gellhorn saw herself as her grandmother's image, for she used virtually the same words to describe Mary Douglas in *A Stricken Field*, who feels she must "pay back" her privileges and good luck by helping refugees fleeing Hitler's persecution.

Martha's urge to see the world came from her father. George Gellhorn, born in Breslau, Germany, was educated at the *Gymnasium* in Ohlau, received his M.D. from the University of Würzburg in 1894, and served as an assistant in clinics at the universities of Berlin, Jena, and Vienna. Respected as a bright young man in the German medical community, Gellhorn also had ambitions as a scientist, and for a time he served as an assistant to Wilhelm Conrad Roentgen, a Nobel Prize winner (1901) noted for his research in physics and famous for his discovery of the X ray.

George Gellhorn was an antimilitarist who was profoundly disturbed by the rise of Prussianism. Possessed with an overwhelming desire to travel, and with letters of introduction to distinguished professors in the American medical establishment, Gellhorn embarked on a trip that he hoped might well help him to decide how to pursue his dual careers in science and in medicine. It was typical of him, however, then to take a detour by becoming a ship's doctor. He sailed the world for a few years before landing in the United States in 1899.

Gellhorn had no plans to stay in St. Louis, but one of his letters of introduction was to Washington Fischel, who had studied at the universities of Prague, Vienna, and Berlin for two years after obtaining his medical degree from St. Louis Medical College in 1871. These two men of medicine and science shared many of the same political and ethical convictions; more importantly, they admired each other. Soon Fischel was urging Gellhorn to stay: St. Louis needed men like him.

Martha's story of her parents' first meeting is colored by a romantic vision of Edna gliding down a center stairway, the light of a stained-glass window showering her golden hair with highlights. George Gellhorn was bewitched by her charm, which she was said to have inherited from her father, and he resolved on the spot to marry Edna. It took him three years to convince her (a telling part of the story for Martha, who always had her doubts about marriage).

George Gellhorn was proud and supportive of Edna's accomplishments. He liked to accompany her to speaking engagements on behalf of women's suffrage and "nod approvingly." He was a distinguished gynecologist and obstetrician, and he never made his wife or his family feel that his career was more important than Edna's participation in social causes and civic organizations. He gave a considerable amount of his time to establishing free prenatal clinics and other medical services for the poor. Dr. Gellhorn was often called away from home on night calls or for emergency surgery. When he was not practicing medicine, he would study and write at home in the evening, with his children often emulating his example.

Dr. Gellhorn's strong support of his wife's public service had much to do with his sophistication. He was well read, had a command of five languages, and a deep appreciation of good music. As a young man, he taught himself Portuguese on a ship headed for Brazil. Many years later, he was able to call on his powerful memory and read a Portuguese medical text to resolve a scholarly question.

Martha believes she was extraordinarily fortunate to have grown up with her three brothers, George, Walter, and Alfred, in a "loving, merry, stimulating" home. At the dinner table, they listened to talk of distinguished guests such as Herbert Hoover, who visited the Gellhorn home during World War I when Edna became prominent in the War Food Administration. The Gellhorn children also found themselves present at debates over the League of Nations. Walter remembers being taken to hear Senator William Borah, Woodrow Wilson, and others, who were stumping the country in favor of the league.

George Gellhorn was not a casual or easygoing parent in the contemporary American sense. Martha describes him as having "set icily high standards. 'Isn't there anything *better*?'" he asked her when she brought home a report card with all A's. His children had no trouble confiding in him, however; indeed, Walter enjoyed conversations with his father in the course of his hospital and home visits to patients.

George Gellhorn was a little taken aback by the forwardness of his children. He did not disapprove of their outspokenness—indeed, he had encouraged it—and yet he could not help but remark upon their openness and confess that he would never have dared to speak to his father using their terms. Everything George Gellhorn did had about it a kind of Germanic precision, although he was not stiff and his children did not feel awkward in his presence. It was like him to drive a car on his medical rounds while listening to Walter conjugating Latin verbs. He was the kind of father who helped his son with his algebra but who never scolded or reminded him about homework.

The most remarkable thing about the Gellhorn household was how permissive these parents seemed and how well their children behaved without any overt discipline. If Edna did not like what one of her children was doing, she would not criticize but would recommend something better to do. This was in accord with Martha Ellis Fischel's "substitution plan" for training children, which her daughter adapted to her own purposes:

> Instead of telling your child to stop what he is doing, suggest something else which he would like to do, instead. When he has picked up an article you do not want him to have, hold out to him something else which will engage his interest before you try to get him to relinquish what he holds. In this way, you will get through the day with as few "don'ts" as possible.

Edna practiced this code of child raising so consistently that it is doubtful she ever forbid her daughter anything—at least in so many words. She could not have been a more encouraging mother. According to Martha, Edna made her children feel they were "wonderful."

No typing by racial or ethnic epithets was allowed in the Gellhorn home. The worth of things was never to be measured in money, and the children were strictly forbidden to report gossip. Their opinions had to be based on what they had witnessed and thought about, not on what so and so had said or wondered. Family discussions followed *Robert's Rules of Order,* with George Gellhorn as Speaker. Disputes were resolved by consulting reference books.

The Gellhorns were not a religious family in the conventional sense. Martha's great-grandparents, Ephraim and Babette Fischel, were members of B'nai El, a small but very active Jewish congregation, and are buried in Mt. Sinai Cemetery in St. Louis. Their son, "Wash," and subsequent members of the family did not practice Judaism or identify themselves with specifically Jewish activities, although, like many Jewish families, they became active in the St. Louis chapter of the Ethical Society, founded in New York City in 1876 by Felix Adler, to promulgate "the supreme importance of the ethical factor in all relations of life, personal, social, national, and international, apart from any theological or metaphysical considerations."

George Gellhorn had concluded that he could not reconcile his scientific research with the tenets of religion. Characteristically, he did not try to sway others to his views and exhibited no hostility toward believers.

On the contrary, his children often found themselves in the company of a great-aunt, Sister Miriam, who had once been an Episcopal nun and who was notorious for her fierce, narrow-minded piety. Born Susan Mary Ellis, Sister Miriam (Martha Ellis's sister) had done missionary work in Baden, "instituting Sunday School classes for children of laundresses at the school" and establishing a "Peace Mission" in St. Louis. She had a rugged dedication the community admired: "I have encountered her far from home at all seasons of the year, all hours of the night. Dark alleys, miserable hovels, lonely county roads, river front jungles, held no terrors for her. She was never afraid," a doctor said of her. She was frequently at the Gellhorn home for Sunday dinner, present through the courtesy of some member of the family who had driven far out into the country to get her. This bigoted woman was absolutely devoted to the Gellhorns, as they were to her, and she never seemed uncomfortable with this group of infidels. Somewhere in her constricted view of things, she had found a treasured place for them. She once admitted to Walter that his parents led such sainted lives that it was a pity they were not Christians. When the astounded child asked her to explain herself, she simply pointed out that the family never received Holy Communion.

Walter and Martha did attend an Ethical Society Sunday school for a few years, and their brother George quickly gained his parents' permission to attend the Episcopal Sunday school, where so many of his friends were to be found. Neither Walter nor Martha seemed especially interested in ethical instruction; sometimes they would play hooky and buy candy with the donations they were supposed to make to the Ethical Society.

As a child, Martha sensed how peculiar her parents were in comparison to their contemporaries. Her mother had not only gone to college—unusual in itself for a woman of her era—she was a Bryn Mawr graduate. She had been east, and that alone was enough to provoke gossip. Then there was Martha's nonconformist father, who refused to join a country club when he learned that all they did was play golf. He wanted it known that he got plenty of exercise walking and did not need more of it swinging at a golf ball. In fact, he was opposed to exclusive clubs; he revered the works of Abraham Lincoln and Thomas Jefferson, and such clubs in his view were undemocratic. Martha claims the Gellhorns were the only important family in St. Louis not to join.

It was hard not to be considered a part of the upper class if your father was a doctor, Martha admits, but no one could mistake the singularity of the Gellhorns. Terribly fond of classical concerts in his native Germany, George Gellhorn relished the food available at intermission. It was his conviction that a pastry fortified the concertgoer and enhanced the pleasure of the remainder of the program. Alas, St. Louis concerts were without nourishment, a deficiency he rectified by bringing his own provisions. His daughter was a little abashed by his deviation from community norms, but she had been taught to act independently of what other people did, and it was not supposed to matter if one's behavior differed from everyone else's.

The Gellhorns were cosmopolitan individualists. They liked to travel with their children cross-country and to Europe. These trips delighted Martha and encouraged her craving for foreign and exotic lands. St. Louis cramped her style. Lighting out for the territory would become the essential story of her very American life.

MOTHER AND

DAUGHTER

1 8 9 4 – 1 9 2 4

At Washington University's Mary Institute, Edna Fischel received the best primary education available for her time. Her reading classes emphasized "clear enunciation." Geography, arithmetic, singing, drawing, writing, calisthenics, and lessons in French were part of her curriculum, which downplayed "mechanical drill and text book routine in favor of methods which are at once more modern and more stimulating to the minds of children." Teachers tried to make grammar "entertaining," and natural science classes encouraged "the powers of observation." Composition exercises were based on topics of interest to the students. Edna was very much the product of a school that believed in the "development of the whole child," and that had liberalized and broadened its courses under a succession of headmasters.

Edna was elected president of her class and was treated with great affection by her classmates. To hear her tell it, there was nothing precocious about her opinions, in spite of the fact that her home received constant visits from men and women at the forefront of social change. When Stanton Coit, leader of the Ethical Culture Society in England, took up the subject of feminism one evening in the Fischel home, young Edna blurted out, "But how can women find time to work for the vote? They have so much to do. It takes them ever so long just to put up their hair, for instance." "Let them cut it off, then," was Coit's decisive reply.

Edna's mother boldly decided to send her east to the Baldwin School in preparation for the following year at Bryn Mawr College. When Edna left St. Louis, "the entire class escorted her to the station and, in the fashion of young ladies of the era, wept copious tears." Four years later, she returned as an ardent advocate of women's rights and with an accent, "clear and unstrident and quite un-Midwestern." She behaved with such "natural and unconscious pride," however, that she won many people to her side. In 1903, visiting the Bryn Mawr campus for her third reunion, she was "trailed" by a group of sophomores who were immensely taken with

> this gorgeous creature. With her masses of golden braids and her blue eyes, she was like a tall, slim Norwegian princess. She wore a Gibson girl skirt and skirtwaist, and always had fresh violets tucked into her belt. It was said she was engaged to a German doctor, who sent her fresh flowers every day.

In her day, Edna had been the most popular student on campus and was "chosen lifetime president of her class." Later she was elected a trustee of the college and was consulted closely by M. Carey Thomas (one of the founders of the school), who wrote her long letters about the selection of a college president and other matters.

Edna was a beautiful woman with an unaffected interest in people. As T. S. Matthews, Martha's third husband, put it, Edna "wasn't the embattled clubwoman or the crusading social worker type at all." In fact, organizations per se did not appeal to her—even though she was always engaged in running them or shaking them up. When Edith January Davis asked her to be president of the Mary Institute Alumnae Association, she replied, "I can't. I have three little children." Most of the Mary Institute graduates had children, Davis pointed out. "But I'm a Suffragist," said Edna, thinking that this would disqualify her. "We can take that," Mrs. Davis assured her—although there was "quite a furor" when Edna brought Sylvia Pankhurst to the school to debate women's suffrage. The Mary Institute was evidently not quite ready to hear from a woman who defended unmarried mothers, attacked the institution of marriage, and herself later bore an illegitimate son.

For Edna, organizations were merely means to an end. As she once said to a neighbor, "political science will not get you very far." It was much better to model yourself after "priests and gangsters," who knew their own people well and got things done. There was never anything academic or snobbish about Edna; she was willing to learn from anyone.

Edna's personality helped her become the most adept of politicians. When she traveled the state in milk-train cabooses conducting voter-education classes, she struck a proper ladylike pose by pretending to knit, thus suggesting that she was never very far from home and that her public work was truly an extension of her domestic life. She kept a maternal eye on things; nothing escaped her. "Now I'm being your mother," she once said to a close female friend. "Your lipstick doesn't match your jacket."

Although she had a strong ego, Edna was selfless in pursuit of her causes and was legendary for never losing her temper. Avis Carlson remembers Edna's visit in 1931 to the struggling Wichita, Kansas, chapter of the League of Women Voters. During an all-day meeting, there had been a number of "grade A personality clashes." At the end of the day, Edna rose to address the gathering. She was now a woman in her fifties—still handsome and "full-blown," with the presence of a great actress. For many years now, she had worn her thick blond braids in a kind of coronet that enhanced the image of her authority. With her deep blue eyes, glowing face, and animated voice, she dazzled her audience. She spoke with both conviction and calculation, having perfected her platform persona over many years of traveling on behalf of the league.

Edna lobbied fiercely for her causes, but she saw no gain in alienating her opponents, for they might be useful as allies in some other campaign. Her correspondence file at Washington University is full of letters from prominent businessmen and politicians flattered by her solicitous letters and invitations to speak to the league or otherwise to contribute to the work of her organizations. She knew how to compliment people in power and to make them feel indispensable to her cause. Writing to Mr. Hornback, an officer of the St. Louis Ethical Society, she noted that sooner or later one had to go to him for an answer. Asking for someone's help usually became an occasion for acknowledging that person's importance.

On one occasion, it does seem that Edna lost her temper in public. To a state convention organized to raise funds from wealthy patrons for women's suffrage, Edna had invited a well-known speaker, who delivered an address on "Men, Women and Civilization." His remarks startled the assemblage: "Modern woman . . . has forfeited man's respect and love.

She is no longer an inspiration to artists. Can you imagine a bobbed-haired Madonna? Horrible thought!" His tirade was greeted by "a few polite hand claps" that broke the grim silence. Edna took the floor, and "without preface or apology she launched into a verbal lashing that fairly withered the gentleman. He squirmed in visible discomfort at the head table." Edna "fixed her gaze" on her male opponent and said, "Several times during the course of the speaker's address . . . I was tempted to let down my long hair and strangle him." The highly amused audience then watched "the speaker of the evening beat a retreat." It was later suggested that he was, in fact, presenting a "subtle satire." Whatever the truth of this incident, it is indicative of how Edna came to be portrayed as a stalwart, imaginative, and engaging leader who lost none of her femininity in pursuit of equal rights.

Virginia Deutch, whose mother, Tess Loeb, joined Edna in a campaign for a pure-milk ordinance in St. Louis, remembers that a newspaper ridiculed them as "Nosey Nellies among the cows." Male politicians might have made fun of Edna's social reformism—but not to her face. They wanted her good opinion and courted her support. "I was very much interested in getting some junior college legislation through in Jefferson City," Mrs. Aaron Fischer recalls:

> I felt I needed the vote of Senator Mike Kinney, a real old-time politician who was very influential. I asked Edna if she would go with me to see him. And she did. He sat there behind his desk and every minute the telephone rang and he did some chore for somebody or got money for somebody else. Behind him up on the wall was a bust of Napoleon. We told him what we wanted and how it was a wonderful thing that we hoped he would support. Many months later the junior college legislation passed, even though Kinney voted against it. When it was all over and we were going down in the elevator, Kinney said, "Now be sure to square me with Edna." And we said, "Why should we do that? You voted against it." And he said, "Ah, but I didn't work against it."

Kinney knew Edna would understand the politician's point—that he paid his respects to her power even when he could not support her on a particular piece of legislation. Both he and Edna realized there would be occasions when they would help each other out, so neither one could afford to offend the other.

There was an underlying sweetness in Edna. She blanched on one occasion when two of her colleagues engaged in an ugly quarrel. She was silent and seemed completely nonplussed by the incident. Personal animosity embarrassed her. T. S. Matthews marveled at how Edna had been able to be a good doctor's wife, a confident mother of "four inquiring and obstreperous children," and a civic reformer. She seemed a miracle of a human being, who combined in one person a serene, soothing tone with firm and unshakable convictions.

Edna did not demand her daughter to be just like her; rather, she expected Martha to be only herself. Each of her children, Edna pointed out, was expected to do his or her best. To this day, Martha has a portrait of Edna over her writing table, for she remains an ideal figure for her daughter, a mother who appealed to "human beings of all kinds" with warmth and generosity.

Edna was a very affectionate woman. As her son Walter remembered, she was happily married to a man who never felt the want of her companionship. "She runs as fast to meet me as when we were first married," George Gellhorn confided to a friend many years after his wedding day. The wonder is that she could care so much about other people and yet never neglect her family. Although her children engaged in normal kinds of "bickering," they never thought she played favorites. On the contrary, she was one of those rare people who seemed to proportion her life perfectly.

Unlike the children of many reformers who decry their parents' fanatical devotion to causes, Edna's children saw the fun, the sporting quality she put into her civic campaigns. She did not bring her social concerns home with her; they were always a part of her domestic life. Committee work in her home was not one of those obligations to be endured, but a joyful time to be "savored." One of her son Walter's first memories is of the "peels of laughter" emanating from her meetings. "She made it fun," one of her friends recalls. "Any kind of league meeting—especially in the evening—was a festive occasion." In Edna's causes, everyone had a part to play. Indeed, she was so good at engaging her children's interest that each thought "she or he had virtually singlehandedly achieved woman's suffrage and had founded the League of Women Voters."

As loving a mother as Edna was, there were aspects of her child rearing that made things difficult for her daughter in St. Louis. As little girls, Martha Gellhorn and Emily Lewis Norcross were best friends. Their families were also very close. The two mothers had gone to Bryn Mawr and then settled near each other in the same neighborhood. From a very early age, Emily was aware that Martha's mother was an outstanding, powerful person, a "doing woman." Although Emily's mother was a writer, active in civic affairs, she did not approach the prominence Edna had already attained. Even more striking was the fact that Martha seemed to be on her own much of the time.

"Marty's mother was away an awful lot," Emily recalls. "So Marty was very independent as a child." She did not have the "governed" homelife Emily and her friends enjoyed. "We all grew up in this little protected community, going to our debutante parties, having our fun, and Martha was not about to do that," Mary Taussig Hall recalls. Martha Love Symington was fascinated by how permissive Mrs. Gellhorn was with the only girl in the family: "Martha went along with her brothers doing anything they did." By the age of eleven or twelve, "she knew the whole city. And we weren't allowed to put our *feet* in busses—unless we were going to school and back." Already a strong personality, Martha was a "hell of a lot of fun." She read everything that came out and was way ahead of everyone else her age. At twelve, her vocabulary was terrific, and she was a sheer delight for her companion Emily, who also had taken up writing. It was already apparent, however, that Martha was "turning terribly against St. Louis."

"Marty's family was half-Jewish," Emily Lewis Norcross points out, "but they were accepted in St. Louis as Gentiles." When Delia Mares went to St. Louis in the mid-1930s and began to work closely with Edna Gellhorn, she remembers the family's Jewish background being mentioned. It was something of which people were conscious—even if they made no great issue of it. Indeed, Mary Taussig Hall—who has known Martha and her family since she was a child—never inquired very deeply into her own Jewishness, but there was a community feeling about it. Another of Martha's friends cannot remember anything being made at the Mary Institute of Martha's Jewishness, but she had to be aware that being Jewish was regarded "with a little more feeling in those days," as Emily Lewis Norcross delicately puts it:

> For instance, our Jewish girlfriends did not go to our dancing classes. They had their own thing. We had a couple of friends who were *intimate* pals, who we were devoted to, and Marty would often talk to me about how "isn't it sad that because they're Jewish . . ." I knew that Marty was part Jewish—

ROLLYSON: She never talked about it?
NORCROSS: *Never!*
ROLLYSON: Never?
NORCROSS: *Never!* This was a very telling thing.

When Emily Norcross and Martha Gellhorn were thirteen and four-teen, respectively, and whipping around to "gassy little Friday-night dancing classes," neither of them was very popular, Emily recalls: "Marty was overpowering to those little boys"; she did not make a debut the way most girls did, since her family "were really sort of above that, and didn't want it, but she missed it. *Really.* She missed it." Martha's parents were great citizens of St. Louis, but they certainly were not in the social mainstream.

Martha attended Mr. Mahler's dancing classes once a week during the winter season. William Julius Polk, one of her companions, cannot vouch for her attitude then, except that he is inclined to think she viewed places such as the Fortnightly Club askance:

It was an exercise in deportment and ballroom behavior. Everyone, in the sense of being everyone one knew, went to Mr. Mahler's dancing school. I think it's in Alexis de Tocqueville's study of the United States—when he comes to St. Louis, he says that in order to understand St. Louis you have to take into consideration the influence of the religion of the sacred heart and M. Sarpi's dancing academy.

"Nice girls" dreamed of pretty social affairs in Mahler's ballroom. "Every girl wants to have a ball, and many of them will have their desires granted," a social column observed.

This kind of niceness would not have appealed to Martha, who was always "slightly rebellious and slightly nonconformist. . . . When we were growing up we felt that St. Louis was somewhat midwestern and provincial. And she thought it would be more interesting to belong to the big world," Polk concludes.

Children her own age often found Martha peculiar. At Mary Institute, Martha remembers eating her lunch alone. No matter how self-reliant she was, it was painful to be shunned by her classmates. It was the period of the Great War, and feelings ran strongly against a child with a German last name and a family engaged in controversial activities. Martha Love Symington, who lived a few blocks from the Gellhorns, remembers that she and her friends used to march up and down the street singing "Kaiser

Bill went up the hill to take a look at France. And Kaiser Bill came down the hill with bullets in his pants."

Martha was an extraordinarily resourceful child who overcame most of this prejudice. Although, even when she could take comfort in close friends such as Emily Lewis Norcross, she could not help but notice that her very freedom from restrictions isolated her. "On Saturday let's go downtown on the streetcar and have lunch," she proposed to Emily. They were about twelve or thirteen at the time. Emily said, "Marty, I can't. I'm not allowed to go downtown alone." So they did something else around home. A week or two later at Mary Institute, a girl they did not know very well came up to them at recess and said, "Listen, tomorrow, Saturday, let's take the streetcar to town." "I'm not allowed to go into town alone," Marty said. It was then that Emily realized her friend was envious. Emily's parents had "certain rules and laws" that Martha would probably have disdained, yet the absence of this kind of discipline at a young age intensified her alienation.

It also made some difference that Martha was a doctor's child. Many of her friends came from business families. These people were not professionals; that is, most of them were not doctors or attorneys. The Gellhorns were not snobs about the world of commerce, but it was a fact that many of Martha's companions' families were less cultivated than her own and less committed to the general welfare. Her parents hosted their share of parties for Martha and her friends, but the Gellhorns did not indulge in many purely social affairs. Martha noticed this and developed a "slight chip . . . well, a sensitivity," as one of her friends puts it.

The first time Martha Gellhorn ever felt truly content and comfortable was during her vacation in Grenoble, France. She was sixteen and chaperoned by a female companion. The boys from Paris and Oxford appeared to be more mature and refined than St. Louis boys. In St. Louis, it did not take much to be popular—just carry a current tune while you danced. Only in France did she feel relaxed in conversation, discussing ideas freely as she had done in her parents' home. At school in St. Louis, children avoided this intellectual prodigy; in France, it was as if she had been welcomed home. What a delight it was to actually watch people weighing her opinions.

Martha also found European topography more appealing. The way city and country seemed to blend into each other was preferable to America's enormous discontinuities, its mountains, plains, and plateaus juxtaposed against cities Gellhorn considered ugly. Back in St. Louis, Martha bided her time, wondering when her life would really begin.

SPECIAL:

JOHN BURROUGHS SCHOOL

1923 – 1926

n the spring of 1923, when Martha Gellhorn completed the ninth grade at Mary Institute, there was no private coeducational school in St. Louis. Almost none of her friends went to the public schools. Instead, the boys went to Country Day, and the girls usually stayed to graduate from Mary Institute, which prided itself on its up-to-date curriculum, its practical and vocational training, its courses in "Civics and Social Problems," in mathematics, foreign languages, and English studies, and its small classes (one teacher for every fifteen pupils). Yet something more was wanted, something that would reflect "the new spirit in education." In the 1920s, "we came to call it progressive education and learning by doing," remarks Delia Mares, who went to St. Louis in 1933 to teach at the John Burroughs School.

Edna Gellhorn and like-minded parents decided to establish a new school where their children could "profit from the best that modern thought and practice had to offer." How to foster the enjoyment of learning and to stimulate "intellectual endeavor"—this was the task these parents set themselves. They were all too familiar with schools where a child was "dragooned to walk single file along corridors" or had to "eat his lunch in bleak silence."

Beginning in 1921, Edna was present (along with her mother) at most meetings for the new school, where she took minutes. A committee was organized to investigate other schools that might serve as models for their own. Edna visited her alma mater, Bryn Mawr, to ask the advice of its president, who convinced her the school should be coeducational. She took friends to dinner parties to discuss "The New School": "Each time we would bring a new guest to inoculate him!" she later recalled. The public received similar treatment: distinguished educators were invited to St. Louis to present lectures on the modern school. Dr. Otis W. Caldwell of Columbia University, for example, was quoted at length in a two-column report in the St. Louis *Globe-Democrat:*

> If we teach children to confer with one another on their subjects of study, we stimulate their understanding. . . . They can teach one another much faster than we can teach them.
>
> Then we are too apt to consider the school plant as existing for the excuse of arbitrary adult techniques. We should permit the children a co-operative part of the school management. I do not mean a pupil-governed school, but a co-operatively governed school.

Edna knew how to build constituencies for her causes, but she could not finesse everything, and soon the community of supporters was rent over the proposition that boys and girls go to school together. She remembered it was like civil war breaking out, "dividing family against family, children against parents, friend against friend." Some people withdrew their support of the school, horrified at the ruin it would make of education in St. Louis.

Edna and a strong group of supporters persevered. By 1922, a site in the country "close to nature and free from pollution" was chosen and the purchase money guaranteed by a group of parents, including Edna. After repeated discussion over the naming of the school, John Burroughs was decided upon in honor of the naturalist who had died a year earlier. As one of the school's founders puts it, "He loved personality for its own sake. . . . He coupled the appreciation of beauty with a rugged spiritual sturdiness. He radiated self-reliance, usefulness, brotherliness. Particularly he admired leadership founded on high motive." Edna became an officer of the school and served as its secretary.

Edna knew that more than good intentions and fine sentiments were needed to make the school a success. When she was asked to supervise the school's executive offices, which were just about to open at the Wall building in the city, she began by paying the back rent and securing the office furniture. She called friends about the school and had them come to the offices. Edna had a way of imbuing everyone with the urgency of her projects. She wanted to know how soon her old friend Amy Scholz could start work: "Tomorrow?" Scholz considered the project for a day, and then returned to give Gellhorn her decision. However, before she could say a thing, she was interrupted by Edna, who heard "the clang of the elevator gate." She directed Amy to sit at a desk and to pretend she was typing. It was 9:00 A.M. and the trustees arrived, observing an office already in action.

Campaigns to raise funds for building the school and for recruiting faculty, administration, and students were remarkably successful, so that John Burroughs was able to open on October 2, 1923, with ten teachers and seventy-five students. Martha Gellhorn was the first girl admitted to the school. Each day, she boarded the 8:00 A.M. streetcar with its sign in front announcing SPECIAL: JOHN BURROUGHS SCHOOL, and traveled from the city to the countryside, out across open fields and through a small village to a narrow paved country lane, full of potholes, from which she would climb a footpath to the school.

In 1923, John Burroughs was a handsome, compact, L-shaped building still under construction. The Spanish-style architecture, the white plaster walls and red tiled roof, were meant to evoke "the thought that St. Louis had always been the gateway to the West." Everything was new; nothing had precedent. The children knew the school had been "the dream" of their parents.

It was "pretty heady living" for the fourteen tenth-graders who had to take the lead in school affairs. They were evenly divided by sex. Although there were separate athletic activities for boys and girls, they ate together in a handsome dining room with Palladian windows, a fireplace, long wooden tables, and straight-back chairs. Even to this day, teachers at John Burroughs are assigned tables and serve meals in a charming area that is also appropriate for the most formal and solemn occasions. Classrooms were odd sizes and shapes; some of them had low or sloping ceilings, windows of varying dimensions, white plaster walls, and dark wood trim. The original library had heavy wooden beams, beautiful chandeliers, and a fireplace.

Along with many other distinguished visitors who addressed students on special topics, Edna Gellhorn would periodically deliver talks at John Burroughs. In Martha's senior year, Edna spoke to a school assembly about "personality." It was Lincoln's birthday, and she wanted to impress the students with the message that this "great man" had an "ineffable and attractive quality . . . greatly influenced by environment." It was characteristic of her to strike a balance between the individual and society—not for a moment denying genius, but suggesting everyone had a share in shaping it.

It is not surprising that these pioneering students had a sense of solidarity and pride in their school. The slightest infractions of the rules seemed terribly significant, and "every joke the epitome of wittiness." Girls found it a "strange and exhilarating experience" to be educated with boys and to be taught by male teachers. If academic subjects such as English, French, Latin, mathematics, science, and social science were required for students expected to apply to college, the school nevertheless gave so-called extracurricular activities, along with fine arts and physical education, equal weight. In the words of Wilford Aikin, John Burroughs's first headmaster, "school life should be interesting, and full of color and variety." Art history, symphony concerts, and art-studio classes were part of the curriculum.

Aikin believed that "school is not only a preparation for life . . . it is life." A geometry student, for example, would learn this subject while studying the architectural design of a house. Roman fortifications and battering rams were constructed for a Latin class. Social-studies classes had students "studying maps and leaflets about city waterworks." At one point, students were even enlisted in planning an industrial-arts shop at the school and later helped to dig its foundations.

When the John Burroughs School building was dedicated on October 12, 1923, the distinguished speakers present at the ceremony included the president of the University of Missouri and a member of the St. Louis Board of Education. The dedication quite consciously lauded the experimental nature of the school and its democratic spirit. Several students who could not afford the tuition were provided with scholarships, and John Burroughs was regarded as setting a new standard for other schools, public and private, to follow.

Given such an atmosphere of high hopes, it was inevitable that Martha Gellhorn should feel herself in the vanguard of change. In the fall and winter of 1923, she was actively involved in drafting the school's constitution. A group of constitutional delegates was elected to write a document that was to be presented to the school assembly, where it saw some heated debate. Eventually, agreement was reached, with students and teachers having equal voting rights as members of the John Burroughs community. The first election under the new constitution was held on March 27, 1924. Martha Gellhorn was elected speaker of the assembly and president of the Girls' Athletic Association.

Throughout her three years at Burroughs, Gellhorn was a conspicuously active member of various groups and took on considerable responsibility for organizing school events. She assisted the stage manager of the school's first play, *The Pot Boiler,* and served on a committee to pick the school colors. She was a senior member of the field hockey team, a member of the dance committee, and president of the dramatic association. As a member of the board of editors of *The John Burroughs Review,* she supervised the solicitation of advertising. She knew it was no fun for student solicitors to deal with tough shopkeepers, and she praised her staff's energy and resourcefulness. Like her mother, she knew how to bestow compliments laced with good humor, and how to make the simplest tasks seem heroic, calling upon Allah to safeguard her sales force in their encounters with St. Louis shopkeepers.

Gellhorn, one of ten seniors who founded *The John Burroughs Review,* was a frequent contributor. "We had a perfectly fantastic English teacher, Francis Seely. He had us *writing—pouring* out literature: poems, stories, everything. We adored writing," Emily Lewis Norcross recalls. Seely, the faculty advisor to the magazine, was a poet himself, who inspired his pupils to think not in terms of journalism but of more enduring work. In Emily's view, Gellhorn was a better talker than writer, a brilliant conversationalist—very witty and amusing—who could "talk the birds off a tree."

Much of Gellhorn's high school writing has a mocking, theatrical tone. Even a trivial incident—such as the difficulties of placing a call from a public phone—is transformed into a play, grandiously titled *A Soul in Torment.* A silly prose sketch extols her cherished old hat. "Ye Exame" presents a bickering dialogue between little brother, big brother, sister, and mother on the eve of a school exam. A sketch entitled "The Sky" has a Stephen Crane–like focus on the hardness and the immensity of the urban environment, which seems to render individual lives meaningless. "Jemima Smyth, Super-Shopper" briefly experiments with dialect writing.

Gellhorn's poetry in this period deals with the poor, slum housing, travel, her Kewpie doll, and sunsets in verse that is serious yet whimsical and gay. It favors simple rhyme schemes and refrains—although she occasionally sounds pompous and stilted when reaching for the poetical.

In her most interesting poem, "Hester, Defiant," the speaker identifies with Hawthorne's scarlet heroine, who rejects the ice-cold men who judge her, emphasizing her femininity and courage. Gellhorn put her most passionate expression into Hester's attachment to her strange, unruly, and taunting love child, Pearl.

Gellhorn herself had a rebellious and irreverent streak. She was appreciated as a "character" and satirized in the *Review,* but her classmates were fond of her sensible and warmhearted temperament, which prompted a tribute to the "magnificent Martie." While most students idolized the headmaster, Wilford Aikin, she called him "Wilf" and sat on his desk and smoked. In her senior year, she was "perfectly cast" as "the courageous Vigdis Goddi" in John Masefield's play *The Locked Chest,* about a woman who leaves her cowardly husband for refusing to shelter a relative falsely accused of murder.

From February 1925 to June 1926, Gellhorn published forty-two poems in *The John Burroughs Review* (enough for a slim volume of verse). This work meant a good deal to her; it was not simply the product of classroom assignments. She was doubtful about its quality, however. She had met Carl Sandburg at Washington University, where he had spoken to a throng of admirers. This had prevented her from saying much to him, but she then wrote him asking his opinion about her poetry, relying on this tough-minded poet to tell her the truth. The letter was both apologetic and aggressive. Full of exclamation marks and parentheses, it revealed a very young writer in agonies of self-doubt and self-assertion. In some ways, she suspected she was setting herself up for failure. She even speculated the poet would send the poems back to her without reading them. To ensure a reply, she had included a stamped self-addressed envelope.

Sandburg's reaction is not recorded in his papers. Several years later, Gellhorn told a Ph.D. student writing about her work that the poet kindly returned her fledgling poetry with the comment that if writing is a necessity, nothing can stop a person from doing it—sage advice, Gellhorn feels, that cannot be improved upon.

It was a curious performance, this letter, filled with pretension and self-criticism, the product of a writer half-formed and impatient to get on to finer work. She wanted seasoning. Better to be brutalized by experience or by the harsh words of an admired superior than not to grasp for the best that was out there and that might also be in herself. She had her goal. From then on, it was only getting there that mattered.

BRYN MAWR

1926–1929

On the face of it, Bryn Mawr College—known as one of the most progressive educational institutions in the country—seemed like the perfect place for Martha Gellhorn. Her mother had graduated from there and had maintained warm relations with the administration. Bryn Mawr was unique among women's colleges in having a graduate school, in establishing a summer school for working women, and for taking a decidedly internationalist perspective on education, inviting scholarship students from abroad and arranging to bring the greatest minds and talents to the campus to lecture and to perform. During Martha's years at college, Willa Cather, Æ (Irish writer George Russell), Bertrand Russell, Edna St. Vincent Millay, James Watson, Norman Thomas, and many other distinguished individuals visited the campus.

Most students, however, showed little concern for public affairs or for social issues. If a student took a term off from school, the reason usually was so that she could return home to make her debut. The last thing Martha Gellhorn wanted was to "come out" to society. At Bryn Mawr, she often could be found in the "smoker," a room in a residence hall set aside for students who seemed to use it with a vengeance. It was the source for all kinds of news. Smoking itself was a big topic. There were many articles in college papers about what it represented: a rebellion against authority, a sign of intellectuality, a "gesture of the brothel." It was in the smoker that a student might really learn something about herself and her classmates; and it was also there that a lovely and entertaining Martha Gellhorn could be found. It was fascinating to hear her talk, because she already seemed to know so much about life. She was sophisticated, far ahead of her fellow students, and was willing to share her experience. She was generous and loved talking about her adventures. Her friends often felt grateful for her presence—probably because she presented such an attractive alternative to the pieties and prejudices of Bryn Mawr society.

Emily Lewis Norcross, a year behind Martha at Bryn Mawr, remembers that her childhood companion's "wings had begun to spread a bit. She had a perfect horror of being regimented in any way. She would sometimes try to defy the rules by smoking where she wasn't supposed to." Martha's transgressions were quite minor and drew little attention, however. The point was that Martha "started having a freer life much sooner than the rest of us did," Mrs. Norcross concludes.

Self-government was *the issue* during Martha's years at Bryn Mawr. It had always meant an elaborate system of chaperonage and privileges. To students in the 1920s, it had almost nothing to do with independence and everything to do with policing themselves. In their view, self-government had become a Byzantine code regulating their lives in the most minute particulars: Special permission was required to attend dances farther away than Philadelphia or Haverford; 10:30 was the curfew for dancing at the "authorized places"; there was to be no smoking in public off campus; students had to register all departures and returns to campus; visits from men were confined to the hours of four to six on Sunday afternoon; trousers could not be worn on campus. Students bridled at four years of compulsory physical education and in general railed at their subjection to the "humiliation of paternal supervision," which did not give them the opportunity to behave as adults.

Gellhorn would later vent her anger at these restrictions in *What Mad Pursuit,* her first novel, and show how they trivialized the notion that young women could govern themselves. Unlike her classmates, however, she wrote no letters of protest to the school paper. Indeed, her absence from most school activities—especially in her first two years—is the most conspicuous part of her record at Bryn Mawr. She did not try out for the school newspaper; she ran for no important office in college; she took no part in team sports. Only on a few occasions when some aspect of school life deeply touched her interests did she make herself count.

Gellhorn was writing poetry—introspective and private verse—some of which she published in *The Lantern,* Bryn Mawr's literary magazine. Most of it she destroyed before leaving college, but the fragments that survive reveal a young writer inspecting nature and the character of her own feelings. The work is fairly conventional, except for the austerity and the clarity of the lines. There are no baroque metaphors employed, no romantic longings expressed. There is, however, disappointment in the mundanity of existence. The futile gestures of human beings are well observed. There is the kind of 1920s awareness of the false brightness and brittleness of conversation that might be found in a novel by F. Scott Fitzgerald. In poem titled "Plea," a sense of the mocking quality of modern life is effectively conveyed in her evocation of a couple smiling and chatting and making fun of things that are attractive but bound to disintegrate.

Some of the poetry is written in free verse; some of it is carefully rhymed. She was experimenting with different verse forms and with the length of lines, which varied anywhere from two to as many as ten or eleven syllables. Speakers in most of her poems are not identified, except in "Yseult," in which a young woman is dishonest with herself in order to suppress her suffering. She cannot have the man she wants and must persuade herself to be content with the man at hand, even though she knows she will grow to hate him.

This early poetry is about human integrity, about people who have trouble facing the reality of their rather sad choices. A more affirmative sequence of three short poems expresses Gellhorn's delight in the sensuality of nature, in a casual wind philandering in the trees. In what looks like her personal credo, she makes a vow to enjoy simple, rather delicate pleasures: a bit of sunshine, a rain-drenched leaf, and a small wind. She imagines herself to be a cavorting geisha girl; the leaf holds within it a kind of jewel box of colors; and the breeze is pictured "somersaulting in the grass." She makes her solitariness a part of her poetic persona—singing alone not in sorrow but as the rain sings, beautiful and forlorn.

By the end of her sophomore year, Gellhorn was one of twenty-one students who were listed in *The College News* (May 2, 1928) as cum laude. She was also elected as a "speaker" for the undergraduate association. As an English major, she had outraged her teachers by writing dismissively about Wordsworth. Feeling the weight of her instructors' disapproval, "Dutchy" (a nickname she had picked up) happily changed to French, which she always had found a pleasure. In April 1928, she proudly wrote

Edna that she had painstakingly produced twenty-four pages of French on Voltaire and his modern disciples. She had received the highest grade and the professor's comment that the work was very interesting.

Edna preserved a few of Martha's chatty letters from the spring of 1928, which were full of gay observations. Martha liked big cities, and New York was a relief after the agony of a visit to the dentist. She enjoyed taking the ferry with a Princeton boy and going out to dinner and dancing. The next summer, she was expecting to have lots of boyfriends. She looked forward to being around them, to making a study of them, for they could be quite amusing.

In her junior year, Martha had a featured role in the French Club production of *Le Professeur,* a one-act comedy. *The College News* (December 12, 1928) gave her a rave review. The setting was a butcher shop "with realistic carcasses." The characters were a "gruff, ruddy butcher; his very French and very efficient wife; their altogether charming daughter; and an ambitious and starving young professor." Gellhorn stole the show:

M. Gellhorn, '30, was the wife. She alone of the cast, managed to hit exactly the right note. Her accent, her gestures, and most difficult of all, her intonation, were completely and miraculously French. Hearing her telephone was, alone, worth paddling through the snow to Wyndham [Hall]. . . . Her acting was splendid . . . and she brought out to the full the comic possibilities of the part.

Bryn Mawr engaged Gellhorn only in so far as it allowed her to make contact with a greater world and with her generation. In early January 1929, she attended the Fourth Annual Congress of The National Students' Federation of America, an organization founded in 1925 by 245 colleges and universities. Her report to the undergraduates in the Bryn Mawr chapel on Friday, January 11, was given extensive coverage in the January 16 issue of *The College News.* The congress had been called to reach an agreement among students about a World Court. The result of the congress, however, was to establish a continuing association dedicated to developing informed positions on national and international issues. The ultimate goal, as reflected in its constitution, was to "foster understanding among the students of the world in the furtherance of an enduring peace."

Gellhorn's fellow students would have had little conception of the convention she had attended, so she compared it to one of their huge events, the annual May Day celebration involving nearly the entire student body. Knowing the energy and the enthusiasm students put into May Day, Gellhorn conveyed the excitement of an altogether different activity in words the others would immediately understand.

This was an incredibly poised performance. In very brief compass, she explained how the congress was organized and accomplished its work. Then she concentrated on a point of particular interest to her audience. Mount Holyoke had a system of governance that was better than anything she had observed. Both faculty and students took part in all aspects of government. Why not? Faculty resided at the college; it was ridiculous to strictly divide students from instructors. Committee work, extracurricular activities—everything that made up campus life—was determined by democratically elected bodies of faculty and students. Obviously, this made for a stronger degree of collaboration and harmony in the college community.

Gellhorn's observations struck hard at just what had been bothering Bryn Mawr for some time. *The College News* had editorialized about bringing more democracy to student government, and implicit in the editorials, student debates, and chapel talks by Bryn Mawr's dean had been a concern over the increasing lack of cooperation among undergraduates. Most of these expressions of concern had been couched in rather unappealing, moralistic language, however. Students were aggrieved; administrators and faculty members were disappointed. Gellhorn was refreshingly direct yet political. Whatever the merits of her observation, it was to the point and without the usual cant. It cleared the air to hear someone say what was nonsense and what was not.

There was nothing smug about this speech, and Gellhorn wanted the students to know she had had some fun. She had been especially taken with one southern lady who had asked her what women's colleges such as Bryn Mawr "did" to their entering freshmen. Gellhorn was mystified by the inquiry but soon learned the woman had in mind the hazing of new students, which now seemed to be in disfavor. In this southern woman's day, freshmen were doused with house paint; now their faces were merely dabbed with some kind of goo that was no trouble at all to remove. Gellhorn and her eastern cohort were aghast, and she told this Southerner rather loftily that freshmen ought to be treated like the human beings they were and not covered in paint. The Southerner replied that freshmen looked forward to this abuse. Gellhorn and her friends were struck silent by this description of a breed they had never encountered.

Gellhorn dispatched in a few sentences those subjects of the congress that did not interest her, giving the gist of what had occurred. The

ROTC report caused much controversy, with students strongly divided between those advocating and those opposing military preparedness. Gellhorn was on the opposing side and felt its arguments were more persuasive, but she let her Bryn Mawr audience know that her judgment just might be biased. She had been impressed by two Italian Fascist students who would be visiting Bryn Mawr soon.

Gellhorn's final words had to do with the significance of the congress. It was her conviction that it had been one of the most impressive experiences of her life. One hundred and eighty-six male and female students had met to consider important public issues, with some of the most dedicated students working late into the night. It was a peculiarly exciting experience, and it made her feel proud of her generation in a way that she clearly had not anticipated. The commitment to improve the lives of people suggested to her that her generation had much more promise than some writers had given people to believe.

Gellhorn was aware, however, of the skeptics in their midst. So she put to herself the question she imagined someone in her audience might ask her. What was the point of it all? What was the point of anything? was her answering query. Her conclusion had a modest, almost self-effacing quality. All she could claim to have done was to have attended an interesting meeting, absorbed certain ideas and hopes, and sincerely sought a path toward progress.

What a shrewd performance this speech was. Gellhorn knew her audience well, knew they would not be swayed by large claims or moved by exhortations to social action. Rather, they might be intrigued by the picture of genuine and modest efforts to make the world better. Judging by the accounts in *The College News,* nothing else so fine as this speech was delivered by a student during Gellhorn's years at Bryn Mawr.

About a month later, on February 27, 1929, *The College News* listed Gellhorn as a Bryn Mawr delegate to the Model Assembly of the League of Nations. On March 13, 1929, J. S. McDonald, Chairman of the Foreign Policy Association, wrote a letter praising Gellhorn that was published in *The College News:* "Miss Gellhorn made a brilliant attack on John Rockefeller's report on the Secretariat and was ably supported by her colleagues."

Campus life was rooted in routines that had become intolerable to Gellhorn by her third year at Bryn Mawr. She took to living in a settlement that cared for the poor. She had decided not to finish college;

she did not want to be the typical Bryn Mawr graduate: settling down, marrying, and pursuing "the vapoury phantom of general culture," as a *College News* editorial put it. She had in mind a self-supporting career and a single lifestyle. By not getting her degree, she could avoid the curse of respectability.

Gellhorn was reading Hemingway and trying to write as he did. The popular press treated the influence of *The Sun Also Rises* like an epidemic. In the spring of 1928, the journalist Richmond Barrett remarked in *Harper's* that young people had adopted *The Sun Also Rises* as their Bible. They had "learned it by heart and [were] deserting their families and running away from college." Their destination was usually the sidewalk cafés of Paris. According to Malcolm Cowley, girls modeled themselves after Lady Brett, Hemingway's version of European elegance and charm, a beautiful young woman already on her way to a divorce, who must forsake her love for Jake Barnes, a stoical newspaper correspondent emasculated by a wartime wound. As Kenneth Lynn suggests:

> In the twenties, the disequilibrium of life gave rise to a romantic sensibility, especially among pacesetting young people. It was their sense of themselves as historical victims that led them to interpret *The Sun Also Rises* in the light of its modern epigraph ["You are all a lost generation."] and to identify with Jake and Brett as fellow lost souls.

During Gellhorn's freshman year at Bryn Mawr, a review of *The Sun Also Rises* appeared in *The College News* (December 8, 1926). Entitled "Pessimism Triumphs," its reviewer noted the source of the novel's title—a passage from Ecclesiastes about the "vanity of vanities"—and bemoaned the attention given to "degraded characters leading a vagabond life who magnify its futility by their perverse views and increase the causes of their self-humiliation by prolonging their unpraiseworthy habits." There was no hope for change, no prospect of "regeneration." The American and English characters simply roamed France and Spain "in the pursuit of pleasure" and of "excitement of a low order." Cabaret touring, fishing, fiestas, and bullfights could not cover up the "drab weariness of life." In short, this was "sordid subject matter." With no hint of Christian or democratic values, the novel stood for "the darker side of life with no note of optimism to brighten it." The reviewer implied that this attitude prevented the author's work from becoming a "classic."

The Bryn Mawr reviewer had failed to engage with the experiences of the novel's characters. Martha had come to feel that Bryn Mawr, on too many counts, had failed to engage with life itself. The college was a cloister. Leaving it, she would imagine herself emerging from a period of confinement.

Part Two

... EXILES AT HOME AND

STRANGERS WHEREVER THEY GO ...

NOTHING EVER HAPPENS TO

THE BRAVE.

ON HER OWN

1 9 2 9 – 1 9 3 0

5

ike many of Martha Gellhorn's St. Louis friends, Mary Taussig Hall
recalls Martha remarking:

> "St. Louis has taught me all I know and I'm leaving." Later, she
> said the same thing about Bryn Mawr. So she was not anyone
> to say "I want the traditional degree, and I want the security of
> home." She had no fear of anything. . . . Adventure—she just
> loved it.

Her parents were upset. Seven years later, Edna referred to the pain of
this episode when she admitted to a reporter: "Her father and I were
disappointed. Just taking an apartment and being independent in New
York we viewed with misgivings and doubts. But she convinced us she
meant it."

Martha persuaded her parents of her sincerity by refusing to accept
their financial support. While still at Bryn Mawr, she was scrupulous
about writing her mother letters thanking her parents for checks that
covered her educational and personal expenses. As soon as she resolved
on a career she knew they would question, self-support became one of
her paramount objectives. Edna was especially impressed when Martha
returned checks during a period of illness and insolvency. Subsisting on

doughnuts and pawning her typewriter to sustain her over weekends, Martha determined to make her own "shoestring living" as a journalist. She would rather borrow money elsewhere than accept "a penny of support from her father," Edna noted.

Edna used the word *disappointed* to describe the reaction she and her husband had to Martha's departure from Bryn Mawr. In fact, George Gellhorn was very angry. For all his support of women's rights and of various liberal causes, he was a traditionalist. It was one thing to campaign for the vote, to support all manner of causes that would make full use of women's talent; it was quite another thing to condone the liberated life Martha proposed to follow. It was immoral. "You don't get something for nothing, and I paid," Martha confessed to Victoria Glendinning. The cost was her father's—and sometimes her brothers'—harsh criticism of her.

Edna was too generous and too loving to take Martha's declaration of independence as a personal affront. She was wounded by her daughter's rejection of St. Louis, but she always defended Martha's right to go her own way. Edna seemed to have an infinite capacity for tolerating differences of temperament and outlook. She had raised her children to think for themselves. How could she complain that Martha wanted a life quite separate from her own? To require obedience from her daughter now would contradict the very attitudes Edna's mother had instilled in her. In Martha's memoir of her grandmother, she paid tribute to Martha Ellis Fischel's unselfish acceptance of her children's various enterprises. She nurtured them like a rather unmanageable garden with a certain proclivity for growing beyond the confines of its plot.

However, the benign image of children gradually abandoning the boundaries of a familial Eden does not quite fit what Martha had in mind, for she chose to jump the fence and—so it seemed to some of Edna's family and friends—repudiate her mother's example. Although no one said it in so many words, Martha was breaking traditions her grandmother and mother had established and threatening their sense of community and of family.

Yet both women had considerable sympathy for Martha. If they had contented themselves with staying close to home—traveling afar but always returning to St. Louis—they knew it was not in Martha's nature to do so. After two generations, this kind of feminine accommodation had played itself out. Moreover, they recognized Martha's radical side in themselves. Edna seems not to have kept many letters from her mother, but two that are in her papers reveal the very complex feelings they shared over Martha's choice to live a life so unlike their own.

Writing to Edna from the Lebanon Hotel in Chautauqua, New York, on August 27, 1931, her mother described a lecture about India she had just attended. It had been a fascinating travelogue, but now she was looking forward to a reunion with her family. These separations did not please her, but the trip had been intellectually and emotionally stimulating, intensifying her compassion for humanity. Four days later, on the eve of her departure from Chautauqua, Martha Ellis Fischel wrote another letter to her daughter expressing most delicately her disappointment in George Gellhorn. It was unfortunate that he did not realize that Martha's desire for independence was not so different from her grandmother's and mother's feelings. Martha Ellis spoke elliptically and with great delicacy, but she did not have to spell things out for Edna, for there had been tensions in their roles as mother, daughter, housewife, and social activist, and they had chosen not to make an issue of their deeply personal feelings and needs. Knowing how much they had sacrificed, they could not ask Martha to conform.

For Martha Gellhorn, staying in St. Louis would have meant giving up too much of herself. She would have shriveled. "She had a certain contempt for all of us who did stay in St. Louis," Mary Taussig Hall suggests: "She said, 'If they are going to sit in that dump of a little city, let them stew in their own juice. But I'm not going to!'" It was the vehemence of Martha's attacks on the city that astounded many of Edna's friends, for to Edna it was her very life; her sense of self and of her heritage were inseparable from her devotion to the city. "Edna loved St. Louis. Even when she was very old, she wanted to keep up with what was going on in town," one of her close friends recalls.

Martha seemed to get up a head of steam out of opposing St. Louis, and this greatly hurt her mother, one of Edna's friends observed:

Edna's relationship with Martha was a fascinating one, and I think for Edna a very painful one. She really loved that girl to distraction, but Martha was always trying very hard to prove that she did not share any of her mother's interests or preoccupations. We all hated the way she treated her mother. She wrote Edna affectionate letters but rarely came to see her.

In St. Louis, Martha's behavior was often looked upon as "self-seeking," and not much sympathy was expressed for a young woman who had to contend with her mother's formidable reputation.

Martha's letters to Edna are as loving as any mother could hope to have from her daughter. Yet Martha kept her distance, because in St. Louis she could not escape identification as Edna Gellhorn's daughter. Staying at home meant risking submersion in her mother's enterprises. Edna's friends remember how being around her was a remarkably seductive experience:

She had a wonderful guile. She knew how to approach a senator, a coal miner, or a child. She appeared ingenuous and had a wonderful ability to put herself on any level while remaining on her own level. . . . You could feel yourself being led right into her trap! She would find a place for you in her scheme of things, you would be sucked up, and you would find yourself the head of the parade. She picked out a few people. You might not know it, but you were tapped. And you wound up with a lot to do.

When Emily Lewis Norcross's mother died, and she returned from Bryn Mawr to St. Louis, her father said, "Now, Emily, I've got to warn you. Our dear, dear friend Mrs. Gellhorn will try to get you involved in many things." Emily's father knew about Edna's tenacity and about her beautiful, powerful presence. To Emily, Edna was

a Viking goddess, like something out of *Götterdämmerung*. I never really felt cozy with her. I saw her as Marty's mother and as my parents' friend. I never really worked with her—like Delia Mares, Mary Hall, and the girls who were under her spell. She was sort of a surrogate mother to them. They revered her.

Having been at the head of her mother's parades, Martha determined early on to set her own pace, carry her own banners, and create her own causes. Giving up St. Louis meant giving up the only social base she had known. For anyone less committed to being her own person and to forging a writing career, leaving Bryn Mawr at the age of twenty would have been terrifying. As one of the girls quitting college in *What Mad Pursuit* remarks, she will never again have that kind of security.

* * *

Gellhorn's first job the summer after leaving Bryn Mawr was at *The New Republic*. To her surprise, work there seemed like a continuation of her college education. She was stuck in a building on New York City's East Twenty-third Street with the likes of Walter Lippmann, Edmund Wilson, and a bright young book reviewer, T. S. Matthews—but she was not impressed. One of her pals was working on the Albany *Times Union*, a Hearst publication, and suggested she join him. Remembering when he first met her in France, Bertrand de Jouvenel portrayed her as *une gamine*, a wanderer, blindly running away from the lofty Gothic precincts of the Bryn Mawr campus, weary of learning to speak the language of Chaucer, and avid to cover the lurid criminal activities of a smoky, stinking town like Albany. She walked into a newspaper office, a blonde in dungarees, and announced, "My name is Martha Gellhorn. I want to work."

Like Charis Day, her fictional counterpart in *What Mad Pursuit*, Martha was hired as a cub reporter covering social events and the morgue. Sometimes she was fortunate enough to get assigned to accidents. At first, editors were struck by how young and delicate the fair-haired Gellhorn looked, so she had trouble getting important jobs. She was probably looked upon as a *lady*—the term applied to Charis Day. Soon, however, Gellhorn's aggressiveness earned her a new title, "The Blonde Peril." In Charis, she embodied her own character, a feisty neophyte who gives orders to the city editor on her first workday. In retrospect, Gellhorn compared her experiences in Albany to *The Front Page*. She claimed to have worked for an alcoholic, illiterate editor who fired his staff nearly every day. Gellhorn would join her colleagues in a speakeasy, awaiting the customary summons back to work. She remembered the whole period fondly, as a lark.

Martha's Albany escapade distressed Edna, for it was hardly the right setting for a Bryn Mawr girl. Consequently, Edna wrote to Eleanor Roosevelt—already a friend as a result of their participation together in various social causes and programs—and Martha was invited to the Governor's Mansion for dinner. She was furious at being treated like a straying child and was in no mood to view Roosevelt sympathetically. Her own memory of the scene is that she was sullen and thought Roosevelt's tiger's teeth necklace was decidedly ugly. Martha did not appreciate presenting herself for Roosevelt's inspection or becoming the subject, no doubt, of a report to her mother.

Judging by *What Mad Pursuit*, Gellhorn's six months in Albany, New York, were lonely. Her decision to try journalism was not as arbitrary as that of her heroine—who is attracted to newspaper work after seeing a movie about a star reporter's adventures—but Charis's isolated, impecunious existence reflects Martha's own plight. She could not have had much more than Charis: a salary of twenty dollars a week, a "cell" in a rooming house, "papered in diseased poppies and furnished with a bed, a dresser, a table and one rocking-chair," and with a "stygian bathroom" two floors below.

The Albany *Times Union* could offer Gellhorn precious few outlets for her ambitions. Most of the major national and international stories were taken verbatim from the wire services. Local news—even of the melodramatic variety—would not have enchanted her, since the squalid and gruesome details of murders and accidents were all too predictable and repetitive. The last thing she was looking for was the sensationalism and formulaic quality of newspaper items: "Death Ends Romance," a front-page story with a picture of the slain female lover; features on "Appetizing Menus for the Week"; serialized novels ("The Story of a Hell-Cat Wife Who Couldn't Be Good"); sections on "News and Gossip of the Stage, Screen and Studio," "The Woman in the Home"; and several columns of society news appeared with boring regularity. In *What Mad Pursuit,* Gellhorn has Charis at work on revisions of news from the competing newspaper; these have to do with meetings of parents about child psychology, a local dramatic group, and the "Mad Hatter Club Sewing Bee."

By express train, Gellhorn could get from Albany to New York City in three hours. She had begun contributing short unsigned book reviews to *The New Republic* and hoped by placing an article with the magazine to establish her journalistic credentials. On one of her trips to the city, she visited the Brooklyn Paramount Theater at Flatbush and DeKalb avenues to attend a sold-out Rudy Vallee performance, the subject of her first signed piece in *The New Republic* (August 7, 1929). Gellhorn affected a rather weary, sophisticated stance toward the Rudy Vallee revue, which seemed no more than tolerable—passable jazz, a girl with a sturdy if not especially attractive voice, a comic at whom one might consider laughing, and so on.

The real object of attention—Rudy Vallee—had a pleasing theatrical style, playing the abashed male surrounded by adoring females. When he picked up his megaphone and crooned "I Kiss Your Hand, Madame," she felt the charm of what amounted to his love letter to each clutching girl in the huge theater. She had to admit he deserved to be called something better than good. He was "swell."

In the spirit of her ironic subtitle, "God's Gift to Us Girls," Gellhorn conveyed both the excitement and the silliness of the Vallee phenomenon. The trouble was she came off a little too superior to her subject. She alluded to a photograph of Vallee in *Vanity Fair,* complete with megaphone and saxophone. Naturally, he was a saxophone player—nearly everyone was, she sneered.

After considering and rejecting many different reasons for Vallee's appeal, Gellhorn finally settled on the American woman's craving for a "beau." American men were too busy working for the money that sent their women to entertainments such as the movies to coo "I Kiss Your Hand, Madame." Vallee's tender, caressing tones attracted all the silly romantic women in the country—which seemed to be the only point worth making, she concluded.

Gellhorn quit the Albany *Times Union* after less than six months. She briefly returned to St. Louis, where she failed to get a job on the St. Louis *Post-Dispatch,* but she made valuable contacts that later resulted in her placing several articles with the newspaper. New York City made her restless. By the end of 1929, she was making plans for a trip to Europe and a future as a foreign correspondent.

LAUNCHED

1930–1931

6

I n February 1930, twenty-one-year-old Martha Gellhorn bartered her way to Europe. In exchange for writing a complimentary article for the trade magazine of the Holland America Line, she was allowed to travel third class in steerage. Headed for Paris with not much more than seventy-five dollars and her suitcase, and knowing no one in this foreign capital, she was cheerfully certain of obtaining a job as a correspondent.

If Gellhorn had a "passion for France," where she had spent three summer holidays, she understood virtually nothing about actually living there. She enjoyed the ambience of the Place de la Madeleine; its stands of flowers appealed to her craving for a pleasant milieu, and the price of a room did little to dent her purse. Her accommodations were sleazy, however, and she was puzzled at what she took to be the French mode of having a mirror on the ceiling. Then there was the uproar in the hallways. Why did the French tramp around their hotels? And why— when she was so happy and gregarious—did the hotel clerk seemed ruder each time she passed his desk?

Gellhorn's mystification was soon dispelled by a kind Englishman, the head of the *New York Times* office in Paris. To his great amusement, she had presented herself as an applicant for a job. When she told him her Paris address, he laughed so hard he cried. Always grateful to be treated to a meal, she accepted his invitation to lunch, during which he revealed that her residence was a *maison de passe,* an establishment that let out rooms to the amorous at hourly rates.

Taking the Englishman's advice, Gellhorn settled on the Left Bank, where she felt more secure in a student community. In retrospect, she pictures herself as the complete naif earnestly absorbing the atmosphere—living on the rue de l'Université in a room with no windows, with a bath four floors below, bothered by her neighbors' crying, bickering, and screaming at one another, charmed by the Chopin that was played on the hotel's grand piano, and shocked to learn about homosexuality when her companion, an "ex-Princetonian," was accosted by another male. She pined in unrequited passion for a magnificent "White Russian balalaika player."

Gellhorn went through a succession of jobs, earning barely enough to support herself. These were the days when she could walk into the United Press office low on funds and secure an assignment. For a short time, she wrote dull copy for an advertising agency. On the Paris staff of *Vogue,* she entered the fashion world of the city:

> Tall, slim, blonde, with a gracefully poised head set off with the smartest of haircuts, it was the delight of Paris dressmakers to dress her up in their newest models and have her parade them, not as the usual mannequin at the race tracks, but as a personality among personages. She wore the first halter neck backless evening gown at the World Economic Congress in London and the Parisian dressmaker's confidence in her ability to show it off was not misplaced. It became a hit that swept the fashion world.

Although her heart was always with the poor, and she was never a part of the snug coterie of American expatriate writers in Paris, Gellhorn did enjoy associating with the gaudy rich and lecturing them about their duty to those whose station in life was less fortunate than their own.

With so little money, and accustomed to working with student groups, Gellhorn found herself thoroughly ensconced in French culture. Her friends were ardently involved in politics, no matter whether they came from the intelligentsia or from the realms of fashion and journalism. They were not insular; politics cut across class and other social distinctions. Questions of "unemployment, underpaid and badly treated workers, the cynicism of old politicians" engaged nearly everyone in her circle. It was this kind of vitality and concern she would find lacking in England and the United States, except during the Depression.

"Real life," Gellhorn supposed, was seeing things for yourself. It meant getting out and touring the country, witnessing strikes and protest marches, visiting slums, mill towns, and mining areas. "Real life was the Have-nots," she concluded. The emptier her stomach, the more she identified with these people. She called her mode of traveling and abiding with the poor "standing room at ground level to watch history as it happened."

By the spring of 1930, Gellhorn was back for a short stay in the United States, surveying the ground, so to speak, with her newly acquired European perspective. In "Toronto Express," an article published in the April 30, 1930, issue of *The New Republic,* she gave a detailed account of a dismal train trip from New York to Toronto. She was struck by the lifeless passengers—by their staleness and seeming lack of interest in the journey itself. Whether in first class or in coach, people behaved like automatons. She had trouble fixing on individuals; there was nothing to distinguish one from the other. Finally, she noticed a yellow-bearded old man reading a Yiddish newspaper and his wife laughing, talking, and eating with gusto. This couple reminded her of how much Europeans relish going on journeys. For them, traveling was an act of hope, an investment in life's possibilities, a departure from routine ways of thinking and behaving. Gellhorn was partial to France, a dynamic culture, where people talk on their trips about where they are going and what they expect to find. On European trains, she had heard many life histories—of a man imprisoned in Siberia and of a German nurse who had worked in a Cleveland hospital. She had discussed writers and the Russian ballet, and argued about whether there would be another war. Even though European trains were often less comfortable than American ones, passengers on the former thrived on the unpredictability and charm of traveling. What infuriated her about Americans was a certain complacency, a reluctance to cross borders and to empathize with other cultures. When she thought of Americans, she pictured shapeless faces in speakeasies and crowds of unseeing subway passengers.

By the fall of 1930, Gellhorn was back in Europe writing for the St. Louis *Post-Dispatch* about the women delegates to meetings of the League of

Nations in Geneva. She presented an appealing portrait of Mary Agnes Hamilton, a stylish, energetic woman, a Labour member of the House of Commons and, like Gellhorn, a militant pacifist. Gellhorn took obvious delight in describing Hamilton's smart black dress and her old-fashioned black beret. This woman moved briskly and nervously. Gellhorn could tell her hair was closely clipped beneath her tight hat. She was the epitome of a slim, tall, athletic, and attractive woman. Gellhorn thought it likely that Hamilton was good at golf, and she was sure Hamilton rode horses. She strode with an uplifted head, leaving a swirling current of air in her trail wherever she went. The effect of a woman's appearance, the way one could seem to alter the climate, intrigued Gellhorn—as did Hamilton's career as a journalist, novelist, and biographer who befriended political figures who then became the subjects of her books. Hamilton told Gellhorn that she much admired young American women but faulted them for relishing their place on the "pedestal." Hamilton did not care much for separate women's organizations. In Britain, female Labour party MPs like herself had worked beside men and merited their appointments.

What must Edna Gellhorn, founder of the St. Louis League of Women Voters, have made of these comments in her daughter's newspaper article? It was apparent to Edna's friends in the league that Martha did not have much use for it and resented the time her mother devoted to its activities. Through Hamilton, Martha was able to express her rejection of what she saw as the genteel pretensions of the American woman, which made her, in Hamilton's view, crave not only equality but also the status of an art object. It was this stasis, this underlying passivity—as Martha saw it—that had to be attacked.

Gellhorn adored Geneva. Her second article on the League of Nations meeting began with a description of the Hôtel des Bergues, headquarters for most of the league delegates. In the course of a conversation, one could hear five languages being spoken. She dwelled on the congregation of different nationalities, the women's colorful clothes as opposed to the men's somber, conventional dress. She was fascinated by the profoundest political intellects of Europe in meetings that were filled to capacity.

The heroine of this second article was Mademoiselle Hanni Forchhammer, the first woman delegate to the league. She was a small woman with white hair, reserved about her personal life and positive about questions of public policy. Growing up in an austere, scholarly environment, she became a teacher, one of the leaders of adult-education programs in Denmark. After twenty thousand women had marched in Copenhagen for women's suffrage, she was selected to speak for them before the king and Parliament. A champion of human rights, she had traveled the world, investigating the white-slave traffic in Asia Minor and working for the protection of women and children in the Near East.

Forchhammer had nothing but praise for the speaking and organizational talent of American women, although she conceded that a significant number did little and were "perfectly parasitical." She referred to the European myth of the pampered American woman, but on her visit to the country she had seen only the grand ones. Gellhorn took Forchhammer's unassuming, quiet competence as the epitome of an agreeable feminism. Some feminists denied their femininity and others traded on it, but Forchhammer was indifferent to the entire matter. In Gellhorn's view, this was the most effective position. Not surprisingly, it was her own.

Gellhorn could not help noticing that Forchhammer lacked elegance. She wore a watch attached to the front of her dress with a safety pin in a rather grand and quaint fashion. The hem of her dress drooped. Forchhammer seemed unconscious of the things that made her appearance "charming or unattractive." For her, work was everything, so Gellhorn was content to judge her not as a woman but as a "worker."

In early 1931, Gellhorn visited striking textile workers in Roubaix-Tourcoing. She was not alone. Accompanying her was Bertrand de Jouvenel, the handsome son of a prominent French politician and diplomat, Henry de Jouvenel. Bertrand was just beginning his distinguished career as a journalist and expert on economic affairs. Following his father's lead, he dedicated himself to the cause of world peace. He had met Martha in the company of one of his friends during one of her backpacking trips through Europe. She and Bertrand were soon engrossed in conversation. When she asked what his life ambition was, he quickly admitted it was to write as many books as possible. He was married, but he simply walked out on his wife (causing a scandal) to follow her. She was touched by his sensitivity and decency, and amused by his impracticality, claiming to his biographer, John Braun, that Jouvenel had trouble taking care of the simplest everyday tasks.

Bertrand adored Martha and worried when he had to leave her in the company of his friend Robert Lange, who was given clear instructions not to lay a hand on her. Lange recalls that they went to a hotel not too far away in southern France and kept to the instructions, though only

Robert's room had a shower and he was astonished to see Martha come in to use it dressed only in a towel. Gellhorn subsequently thought of this period as still part of her girlhood.

Bertrand and Martha traveled in Europe for four months, working closely with pacifists dedicated to a rapprochement between France and Germany. These two fervently wished to overthrow the older generation that was obviously heading toward a second world war. Terribly conscious of their youth, and of what it meant to be in love and to fight for their ideals, they were a transatlantic couple devoted to the dream of an international community.

JOUVENEL

1 8 7 6 − 1 9 3 0

7

The Jouvenel family traced its descent from fourteenth-century Limousin barons. Bertrand's father's full name was Bertrand Henry Leon Robert de Jouvenel des Ursins. Shortening his name to Henry de Jouvenel was not simply a matter of convenience; it bespoke a desire to retain just enough of an aristocratic appellation to impress without offending a democratic age. The Jouvenels were notable for their support of royalist causes; they claimed descent from the Italian family d'Orsini. In the sixteenth century, the Jouvenels converted to Protestantism and were out of favor, but by the 1800s they had recovered both their Catholicism and their position in affairs of state.

All of his life, Henry de Jouvenel had "the talent for being loved." Henry's son, Bertrand, would inherit his father's princely, slender figure, which women found hard to resist. At an early age, Henry developed a gift for diplomacy, fashioning arguments that reconciled different points of view. As ambassador to Italy, editor of *Le Matin,* and parliamentary politician, he usually played the mediator. He had an eloquence that could "overwhelm assemblies split into hostile factions." His aristocratic aura contributed to the feeling that he was above the fray. A man of principle dedicated to the French republic, he was by nature a compromiser. He could get warring parties to settle their disputes by negotiation, but his triumphs were usually short-lived and, in retrospect, seemed ambiguous and indeterminate. There was nobility in his opposition to factions, in his call for "a broader community," but he was often ineffectual precisely because he would not stoop to the tactics of partisan contests. Like Henry, Bertrand would work tirelessly to stave off a second world war, yet in the very effort of diplomacy father and son obscured forces of evil that Gellhorn and her generation came to see as irremediable.

Bertrand was eight years old in 1911 when his father fell in love with the novelist and actress Colette. Claire Boas, Bertrand's mother, had become an important journalist and had retained the name of Jouvenel while safeguarding her son from his rakish father. Henry did not object to this arrangement until his son was sixteen. By then, Henry was married to Colette and beginning to miss Bertrand's company. If Bertrand were not allowed to visit Henry's household, Henry would deprive his ex-wife of the use of his family name—a threat she had to take seriously or suffer certain diminution of her influence as a journalist.

What Henry had not reckoned on was the enormous hold Colette would come to have on his son. Although Bertrand had been brought up in the society of such famous figures as Claudel, Bergson, D'Annunzio, and Anatole France, he was not prepared for his stepmother's worldliness. He might have the name of a Limousin aristocrat, but he was brought up within the confines of the Parisian Jewish bourgeoisie. His grandfather, Alfred Boas, had prospered manufacturing headlights for the emerging automobile industry in France. Bertrand was a bookish boy who loved horseback riding and tennis but who had grown up among servants and fashionable society. He had few contacts with children his own age and knew nothing about women. At sixteen, he was a timid, trembling, awkward boy, who "hid behind a piano, in the darkest part of the room," clutching a bunch of flowers he had brought for his first visit to Colette. This spoiled and very shy child, "educated at home by private tutors" and protected "by an Irish governess in his mother's spacious apartment," provoked Colette's curiosity. She found him enticing, and he spent his next summer holiday at her house.

It was 1920. Bertrand was seventeen; Colette was forty-eight. She gave him massages, filled him with food, and tanned him in the sun. She taught him how to swim. When she stroked his hip as he emerged from the water, he shivered with a "thrill he [had] never experienced before." She gave him a copy of her latest novel, *Cheri,* about a young man who falls in love with an older woman. She was firm with him, a source of strength, but also very tender. Before retiring for the evening, she would kiss him on the cheek. On one occasion, she kissed him on the lips. He was so startled, he almost dropped his oil lamp. "Hold the lamp steady" was her only reply.

Colette and her female companions joked about Bertrand's innocence. It was time, they thought, that he "became a man." After failing miserably with one of her friends, he found Colette waiting for him in the middle of the night, and they became lovers. For the next six years, she was his passion, his teacher, and his confidante. If she was doomed to see him eventually outgrow their attachment, she savored the pleasure it was in their power to enjoy. By this time, her husband lived much of his public and private life away from her, intensely involved in the politics and diplomacy that bored her, and with the mistresses that made her jealous. To fashion Bertrand into a mature figure was a temptation she could not withstand—even after Henry and Bertrand's mother detected the affair. Not until Bertrand showed signs of embarking on his own career did she deliberately break off their liaison.

Bertrand's political interests had developed early. His Uncle Robert had died in the First World War, and Bertrand was strongly influenced by the antiwar novels of the time. An enthusiastic supporter of the League of Nations, he attended an international conference in Genoa in 1922, taking a leftist and internationalist position that emphasized the economic reconstruction of Europe and opposed the heavy reparations the Allies were forcing Germany to pay. In the mid-1920s, he was intensely involved in debating questions of disarmament and national security, but he had not yet developed the expertise that would later make him an authority on international affairs. His plans to become a lawyer were halted when he failed his exams. By 1924, he was a journalist, but in the next few years he was known more for his heavy drinking and womanizing than for his professional work. Married in December of 1925 to Marcelle Noilly-Prat, from an aristocratic family in Normandy, he carried on a rather frivolous life that included an apartment with lily pads in the tub. Jouvenel had become a devoted hedonist.

By 1928, Jouvenel was actively involved in politics, losing his bid for election as a Radical party deputy, pursuing his career in journalism, attending a World Youth Congress meeting in Holland, and writing a novel, *La Fidelitie Difficile,* which explored the agony of a young man, René, who was divided in feeling between his mistress and his wife. Jouvenel had not been faithful to Noilly-Prat any more than he would be to Gellhorn. The novel represents the epitome of his hedonistic period and is his only work that does not address social or political issues.

When Bertrand de Jouvenel met Martha Gellhorn in 1930, he was once again fully committed to public life. He had been part of the rejuvenation of the non-Marxist left in late 1920s France. Editor of a daily newspaper, *La Voix,* an organ of the Radical party, he argued that France should follow the example of the United States: Only an enterprising, innovative culture heavily involved in the development of financial markets could make France once again a great nation. Similarly, Europe as a great entity could progress only if it united—at least in economic terms. By the summer of 1929, he had rejected his earlier enthusiasm for the League of Nations. It had proved powerless in the face of national sovereignty, and Jouvenel had to abandon his naïve belief that personal contacts between league leaders would help to ensure peace.

Jouvenel's renewed commitment to economics and politics did not mean he had forsaken the sensuous pleasures he had shared with Colette. On the contrary, his love life was as complicated as ever, but now he had adopted his father's attitude, taking his romances and his politics as all of a piece. Jouvenel carried his typewriter everywhere, making no distinctions between vacations and work periods. He would still enjoy his days in the sun, pursue the fashionable life of Paris, but his pleasures would no longer interfere with his social and political projects.

In 1930–1931, the first year that Jouvenel and Gellhorn spent together, he was reading voraciously in U.S. economic history. Later he would produce a classic text on the Great Depression in the United States. At the same time, Colette was still very much on his mind, even though they had not seen each other for nearly five years. Indeed, in his eighties, he continued to speak reverently of her and of their time together. He had been ready to spend his whole life with her before she ended their amour. As Martha said several years later to his half brother, Renaud, Bertrand "still loves her. He is still in love with her."

With this kind of romantic past, Bertrand de Jouvenel was a most appealing figure. He had, in a way, apprenticed himself to Colette and cultivated a very sophisticated sense of society. His world was more literary than his father's. Under Colette's influence, Bertrand had written stories about his childhood and a play at the age of eighteen. It is no accident, for example, that while Henry wrote a book about Mirabeau,

Bertrand wrote one about Zola. Both father and son were dilettantes in the best sense of the word, but Henry had little patience for Colette's literary soirees or for the sheer enjoyment she could derive from entertaining friends. Colette, Henry, and Bertrand all wrote journalism, but Bertrand was the most catholic in his tastes, which reflected (in the words of his memoir) *"cet esprit eclectique et curieux."*

A spirit that was eclectic and curious tended to view politics with a generous and conciliatory attitude. By 1930, Jouvenel could see another world war approaching, and he worked furiously for *"la reconciliation franco-allemande."* The enmity between France and Germany had only grown worse in the years since 1919. Germany, in his view, had been treated by all of Europe as a scapegoat for its problems. This is why he sought the company of a new generation, especially students, who would foster mutual understanding between nations and peoples. Like Gellhorn, he came from a family of mixed background, of Gentiles and Jews, which fought against excluding or discriminating against any individual or group. His father and uncle had been actively involved in protesting the Dreyfus Affair (1894–1906), the case of a Jewish army officer falsely accused of treason. It was odious to think that a man could be condemned simply because he was Jewish. Bertrand's two grandfathers, Alfred Boas, a Jewish industrialist, and Raoul de Jouvenel, a Catholic and royalist, composed in his mind an image of France at the time of the affair. In order to live with these different heritages—really different aspects of himself—Bertrand had to locate reconciling principles in the world around him.

How fascinating for Gellhorn to find on French ground a man with a background so different and yet so like her own. Not willing to subject herself to further schooling or to conventional employment, she had become a journalist, intent on satisfying a spirit that was at least as eclectic and curious as Jouvenel's. Like his father, he was a dashing figure, a duelist, an adventurer. As a child, he dreamed about Buffalo Bill, a Buffalo Bill who delivered Napoleon from his imprisonment in a cave. Bertrand's uncle, Robert Boas, had it in mind to train his young nephew for the cavalry.

They were a cosmopolitan couple, Bertrand and Martha. He had grown up in a household supervised by an Irish governess, and she been cared for by a German housekeeper. They felt at home in a multicultural world and craved contact with other societies as a way of informing their own. The narrowness of nationalism disturbed them. Not willing to concentrate on German militarism as the cause of the First World War,

Jouvenel pointed to the rivalry between czarist Russia and the Austro-Hungarian Empire; their designs on the Balkans and on the disintegrating Ottoman Empire had (as much as anything else) led to war. He believed Germany had been forced to issue an ultimatum to Russia because of the Russian mobilization that put pressure on the German frontier. Naturally Russia then appealed to its ally France, which mobilized its army on August 1, 1914. How could Germany fight Russia without preparing for a French offensive? Jouvenel asks in his memoirs. The tragedy of the war's aftermath was the Allies' dogged insistence that Germany alone should be held responsible for the war and for reparations. He was scandalized that the Germans were not allowed to take part in the discussion of the peace treaty. He noted that even though the Napoleonic Wars a century earlier had inspired much hatred for France, the defeated French were still invited to negotiate a treaty that provided Europe with fifty years of peace. In 1919, however, all was done in the spirit of revenge, a spirit of revenge that haunted Jouvenel's youth.

This history is important for understanding the fervor Jouvenel and Gellhorn brought to their internationalism. They felt they were combating deep forms of prejudice that divided the world. They rejected everything that seemed provincial about personal and public life. Politics, in their view, was not simply a matter of how the state was governed, it was, on a much more profound level, about the organization of human lives. As Jouvenel concluded many years later in his memoirs:

> *A mes yeux, le concret, le positif, le vivant, l'humain, c'etait "les gens,"*
> *et l'Etat une bienveillante abstraction.*
> *J'apprendrais qu'il n'y a rien de plus vivant, de plus humain, que la scene*
> *politique.*

Jouvenel and Gellhorn saw in political life an incredibly moving human drama and insisted upon treating any proposal for social or economic change in terms of human costs and benefits. They were not willing to sacrifice lives for the greater good. No doctrine justified elevating the welfare of the state over the health of its citizens. Thus Jouvenel deplored the punitive damages assessed against Germany because it degraded the German people.

Jouvenel was inspired by his friend H. G. Wells, whose grand world vision Jouvenel termed *"la marche future de la famille humaine."* Jouvenel would later become a pioneer in the field of "future studies." Informing all his work would be a principle he and Gellhorn pursued in their peace efforts: "politics cannot be reduced to institutions . . . power lies above all in the initiative of men moving other men." This was the role of the writer; the role model was H. G. Wells. Wells was an exhilarating presence. With his youthful laugh, his jokes, his energetic, erudite manner, and his floundering in a French that was virtually impossible to understand, he was a touchingly human and powerful example of the international man. It was Wells's contention that intellectuals had to articulate the political, social, and moral ideas that already existed in a vague form among the people. He opposed violence as a means of achieving social justice and rejected the dangerous doctrine that the end justifies the means. In a few years, he would be championing Gellhorn's great book *The Trouble I've Seen*, because she used her talent as a writer to provide witness to the suffering and aspirations of the people.

Wells exemplified generosity of spirit—the very thing that was lacking in *"le drame de l'entre-deux-guerres,"* as Jouvenel characterizes it in his memoirs. Was not the period between the two world wars the moment to extend a hand to Germany? Jouvenel asks. Such magnanimity would have been prudent, he observes. When this failed to materialize, and when the Nazis took advantage of the spirit of revenge, a world crisis resulted. What Jouvenel does not say in his memoirs is that the defeat of his hopes for a united Europe also doomed his union with Gellhorn, for their love was predicted on a sense of conciliation and common interests that their personal and political lives could not sustain. Their love was like a political alliance subject to the pressures of competing powers, of other spheres of influence, and of an international community over which they could have little control. Theirs was a mutuality that depended on their sense of bridging gaps between countries and peoples. It is significant that Jouvenel should title his memoirs *Un Voyageur dans le Siècle*. Pierre Hassner points out that Jouvenel selected "the metaphor of the traveler exploring uncharted roads, announcing opportunities and dangers ahead" as the central theme of his life and work. No more than Gellhorn could he stand still. As an internationalist, it is difficult to commit yourself to only one alliance or to one point of origin.

As happy as she was in her four months of travels with Jouvenel in late 1930 and early 1931, Gellhorn left him for a trip home. He would follow shortly. They would journey in tandem and then explore various routes separately, sometimes closing the loop in their lives, sometimes enlarging it, until finally the tie between them wore out.

CROSSING THE CONTINENT

1 9 3 1

8

By the early spring of 1931, Gellhorn had embarked on a cross-continental tour of the United States. She adored traveling. Nothing else gave her the same lift as the prospect of a journey. Yet she was often in a foul mood—upset with the Americans she encountered and disappointed in herself. Part of her problem was writing. She had not found the right subject, and herself as a subject soured her. Her feelings were summed up in a poem, "Spleen, 1931." She wrote about going through Bismarck, North Dakota, the oil fields of Texas, and the prairie. Much of what she saw was a grayish-brown world viewed from the windows of her train. She was troubled by the mediocrity of the people and the towns she visited. She wanted to see something more than tired-looking roads, crummy stores, and heavily made-up girls flirting with train conductors. The banality of the conversation bored her. Who wanted to listen to a bow-tied youth piously praising the Deity as the creator of nature? She longed for some kind of robust emotion or deed that would wear away this insipid world.

Gellhorn sent her poem to Joseph Stanley Pennell. He had come to St. Louis in the mid-1920s from Junction City, Kansas. In St. Louis, he had worked for radio station KMOX and the *Post-Dispatch,* and had taken roles in several amateur theatricals. He was a poet. Desperately trying to write a novel, disappointed that much of his work was not published, worried about making a living, hostile toward the insularity of his midwestern upbringing, and itching to travel to more stimulating places, he was nearly the perfect male counterpart to Martha Gellhorn. Fond of George and Edna Gellhorn, he wrote them letters echoing Martha's unquenchable urge to get somewhere. On stationery of the Santa Fe Railroad Observation Car, he placed three question marks after the letterhead's words *En Route,* for he wondered where he was really going. He was in San Bernardino, California, and he felt stranded by the rain in the normally arid climate. Much like Martha, "Stan" (as she called him) wanted to make literature out of his predicaments. In his diary, as in her letters, there is a sense of a very young and aggressive personality pushing against environment and arguing with the grounds of existence that others take for granted.

Pennell was the same age as Gellhorn and knew many of her friends, especially Erna Rice, a John Burroughs classmate. Rice's family had an Ozark lodge that Gellhorn liked to visit, and Pennell was sometimes included as an extra man. He held some appeal for her, since she favored artists and journalists—anyone who might have a fresh outlook. She had little use for most of the young men with whom she had grown up; they were too conventional, too bound by St. Louis. She preferred her own company if no one of interest was available. One St. Louis winter, as one of her friends remembers, Gellhorn rented a room in which she could write. For a brief period, she and Pennell were close and she became the subject of a sonnet sequence he deeply cherished and continually revised, memorializing her beauty. Visions of her haunted his nights as he remembered the way she turned her "golden head," the way she slept, her voice, and the transience of their time together.

By 1931, they were no longer as close, but the bond between them was still strong. She wrote him from California in the middle of April about how fed up she was with people praising their climate, their land, their big buildings, their clubs, and their salaries. It all seemed so arid. She was not going to stay. Things were not as wonderful as people seemed to think. She was having trouble keeping her left eye open—a curious ailment similar to one Pennell would experience a few years later on his depressing return to Junction City, where he was trying to get some writing done. Why keep traveling? Well, she had to admit she liked observing the hills rising from the ground and feeling the wind blowing.

From Reno (April 27), Gellhorn reported to Pennell on the lotus-eating natives. She was disgusted with women in their department-store, mail-order clothes but charmed by the magnificence of the land. Even St. Louis now seemed appealing as a refuge for weary travelers. She had been harried by amorous males and was actually looking forward to going home. She consoled herself with a copy of Pennell's verse he had just sent her and luxuriated in lines that sounded like Thomas Wolfe, paeans to the fertile, dark land.

By early May, she had made it to St. Louis, limping into town on a badly bruised foot that needed treatment in Saint Luke's Hospital. It was an old injury, the result of a fall on the side of a mountain in Italy. She wanted to write Pennell about her feelings, but she distrusted words. She wanted to write, period. Although she does not say so, she was beginning to formulate the themes of her first novel, for she alluded to the lines from Hemingway and Wolfe that would become the epigraphs to her novel:

Nothing ever happens to the brave. —*A Farewell to Arms*
The hunger that haunts and hurts Americans and makes them exiles at home and strangers wherever they go. —*Look Homeward Angel*

There it was: a feeling that she would somehow survive her sojourns so long as she remained intrepid; a gnawing need to be on the move, even though a sense of estrangement dogged her no matter whether she was in St. Louis or elsewhere.

On May 14, she was writing Pennell from Indianapolis, where she was changing trains for Pittsburgh. She thought of him holding her as a male gave her a look-over; but he was not to think of coming after her. It was best for him to remain at his job. She was tiring of American train travel; somehow it did not inspire her the way European trips always did.

From Dayton, Gellhorn groused about the abominable food, which looked as though it been put to torture. How could people put up with such crap? If she had not grown up to appreciate the comforts of the middle class, what kind of criminal might she have become in such sorry circumstances?, she wondered. She was looking none too good herself— rather wrinkled and flattened by the long hours of travel. She felt that Pennell would not find her very appetizing if he could get a whiff of her right then.

Finally, Gellhorn found respite with the rich. On May 19, she wrote Pennell describing the bucolic setting of a country estate in Bryn Mawr, the home of Kitty McVitty, Bryn Mawr, class of 1928. She enjoyed the garden, the yacht, and the dinners—everything that made this kind of life comfortable, if not useful. She reveled in luxury, yet she doubted she deserved it. It was so pleasant to linger among the cherry trees, the magnolia blooms, and the wind invading the Bryn Mawr campus. She was visiting friends, including Emily Lewis, her schoolmate at the John Burroughs School who had entered Bryn Mawr a year after Martha. She was thinking of Pennell—she missed him—while having to confess a compulsion to escape from what she cherished. It was a kind of self-torture she had trouble comprehending. She could be his only on occasion, for she was always leaving one place for another. Russia might be her next objective.

In New York City by the end of May, she found herself still wishing she could put her arms around Pennell just so she could fill the void. She was shocked to find the fight taken out of herself. There was a kind of oblique warning to him in her reference to having been in love with a man for nearly a year who so captivated her that she was incapable of feeling anything for anyone else. The same might happen to Pennell.

In Mexico for the summer, it was a relief for her to learn in late July that Pennell had accepted a teaching position at the John Burroughs School. She imagined him making his peace with St. Louis and absorbing its life. It was the only way to have a tolerable existence there. As for her, she was getting a lot of sun and exercising. She hoped he might come for a visit and presented an enticing picture of herself, without clothing, lying about in the sun. She was getting no work done—a problem only because she had to have sufficient funds to finance her trips.

Luxuriating in the Mexican climate gave Gellhorn time to think about herself. Although she had a wonderful gift for friendship and took a deep interest in the affairs of others, she wondered at her lack of commitment to people, at her reluctance to couple herself with anyone. It gave her the shakes to suppose she was such a superficial person and it bothered her that she could not find a calm within herself. She longed for the kind of stasis Keats evoked in "Ode on a Grecian Urn." She would use a phrase from the poem, "what mad pursuit," as the title of her first novel, which she was about to begin. She suspected her life was out of control and feared the same for Pennell.

Mexico was lovely and old. It reminded Gellhorn of Europe. It did not cost much to live there, or to buy things such as flowers or lovely handcrafted objects. The Mexican countenance was worthy of study; it revealed character. She had accustomed herself to being alone, and the art and architecture delighted her. She was going to do an article on

Eisenstein, who was filming in Mexico. She worked on four other articles, but only the Eisenstein piece was published in the *Post-Dispatch* (August 9, 1931).

Entitled "Mexico's History in a Film Epic," Gellhorn's article explained the Russian director's efforts to capture the customs of the country truthfully and esthetically. Constructed as a series of discrete but connected episodes, the film sought to portray the nation's development. In the Yucatán, Eisenstein concentrated on the life of a people descended from the Mayans. Shots of Indians alongside ancient statues established the sense of continuity between past and present. Eisenstein was using more than six hundred natives to convey an authentic picture of daily life and to emphasize, in Gellhorn's view, a theme of the director's other works: the heroic nature of the people. The attention to details—to dress, to setting, and to many other indigenous elements—was impressive. So was Eisenstein's focus on the Spanish invasion that oppressed the people and exploited the country's resources. Yet old Spain's romantic aura and the splendor of its architecture, dress, and customs were given full play in an episode that Gellhorn obviously enjoyed. She was hardly a Marxist, but after her own recent experiences with the rich, idle ruling class in Bryn Mawr, she was taking some measure of satisfaction in viewing Eisenstein's version of historical process, in which the people become aware of their strength and inevitably press forward into revolutionary action. There were more scenes—glimpses of the postrevolutionary world—and Gellhorn left no doubt in her readers' minds that some of the authentic Mexico had been successfully recorded for the cameras. This is a neat, straightforward piece of reporting that does not reveal the feeling she vouchsafed to Pennell at the beginning of her assignment: that Eisenstein's work seemed rather peculiar. She thought it might be fun to work with him, but then again, she felt her assignment might be to do the washing.

Mexico provided easy living and Gellhorn enjoyed being alone. She did not want any men in her life just then. Besides, she was having trouble adjusting to the altitude and the food. She felt a little queasy, and was disappointed that she was not picking up Spanish more quickly. She had decided to move to a lower altitude, watch her diet more carefully, and work on her articles.

Sometime in mid-August, Gellhorn let Pennell know that she was going to marry Bertrand de Jouvenel. Pennell did not accuse her of betraying him, but she interpreted his rather mean tone as implying her perfidy. She claimed to have been as open with him as she was with herself, having heard about the marriage announcement just a week before he did. This was a curious way to refer to her own wedding plans, but not unlike a woman who would always seem at some remove from her own marriages, wishing to give herself wholeheartedly to them but demurring nevertheless. It was clear enough from her letters that she would not go back to Pennell, but her encouraging words naturally aroused his hopes.

In late September, Gellhorn wrote Pennell about her plans to stay in New York City at the home of Mrs. Frederick Vanderbilt Field. She was not looking forward to the filth and ugly stickiness of cities after such a sumptuous summer. Mrs. Vanderbilt had become a friend of Martha's brother Walter during his law-school days and subsequently formed a close friendship with her. Frederick Vanderbilt Field found Martha an interesting, attractive, and entertaining houseguest. Field liked to talk politics, and he learned that she was reading Communist writers. But there was little he could discern about her leftist sympathies, except to say that she was a "very liberal and observant person."

At the end of September, Bertrand de Jouvenel arrived in the United States on the *Ile de France.* It was a moment of grave economic crisis for the country—as he puts it in his memoirs—and he had come to observe it firsthand. Gellhorn met him at the dock in New York, dressed in a sleeveless blue linen shirt. It was an outfit that he would become most familiar with during their travels from October to April. To Europeans suffering the deprivations of the post–World War I period, the United States was Eldorado, a land of the rich, Jouvenel explains in his memoirs. Shortly, he would be writing for French readers about men sleeping on park benches, about beggars in the streets, and about unemployed auto workers in Detroit. Everywhere he went, he was struck with the spectacle of men, women, and children sitting on sidewalks, waiting. Waiting for what? he asked. They were in soup lines, out of work, miserable, and hungry. Nine million people were looking for jobs.

Gellhorn wanted to show Jouvenel poverty that was even worse than the urban distress he witnessed. Much to his delight, she proposed they tour the South. He remembered them purchasing *une immense torpedo* in New Jersey for the sum of fifty dollars. In an article published in *The Spectator* (August 1936), Gellhorn recalled the sum as $28.50 for an "eight-year-old Dodge open touring car." Their accounts agree that the backseat was full of fallen leaves. For Jouvenel, the car became a prized possession and one of his fondest memories.

Jouvenel found the South a fantastic phenomenon. They drove with their car leaning to one side as he welcomed their penetration of the Cotton Kingdom. It was like a "palette" on which was arranged every tint from chrome to vermilion. The rivers and ponds were the color of iodine, with their banks a paler shade underneath a copper sky. Gellhorn remembered the heat and dust. A powderlike coating stuck to their faces and hair. Both were struck by the contrast between the beauty of nature and the poverty of the people, the ramshackle buildings made of planking and the thin people standing in the fields, as if immobilized by "semi-starvation."

As much under the influence of Thomas Wolfe as Gellhorn was, Jouvenel imagined his trip across America as a great epic, the stuff of an immense novel, with the railroad serving as the symbol of the traveler's quest to cover the whole of the enormous American expanse. He even had his share of adventures in Hollywood, where he met Gellhorn's friends Martha Love Symington and Emily Lewis Norcross. Much to his amusement, he was hired as an extra. A handsome man with a long face faintly reminiscent of Valentino's, he was picked to play figures in society, even though his body still bore the marks of his failed efforts to become a boxer. He learned quickly how to assume the airs of a French gentleman. It was necessary to enter a scene quickly flapping his elbows as if they were the wings of a penguin, then to seize a lady's hand in order to kiss the inside of her wrist. He raised objections to this practice and was told it did not matter what he had done in France: "Here you must have the bearing of a Frenchman." Jouvenel enjoyed acting, which was mostly waiting around for the star to appear. The company was agreeable, however, and he earned seven dollars a day. Martha also may have worked as an "extra," for Joseph Pennell noted in his diary (September 23, 1932) that she was supposed to have a part in *Movie Crazy,* Harold Lloyd's latest picture. When he saw the film, he could not find her, however. Jouvenel had many entertaining memories of California, including the time he and Martha were recruited by a local sheriff who spent his free time looking for gold.

When she was not traveling with Jouvenel, Gellhorn was off by herself writing fiction, the only thing besides traveling that really appealed to her. She wrote Pennell on December 28 to say she was about midway through writing what seemed like one of the most turgid novels on record. She was preparing to set off for the Yucatán, having found a place for herself in steerage. She liked the work Pennell had recently published in *Poetry* magazine, although it was not his best. In a typical jab at St. Louis, she wondered whether it was still the hub of the universe.

WHAT MAD PURSUIT

1 9 3 2 - 1 9 3 4

9

Since leaving Bryn Mawr in 1929, Martha Gellhorn had been on a kind of mad pursuit. She had climbed the Pyrenees with a group of Basques, written for French newspapers, and begun work on her first novel. Sometimes during this period, she lost her literary journal in Switzerland's Lago Maggiore. Never staying in one place very long, writing in fits and starts, in search of an ideal way of life, Gellhorn was restless. This suited Bertrand de Jouvenel, who would later write "a certain indiscipline qualified me for this role of explorer." Like him, she "was always fascinated by the phenomena of my time and the most diverse ones." They had minds that fastened on events and plumbed public affairs for what these revealed about a conflicted civilization they hoped to heal. Taking its inspiration from "Ode on a Grecian Urn," *What Mad Pursuit* reflects Gellhorn's "struggle to escape" the clutches of her time and place. Charis Day, Gellhorn's heroine, quits college in protest over the "double standard": a coed is expelled for having slept in a male student's dormitory room, while he is allowed to remain in school. This is the first of many incidents in which Charis fights against the foul corruption of things and against the way most people live. Whether the cause is a strike or the defense of a radical who has been framed, Charis is prepared to seek justice—notwithstanding the trouble she makes for herself.

65

Gellhorn presented her heroine as a complete naif—certainly more ignorant of the world than Gellhorn herself was when she decided to leave college. Unlike Gellhorn, Charis has no family background or experience abroad that might ease her initiation period. When she is confronted with a corpse in the morgue during her brief career as a cub reporter, she rebels against the sight of a grotesque and destitute-looking body, stinking of chemicals. Life must amount to more than this, she exclaims. However, if Charis is less sophisticated than her author and has fewer resources upon which to draw, she expresses much of the loneliness, anger, and disappointment Gellhorn felt in her first years on her own. When Charis tries, as Gellhorn periodically did, to enjoy the dances, parties, and other social activities of her generation and class, she chafes against the utterly prosaic expectations of her contemporaries and be-moans the perpetual emptiness of a merely social life. When Charis gets involved in defending a labor leader modeled after Tom Mooney (con-victed of bombing and killing people in the 1916 San Francisco Prepared-ness Day parade), she is disillusioned by his plodding, shabby, ordinary supporters, who turn his catastrophe into a boring propaganda campaign, writing drab, shoddy tracts on his case. Charis sees herself, as Gellhorn did, in quest of a higher calling, to achieve, in Charis's words, "a triumph of living."

Possessed of Gellhorn's high spirits and of a romantic belief in taking setbacks courageously, Charis abides by a Hemingwayesque code that asserts nothing can really be amiss so long as there is "one grand person." This is a conviction Gellhorn would invest in various figures from Hemingway to John F. Kennedy, and which saves Charis from utter despair when she finds she has contracted syphilis from her first sexual encounter in Paris. Michael, Charis's somewhat older mentor and lover, carefully manages the scene in which her disease is revealed to her, so that she does not entirely lose the "shine" that has distinguished her idealistic persona. The ending of *What Mad Pursuit,* which gives a brief glimpse of a chastened but still determined Charis, suggests the psychic toll Gellhorn's own hectic travels took on her.

What Mad Pursuit was completed by the end of 1932, but Gellhorn had trouble placing it with a publisher. Three chapters in particular were offensive to the tastes of the time. She wanted to write a sexually explicit novel and go into the consequences of Charis's disease, but the author finally accepted a friend's advice to revise the offending passages. Better to have one's first novel published—even if it meant making "concessions."

These days, Gellhorn is chary of acknowledging *What Mad Pursuit.* She admits that her father disliked the book with good reason. He once complained of it to Emily Lewis Norcross, who tried to console him with the suggestion that it was a book his daughter had to get out of her system. Gellhorn would like to expunge it from history; she never lists it among her published works. As the reviewer in *The New York Times* (November 18, 1934) suggests, the novel is "palpably juvenalia," although it is readable because of the author's great vitality. The trouble is that Gellhorn was very close to her heroine but contemptuous of nearly everything in the heroine's environment. Nothing measures up. The college Charis attends has almost no distinguishing features; and the same is true of the newspaper that employs her and of most of the other American and European settings. The best parts of the novel are when Charis is by herself—mountain climbing, for example—because there the rhythm of the scene actually evokes her fitful, reckless nature. Otherwise, episodes are introduced only to dismiss other characters and places as unworthy of Charis's noble aspirations. Although Charis is criticized for her heedless pursuit of the ideal, in the end she is practically worshipped as a sojourner after truth. The novel lacks the tension and self-criticism of mature work. The truth is that Gellhorn was not perceptive enough about the very things she rejected to make them come alive in fiction.

Bertrand de Jouvenel, interviewed by Olga Clark in July of 1934 for the St. Louis *Globe-Democrat,* professed to be "proud of his wife's first book." They had been married the summer before in Spain at the home of an old friend of Colette, the portrait painter José Maria Sert, whose wife, a sculptress, had just completed a bust of Gellhorn. The couple were separated while Martha (in the Midi since the early spring of 1934) worked on a second novel, which she was never to publish, the story of "the Franco-American clash, or temperamental differences between the two nationalities."

Edna, more worried than she would admit about her roving daughter's fate, was relieved to see her married to such a distinguished Frenchman. At a Bryn Mawr Club meeting in Emily Lewis Norcross's home, Edna was called to the telephone. She came back looking very strange, with her head held extremely high. It was the St. Louis *Post-Dispatch* calling to confirm that Martha was married to Bertrand de Jouvenel. Everyone looked up and said, "What!" "Yes," Edna affirmed, obviously pleased with her news, "Martha was married two weeks ago in Spain."

On October 8, 1933, Joseph Pennell received a letter from Gellhorn, who was staying in Capri. In his diary for the next day, he recorded her announcement that she had become Madame Bertrand de Jouvenel and that she planned to stay in Paris to bring up her husband's young son. She was deeply in love, but Pennell could not resist observing that her pleasant note had something of the lofty tone she used to take with him.

In the summer of 1934, Bertrand met Edna and some of Martha's friends and satisfied his curiosity about her birthplace. Martha Love Symington, who showed Jouvenel around the city, recalls that he was madly in love with Martha, and that she gave every sign of feeling the same about him. Martha Love took him to an intersection where there were four churches. He wanted to know about them. She explained to him about Methodists, Jews, and the other religions that were represented there and in other parts of the city. To Martha Love, he seemed thunderstruck by the great variety of Christians, as if he had never heard of the Reformation: "Here was this sophisticated Frenchman, and he did not seem to have any idea of these splits in the Church." Soon she was talking about Lutherans and Presbyterians. " 'Oh,' he said, 'how confusing!' " This was his first trip to the United States, and he was not used to seeing different churches at each corner of an intersection, like so many filling stations.

Given the grim news coming from Germany in 1934, Edna was astonished at Jouvenel's friendly attitude toward Germans. He had already been branded as a Fascist in France, but he defended himself by suggesting that "the best way not to fight with the Germans is to be friends with them." Martha's attitude had changed after their visit to Nazi Germany in January. They were traveling with a group of French pacifists of various political persuasions on the left and the right. As a "liberal-reformer," Gellhorn was outraged when German police entered their third-class train compartment and seized the group's newspapers. At the station, they were met by clean-cut, light-haired, regimented Nazi youths parroting the latest Fascist cant. Their barbaric behavior was inexcusable. An angry Gellhorn left the home of von Shirach, the leader of these young Nazis who passed themselves off as socialists, when she witnessed his assault on a servant for spilling coffee. Martha Love Symington, who spent part of the early 1930s in Germany, remembers Gellhorn's letters pestering her for information about the Nazis. It was clear Gellhorn wanted to hear negative news and that she was profoundly disturbed by the treatment of the Jews.

Jouvenel worried about anti-Semitism as well, but he was still fascinated with Nazism as a youth movement. Most of his contacts had been with young Nazis who impressed him with their physicality and equal treatment of each other regardless of class. He seemed taken with their vitality and concerned that they should not feel rejected by their fellow Europeans. The worst outcome would be to isolate Hitler and his followers, Jouvenel thought. In power, Hitler would have to temper his more outrageous proposals. He would have to behave more like a rational politician. In other words, his movement would be demystified and treated like any other political program. This was the time to "revive proposals for international cooperation through trade," Jouvenel argued.

In retrospect, this reasoning seems naïve in the extreme, but Jouvenel was responding to the Nazis from the point of view of a European aristocrat with a strong bourgeois background who felt exhilarated by the camaraderie of Hitler youth groups. Many years later, Gellhorn noted that there was an air of unreality about Jouvenel's politics; he roamed among different political camps, and she doubted that his positions were treated with much respect. Gellhorn, after all, had lived in a much more open world. Her childhood was not spent in the isolation that so clearly marked Jouvenel's. What is more, she was outgrowing the almost mystical faith he had in analyzing history by generations. He believed, for example, that French and German youth shared a sense of solidarity that marked them off from generations of the past. The war and certain public events formed a common bond. Modern technology—the speedup in communications accomplished by the telephone, the radio, and the automobile—meant that a new generation was impatient with tradition and mandated that changes occur more rapidly than before. Misjudging the thrust of Hitler's national socialism, Jouvenel contended that the Nazi youth were part of a European generation that believed in the welfare state, which would address quality-of-life issues. Much of this seemed wishful thinking to Gellhorn, who was now moving toward a nationalistic focus, toward the United States, after finding it impossible to work with this new European generation.

The changes in Gellhorn's thinking are reflected in "La Plume et l'Epee," an article she published in Jouvenel's journal, *La Lutte des jeunes,* on June 10, 1934. *La Lutte* had begun by advocating a national plan for youth, recommending mandatory retirement at age sixty and the establishment of communes for unemployed young people (*maison de jeunesse*), which would put them to work on New Deal–type projects. Gellhorn had contributed articles on Diego Rivera's controversial American murals (May 31, 1933) and on the civil war in Vienna (February 25, 1934) between socialists and the Austrian government. Now she turned her attention to a frank discussion of pacifist writers and revolutionary painters. Why was it, she wondered, that they had been unable to endow pacifism with a sense of glory and myth that would animate the multitudes the way Hitler and Mussolini were doing with their propaganda? She knew that it was not the proper calling of an artist to propagandize, yet she longed for someone to compose a marching song that would galvanize a new generation's hopes for a humane revolution in human affairs. She pointed to the powerful scenes in Rivera's murals evoking the suffering and the struggle of the masses for expression, and to Roosevelt's employment of artists who were transforming American life with pictures of laborers in strong colors, in simple designs, and in a muscular, virtually photographic style that amounted to a hymn to work.

While Jouvenel continued to argue that much could be learned from the development of Fascist states in Germany and Italy, Gellhorn was preparing to return to the United States to work for the New Deal. Jouvenel wanted to reconcile left and right in France and to restrain the more extreme elements of the left. For Gellhorn, it was much too late to speak of compromise, and she felt her own country was in trouble. Suddenly struck by the enormity of the Depression, she realized that the United States was no longer secure and wealthy and isolated from the rest of the world. So she reversed direction—in search of an America that now needed her energies every bit as much as Europe, which, she had thought, specialized in trouble. In his diary for July 8, 1932, Joseph Pennell noted the dejected appearance of people in the Kansas City Union. With little money and few prospects himself, he dreamed of making his fortune, and he clipped out of newspapers articles detailing the exploits of various extravagant and wealthy characters. Pennell thought of Gellhorn often and of what her life in Europe must be. He still believed she was a magnificent girl who had inspired his best poetry, and he still loved her, even though he realized there was no likelihood of their ever getting together.

Gellhorn's relations with Jouvenel were in flux. In spite of her letter to Pennell announcing her decision to live a married life in Paris, she did not stay in the city or take care of Jouvenel's young son, and the very idea of marriage soon lost its appeal. In February 1935, Jouvenel would challenge Julien Duvivier, a film director, to a duel for "an alleged insult to his honor and fair name as a critic," but he was worried that "his wife . . . now in the United States might fear for his safety." The marriage was not so much over as it was attenuated by her lack of commitment to the cause and to the vision of the world he espoused.

THE TROUBLE

I'VE SEEN

1934 − 1936

10

October 16, 1934: It was a sunny day. Martha Gellhorn had arrived in New York from Paris six days earlier on a pathetic little ship. An eighty-five-dollar passage, it was all she could afford. Marquis Childs, a St. Louis friend and newspaperman, had taken her to see Harry L. Hopkins, director of the Federal Emergency Relief Administration (FERA). Hopkins was looking for field investigators to report to him on how people on relief were faring. He wanted detailed accounts concerning their health, nutrition, housing, likelihood of employment, and mood. The blond, slender Gellhorn did not appear to be a credible candidate for the job. Someone more sturdy-looking was wanted, he thought. She had the polish of a "young society matron" and "distracting" long legs.

Gellhorn told Hopkins two things that made him revise his initial impression: She knew a lot about unemployment and she was an experienced journalist. Certainly her European travels with Jouvenel qualified her to make the first claim, but by her own estimation, she exaggerated her reportorial skills. She was willing to accept employment that would probably last less than two months at thirty-five dollars a week plus traveling expenses. Gellhorn detected a glint in Hopkins's eyes that made her think he might be amusing himself when he offered her the job.

She was probably right. Hopkins was anything but a stuffy govern-

72

ment bureaucrat. He had spent his boyhood in small midwestern towns, brought up by a wandering father with a "weakness for poker and bowling" and by a Methodist missionary mother. This combination produced in Hopkins "a militant social conscience" and an "easygoing gaiety"—a description that would fit Gellhorn pretty well, too. Like her, he had spent some time working in settlement houses; and like her grandmother, his social work with children made him particularly sensitive to the plight of the poor. Gellhorn could not have picked a better boss. The "lean, loose-limbed, disheveled" Hopkins, with "sharp features and dark, sardonic eyes," had a penchant for profanity and "concise, pungent" language. His assistants called him Harry. He was informal and direct, the very model of a brash man she could admire. Like her, he was possessed of the conviction that "all walls would fall before the man of resources and decision."

Gellhorn's first trip as an FERA field investigator was to a textile town in North Carolina. Conditions were appalling. A typical case involved a woman with five children. She received a relief check of $3.40 a week. The family had no shoes. Nearly all their furniture had been sold. The price of food had doubled in some areas. The diet was so poor that pellagra had become commonplace. With no money for medicine, many people were degenerating mentally and physically, succumbing to syphilis and infectious diseases. Cripples and imbeciles often were the result of inadequate diet, inept medical treatment, and plain ignorance.

There was no sanitation to speak of. Latrines frequently fed right into a community's drinking water. Why everyone had not succumbed to typhoid was more than Gellhorn could understand. People lived in shacks with shattered windows, no plumbing, and rats. The tenements were worse than anything she had seen in Europe. Yet tenants were forced to pay high rents and to purchase food at exorbitant rates from the company stores.

Union workers on strike were not rehired and had no clothes for the winter. People were being evicted from their homes. Those still on the job were punished with "stretch-outs" (heavily increased work loads and schedules). Workers were fainting and dying beside their looms. After work, they could not stop their hands from shaking. This was just like a Dickens novel, Gellhorn wrote Hopkins on November 11. Women ate their lunch standing up next to their machines. She found them lying on the cement floors of bathrooms, snatching some respite from their cruel regimen.

Gellhorn cited statistics and gave Hopkins precise descriptions of what she had seen. From her interviews with these people, she could tell they were not complainers. Indeed, they were wonderful, good-humored, and tremendously loyal to the President. They relied on his promise to relieve their suffering. They felt a deep kinship with Roosevelt, often putting his picture in a place of honor. Their main problem was that they were ill, ignorant, and out of work—or exhausted by the employment they could find. It made Gellhorn savage to hear them accused of bolshevism—although a year earlier a relief investigator, Lorena Hickok, observed examples of Communists organizing "farmers and working like beavers." According to Gellhorn, there was no chance of an insurrection among these people, for they were mired in feudal conditions, a shameful thing for her to admit in a country with such lofty democratic ideals.

On November 26, in Boston, she reported to Hopkins that she was seeing as many as "five families a day." More examples of malnutrition, tuberculosis, rickets, retardation, anemia, and a multitude of other diseases and maladies disgusted her—especially when she discovered that the local relief administrators were often corrupt and inept. She would quote verbatim the desperate expressions of families who could not live on the pittance supplied by the government—on the average, no more than half a dollar a day. In early December, after a trip to Rhode Island, she wrote Hopkins to support mill owners' accusations that only Catholics who were Democrats could become federal administrators. In New Hampshire, she saw further signs of graft in the way men were hired to work on certain projects.

The first two months in the field were grueling for Gellhorn. She lost weight. She got angry at what she saw. Her meticulous observations and citations of facts and figures sometimes gave way to livid denunciations of the politicians and mill and factory owners who perpetuated a brutal economic system. She stormed back to Washington full of "blood and thunder." Hopkins tried to calm her and talk her out of resigning. He commiserated with her and knew FERA was not doing enough, that it was doing, at best, a "minimal job." State welfare budgets and private charitable funds were depleted, and the federal allocation was only $500 million for the whole country. He suggested she speak with Mrs. Roosevelt, which she proceeded to do, using the same crabby words she had used with Hopkins. In retrospect, she saw the humor in her high dudgeon and found it remarkable that Hopkins could contain his mirth and not laugh uproariously at her. Always a sympathetic listener, Mrs. Roosevelt convinced Gellhorn she should tell her story directly to the President.

Many years later, Gellhorn wrote fondly of her first visit to the White House. She was invited to dinner and went in a "black sweater and skirt." She was irritated at the fine dishes, the splendid meal, the complacent guests in their formal clothing. All she could think about were the Depression-deprived millions lacking the basic decencies of food, shelter, and work. Hard of hearing and in the habit of shouting, Mrs. Roosevelt stood up at the far end of the table and urged the President to "talk to that child at your left. She says that all the people in the South have pellagra or syphilis." This announcement brought conversation to a halt. Almost immediately, the table was convulsed in laughter. Mrs. Roosevelt had not meant to be amusing, but, rather, to get her husband's attention. Gellhorn was furious. She wanted to leave right then. But the President was fascinated and pleased with her. He was not going to let his wife's awkwardness spoil things. Instead, he listened to Gellhorn's brief words— she was still choking with anger—and invited her to visit him again.

The Roosevelts talked Gellhorn out of quitting her FERA job. She was to go back into the field so that they could learn more about what was actually happening. She was assured that her reports would result in action. She kept at it for nearly a year, traveling across the country, investigating every region, and writing to Hopkins at lightning speed. By April 25, 1935, her mood was changing, along with the feelings of people who could not get off the dole; it was like that period of a protracted war during which people's spirits sagged. Roosevelt's support seemed to be dwindling; people were no longer sure things would get better.

On August 22, 1935, Bertrand de Jouvenel arrived in Washington for another tour of America. He interviewed Senator Borah about the Neutrality Act that had just passed the Senate and J. Edgar Hoover about organized crime. He made several visits to relief investigators, including Gellhorn. In fact, his main purpose was to see whether they could reconcile their differences. They toured Moscow, Idaho, and visited "Psychiana," a community founded by Frank B. Robinson, who declared he had communicated personally with God. Gellhorn made it clear she was no longer interested in living with Jouvenel. But she was still fond of him, and they would remain close friends for the rest of his life,

Jouvenel becoming a steadfast supporter of her books and writing admiring articles in the French press such as "Avec Martha Gellhorn, Collaboratrice du President Roosevelt."

By the fall of 1935, Gellhorn's attitude toward her relief work had turned rebellious. No, she kept telling the dullards in Washington, there were no agitators stirring up dissent. She was beginning to wish there were. In a small Idaho town, she encountered an all too familiar situation: unemployed men exploited by a dishonest contractor. The men had lost their farms and ranches and were now digging dirt for a contractor who took their shovels, tossed them in the lake, and benefited from a commission for the order of new ones. The men had to wait for the next shipment of shovels with no means of support unless they were willing to submit to a humiliating means test. Gellhorn bought them beer and lectured them. She taunted these hardy Westerners and questioned their manhood. Only by making some kind of disturbance, she assured them, would they get the government's attention to their complaints.

Gellhorn was in Seattle by the time the FBI caught up with her. The men in Idaho had broken the windows of an FERA office—incited by her, they said. The contractor's scam was stopped, and Gellhorn was returned to Washington. She was delighted to get word from Hopkins's deputy that the men now balked at the status quo and went around repeating her arguments. To her parents, she wrote an exuberant letter about how she was now regarded as a "dangerous Communist." It was obviously a thrill to be taken so seriously. Hopkins regretted it, but he had to fire her. She was happy to be free of government work and immediately determined to write the exposé of the relief program that she had intended to publish nearly a year earlier when Hopkins talked her into staying on the job.

In the midst of cleaning out her office, Gellhorn got a call from the President's secretary. The Roosevelts were concerned about her and wanted her to stay at the White House. She was a quick-tempered revolutionary spirit who might seriously run awry by alienating the very people who could help her. "She [Martha] must learn patience & not have a critical attitude towards what others do for she must remember that to them it is just as important as her dreams are to her," Eleanor wrote to Lorena Hickok. It was December 1935, the end of an arduous year for Gellhorn. She was near collapse and verging on anemia. In January, her

father died before getting to see her first major work—which she dedicated to him—in print. From St. Louis, she wrote Eleanor Roosevelt that
she would remain with her mother as long as she was needed; none of
her family had yet come to an understanding of how to cope with their
terrible loss. Later she would admit she had found no way to accept death
and did not want anyone's words on the subject.

In early February, Martha wrote Eleanor about her need to look for
another job. She would probably go to New York, since St. Louis seemed
to specialize in women who sold dresses in fashionable stores. The Roosevelts thought Martha needed time to consider her next step, and they were
sure her finances were shaky. They sensed that she did not like the White
House that much, but Mrs. Roosevelt assured her she had to show up for
meals only when it suited her. Otherwise, food in her room would be
fine, and so were visits from friends or anything else that would make
her comfortable.

Gellhorn accepted the invitation, but it was rather unnerving for her
to be put in Abraham Lincoln's room. This all seemed so out of scale with
her kind of life. She dashed down a corridor late one evening, woke up
another guest, Alexander Woollcott, and confessed her uneasiness about
occupying Lincoln's bed. "Shut up and go back to sleep. Edna Ferber slept
in it last week," he said. Woollcott had been present at Gellhorn's first
White House dinner and was quite aware of her moral earnestness and
sense of mission.

The Roosevelts' hospitality did not seem unusually generous to Gellhorn at the time, and it was so like them to join her in making fun of
the FBI. They were a down-to-earth couple concerned with the everyday
problems she faced. Gellhorn points out that the White House was not
the protected mansion it has since become. More like a "great big house,"
it was not much different from what the Roosevelts had lived in all their
lives. Remarkably little attention was paid to security. Some of the
furniture, Gellhorn remembered, was quite old and faded but comfortable, and like most of the furnishings, reflected the Roosevelts' plain but
pleasant tastes. The old-fashioned bathrooms with brass fixtures and huge
claw-footed tubs befitted their unpretentious, homey style. Gellhorn
found Mrs. Roosevelt's own room austere and unattractive, with rather
dull features. Besides the bed, there was not much more than a few chairs,
a modest desk, and bookshelves. Mrs. Roosevelt obviously cared little for
her own decor. The White House lacked the pomp and splendor initiated
by later presidents.

The more Gellhorn saw of Mrs. Roosevelt, the more she grew to love her as a second mother. Nothing pleased Eleanor Roosevelt more than to help other people; caring for others was something she *needed*, Gellhorn realized. She did not like to be waited on and would fetch things for herself. Gellhorn would stay up with her some nights to read the mail. She had the impression that Roosevelt answered these letters, many of which addressed her as a friend to whom people could confess their cares and expect help. This "pathologically modest" woman never claimed the privilege of another's love. While her husband mixed "lethal Martinis" and entertained his cronies after dinner, she retired to her room to work. To Gellhorn, "he was a charmer, but she was the moral true north." He was not especially "cozy or comforting" with his wife, but he acknowledged her as the conscience of his administration. He treated Gellhorn as "a sort of mascot or pet or poodle or something in this galere," she later suggested in an interview. Although he was "nice" to her, she was not especially fond of him. She knew he was a great and powerful politician, but her emotional tie was to Eleanor, for "she was love."

The White House served Gellhorn quite well as a quiet setting in which to work on her first draft of *The Trouble I've Seen.* When a friend made available his vacant, isolated Connecticut home, she left the Roosevelts, full of gratitude for their sensible and loving support but bent on finishing, in complete solitude, a fictionalized version of her relief work. The book put an end to a chapter in Gellhorn's life. It was like a catharsis, as if she had thrown off some wicked disease. Only by disgorging the experience in an article or book could she return to health and hurl her resources into another assignment. Her job with FERA would turn out to be her most sustained period of commitment to working beside her countrymen. She would never feel quite this close to Americans again— and certainly not to the presidency. In her view, the Roosevelts were unique in their personal and civic courage.

By early June 1936, Gellhorn was in England, the guest of H. G. Wells, whom she had met at the White House. He was known for his "free and open hospitality" and his eagerness to share his views with "nearly anyone." He was especially taken, however, with young women, who found him quite intriguing. It was a heady experience for them to be treated as his equal. He was susceptible to their charms but sometimes was able to restrain himself. To Sinclair Lewis, he wrote that Gellhorn had not "seduced him." His interest in her was "purely friendly, although she is 27 and quite attractive."

Since Wells had befriended Bertrand de Jouvenel and shared his misgivings about the world economy and the fate of mankind, Wells proved a sympathetic—albeit trying—companion for Gellhorn. Wanting to luxuriate in the aftermath of completing her book, she was irritated by his criticisms of her writing habits; he felt she should follow his example and write every day at regular intervals. More interested in parties and dances and dates with her young male friends, Gellhorn tried to explain that she wrote by inspiration. She would never be able to compose on schedule. Almost on a dare, she did draft one article, "Justice at Night," her account of a lynching she claimed to have witnessed in 1931.

In July, Gellhorn moved on to Germany to do further research on her next novel. It centered on a young upper-class French couple committed to helping striking coal miners and to using their militant pacifism to conciliate France and Germany. However, Gellhorn was now a committed anti-Fascist. Civil war had broken out in Spain, and she knew that only a world war could now stop the spread of Nazism. Like her love for Jouvenel, her novel of their time together had lost its conviction. Although she did not abandon the novel, it was superannuated by an utterly changed world.

By mid-August, Eleanor Roosevelt had received an advance copy of *The Trouble I've Seen* and was writing about the book in her syndicated newspaper column. She explained she had been reading it to friends on the U.S.S. *Potomac* and at Hyde Park. She described Gellhorn as "young, pretty, college graduate, good home, more or less Junior League background, with a touch of exquisite Paris clothes and 'esprit' thrown in." Of course, Gellhorn had not graduated from college, but she had the demeanor of a privileged member of society speaking for the hungry and the unemployed: "She has an understanding of many people and many situations and she can make them live for us. Let us be thankful she can, for we badly need her interpretation to help us understand each other." The Roosevelts were immensely taken with her, for she was doing their work and had the "aristocratic" manners she would later attribute to them.

On September 25, Edna wrote Eleanor about her pleasure in knowing that Martha was returning home to work on her next book; and on October 5, Eleanor replied, praising *The Trouble I've Seen* once again and wishing it every success. On October 15, Edna wrote Eleanor to say her letter to Martha had been sent on to the *Queen Mary*, which was due to dock on the morning of October 19. Edna knew her daughter would take joy in Eleanor's note of greeting, for Martha's recent correspondence had been full of praise and fondness for Mrs. Roosevelt. Martha could not understand why Mrs. Roosevelt had been so helpful to her, a sentiment Edna was sure was shared by thousands of others.

With a laudatory preface by H. G. Wells, *The Trouble I've Seen* received rave reviews. For a while, Gellhorn was a national figure. On September 30, Joseph Pennell, still struggling with his own writing and bitter over his brief, unsatisfactory teaching career at John Burroughs, confided to his diary the shock of seeing Gellhorn's glamorous photograph on the cover of *The Saturday Review of Literature*. His first impulse was to call a friend to talk about her picture and marvel over her beauty. Then he considered getting drunk, and was close to tears as he went over various schemes for making money. In the end, he went to a movie and out to dinner, presenting Martha's cover photo to the waiter and asking for his judgment on her looks. The waiter conceded she was attractive but stopped short of calling her a beauty. In Pennell's opinion, the waiter lacked discrimination. After trying to contact a few friends about Gellhorn and looking for her book, Pennell felt it might have been better if he had not noticed the magazine cover.

In the depths of the Depression, the way Gellhorn looked and what she had to say were fused in the public mind. Her glamour and the grimness of her subject matter somehow spoke to the aspirations of everyone like Pennell who wanted to rise above this penury and be recognized for his own shining self-worth. In his syndicated column, Lewis Gannett compared Gellhorn's dust-jacket photo with the pose of a Hollywood actress starring in a film that was to be titled *The Virgin's Prayer.* Other reviews referred to Gellhorn's "young and wistful" expression. Even better, Gannett said Gellhorn was as good as Hemingway in her use of authentic American speech and in achieving "economy of language."

In early October, Marguerite Martyn wrote an article for the St. Louis *Post-Dispatch* that offered a reprise of Gellhorn's career to date, making her seem adventurous, romantic, and somewhat mysterious:

And, oh yes. She married into the old noblesse, a young French Count, a journalist, economist and political commentator. But that seems to have been a transitory affair, a more mental rather than sentimental attachment which waned as he became more Fascist, she more liberal in political views. "They simply are not married now," one is told.

Above all, Martyn wanted to show Gellhorn's independence, dramatizing her departure from college and her journalism and travels abroad as manifestations of her enormous vigor and resourcefulness.

In his preface to *The Trouble I've Seen,* H. G. Wells comments on how "plucky" Gellhorn's characters are. She had traveled in every region of the country and everywhere she saw both the degradation of a people and their determination to reclaim their integrity. North, South, East, and West, children, young people, the middle-aged, and the elderly—all received equal treatment in the four parts of her book. In *The New York Times* (September 27, 1936), Edith H. Walton expressed astonishment at how well Gellhorn identified with all of her characters. Having read *What Mad Pursuit,* the reviewer expected to find a sensibility that patronized and remained aloof from them. The difference between the first and second books was that the author was now willing to live with her characters and not just to view them as literary material. They were people with stories to tell through her, and to a large extent Gellhorn put her style at their service, using their words and expressions in her narrative even when she was not directly quoting or describing them. As Mabel Ulrich put it in *The Saturday Review of Literature* (September 26, 1936), *The Trouble I've Seen* had been fashioned "out of the very tissues of human beings."

Perhaps the best single page of *The Trouble I've Seen* is the first. Mrs. Maddison stands before her mirror trying on her hat, tilting it toward her right eye, then toward her left. Her face appears confused in the cracked mirror. This cheap thirty-cent white straw hat shaped like a pot has been trimmed by Mrs. Maddison herself with a "noisily pink starchy gardenia, in the centre front, like a miner's lamp." When she walks outside, the flower (safety-pinned to her hat) nods as she walks, bows before she does, and sometimes blows "from side to side petulantly." This is her best hat, the one she wears when she goes to pick up her relief check. It is important to Mrs. Maddison that no one should suppose she needs things. She will get what is coming to her, but no one is going to think she should be pitied.

Nothing approaching this sort of intimate, involved writing appears in Gellhorn's earlier work. Without commentary, the author conveyed her character's dignity, her effort to achieve balance in her life by setting her hat on her head just so. Mrs. Maddison has a sense of style. Accepting relief is a blow to her pride, but she will find an honorable way to deal with it. Only a writer who had lived with someone such as Mrs. Maddison could describe her most characteristic features in such precise and evocative prose, or would think to include the detail about the safety pin in the hat, which rubs against her forehead. The enormous care the character takes with her own person is paralleled by the author's concern to find just the right words to describe her.

Although H. G. Wells commended Gellhorn for her lack of sentimentality, there is a kind of "salt of the earth" quality to all the stories in the book. As Edith H. Walton noted:

> Few of Miss Gellhorn's characters belong among the naturally idle and supine. Most of them have been, all their lives, self-respecting and hard-working; they are bewildered by what has happened to them; they look back, pathetically and nostalgically, to the day when they were "real folks."

Mrs. Maddison is hardier than most. She agrees to take over an abandoned Negro shack and begin farming with her son and daughter-in-law. When the backbreaking, enervating effort of working the land and rebuilding the flimsy shack results in the destruction of the young couple's dedication to the farm, they blame Mrs. Maddison for bringing them there. Deprived of any continuity or commitment to work, the male characters in this book dream idly of prosperity and condemn the dole and other institutions of society for providing so little support. As Gellhorn noted earlier in her reports to Harry Hopkins, the very bonds of community were being destroyed in the uprooting and displacement of millions of people. In *The Trouble I've Seen,* Mrs. Maddison fears that the wind will carry everything away even as she waits for her relief check.

In Part Two, "Joe and Pete," Gellhorn dramatized the efforts of workers to organize their own unions and to help themselves rather than accept relief. At first, there is sheer exhilaration in acting for oneself. Pete welcomes the feeling of being a strong, independent man, striking out for himself and his buddies. Joe is the idolized leader who will fight for workers' rights and a decent wage. Working men feel they cannot lose because they are supported by Roosevelt, who understands their plight. When Joe is compelled to settle for a token wage increase and workers such as Pete are let go and blackballed, Pete's vision of a society where he can always find a job, where he can support himself, is annihilated. Too ashamed to accept relief, to answer the prying questions of the relief official who visits his home, he runs away from his nagging wife and his responsibilities.

In Part Three, "Jim," Gellhorn concentrated on the romantic illusions of young people. Jim dreams of becoming a great doctor or a musician, and ends up driving a delivery truck. He desperately wants to attain some kind of distinction in his life and resorts to stealing clothes for his marriage to Lou, already pregnant and anxious not to put off their life together for better times that may never come. His idle fantasies about fame and fortune are not merely pathetic, because they arise out of a hardworking, fiercely moral spirit.

"Ruby," the last section of *The Trouble I've Seen,* horrified and impressed many reviewers, for it is about an innocent eleven-year-old girl who turns to prostitution as the only means of gratifying her simple desire for roller skates and other things that delight her still-childish imagination. The first page of "Ruby" sets her in motion as a perfect portrait of youth, an exact counterweight to the opening of "Mrs. Maddison." Ruby enjoys the wind snapping her head back. Her coat, fashioned from her father's castoff, waves in back of her as her coaster skips over the bumpy pavement and she shouts "hoo-wee," with one stocking crumpled down around her ankle. Ruby rides her coaster as if she were flying. She borrows it from a boy who worries she will break it. And indeed there is a reckless, high-spirited quality in the girl that is predictive of her fate. She will do almost anything to attain these emotional highs, these feelings of absolute freedom. "Lookit me," she says, "I'm flying." When she flies, she imagines "the wind yelling" at her.

Poorer than most children from families on relief, Ruby has few friends. Most of the kids make fun of her unkempt and unwashed appearance, and she pretends that she wears rags because she prefers them and does not want to soil her dresses. Her father has abandoned the family, ashamed that it has to accept relief. Ruby is out on her own most of the time, inventing games and pastimes until she is taken up by a group of young girls who have set up a part-time whorehouse. Although her first sexual experience is painful and bewildering, she steels herself to the "work" in order to earn the money that makes her existence a little more pleasant. Eventually, she is caught and taken away from her mother.

Gellhorn told Ruby's story without pathos. It is what Ruby feels she has to do, and Gellhorn had to respect the fact of Ruby's adaptability. Bernice Kert reported that Ruby "was based on a waif Martha had encountered in a Hooverville, Illinois shanty." Ruby was probably a composite of many children Gellhorn observed, including some she had seen in St. Louis. "I knew the riverfront pretty well and the tragic lives of penniless people camping there," Mary Taussig Hall recalls. One of the sights she shared with Martha was of a little girl going "clickety-clack" down the street on her scooter. "Now here's Martha, she comes home for a few days. She goes down to the riverfront for two hours where I've lived and still she's able to write that story ["Ruby"]. She can do more for those people than all the social workers in the world." Martha had her impractical side, wanting to "change all that and get a house for that man who didn't have a house, but she soon found she couldn't do all those good things. Then she left, and we went on dealing with all those people," says Mrs. Hall.

It was the imaginative power Gellhorn could bring to reality that impressed friends. Emily Lewis Norcross has always suspected Gellhorn of fictionalizing her journalism and journalizing her fiction. In at least one instance, the suspicion was well founded. "Justice at Night" purports to be an eyewitness account of a lynching during Gellhorn and Jouvenel's 1931 southern trip. In the article, however, Jouvenel is not mentioned, and his memoirs do not contain any reference to this incident. Taking his place is a companion identified only as "Joe." When the car Gellhorn and Joe are traveling in breaks down somewhere on the way to Columbia, Mississippi, they are picked up by two men on their way to lynch a "goddam nigger" who has raped a white woman. None of it makes sense. The raped woman is fifty; her accused assailant, nineteen. She is a mean, physically unattractive woman, but her word as a white person has to be respected. How would things be if white people were called liars and if "niggers" were truthful? their driver asks. When Joe objects, when he tries to demonstrate how irrational the accusation is, he is threatened and told to shut up.

In this grim, emotional story, Gellhorn maintained control by making her descriptions terse and by reporting as sparely as possible the dialogue and observations of the characters. Although the events are presented as fact, clearly they have been fictionalized to make her point about a community's need for a scapegoat and its hunger for revenge. The lynching itself is rendered in precise detail, so that it is not difficult to imagine oneself there, watching the black man trying to fight the rope and twisting until his head falls to the side. Gellhorn did not give herself a reaction; instead, she described Joe making stifled noises next to her, weeping in anger and in frustration. Her only response was to express her incredulity that such a monstrous thing could have happened, and to end the story with the driver's comment that he will now get them to Columbia.

"Justice at Night" aroused considerable interest. It was a very good piece of writing; it moved people and was reprinted in two magazines. Gellhorn was invited to appear as a witness before a Senate committee drafting an antilynching bill. She was embarrassed, for she had gotten her information from a drunken truck driver who had given her a lift after a lynching, and from a black man whose son had been lynched. She wrote Eleanor Roosevelt, treating her ruse as an amusing mix-up, a product of a rather confused mind. The First Lady advised her not to confess, sensing that the story derived much of its power from Gellhorn's first-person testimony and from the persuasive realism of her imagination. Still fond of the story, Gellhorn included it in *The View from the Ground,* her recent collection (1988) of journalism, with the disingenuous comment that she was not sure it should appear with her nonfiction, since it was based on a memory that might be faulty.

Having returned to the United States on November 1, 1936, Gellhorn was now a public figure, lecturing, lunching with Eleanor Roosevelt, working—with difficulty—on her novel, and writing articles. As always, Mrs. Roosevelt was eager to get Gellhorn through her periods of self-doubt, praising her for her uncanny knack for making readers visualize events and characters.

On November 17, Gellhorn was part of a panel ("Listening to America") appearing under the auspices of *The New York Times* National Book Fair at Rockefeller Center. There was talk of dramatizing *The Trouble I've Seen* for Broadway. Nothing came of it, but a new magazine, *Book Digest,* did publish a condensed version of the work in one of its winter issues. She spoke at a preview of a Group Theatre production and wrote an article on the "Federal Theatre," for the July 10, 1936, issue of *The Spectator,* praising the Works Progress Administration (WPA) for putting more than ten thousand people back to work. There were theater projects in thirty-one states, performing both the classics and new, experimental plays, drawing on the experience of various racial and ethnic groups. She especially enjoyed a midsummer performance of *Macbeth* by an all-black cast, featuring a rather lush, tropical, and lavish interpretation of the play. Earlier, in April, she had written Mrs. Roosevelt about a production of T. S. Eliot's *Murder in the Cathedral,* noting how the audience responded to the play just as readily as the public responded to mystery stories.

Finding all the "promotional hoopla that went along with the publication" of her book distasteful, Gellhorn returned to St. Louis to be with her family. It would be the first Christmas without her father. Martha suggested they take a vacation in Florida. The trip would change her life, eventually resulting in more fame than any of her books would claim, making her personality, not just her writing, part of a myth—the myth of a great writer's career.

Part Three

...WE WERE ALL IN IT
TOGETHER....
...THE GREAT UNENDING BATTLE
BETWEEN MEN AND WOMEN.

BEAUTY AND THE BEAST

1 9 3 6 – 1 9 3 7

11

Florida meant Miami to Martha, Edna, and her brother Alfred, who was on vacation from medical school. They hated it. Off on his own to do a little exploring, Alfred saw a bus heading for Key West. They had never heard of it, but something in the sound of the name appealed to them, especially when the driver mentioned it was south of Miami. The Gellhorns were attracted to things off the beaten path, and in those days Key West still had a rather rough side to it—just the place for an adventure.

With as much of an eye for local color as her daughter, Edna noticed a bar named Sloppy Joe's. This was a curiosity she just had to investigate. Sitting in the bar was Ernest Hemingway, his body darkened by the sun. Lounging in a "grubby T-shirt," "odoriferous Basque shorts" held up by a bit of rope, and barefooted, a bulky figure weighing about two hundred pounds, he struck Martha as nothing more than a "large, dirty man." She remembers him speaking to the Gellhorns first.

In that crude setting, the family made quite an impression. Martha was very fond of her younger brother. He was her favorite. They loved joking and horsing around and traveling together. Edna, a handsome woman in her mid-fifties, could easily hold her own with her diverting, intelligent children. Many of Edna's friends observed how much she enjoyed her daughter's company and how witty Edna seemed when

Martha was around. Martha, naturally, got plenty of Hemingway's attention. She was dressed in a "one-piece black dress and high heels." It was
one of her favorite traveling outfits. "Marty went through a phase in her
late twenties when she wore nothing but the little black dress. With her
golden hair, she looked very effective in her black and white" ensembles,
one of her friends remembers. Her "shoulder-length hair, high cheek-
bones, and full-lipped mouth" gave her an elegant and sensuous look.
Another friend notes that "Martha was a very beautiful woman. When
she walked into a room with her carriage and bearing, everyone knew
she was beautiful and they were in awe of her." "Very blond, beautiful
skin, tall, thin—very dramatic and very amusing in her speech" with a
"low, husky, eastern-seaboard-accented voice," it is not surprising that
Hemingway was shy at their first meeting and mumbled by way of an
introduction that he had "known St. Louis in the days of his youth. Both
his wives had gone to school there, and so had [his friends] Bill and Katy
Smith." Skinner (Sloppy Joe's bartender) watched Martha take a seat
beside Hemingway. It reminded him of "beauty and the beast."

If it was truly a surprise for Gellhorn to find Hemingway in Key West,
she soon warmed to his charm. It would have been hard not to appreciate
him as he sat there enthralled, encouraging her to talk. They drank "Papa
Dobles," made out of "two and a half jiggers of white Ron Bacardi rum,
the juice of two fresh limes, the juice of a grapefruit half, capped off with
six drops of maraschino" mixed in a "rusty electric blender near Ernest's
end of the bar." She had read his books, and he had been her "literary
hero" since her college days. She talked about a novel she was trying to
finish. The thirty-seven-year-old Hemingway seemed a little old to her
(she was seeing a younger man at this time). She impressed Hemingway's
friends as looking a very youthful twenty-eight. In contrast to her fiery,
still almost teenage temperament, he "talked older. He acted older."

As he learned about Gellhorn's background, Hemingway was stirred
by how many different elements of her experience touched his own.
Hadley, his first wife, had attended but did not graduate from Bryn
Mawr. He had met Hadley just after her mother had died; he was meeting
Martha after the recent death of her father. Although he was younger than
Hadley, he "compensated, in part, for the loss of the parent," by adopting
a paternal attitude. Pauline, his second wife, had been educated in a St.
Louis private school. Trained as a journalist, she was an alluring, stylishly
dressed woman when he met her. She had cleverly "insinuated herself into
[his] household" and "courted" him while Hadley was trapped in the role

of dutiful housewife. Martha, however, was more talented, bolder, and better looking than his previous women. In terms of daring, she was most like the stunningly attractive Jane Mason, with whom he had just ended a four-year affair. Jane had been a problem—too unstable and prone to self-destructive acts, married, and close to Pauline in a way that "inhibited her intimacy with Ernest." Martha was a solid woman, very much at home with herself, and thirteen years younger than Pauline, who now found herself relegated to the domestic routine that had done in Hadley.

That December afternoon and evening, Hemingway and Martha talked their way agreeably through "a run of Dobles." She was an intense conversationalist who could range widely over her travels and adventures, giving one the feeling of access to inside information about events abroad. She had a winning smile and a charming manner. Hemingway was certainly mesmerized. He was supposed to be home for dinner with Pauline and his friends Charles and Lorine Thompson. An angry Pauline asked Charles to haul her husband home so they could eat. When Thompson realized he could not budge Hemingway from his place at the bar next to Gellhorn, he reported to Pauline, "He's talking to a beautiful blond in a black dress." It would be very difficult for Pauline to compete with Martha. "If Pauline, as Hemingway wrote in *Green Hills of Africa,* was like a little terrier, then Martha could be compared to a wolfhound: 'lean, racy, long-legged and ornamental,' " Jeffrey Meyers has suggested.

It was to Gellhorn's advantage that Hemingway met her in the company of her mother. Edna delighted him. She was shrewd, gay, and open with him. Although she had been the wife of a physician, she was nothing like his own mother (also a doctor's wife), whom he found bigoted and dictatorial. Edna was generous and never demanded her children's love. Hemingway always labored under the grudging feeling that his mother believed he owed her something. His parents had fought over money and child rearing. Dr. Hemingway had taken on most of the shopping and cooking and relied on servants to keep up a house that otherwise suffered from his wife's slovenly habits. Hemingway had chafed under his father's religiosity and his mother's artistic pretensions. How different it had been for Martha to be a doctor's child and yet enjoy so much freedom and encouragement of her creativity. Edna radiated love.

Hemingway was eager to take the Gellhorns on a Key West tour. He wanted Pauline to meet them. As he was driving Martha and Alfred around the island, he spotted Pauline on the street, stopped the car, and invited her to join them. "She was very grumpy," Martha told Bernice

Kert several years later, and "he was very sharp. . . . It never occurred to me that she could be jealous, and who knows if she was; [she] may have had other reasons for being cross." Pauline's friends quickly suspected Martha's intentions. As Lorine Thompson puts it:

> Martha was a very charming girl and if I had known her under other circumstances I would have liked her very much. She said she came to see Ernest, she wanted him to read a book she had written, she wanted to know him. There was no question about it; you could see she was making a play for him. . . . Pauline tried to ignore it. What she felt underneath nobody knew.

Leicester Hemingway, Ernest's younger brother, also believed Martha was the aggressor and that she made the most of their bond as writers, talking up the opportunities and the hazards of a trip to report on the Spanish Civil War.

Gellhorn particularly admired Hemingway's early work. For her, this was his writing at its cleanest. She was herself still in the initial stage of her writing career—a point he could not fail to notice. He was moved by her profound conviction that writers should use their talent "to make the world a better place in which to live, and that included fighting for human freedom wherever it was threatened." *A Farewell to Arms* was her favorite Hemingway novel—the one from which she had picked her epigraph for *What Mad Pursuit.* Could it be that she had found the brave man who would share with her the adventures of war?

Gellhorn has made light of these first days with Hemingway, claiming, according to Bernice Kert, that "she never saw him in the evening and remembers only one visit to the Key West house. Neither by word nor gesture did Ernest show anything beyond friendly interest." Yet Martha later wrote to thank Pauline for her hospitality and admitted she became an addition there, something akin to a big-game trophy. Miriam Williams, Hemingway's cook, saw Ernest and Martha "outside . . . kissing and carrying on."

Edna and Alfred left Key West after New Year's Day; Martha checked into the Colonial Hotel for another week of sunshine and swimming. Ernest accompanied his "mermaid" on her jaunts, while Pauline plaintively remarked, "I suppose Ernest is busy again helping Miss Gellhorn with her writing."

On January 5, 1937, Martha wrote Mrs. Roosevelt, excitedly telling her about Key West and her new companion. Hemingway liked to exaggerate; his stories were marvelous and clearly a product of his genius. His new book, *To Have and Have Not,* was finished, and she had made a few comments on it. She was worried about her own work and realized it was much easier to be a critic of someone else's. She sensed that war was coming and wanted to make the most of the moment. Things went quickly to hell in this tropical land, but no one seemed to mind. It was poor country, but people made do with fish and coconuts, and relaxed.

On January 10, Gellhorn left Key West by car en route to St. Louis. Hemingway caught up with her in Miami and accompanied her by train as far as Jacksonville. Now there could be no question in her mind that he was after her. As soon as she got to St. Louis, she wrote Pauline about a delightful steak dinner in Miami with Ernest and his friend Tom Heeney. She was reading all of Hemingway's work, but she made a point of saying for better or worse she would have to find her own style. She meant it. However, she did not confide in Pauline that Hemingway held a peculiar fascination for her just then because she was going through a tremendous crisis of confidence in her own work. The signs of it may have been apparent to Pauline, since Martha had begun her letter by saying she was writing twelve pages a day, which she would toss into the toilet as soon as her book was finished.

Patrick, Gregory, and Pauline had made Key West a lovely place for Gellhorn. The boys' wonderful behavior had provoked her to consider motherhood seriously until she took a ride to Miami with Mr. Van Hining's eldest daughter, who would make anyone anxious. Martha hated to think she might have a child like that, who was enough to drive her to thoughts of murder. Family life at the Hemingways, on the other hand, left her with nothing but praise for Pauline and fondness for her boys.

Martha's stay in rainy St. Louis was brief but upsetting. She had the itch to travel, to go somewhere that would test her restless spirit. Enclosed in her letter to Pauline were two photographs of a very handsome Jouvenel, who was looking rather dissipated these days. There had been incidents in her life with him that merited comparison with a French farce.

Writing to Eleanor Roosevelt at about the same time, Gellhorn confided only her feelings about Hemingway the writer, about his devotion to precision and craftsmanship. She felt her new work was static, and he suggested she had fretted too much and that she should simply write and have the courage to throw away inferior material. She was going on doggedly at the rate of ten pages a day but felt she was missing every-thing. Spain was the place to be: She was certain war would start there just as surely as it had in the Balkans in 1912.

In New York, Hemingway signed a contract with the North American Newspaper Alliance (NANA) to cover the Spanish Civil War. He also convinced his editor, Maxwell Perkins, to buy Gellhorn's story "Exile" for *Scribner's Magazine*. "Exile" is about a German refugee who flees the Nazis because they have ruined his country. Heinrich is not a Jew or a Communist or a pacifist—just a quiet man who has spent his life in libraries researching the history of the postal system. In his view, the Nazis are barbarians, noisily marching in the street and mixing up "history and truth." Newspapers are unintelligible. The libraries have no new books. The final blow is the Nazi assertion that his beloved Heine, a Jew, can no longer be considered a poet. But Heinrich is no happier living with his cousin in the United States. His presence crowds her home, and he has no means of support. She thinks of the Nazis only as persecutors and cannot grasp Heinrich's point that his leaving had more to do with their pollution of an entire culture.

Having lived in Germany, Gellhorn had a feel for day-to-day existence there, and she realized Americans did not have the faintest notion of what the Nazi takeover meant, not just for politics and international affairs but for learning and art. Heinrich is no hero—in fact, he merits his cousin's accusation that he is a "dirty, messy old German"—but his rather mun-dane personality was an effective way of exposing how the Nazis infected the very core of civilization. It often frustrated Gellhorn that Americans did not grasp how easily groups such as the Nazis were able to destroy democratic values. Most of her life would be spent in a kind of "exile" from the United States. It is no surprise that she had Heinrich wonder how a man can establish a sense of home. It was a question she constantly put to herself. The story had its effect on Hemingway, who would eventually write *For Whom the Bell Tolls,* with its famous epigraph from John Donne: "No man is an *Iland. . . .*" "Exile" bore witness to the consequences of an aggressively expanding Fascism; the story played its part in spurring Hemingway on to Spain.

On the phone to Gellhorn, Hemingway encouraged her to come to New York. He was certain he could arrange her trip to Spain. She demurred, "flattered and amazed by his attentions" but not ready to put herself under his protection. Besides, she had a book to complete and was involved in the relief efforts of the Red Cross for flood victims in southern Missouri. Looking for some kind of action to relieve her St. Louis "horrors"—what felt like Siberian exile in an ugly, dismal, polluted city—she marched in a picket line of female workers striking the National Underwear Company. Joining a group of faculty wives at Washington University, she negotiated with management on behalf of the union. Try as she might, Gellhorn could not get her novel moving. Her habit was to keep writing the same chapter until she got it right. Eleanor Roosevelt sent a soothing letter, encouraging her to write more chapters and to save the revisions for later. Gellhorn was able to finish her novel, but she put it away, deciding never to publish it.

Gellhorn's letters to Hemingway continued—even after he returned to Key West. A week before he was to depart for Spain, she expressed the hope that they would find themselves in the same boat when the "deluge" began. She did not want to get stuck with the St. Louis Wednesday Club. On February 15, just as he was leaving Key West, she wrote him as her fellow conspirator plotting to get into Spain—obtaining visas had become difficult since the advent of the Franco-British Non-Intervention Pact. She had gotten herself a disguise—dark glasses and a beard. They were to remain silent and appear stalwart. Then her humor gave way to jitters and to terms of endearment. He was her "angel," and she had so much to say to him. He should leave a message for her in Paris if she failed to catch him in New York. There was still a word for Pauline: Martha sent her "love." However, the letter concluded with an injunction to him not to forget her, for after all they were in the same league, and she doted on him. She was beginning to lapse into his jargon, referring to him as "Hemingstein," one of his pet names for himself.

Hemingway and Gellhorn were both approaching a new relationship with divided minds. He was by no means ready to abandon Pauline, and the last thing Gellhorn could afford to do was pressure him about it— especially when she prized her own independence so much. On February 9, Hemingway had written Pauline's parents, expressing his sense of urgency about Spain and his devotion to their daughter: "me and my conscience both have known I had to go to Spain. . . . I'm very grateful to you both for providing Pauline who's made me happier than I've ever been." Many of Hemingway's friends believe he was still deeply in love with Pauline even as he pursued Martha. Pauline had been an astute editor of his writing, a good wife and mother, yet the sexual tensions of their marriage and her lack of sympathy for the Republican government in Spain that was fighting off Franco's insurrection were driving them apart.

By the end of February, fed up with St. Louis and feeling that her novel was a failure, Gellhorn decided to join Hemingway in Spain. She arrived in New York, to find that he had sailed for France several days earlier. Contrary to her expectations, he left no instructions about how she was to get into Spain. Whether he intended it or not, Hemingway's lack of help was the very thing that aroused her. Now she would go after him and forsake the caution she had shown thus far. At Fred Field's country home in Connecticut, "clad in black silk and pearls," she bragged about what an "extraordinary man" Hemingway was and "praised his barrel chest, his enormous potency and his skill as a lover."

On March 3, she had a letter in hand from Kyle Crichton of *Collier's,* identifying her as its correspondent. She was no such thing, but she hoped the letter might be good enough to get her into Spain. At about the same time, in Paris, Hemingway—just about to enter Spain—met Joris Ivens, the director who was to become his collaborator in the filming of *The Spanish Earth,* a documentary that would be used to raise funds for the defense of the Republic. "My beautiful girl friend is coming. She has legs that begin at her shoulders," he told Ivens. Arriving in Paris a few weeks after Hemingway's departure, Gellhorn is reported to have told P. J. Phillips, a *New York Times* correspondent, that she was "going to get Hemingway come hell or high water."

In the middle of March, with a knapsack and fifty dollars, and only the clothes she had on ("grey flannel trousers, sweater, warm windbreaker") Gellhorn got off a train at the Andorran-Spanish border and crossed into Spain. From there, she took an antiquated train—full of Republican soldiers—to Barcelona. They offered her food and did not behave as though they were going to war—these young, boisterous, but well-behaved Spaniards whose language she had yet to learn. Barcelona was radiant not only with the sun but with red streamers, the cabbie refused to charge her a fare, and the brotherhood of man seemed to reign everywhere. She was benevolently passed around like a welcome parcel until she reached Madrid (via Valencia), where wintry, dark, bomb-cratered streets suddenly shocked her with the reality of war. The city had become a battlefield. Threading her way through the debris called for acute attention. She could sense the entire city expecting another attack, the thrill of living so close to the margins of death.

Hemingway was having his supper in the basement restaurant of the Gran Vía Hotel when Gellhorn and his friend Sidney Franklin arrived, having met in Valencia and driven up to Madrid. She remembers Hemingway lifted his arm and put a hand on her head. She felt as though she had been annexed. She interpreted his gesture and his words as condescending, yet she was not resentful. Indeed, years later, she could not recount the incident without smiling. She might have forgiven his chauvinism and welcomed his protection; after all, he was the more experienced writer, and his expertise would be especially valuable in war-torn Madrid. He overdid it, however: "I knew you'd get here, daughter, because I fixed it so you could." She was enraged. After days of tough traveling, bitterly cold and exhausted, she doubtless felt a word or two about her own resourcefulness would have been in order—not a boast about his connections and a fatherly tone that put her in her place as one of the Hemingway brood. The best she could do was tell him precisely how she had gotten into the country. Even though she was much better informed about politics and had been following the rise of Fascism far more closely than Hemingway, she was in an awkward position—with virtually bogus credentials as a correspondent and with nothing else to match his authority and high spirits.

Gellhorn had no choice but to defer to Hemingway and to other seasoned correspondents. She knew nothing about war and admitted it. She was enthusiastic, though, and plunged right into things, determined to learn about warfare and to make herself an obliging, useful, and entertaining companion. Even before her meeting with Hemingway, she had surprised correspondent Ted Allan with her forthcoming, winning personality. Assigned the task of briefing her on the war, he "made a face" in expectation of a "dull" meeting. Instead, he "flipped" for her. He was bewitched by her "wonderful smile, the hair, the great figure" and had a splendid time "giggling and cuddling for warmth" in the backseat of the car that sped her to a rendezvous with Hemingway.

The day after Gellhorn's arrival in Madrid, Hemingway took her to Arturo Barea and Ilsa Kulcsar, government officials in charge of censorship who also dispensed such necessities as fuel vouchers and safe-conduct passes and arranged for accommodations. Dumbfounded, these desperately overtaxed officials gaped at Gellhorn, "a sleek woman with a halo of fair hair, who walked through the dark fusty office with a swaying movement." She was like a movie star. It was an eerie moment. For the past five months, Madrid had been under siege and its people had continued to go to the movies, even snickering at the sound of bombs falling so near them, finding what amusement they could in having cheated death for a short time. Hemingway told Barea, "That's Marty. Be nice to her. She writes for *Collier's*—you know, a million circulation."

Josephine Herbst, Lillian Hellman, and other women were impressed with Gellhorn's "Saks Fifth Avenue slacks, the chiffon scarf and her perpetually scrubbed look." Diana Forbes-Robertson, the wife of correspondent Vincent Sheean, thought that the usually "domineering" Hemingway was "weak for allowing himself to be trapped by women." Martha "dressed too showily for a war correspondent," Diana suggested, and was "too assertive in her relationship with Ernest." Stephen Spender recalls that war correspondents in the hotel in Valencia thought it was funny the way Gellhorn was always looking for Hemingway. Often he had departed with Joris Ivens for the front. "They saw Hemingway as being pursued by this tough, aggressive lady. That was their joke."

The physical disparity between Gellhorn and Hemingway was striking. According to Virginia Cowles, a correspondent who became a close friend of Gellhorn, Hemingway "went around Madrid in a pair of filthy brown trousers and a torn blue shirt. 'They're all I brought with me,' he would mumble apologetically. 'Even the anarchists are getting disdainful.' "

Gellhorn and Hemingway stayed in the Hotel Florida—a constant target of heavy-artillery bombardment and a mere "seventeen blocks from street battles." Many of its rooms were destroyed, the elevator rarely worked, and hot water was only intermittently available. Martha had been forewarned about the "filth and vermin of Spain" and had been sure to pack in her knapsack "her most prized possession, a new cake of soap." The food was horrible. Her first meal was "a tiny portion of chick-peas and odoriferous dried fish," relieved only by the private store of provisions in Hemingway's room that had been brought in from Paris.

On Gellhorn's second night in Madrid, heavy bombardment interrupted her sleep. Not wanting to be alone, she got up and realized she had been locked in her room. No one heard her banging and shouting until the shelling stopped. Then a stranger opened the door. She found Hemingway in a back room playing poker, where he confessed bashfully that he had locked her in "so that no man could bother her." His "possessiveness" annoyed her, but she also took pleasure in his sense of command. She liked the "big, splashy, funny" side of him. Having sized him up as "instantly leavable" and "not a grownup," she had little doubt she could handle him. The trouble was, he thought the same of her.

Many years later, Gellhorn was to say of these days with Hemingway, "in that pre-historic past, we tried steadily though in vain to be discreet." When the hotel's hot-water tank took a direct hit, the escaping steam "made the place look like a corridor in hell," and "all kinds of liaisons were revealed," said correspondent Sefton Delmer. "[P]eople poured from their bedrooms to seek shelter in the basement, among them Ernest and Martha."

Living with Hemingway had its privileges. He did not assume her expenses, but she certainly profited from his easy access to automobiles and fuel, for which other correspondents went begging. She got her quota of his Chesterfields and the whiskey from the "huge famous silver flask engraved, 'TO EH FROM EH.' " She was hardly immune to danger or hardship, however. She proofread his dispatches and dashed down bombed streets to deliver them to the government censors. She drove a station wagon for Dr. Norman Bethune, distributing blood to his transfusion unit. There were times when just like every other correspondent she had to scavenge for food. While Hemingway thrived on figuring out the strategy of the war and scheming to get as close as possible to the front, Gellhorn worked with "nurses in evil-smelling hospitals," consoling grievously wounded young men. As she subsequently observed, Hemingway never went near the dreadful military hospitals that she visited often.

On the first warm spring day in late March, Gellhorn and Hemingway left Madrid, swerving around vehicles, sounding the horn, and shouting as though they were on their way to a fire. Out past the street barricades, they plowed over "gutted country roads" on a trip north to the "red hills of the Guadalajara sector," taking blood to poorly supplied field hospitals. They were exhilarated, swallowing dust and liking the rocking ride, wondering what they would discover when they arrived. In the distance, the shelling sounded like a collapsing mountain. Franco's army was digging in against a Loyalist attack. The Loyalists' spirits were high. They smoked and laughed, "sunbathing and seam-picking" as the correspondents circulated among them. Visiting the American trenches at Morata, Gellhorn joked easily with the soldiers, saying she had arrived in a Ford station wagon "camouflaged in such a way that you could see it ten miles off; it looked like a moving rainbow." Milton Wolff, the last commander of the Abraham Lincoln Battalion, remembers her as a beauty who had a knack for brightening a soldier's day. She wondered whether the men were homesick. Their trenches prompted her to think of "flimsy ditches found in empty city blocks, where slum children played." At the field hospital, "a white farmhouse covered with vines and invaded by bees," she watched a doctor applying peroxide to an injured soldier. The foaming liquid in the wound looked like eroded soil, "ridged and jagged and eaten in." There was nothing to romanticize in this hospital full of

"desperately tired" men and stinking of "ether and sweat." Gellhorn saw
a nurse seated on some steps, haphazardly running her fingers through her
hair, obviously exhausted. At another hospital, she entered a dim room
and tripped over two stretchers filled with wounded soldiers. Both armies
had spent the day tediously scraping away at each other. The little town
of Morata had become "the hub of the world struggle against Fascism"—
as Herbert Matthews put it—the thrilling place where Americans and the
other soldiers in the International Brigade were stationed to thrust
Franco's troops back from their march on Madrid.

Spain was not a depressing experience for Hemingway and Gellhorn.
Herbert Matthews has suggested it was "one of the happiest periods of
Hemingway's life." Profoundly convinced of the Spanish Republic's
right to defend itself against Franco's Fascist rebellion, all three felt, in
Matthews's words, "the joy in man's tragic struggle against the forces of
evil." Before going to Spain, Hemingway had been much influenced by
Matthews's *New York Times* reports, and Matthews had quickly befriended Hemingway in the Florida Hotel, writing afterward that Hemingway "exemplifies . . . much that is brave and good and fine in a
somewhat murky world." He was "great-hearted and childish, and perhaps a little mad," but he had saved Matthews's life on one occasion and
proved many times over his resourcefulness and daring during the war.

Hemingway added spice and color to everything. When Matthews,
Hemingway, Gellhorn, Virginia Cowles, and other correspondents
watched a Loyalist attack from "a much-battered apartment house on the
Paseo de Rosales," it was Hemingway who dubbed it "The Old Homestead" because it reminded him of his grandfather's house. In the precarious, unpredictable climate of war, he claimed to know the score. His
assertion of authority had a curious calming affect on people—even when
his pretensions were ludicrous. Claude Cockburn, war correspondent for
the British *Daily Worker* remembers:

> At breakfast one day in his room at the Florida Hotel, Ernest Heming-
> way was very comforting about the shelling. He had a big map laid
> out on the table, and he explained to an audience of generals, politi-
> cians and correspondents, that for some ballistic reasons the shells could
> not hit the Florida. He could talk in a very military way and make
> it sound very convincing. Everyone present was convinced and happy.
> Then a shell whooshed through the room above Hemingway's—the
> first actually to hit the Florida—and the ceiling fell down on the
> breakfast table. To any lesser man than Hemingway the occurrence

would have been humiliating. While we were getting the plaster out of our hair, Hemingway looked slowly around at us, one after the other. "How do you like it now, gentlemen?" he said, and by some astonishing trick of manner conveyed the impression that this episode had actually, in an obscure way, confirmed instead of upset his theory—that his theory had been right when he expounded it and this only demonstrated that the time had come to have a new one.

Every evening, around eleven, reporters would gather at the Hotel Florida in Sefton Delmer's sitting room and carry on until the early hours of the morning. Sometimes there was food that would be "distributed gingerly," and always there were enormous quantities of beer and liquor. When it got hot, Delmer would shut off the lights and open the windows, turn on the gramophone and play Beethoven's Fifth Symphony punctuated by the distant thunder of artillery. This continued until Delmer's rooms were demolished by an incoming shell. Luckily they were empty at the time. The hotel manager would not admit the hotel had been hit, fearing he would lose his guests, but he had little cause for concern. Where could the correspondents go? In any event, there was Hemingway—cajoling and bullying everyone to stay put and not give way under "fascist pressure."

It was such an intimate war; no one could expect to stay and come out unscathed. There was no real division between the war and the civilian populace: This is what was unique and "prophetic" about Spain, Gellhorn points out in *The Face of War.* The correspondents and the soldiers and their officers were familiar with each other and could gossip on a first-name basis. In "Visit to the Wounded" (1937) she remarks that walking to the front from her hotel was accomplished as simply as strolling from the Metropolitan Museum to the Empire State Building. She could see all aspects of the war in a single day in her travels from the trenches to the hospital to the hotel. When she returned to her room one day, she found "a neat round bullet-hole in her window . . . the maid had forgotten to draw the curtain," and the police had shot into her room as a reminder of the blackout restrictions.

Virginia Cowles kept a diary that shows how various a day in Spain could be. She terms her entry for April 11, 1937, "perhaps a routine day":

At the hotel we ran into Martha Gellhorn and Hemingway and arranged to meet at twelve to go to a festival for the benefit of the FAI [Federacion Anarquista Iberica] and hear Pastoras sing. Pastoras never sang and the show was bad; a tap dancer in tails and top hat, a very old flamenco singer and a skit between a priest and a housewife, both of whom kept their backs turned squarely on the audience so that no one could hear what they said. Everyone cheered a lot, so it was evidently a success.

In the afternoon joined Herbert Matthews and Hemingway at the Old Homestead, to watch the battle on the *Casa del Campo*. The Republicans are trying to take three houses in which the Rebels are entrenched. We watched them shelling the houses, then saw two tanks come down a narrow path. One of them caught fire and turned into a sheet of flames and the other turned back. Herbert thought we might see a big offensive, but nothing doing, so finally went back to the hotel.

Matthews later noted they were "within a thousand yards of the group of houses that the Loyalists were trying to storm. We had grandstand seats in a great show." In "Night Before Battle," Hemingway remembered watching from this "shell smashed house . . . the clouds of smoke and dirt that thundered up on the hill crest as the bombers droned over." The tanks looked like "small mud-colored beetles bustling in the trees and spitting tiny flashes and the men behind them were toy men who lay flat, then crouched and ran, and then dropped to run again, or to stay where they lay, spotting the hillside as the tanks moved on." He was trying to get footage for *The Spanish Earth,* to film "the sudden fountainings of earth, the puffs of shrapnel, the rolling clouds of smoke and dust lit by the yellow flash and white blossoming of grenades." He was close enough to smell and to taste "the dust of it." Hemingway loved to watch war, while admitting its horror: "It's the nastiest thing human beings can do to each other, but the most exciting," he solemnly told Virginia Cowles.

When journalists were not occupying Sefton Delmer's suite, they were in Hemingway's. Virginia Cowles saw every manner of man and woman at these gatherings: "idealists and mercenaries; scoundrels and martyrs; adventurers and *embusques;* fanatics, traitors, and plain down-and-outs." Photographers, airmen, refugees, ambulance drivers, picadors, and various strains of Communists frequented the Florida Hotel. Hemingway had his own impresario, Sidney Franklin (born Frumpkin), a bullfighter from Brooklyn who gathered the loot and gossip that nourished Hemingway's entourage. Franklin was loyal to Pauline, hostile to Martha, and probably jealous of her as well, since he sensed her arrival boded tremendous changes in his "master's" life.

Gellhorn was not content to see the war through Hemingway's eyes or to serve as his appendage. This became evident when they visited Mikhail Koltzov, a *Pravda* correspondent close to Stalin. Koltzov ran his own salon at the Gaylord Hotel. Hemingway was fascinated with this brilliant journalist and realized he could learn a great deal from him about how the war was going "from the inside." The Russians had provided important military supplies and advisers—although Hemingway shared Gellhorn's view that the Spanish Republic was "neither a collection of blood-slathering Reds nor a cat's-paw of Russia." Yet Hemingway disliked the Gaylord ambience; it was too cozy, with "too much butter, too much meat, too much vodka." The rooms were actually warm and the elevator operated regularly, if sluggishly. This was no place for a soldier, or for a writer who fancied himself a warrior. It was foreign territory for a mind that really did not know how to fasten on politics. Gellhorn, on the other hand, relished the intrigue and the luxury. Her consort could not forgive her for it and parodied this side of her personality in *The Fifth Column,* a play he would soon begin writing about this period in Spain.

There were, however, things Hemingway knew and instincts of his that kept Gellhorn out of trouble. When Frederick Voigt, Berlin correspondent for the Manchester *Guardian,* gave Gellhorn a sealed envelope as she was about to leave Spain, Hemingway became wary. Voigt had gone around claiming there was a "terror" in Madrid: Thousands of bodies were being found—although when pressed by Hemingway, Voigt had to admit he had not seen any himself. Voigt assured Gellhorn that the envelope contained "only a carbon copy of an already censored dispatch." He was just making certain his newspaper would have it if the original did not arrive. Hemingway insisted on taking the envelope to the censor's office. The censor opened it and read an article about the terror in Madrid: Voigt had put Gellhorn in the position of smuggling an uncensored dispatch out of the country. Hemingway was so furious that he had to be restrained from punching Voigt.

In the last week of April, Gellhorn joined Hemingway in a tour of what he described as "ten hard days visiting the four central fronts." They climbed the 4,800-foot Sierra de Guadarrama. From horseback, they surveyed the Loyalist armies. It was often impossible to return to Madrid for the night, so they took their sleep in crude encampments or just pulled off the road. At one point, they ventured out in an armored vehicle, "hunched in the dark interior," hearing the Rebel machine gunning rattling against the sides of the car. This was the trip on which

Hemingway taught Gellhorn about different kinds of gunfire and when to hit the ground. If anything, she showed more courage than he did, for he proceeded with a caution born of wounds he had suffered in World War I. Her bravery moved him, and his devotion to the Republic touched her. Without the bond of this common cause, Gellhorn doubted she could have become so "hooked" on him. She remembered feeling the following:

> We were all in it together, the certainty that we were *right*. . . . We knew, we just *knew* . . . that Spain was the place to stop Fascism. This was it. It was one of those moments in history when there was no doubt.

THE SPANISH EARTH

1 9 3 7

12

Martha Gellhorn had come to Spain in a spirit of fellowship. She would consider herself fortunate if she escaped with her life. Once there, however, it seemed inadequate just to absorb some Spanish, witness the war, and comfort the wounded. She was a writer; she should write, Hemingway and Matthews both told her. But what were her qualifications to write about war? she asked herself. And who would want to read what she had to say about it? What could she possibly report that would be newsworthy? Surely she would have to focus on some turning point in the war, and all she knew about was the daily shelling—a fact of life for everyone who lived in Madrid. Yes, but being bombarded every day would certainly not be what most people in other parts of the world were accustomed to, Hemingway pointed out.

All right, Martha would confine herself to what she had seen and heard. To her amazement, she wrote a piece that *Collier's* called "Only the Shells Whine" and published on July 17, 1937. "High Explosive for Everyone," the title she gave it in *The Face of War,* her collection of war correspondence, more accurately conveys her feeling that the conflict in Spain excluded no one. It was total war, presaging a world cataclysm in which not just nations but whole peoples would be destroyed. It is an extraordinary dispatch—better than Hemingway's reports about Spain, because it

105

is so direct, so concrete, and so deeply felt. Gellhorn's point of view, her sympathy for the Republican government is implicit, but there is no editorializing; the writing appears to be transparent—a window on war. In this respect, it resembles *The Trouble I've Seen*, for there is no doubt that the author had experienced what she had written.

Constructed like a story, "High Explosive for Everyone" begins with a "thud," the sound of the shells leaving the Rebel artillery with a kind of "groaning cough" until they are heard "fluttering toward you." Then there is the quick acceleration of sound and the huge boom of the explosion. Shifting to the second-person "you"—as Hemingway frequently did in his dispatches—Gellhorn brought home the dreadful closeness of war. When the shells land very near you, they seem to whistle and whirl and spin, whining higher and higher like a "close scream" until they tear up the streets in "granite thunder."

Using understatement the way Hemingway or Dashiell Hammett would in a story, Gellhorn alluded to her own hysteria by changing to the first person, describing her descent to the hotel lobby, concentrating on her breathing because the air stuck in her throat. The strict controls she put on her language are themselves indicators of the discipline she had to maintain during the constant shelling. War is given a face, an intimacy and immediacy: a window shatters "gently and airily, making a lovely tinkling musical sound"; in doorways people await the next bomb with "immensely quiet stretched faces" while the "whistle-whine-scream-roar" of the shells vibrates in Gellhorn's throat; a sliver of coiled steel is sheared off an incoming shell and "takes" a "little boy in the throat." There is a delicacy, a light touch in the prose, that makes the ugliness of death and destruction all the more appalling. It is not just these people, this earth, that has been violated; it is Gellhorn's representative human sensibility that is under attack.

Having plunged her readers into the daily bombing of Madrid, Gellhorn turned to other vignettes of war: Pedro, a janitor, and his family are staunch supporters of the Republic, proud of the fine apartment they will not abandon in spite of the heavy shelling and hopeful about a government that has made it possible for women to have careers; four men in a military hospital—one with a bad chest wound, one with his face shot off, two others with a smashed knee and a head wound. The soldier with the bad chest smiles, but it is too painful for him to speak. The one with the smashed knee sits and props his leg on a chair, talking about his friend with the head wound, who is also out of bed painting a portrait. Jaime has always had a dream of becoming an artist, Gellhorn is told. Now is his opportunity. The irony is that he is encouraged to paint because the damage to his head has dimmed his vision. He must be encouraged to think his eyesight is all right. Without making a point of it, Gellhorn mentioned that one of the men was Hungarian, and this scene concludes with the entrance of a Pole carrying flowers, for she wanted to convey the extraordinary diversity of the men fighting for the Republic and for (as far as she was concerned) the fate of all free human beings.

After the depiction of the military hospital, Gellhorn gave a brief account of her visit to a play put on by soldiers, one of whom has trouble remembering his lines but who steps forward to recite a poem he composed in the trenches. As in most of her pieces about Spain, this first one emphasizes the craving for human expression that waxes even as the bombs obliterate it. Each night, she heard the gunfire, the explosions, and imagined what it was like at the front, thought of the calm, courageous, civilian population that carried on. When the city finally quieted from the last artillery exchange, she knew it was only reasonable to return to bed.

Gellhorn has never made great claims for her war correspondence. She was not trying to create a style; it simply emerged out of her rapid compositions. The problem she had to solve was choosing out of the welter of information precisely those details that best told the story. Her choices were superb—highly particularized and yet exemplary, speaking for both herself and her subjects. Her letters to her editors at *Collier's* give ample evidence of how passionately she cared about the shape of her reports; they were accounts that had to be as concrete and as vivid as possible.

In some ways, Gellhorn was more fortunate than Hemingway, since he came to the war with a well-known style and an identity as a novelist, war correspondent, and man of action. His dispatches show that he had become a prisoner of his public persona. Although he achieved many of the same effects as did Gellhorn—describing the "heavy coughing grunt" of shelling, "the high inrushing sound, like the ripping of a bale of silk"—his pieces have a curious jocularity, with references to himself as "this half asleep correspondent." His writing is just as striking as hers in describing the dead, lying "like so many torn bundles of old clothing in the dust and rubble," and his is more graphic about war's atrocity—the driver of a bombed car lurches out of it, "his scalp hanging down over his eyes, [sitting down] on the sidewalk with his hand against his face, the blood making a smooth sheen down over his chin." He was a more comprehensive reporter, explaining the strategy of individual battles and giving close-up pictures of infantry attacks. A brave man putting his heart into the Republican cause, he never quite leveled with his readers, never told them that his side was fighting a defensive war, and that its victories slowed but could not stop Franco's envelopment of the entire country. Hemingway presumed an authority, a self-importance, that paradoxically makes his dispatches less compelling. His work in Spain lacked Gellhorn's intensity, focus, and unity—in part because he was expected to supply newsworthy articles, whereas she wrote for a weekly magazine that wanted human-interest stories. She did not have to key herself around major battles or significant events.

Between them, Gellhorn and Hemingway employed what Phillip Knightley has identified as the "two distinct techniques" of war correspondents. Hemingway presented himself as a "battlefield correspondent trying to report the overall scene, to give a contemporary observer's account of how a battle was lost or won." He opened up this technique by making himself and occasionally a friend like Sidney Franklin into characters with whom readers could identify. Gellhorn, on the other hand, concentrated on war's "effects on the individual," and followed the intimate destinies of combatants and noncombatants alike. Her range was narrower but more profound. She never approached her material with the great novelist's glibness—conscious of saving his best words for *For Whom the Bell Tolls,* which he hoped would be regarded as the definitive work of fiction on Spain. Everything she had was put into her miniatures of war.

According to Leicester Hemingway, some of the writing in Spain was a joint effort: "Ernest worked on his own material, worked over Martha's; she in turn copied out his material, and they combined their thinking and sometimes their phrases in magazine pieces under one by-line or the other." The style and point of view of their pieces is quite different, however. While they were together much of the time, they also went their separate ways and developed distinct areas of interest and expertise.

In May 1937, Gellhorn and Hemingway returned to the States. It was time to edit the footage of *The Spanish Earth* and to prepare it for distribution. Joris Ivens was sending Hemingway telegrams reminding him of the narration he was supposed to write for the film and of the Second American Writers' Congress in New York he had promised to address. Gellhorn took an important role in seconding Ivens's pleas. She was exasperated with Hemingway but still his admirer, so that any sacrifice she had to make seemed worth it. She knew Ivens was associated with Communists, and she was leery of their efforts to insinuate themselves into the Spanish *causa,* but they were on the right side in the battle to save the Republic. As Eleanor Roosevelt put it in her newspaper column, Gellhorn had returned from Spain with the profound belief that "the Spanish people are a glorious people and something is happening in Spain which may mean much to the rest of the world." On May 21, the St. Louis *Globe-Democrat* carried a news item quoting Gellhorn's prediction that the Loyalists would win because of their "unlimited supply of courage." It had been a "tough bloody winter," with shortages of food and fuel, but the morale in Madrid was "so good it [was] almost incredible."

On June 4, a nervous, flushed, halting Ernest Hemingway prepared to speak to a capacity audience of 3,500 people at the Writers' Congress in Carnegie Hall. He "stood in the wings, muttering he was not a speechmaker." Archibald MacLeish introduced him to deafening applause. In the huge, hot, smoky hall, with his glasses fogging over and his face breaking into a sweat, he jumped to his feet, tearing at his tie as if it were gagging him, and launched into a seven-minute oration before the clapping had stopped. The problem for the writer, Hemingway told the Congress, is always the same: how to tell the truth. He opposed Fascism because it "is a lie told by bullies. A writer who will not lie cannot live and work under fascism." There was not much more to the speech than that—except for Hemingway's moving statement that "it seems a nasty sort of egotism to even consider one's own fate" when the destiny of the world was at stake. Hemingway's presence, his words, filled the hall with excitement. Rounds and rounds of applause followed him as he "rushed to the wings." Gellhorn was thrilled and wrote to Eleanor Roosevelt about her satisfaction in seeing him put his enormous prestige at the service of a crusade greater than himself.

As Frederick R. Benson has suggested, "in the fascist threat of the 1930s, it seemed that the Dark Ages might return." Fascism appeared intent on reversing whatever progress had been made in the past two hundred years in democratic and liberal societies. Fascism meant a new inquisition, a reign of irrationality, and nihilism—in the words of a

Fascist general: Death to the intelligentsia. It was to this fear that writers would be silenced that Gellhorn addressed herself when she spoke on June 5 before an "afternoon closed session" of the congress at the New School for Social Research. She spoke not as a public figure but as a modest participant in the *causa*. She marveled at how little attention writers paid to themselves in Spain. They had come as a testament to their belief in freedom and individuality, expecting no recognition. At the front, they had created their own newspapers, which had become a vital element in soldiers' lives. The writers were there to witness history as it happened, to give it a shape and an interpretation. It was like her to feel that journalism would make a difference in the way people perceived and created their own world. Like Hemingway, she emphasized the selflessness of writers, but she identified with the way they exchanged information, expressing the sense of solidarity everyone felt who covered the Republican side of the war.

Splitting up as soon as the congress was over, Hemingway headed for Bimini to finish revisions of *To Have and Have Not* and Gellhorn stayed in New York pestering her contacts in government and labor to do something about Spain. She implored the Roosevelts to send wheat, if nothing else, to the Spanish Republic. It seemed to Gellhorn that the President did not dare alienate American Roman Catholics, who were sympathetic to Franco and shocked by stories of Republican atrocities, including the raping of nuns—a charge Gellhorn vehemently denied. Dealing with crazy, makeshift committees aggravated her. Then she was devastated to learn that one of her close friends had been killed in Spain and another gravely wounded. She thought she had become inured to war; yet when her companions died, it was a shock she could not absorb.

By the end of June, Hemingway was back in New York to record the narration for *The Spanish Earth*. Gellhorn had helped in the creation of sound effects to simulate the terrifying noise of exploding shells, and she was enormously moved by the young men who worked with her most of the night to get it right. She felt like a mother of a million children who had all been successful. She poured out her enthusiasm to Eleanor Roosevelt and wrote her several letters to set up a showing of *The Spanish Earth* at the White House.

Gellhorn had absolute confidence in the Roosevelts, particularly in Eleanor, and enjoyed relating her adventures—such as her visit to an extravagant beauty salon in the hope that something could be done about her flaking skin. She had come in carrying a copy of the *Daily*

A hundred feet ahead, we found the tidy white cottage, serene in its white-railed enclosure, sitting upon flat, greenish tan ground. (*Author*)

Martha Gellhorn and her mother, Edna, with St. Louis suffragettes campaigning for the vote in 1916. (*League of Women Voters*)

In 1923, John Burroughs was a handsome, compact, L-shaped building still under construction. The Spanish-style architecture was meant to evoke "the thought that St. Louis had always been the gateway to the West." (*John Burroughs School*)

In her senior year, Gellhorn was "perfectly cast" as "the courageous Vigdis Goddi" in John Masefield's play *The Locked Chest*. (*John Burroughs School*)

Gellhorn had a rebellious and irreverent streak. In high school, she was appreciated as a "character" and satirized in *The John Burroughs Review.* (*John Burroughs School*)

In her fifties, Edna Gellhorn was still handsome and full-blown with the presence of a great actress. She spoke from both conviction and calculation, having perfected her platform persona over many years of traveling on behalf of the League of Women Voters. (*St. Louis Mercantile Library*)

Bertrand de Jouvenel met Martha in the company of one of his friends during one of her backpacking trips through Europe. He was married, but he simply walked out on his wife (causing a scandal) to follow Martha. (*Bertrand de Jouvenel*)

A poet desperately trying to write a novel, and hostile toward the insularity of his midwestern upbringing, Joseph Pennell was nearly the perfect male counterpart of Martha Gellhorn. (*University of Oregon Library*)

In mid-October, 1939, Gellhorn got a call
from *Collier's*. Would she go to Finland?
It looked as though the Russians might
invade. (*UPI/Bettmann Newsphotos*)

Sun Valley Lodge in Idaho: Hemingway enjoyed his stays at this new resort, whose owner, Averell
Harriman, appreciated the "publicity value" of the presence of a famous author. (*John Fitzgerald Kennedy
Library*)

Gellhorn learned how to shoot a shotgun. As Lloyd Arnold put it, she "responded to [Hemingway's] wishes with a firm will." (*John Fitzgerald Kennedy Library*)

The Heart of Another was published in the fall of 1941 at a time when Gellhorn and Hemingway were enjoying a healthy holiday in Sun Valley. (*John Fitzgerald Kennedy Library*)

Edna's presence, as always, calmed tempers in Ernest's and Martha's Cuban home. (*John Fitzgerald Kennedy Library*)

Nine-year-old Gregory Hemingway, who had had a difficult childhood, responded affectionately to Gellhorn's warmth. Patrick was the quiet one who regarded Martha "more as a friend than as a stepmother." (*John Fitzgerald Kennedy Library*)

Patrick observed that his older brother, Jack, and Martha were a lot alike: "handsome young people, blonde and radiant and pleasing everyone with their charm and high spirits." (*John Fitzgerald Kennedy Library*)

At Sun Valley, Gellhorn followed the Hemingway regimen: writing in the morning, riding, tennis, and shooting in the afternoon. (*John Fitzgerald Kennedy Library*)

Worker—quite a shock to one of the wealthy patrons but a welcome diversion to a girl working in the salon, who became involved in Communist meetings.

If Mrs. Roosevelt had any criticism of Gellhorn, it was that she was high-strung, sometimes allowing her feelings to get in the way of a more objective analysis of political and social issues. Gellhorn took the criticism well; indeed, she seemed to crave Roosevelt's steady, compassionate, but sober interest in her affairs, for Gellhorn was often in despair over her ability to persuade people on the subject of Spain. She had just addressed a convention of private librarians (most of them working in law libraries, corporations, and foundations). She found public speaking loathsome, and she was not at all certain that her listeners understood her or were equipped to empathize with her experiences.

To Joris Ivens and some of Hemingway's other friends, it looked as though Gellhorn "was doing most of the courting" of Hemingway. They saw her as a spunky woman to whom it would come naturally to go after what she wanted. She also seemed quite carefree and candid with Hemingway and confident of how he felt about her. She had irrepressible energy. She was vexed, however, about her writing. She had spent ten days in Hartford, Connecticut, with the Fields, trying to write a book about Spain. She had no trouble filling up pages with words, but they were no good. She was beginning to think she was another Dreiser.

On July 8, Gellhorn, Hemingway, and Ivens met at the airport in Newark to fly to Washington for a White House dinner and a showing of *The Spanish Earth*. Ivens and Hemingway wondered at Gellhorn's eating three sandwiches at the snack bar. She warned them that White House suppers were inedible. As Hemingway later described it to his in-laws, the White House was hot, except for the President's air-conditioned study, and the dinner was abominable: The soup tasted like rainwater, the squab was rubbery, the lettuce wilted, and the sorry cake (supplied by a Roosevelt supporter) beneath his comment. He was deeply appreciative to the Roosevelts for giving him a hearing but not especially taken with them. He was far more impressed with Harry Hopkins.

While Hemingway and Ivens flew to Hollywood for another showing of the film, which was being used to raise money for ambulances in Spain,

Gellhorn remained in Manhattan, writing to Eleanor Roosevelt to thank her on behalf of Ivens and Hemingway. Gellhorn was again in a motherly mood and grateful to Eleanor for her warm response to two men who seemed like lovable, bright children. It was tough going trying to get *The Spanish Earth* accepted by movie distributors who regarded Gellhorn as a "cuckoo idealist."

Finally, on July 26, tired of her work, Gellhorn visited her mother in St. Louis. She had abandoned her book on Spain, concluding that she was too directly involved in events there to write about them, and too upset to do anything except contemplate a return trip to the war. She was considering a revision of the novel she had written the previous winter.

By mid-August, Gellhorn and Hemingway were reunited in New York and preparing to sail for Spain. Archibald MacLeish and John Dos Passos were both upset to hear that Ernest planned to divorce Pauline and marry Martha. She and Ernest had been able to elude the two writers and then had called newspaper publisher Ralph Ingersoll from a West Side bar in the hope he might be able to arrange the commercial distribution of *The Spanish Earth*. He felt it was a "gem" but too short to be distributed as a feature film. Gellhorn was angry. Ingersoll had once declined to hire her as a researcher for *Fortune* magazine. He thought her beauty "would be disruptive in the office." When he told Hemingway and Gellhorn that no one had had any luck in getting theaters to take *The Spanish Earth,* she let him have it. "She took a whole morning off to give me the most thorough tongue lashing I can ever remember getting from anybody. I was incompetent, unappreciative (of the sacrifices Ernest had made) and a phoney slob," Ingersoll later remembered.

On August 17, Hemingway sailed for Spain on the *Champlain*. Two days later, Gellhorn left on the *Normandie*. They were still keeping up the appearance of leading separate lives. On board, she met Dorothy Parker and her husband, Alan Campbell, who took an immediate liking to Gellhorn, although they did not share her "idea of shipboard fun . . . an energetic workout in the gymnasium." Parker admired how fit Gellhorn looked. Even better was the fact that she was a spirited, courageous, and decent human being. They had a great time together, except for the sulking company of Lillian Hellman, who tagged along with the Campbells.

In early September, Gellhorn, Hemingway, and Herbert Matthews got together at the Café de la Paix in Paris to discuss the grim war news. The Republican government had lost two-thirds of the country to Franco.

While preparing to reenter Spain, Gellhorn went off by herself to a swim at Lavandou on the Riviera. The temperate, tranquil sea, the immaculate beach: She would have this pleasure to think of in Madrid, where people were girding themselves for another Fascist attack. All three "gloomily comforted [themselves] with the knowledge that there was always Madrid to be reckoned with."

Nevertheless, Gellhorn and Hemingway spent six happily private days in Paris—broken only by what he felt to be an obligatory visit (an "anti-gossip ploy") to Dorothy Parker and Lillian Hellman. Still trying to be discreet (according to Gellhorn), he went by himself. She remembered him returning for a meeting with her and Herbert Matthews, approaching them with smudged lipstick on his collar and the gait of a horse fleeing a "burning stable." While such incidents amused Gellhorn, she was miffed when she realized she would not be sleeping with him in the wagon-lit compartment on the train to Spain.

The strategic situation looked improved when Gellhorn, Hemingway, and Matthews visited Belchite, recently taken by Loyalist troops. The first American reporters to conduct a thorough inspection of the Belchite sector, they scaled "steep, rocky trails on foot and horseback and followed raw new military roads in trucks and borrowed staff cars." There was not much to eat, except for the bread and wine given them by Spanish peasants. Cooking had to be done over fires. They slept in open trucks on mattresses and blankets. It had started to snow, but Gellhorn took it all without complaint. Hemingway was impressed.

For her *Collier's* readers, Gellhorn described Belchite before the attack: a walled town, looking like a gray boulder set atop a hill. It had collapsed from bombing and shelling; the streets were impassable and the houses sagged. The smell of decomposing corpses arose from the mounds of wreckage. Household items were scattered everywhere: furniture, kitchen utensils, a sewing machine in the middle of the street. Soldiers had to work with their mouths covered. Gellhorn was full of grit—eyebrows, teeth, hands, clothes—there was no escaping it. She recognized some of the soldiers in the American Brigade, a part of the original 450, some of whom had never handled a gun before they went to Spain. Some had died before ever really becoming experienced soldiers.

In the spring and summer, more Americans had arrived, having trekked in small groups across the snow-covered Pyrenees. It was odd to hear these

American voices from different regions sounding just the way they might at a sporting event or a hamburger stand. She was especially impressed with Bob Merriman, the chief of staff, who talked like the college professor he was, and who became the model for Robert Jordan, the hero of *For Whom the Bell Tolls*. He explained the strategy of the Belchite attack, marking it out on a dirt floor, and he described the house-to-house fighting, the advance backed up with hand grenades and bombing, and how the Rebels made a last-ditch stand with their machine guns in the cathedral tower. He told the story shyly, a little awkwardly, and Gellhorn obviously liked his lack of bravado. He had pressed forward in spite of multiple wounds that were not treated until the battle ended. At this point, the correspondent could not resist remarking on her enormous respect for her fellow countrymen. The soldiers enjoyed talking with Gellhorn, who had a gift for engaging them in conversation. It was just chitchat, but they were pleased that this attractive woman had come to visit them—although they were not particularly impressed with Hemingway's celebrity.

From Belchite, the three correspondents drove north toward Brunete, the site of a great battle in July. As they swung west and descended into a plain, Gellhorn felt the cold air that had been blowing over the tailgate of the truck giving way to summery breezes. High up on an observation post, she tried to imagine what it had been like in midsummer, the sun and the bombers bearing down on the plain, pursuit planes shelling the roads, and the Americans rushing up Mosquito Ridge into machine-gun fire. Now it was "as quiet and beautiful as wheat country in Idaho." In camouflaged cars dodging shell craters, Gellhorn, Hemingway, and Matthews were trying to plot out exactly how the offensive had taken place. There was nowhere to take cover on the exposed plain, with houses being blown up even as the Loyalists surrounded the village.

One of the correspondents' cars had British and American flags on its fenders as a sign of neutrality, but it was evidently picked out by Fascist artillery men as a Loyalist staff car. As the car bounced down the road, a shell hit the dirt about a hundred yards away. The next one was nearer and tore up more earth. Leaning against a shattered house, the correspondents watched the earth spray upward, the road churning into a column of explosives. In July, the bombs had burned the fields, and afterward little "purple flowers like crocuses" had sprung up. Having observed these bits of life, it was time to get out and to leave the Fascists to their shelling.

On the way back to Madrid, Gellhorn, Hemingway, and Matthews visited the Teruel front. The Loyalists had "shut tight and strongly barred" what had been called the "open door" Franco might have entered in a "drive to the coast." Soldiers were slowly loading donkeys with blankets for the winter; women in dark clothes were walking quickly down the road on "strong bowed legs, chattering like birds," devouring grapes they had gathered in the fields. They had fled Madrid and gone from Barcelona to Valencia, carrying essential household items on two donkeys, and mourning for the anguish of Madrid, for its beautiful past.

It was a quiet October in Madrid. Fascist attacks were aimed at the Aragon front. There was good weather and the bars were packed. Writing to her mother on October 8, Gellhorn mentioned a wonderful dinner with Dorothy Parker in Herbert Matthews's room. When it rained, Gellhorn and Hemingway diverted themselves by gambling at dominoes. Then there was the Sunday flea market, where one could buy canaries or silver watches that never worked. All through this period, Gellhorn remembers Hemingway as a jolly, joking companion, although they had their quarrels, such as the one on October 15, when they stormed off with Sefton Delmer and Herbert Matthews to spend an unproductive day trying to find the front lines at Aranjuez. There were other boring days like this one, hanging around the press office hoping for something new to report on.

It made Gellhorn nervous, but she did some broadcasting from Madrid. Her mother picked up one of her reports on November 21. Still identified in the St. Louis *Globe-Democrat* (November 22, 1937) as Mme. Bertrand de Jouvenel, Gellhorn stressed for her radio listeners the composure of Madrid's population. Every day, she watched "a girl with a shawl around her shoulders" work in a house burned and gutted by shell fire. She had stripped the woodwork and built a fire for cooking. She dried the family laundry on a rope hung from the balcony "in front of the gaping windows." Madrid still had a million people who continued to market and clean and go to school. While various staples were scarce, it was possible to purchase "furs, fine silk stockings, and beautiful clothes, French perfume, victrolas, wrist watches and every imaginable luxury." The beauty salons were always busy. Children studied and played as they did in every part of the world.

Tired of war, Hemingway and Gellhorn managed to get into the Madrid zoo. It was closed, but the keepers could not resist the compliments from foreigners who had come so far to enjoy the lovely grounds. Once inside, observing the handsome baby llama, a magnificent yak, and the admirable hippopotamus, they began to speak about the war. How would anyone at home ever comprehend or sympathize with this unique event? In one of her *Collier's* articles, Gellhorn had tried to accustom her American readers—so used to the regularity of life, to the normal sounds of elevated trains and people walking safely on sidewalks, to the acute small sounds of a country night—to the idea of their compatriots who had come to fight for freedom in Spain. How could the people at home visualize a world where such different things got combined: a zoo and gun sites in back of a monument to Alfonso XII; a café occupying part of a smashed building, a shaky divider set up to hide the mess; four women getting permanents, who stayed put even after the floors above them were hit by artillery fire. You could follow new traces of blood to the popular bars, but the people of Madrid simply refused to be cowed by these assaults on their existence.

During the breaks in the fighting, Hemingway worked on his play, *The Fifth Column,* which is about Philip Rawlings, a Loyalist secret agent in love with Dorothy Bridges, the beautiful woman with whom he lives. Set in the Florida Hotel in a room identical to Hemingway's and Gellhorn's, *The Fifth Column* is a curious exaggeration—sometimes an inversion—of their complicated relationship. Bridges is a Vassar girl and speaks in a cultivated voice. She is obsessed with cleanliness and comfort. She dreams of seaside resorts and luxurious trips. Although she has talent as a writer, she is lazy and freely admits she knows almost nothing about the war. She rarely thinks of how dangerous it is to be in Madrid, and when the danger is pointed out to her, she accepts the imminence of death in matter-of-fact fashion. She is such an enthusiast and romantic that she tends to gush, calling everyone "darling." She has very beautiful long blond hair ("like a wheat field") and loves to brush it. Rawlings remarks that "she's got the longest, smoothest, straightest legs in the world." She is vain about her appearance, but that, too, she pretty much takes for granted. She has her moments—when she is passionately sincere—but on the whole she is a superficial hedonist. Rawlings knows he should not tie himself down to this woman, but he confesses, "I want to make an absolutely colossal mistake." He sums her up this way: "Granted she's lazy and spoiled, and rather stupid, and enormously on the make. Still she's very beautiful, very friendly, and very charming and rather innocent—and quite brave." Although she cannot cook, Bridges has a knack for making things cozy and homelike, and Rawlings dreams of making a family with her.

As a Loyalist agent, Rawlings is assigned to investigate fifth columnists within Madrid, traitors actually working for Franco. He has a bad conscience because he has had to kill for the cause and because he has lost a good man through a mistake he could have averted. He has trouble maintaining discipline among the men of whom he is in charge. He comments bitterly, "I'm a sort of second-rate cop pretending to be a third-rate newspaperman." He is also a rather big, sloppy man, self-important and condescending, and there is some merit in Bridges's accusation that he is a "conceited, *conceited* drunkard. [A] ridiculous, puffed-up, posing braggart." Rawlings ends their romance, knowing she represents a soft, humane side of himself he cannot afford to entertain so long as he is "signed up" not only on the Loyalist side but on the side of the "fifty years of undeclared wars" he expects to be fighting. Rawlings realizes, in other words, that Spain is just the beginning of the Fascist assault on democracy. Yet there is no question that when this couple parts company, they are still deeply in love with each other. Something in their affair, and in the play itself, is unresolved, making *The Fifth Column* one of Hemingway's least satisfying works.

Martha Gellhorn was not stupid, and Ernest Hemingway was no Loyalist agent. Otherwise, the portraits he limns in *The Fifth Column* are recognizable caricatures of himself and Martha. She was as fastidious as he was slovenly. While he figured the safe angles in the Hotel Florida—as Rawlings does—Gellhorn calmly accepted their vulnerability to bombing. She had gone to Spain not knowing much more than Dorothy Bridges, and she had a lazy, luxury-loving streak, a gregarious, ingratiating manner that men found irresistible.

Everyone to whom Hemingway showed the manuscript recognized that he had used Gellhorn for his depiction of Dorothy Bridges. A very confident woman, she did not let the burlesque of their liaison bother her. She considered his "impish humor . . . one of his most enjoyable assets. . . . If he needed to portray her in such a light, perhaps it had something to do with his own conflicts," Bernice Kert has suggested. At any rate, Gellhorn did not think Bridges was a credible character. She was an extension of the divisions in Rawlings's own psyche; she did not quite have a full life as a dramatic character.

This troubling focus on Bridges mirrored Hemingway's uncertainty about Gellhorn. While he was proud of her, he also wanted her to be regarded as his protégée, as was apparent to Stephen Spender, who remembers lunching with Hemingway and Gellhorn in Paris during the

Spanish Civil War. Hemingway boasted about taking her to the Madrid morgue every day to inure her to the grim realities of death. Gellhorn has vehemently denied Spender's account, accusing him of being an "apocryphiar." She dearly treasures the image of herself as Hemingway's equal in Spain, but it would have been just like him to exaggerate his command over her. Her rejoinder to Spender that she had already visited morgues as a reporter in Albany, New York, and that Hemingway would not have gone near one is irrelevant. As Spender has observed, Hemingway was adept at tall tales, at fictionalizing his life, and in conversation with an admiring, gullible young poet (Spender has admitted to being as much), he could easily have gotten away with this silly lie.

While Hemingway and Gellhorn never wavered in their support of the Republic, *The Fifth Column* reflects a weariness that had set in during their second sojourn there. The November weather was dismal. Constant rain turned the streets into a yellowish mud. Although everyone talked of a new offensive, they got bogged down in a mood that was of a piece with the Republic's failure to throw off the Fascist incubus. The city was abuzz with rumors. As Gellhorn later put it in a story, war seemed to endure forever, with each day dragging on in the intervals between fighting, when nothing appeared worth doing, and no topic other than war engaged anyone. Sometimes the only way to survive was to dwell on intimate, private matters. The enormity of it all got to be too much for any single person to absorb. It was at one of these moments that Hemingway, having lunch with the head of the secret police, suddenly left, fearful for Gellhorn's safety. He had to know where she was. Searching through the mud and the debris, he found her. She acknowledged his concern, but it surprised her. Usually her safety did not worry him. After all, every day they walked to the war and joked with the men in the trenches. The worst thing that had happened was the bruising her head received when she clambered out of a dugout. It was difficult negotiating one's way through dark trenches, putting one's hands out to the walls, ducking the tunnel supports, and skidding on duckboards or foundering in the mud.

In December, Gellhorn reluctantly agreed to return to the States to lecture on the war, with her fees designated for medical aid to the Republic. She was an extraordinary speaker and was certain to do the cause some good, but she put so much of herself into such trips that she became exhausted.

Her mixed feelings were compounded by Hemingway's nagging. He did not want her to go but did not explain why. He may not have been able to give a reason, but Jeffrey Meyers is probably right in suggesting that he treated Gellhorn's leaving as an act of betrayal. Meyers has pointed to "the theme of personal loyalty" in *The Fifth Column*. For Hemingway, Gellhorn was acting too independently; she was a traitor to his profoundly personal world. With considerable justification, Meyers has implied that Philip Rawlings's proposal to Dorothy Bridges parallels the offer Hemingway thought he was making to Gellhorn: "Would you like to marry me or stay with me all the time or go wherever I go, and be my girl?"

In mid-December, when Gellhorn and Hemingway were in Barcelona, the Loyalists surprised Franco with an offensive against Teruel. Hemingway, Matthews, and Delmer rushed to the front to cover what turned out to be a government triumph. Then Hemingway returned to Gellhorn in Barcelona for Christmas dinner at the Hotel Majestic on the eve of her departure for Paris. Although he did not yet know it, Pauline was in Paris awaiting him and an opportunity to save their marriage. She fashioned her hair in an imitation of Martha's. When he got to Paris, however, she could not control her temper. Nothing moved him—not even her threat to throw herself off the balcony of their hotel room. Yet they sailed home together to spend three fitful months in Key West. He had trouble writing. Making a home with Pauline no longer seemed to interest him. He was fixated on Spain, recalling in a letter to her parents that in Madrid he had felt free of his family, possessions, and obligations. He had been on his own and truly his own man.

Gellhorn was not faring much better. She had left for Paris the day after their Christmas dinner. She got sick from the rich French food and became disgusted with friends who cared little about the Spanish Republic's plight. She cashed a royalty check for *The Trouble I've Seen,* using part of it to pay what she owed Hemingway for her time in Spain. On board the *Normandie,* bound for New York, she wrote him that her baggage had been temporarily misplaced and her compartment was loathsome. She would make the effort to work anyhow. It was a glum letter. She wished him well in the holiday season but was vague about when they would see each other again. It was not exactly a hopeful or an encouraging note.

FOR WHOM
THE BELL TOLLS

1 9 3 8 – 1 9 3 9

13

On January 7, 1938, Martha Gellhorn addressed three thousand people on the University of Minnesota campus. She compared Spain to a "single cell where the body's illness could be fought and arrested." On January 23, Edna Gellhorn wrote to Eleanor Roosevelt describing Martha's exhausting lecture tour. Edna had heard her daughter speak in Minneapolis and Milwaukee and assured Mrs. Roosevelt that the accounts of Martha's superb speeches were accurate. Eleanor would shortly hear from Martha herself, who returned home soon for a brief break in her punishing schedule, having lost twelve pounds and feeling depleted. On January 28, she spoke to an audience estimated at about a thousand at the Sheldon Memorial in St. Louis. Just before taking the stage, she was interviewed by the press at her mother's home. Taking heart from the victory at Teruel, she predicted a Loyalist victory. She also warned that the war might provoke a "world crisis." Franco had the aid of 140,000 men supplied by Hitler, yet the Republican government had endured thus far. She had returned home to correct "misinformation" and to caution people that "their own democracies will surely be threatened if the Spanish democracy is defeated."

Gellhorn lectured to a Chicago audience, including an enthusiastic Grace Hemingway, who promptly wrote her son about what a pleasure it had been to meet Martha. Altogether, Gellhorn lectured in twenty-two cities in a two-month span that left her sapped of energy and filled with frustration. There was no way in an hour to explain to her contented audiences what it meant to save Spain. She disliked being treated as a celebrity, and the pace she assumed for her road trip proved too great a strain. A doctor urged her to quit the tour before she broke down completely. Therefore she forfeited the fees for the rest of the lecture circuit, returned home for a short stay, and left on February 13 to recuperate in the Bahamas.

When Gellhorn arrived in Paris at the end of March, she found Hemingway in the company of correspondent Vincent Sheean and his wife, Diana Forbes-Robertson. The fortunes of the Loyalists seemed very grim. They had lost Belchite, over which they had fought so bravely, and were in retreat. Sheean and Hemingway went off without the women to discuss their entry into Spain. When they returned, they withdrew their invitation to Diana to come along. She accused Martha of engineering this sudden volte-face—although Martha was also excluded from their plans. Both Martha and Diana complained. Sheean left it to Hemingway, who stupidly remarked, "Spain's no place for women." To this, Gellhorn rejoined, "If Diana puts a foot on that train, so will I." To Diana, Martha seemed like a "boy-woman" who allowed Hemingway the upper hand in this instance. The revised plan was for him and Sheean to take the train to Barcelona and then "phone to say whether 'the women' might come."

Gellhorn, now a seasoned reporter, was beginning to get some perspective on Hemingway's "military pretensions," teasing him in the company of Robert Capa, the great photographer, who got to know her and Hemingway well. Hemingway's room in Barcelona's Hotel Majestic was the scene of regular skull sessions, with Martha frequently taking issue with Ernest even as she aped his gestures—flinging herself backward as she sat down, stretching "her legs in the elegant black slacks," running a hand through her hair, and announcing, "Jeez, I'm pooped." Sheean and his wife "smiled. Martha sounded like Ernest's echo."

Gellhorn acquitted herself well in the six weeks of arduous, dangerous reporting she and Hemingway conducted in Spain. Pink almond blossoms signaled spring as "Martha and her companions dove from their small, open car into a ditch to avoid being strafed by a Rebel monoplane." It was difficult to travel on roads congested with refugees, carts, lumbering animals, and tired soldiers. Frequently changing battle lines and careful negotiation of narrow roads and bridges lined with dynamite made the trip hazardous.

Gellhorn wrote Eleanor Roosevelt to tell her what it was like. Although the Loyalists were outgunned and vulnerable to bombing, they had fought their way out of defeat and managed to regroup, retreating in good order. In one bombing raid alone, she had seen more than thirty silver Italian planes in wedge formations dropping bombs over Tortosa. The civilian population seemed remarkably calm. She had heard a man walking down the street, singing to himself after the bombers left. She was amazed and heartened by the good humor and steadiness of the soldiers.

Good Friday, April 15, 4:00 A.M.: Gellhorn, Hemingway, and Delmer left Barcelona under a bright full moon. Overhead they spotted Italian bombers and leaped into the ditches once again. If there was ever a time for Gellhorn to crack, this was it. There were stories about the torture Franco's Moors inflicted on male and female captives, but she never wavered, and Hemingway was proud to have this poised woman beside him. Returning to Barcelona only for a bath and some sleep, she was ready at dawn to accompany him on the approach to the Ebro River, now in Franco's possession. They had to make a run for it through an irrigation ditch as machine-gun fire came closer and closer.

Whatever doubts Hemingway had about Gellhorn seemed to vanish in these days of her intrepid behavior. For the first time, he raised the possibility that they would marry. She was reluctant, realizing his attitude toward her might quickly change when she was a wife, not just a lover. She could tell that making love to her gave him intense pleasure. However, the physical side of it seemed "the least important part of their relationship" to her. She had the best times with men who were her chums, "chaps" who had no special claim on her.

Gellhorn and Hemingway bided their time in Barcelona, then in Paris, before he returned home to Key West. In May and early June, she prepared for *Collier's* assignments in Czechoslovakia, England, and France, writing her editor at *Collier's* about her premonitions of war. It could break out at any time, probably in Prague, and she would take a quick look at conditions there before the shooting started. In a letter to Eleanor Roosevelt, she mentioned her need to earn money (she had given some of her earnings away to needy soldiers), but she vowed to return to Spain to see the war to its end. Although the Loyalists suffered severe equipment shortages, she assured Roosevelt that the Republic would fight on—if only American aid were forthcoming.

Hemingway was dispirited and doubted he and Gellhorn would be together again. As Bernice Kert has observed, "he was sinking into the same state of helplessness that had overwhelmed him in 1926, when he was tied to one woman, in love with another, and wishing for something wholly unpredictable to rescue him." In Key West, he found himself writing again—short stories and political articles that primed him for writing his next big novel. At first, Pauline was polite, but after a few of his tantrums, she turned sour. In the damp August heat, the couple quarreled continuously. He was beginning to locate his loyalties, writing a dedication to *The Fifth Column*— "To Marty and Herbert [Matthews] with love"—that he later dropped.

Gellhorn's editor at *Collier's* saw a world war coming: Fascists attacking Spain; the French army preparing to defend itself along three frontiers; the German army triumphantly marching into Austria; Britain, now extremely vulnerable to air attack, furiously rearming itself. Gellhorn was to find out what the British were thinking. What was the reaction to Fascism? What did they think of the prospects for war?

Gellhorn and Virginia Cowles traveled in England in the month of June, seeking answers to these questions. London appeared to be a bustling, fashionable, thriving peacetime city. Unemployment had dropped dramatically as soon as the government began to rearm. Workers had enough extra money to enjoy themselves on a Saturday night with a few drinks. Housing was decent and not too expensive. There were the usual entertainments—such as a Sunday cricket match. It was unreal, Gellhorn thought. The great London newspapers avoided playing up the troubles abroad; so did the radio; and newsreels were edited so that the public was scarcely aware of the bombing of China and Spain. Everything possible was being done to maintain the fiction of England as a "fine green island" that had nothing to do with the ugly affairs of foreigners. It had been a thousand years since England had been occupied by a foreign power. The British just did not lose wars.

Gellhorn desperately sought some sign that the country recognized it was in mortal danger. She heard of a meeting of workers to discuss the imminence of war. Good—finally she would be able to talk with people who shared her worries. In the run-down, barren streets, she passed houses looking all the same, where inside tired men and women washed up after a difficult working day. Children played rowdily and scooted around streets devoid of trees. It was hot. At a snack bar (a small filthy place smelling of fried fish), she listened to neighborhood men discussing Joe Louis's knockout of the Nazi pride, Max Schmeling. Sports, not politics, held their interest. One of them asked if Gellhorn knew Robert Taylor. Another had read a detective magazine and had a vision of silly Americans all carrying firearms. Still another wanted to know whether it was really true that fabulous amounts of money could be made in the United States fixing radios in a worker's off-hours. Even though Britain was spending close to $2 billion in armaments, nobody mentioned Spain, Austria, or China; nobody wondered what Britain meant to do with all of its new weapons.

It was bizarre. The ARP (Air Raid Precautions Plan) was designed to train more than a half million people as wardens to manage the population when the bombs began to fall. Fire brigades were being organized, Gellhorn thought, because the British government had learned from the incineration of Guernica. Yet the British public did not have the wit to see they were being prepared for war. The poor were indifferent and the rich were incredibly smug, thinking the proper response to bombing was simply to organize evacuations and supply everyone with cheap, doubtfully effective gas masks. Gellhorn was amazed at the antiwar argument: Why would Germany bomb England when it knew England would retaliate by bombing Germany? In other words, rearmament was intended to scare Germany, to demonstrate that it could not win.

In Birmingham, Gellhorn and Cowles interviewed people in a standard working-class English pub looking somewhat dingy and equipped with the customary dart board and shabby racing prints. People were reserved at first. The talk turned to aching feet, the weather, and England's invincibility. Finally, Cowles and Gellhorn succeeded in getting them to discuss politics. A charwoman, employed in a café, vowed she would never live in a Fascist country, where, unlike England, there was no respect for individual liberties. She thought those flag-waving, uniformed, marching foreigners were different, and England had no right to interfere in their affairs. This robust woman was ready to fight England's enemies, but she was a little muddled about exactly who they were. No one referred to Czechoslovakia. To Gellhorn, these sallow industrialized workers in their cheap but solid homes, in their dirty smokestack city, seemed repulsively complacent.

Even the Communists ducked the issue of war and were willing to fight only if England was attacked. In Sheffield, Gellhorn was courteously but resolutely expelled from an arms factory. An ARP official told her quite confidently that people were not afraid of bombing. When she pointed out to him that Sheffield was only a short distance from the sea and was certain to be a strategic target, he took off his pince-nez and gravely replied that the authorities knew what they were doing.

Were the British willing to fight for the Czechs? Cowles and Gellhorn got no clear answer. Nobody seemed to want to fight on foreign territory. Of course they would defend their own land, but it was best to leave all this talk to the authorities, those government chaps engaged in secret negotiations; they would know how to maneuver the country out of war. More than she could say in her *Collier's* article, Gellhorn was outraged. She found it appalling that the laboring classes in England felt no solidarity with workers in Spain or Czechoslovakia.

Cowles watched Gellhorn's survey of public opinion turn into a round of speech making. When Gellhorn got to the subject of war, she lost all patience and harangued people about Hitler's military might. They were hardly startled and treated her as though she was an eccentric. She was ready to explode by the time they arrived in Yorkshire at Lord Feversham's house. Why was it, she asked Feversham, that everyone was obsessed with racing and the weather? He was amused. What an odd thing, he said, going about the country goading people to give their opinions. He accused Gellhorn and Cowles of being "warmongers"—not the first time this charge had been brought against them. Gellhorn was beside herself. She threatened to rile up his "peasants." They were called "farmers" in England, Feversham replied. She knew that, Gellhorn said, "That's what you *call* them." Feversham took them on a jaunt around his estate and stopped to speak with one of his tenants, old Geoff, who simply affirmed ("Yes, m'lord") every argument his master made in favor of the belief there would be no war, and that talk cf war was "rather silly." Gellhorn erupted: "Just try coming to *my* country some day. . . . You won't get all that bowing and scraping, and imagine putting those ideas into that poor old man's head! When the war *does* come, your corpse will be found bobbing about in the river and we'll know who did it. But you can rest assured *I* won't give him away."

She was not far from the mark. About a year and a half later, when Feversham was about to go off to war, old Geoff paid his respects to his master, then "glared ferociously" and said, "I suppose we must pay for our mistakes. Isn't that so, m'lord?" Feversham had been so impressed with Gellhorn's perceptiveness that he asked Cowles to find out whether

Gellhorn thought England would lose the war. Cowles remembered Gellhorn remarking after her English visit, "And the worst part of it is, their skulls are so thick, you can't crack them. If the world comes to an end tomorrow, and there's only one person left, I know it's bound to be an Englishman!" In milder form, she had concluded her article for *Collier's* by observing that the English had such a strong belief in their own salvation that perhaps they were right and the Lord would "provide for England."

The French were not nearly so sanguine about their fate. Belgium, Switzerland, Holland—would any of these nations' frontiers be respected in a Fascist thrust towards France? Unlike England, there was no government effort to prepare the populace for war. No gas masks were being distributed. Gellhorn was relieved to find that the French still made politics a part of their daily life. The problem was that the country had no foreign policy. The government appeared prepared only for appeasement—as long as that would maintain the peace, no matter how dishonorable. Even worse, it had neglected to ally itself with Russia, a powerful military force. There was a slowly growing Fascist party within France that was encouraged by the government's cowardice.

France was busy mechanizing its army, concentrating on mobility and speed, and building up its navy. The air force was pathetically weak, but new planes were in production. Gellhorn observed but did not seem especially impressed with the Maginot Line. France could not go it alone. It was depending heavily on its allies, especially England. Unlike the workers in England, the French were well informed. They understood the grim precedents set in China, Spain, and Czechoslovakia. They impressed Gellhorn as conscientious citizens who realized that someone had to put an end to aggression.

You did not have to penetrate very deeply into the French countryside to find monuments to the Great War. There were still dangerous areas of explosives marked off with barbed wire. Northern France had buried within it the bodies of thousands of soldiers from England, France, and Poland. The French lived every day with the tragedy of war.

August 1938, Czechoslovakia: On a Sunday morning, Martha Gellhorn watched a parade of Social Democrats go down the main street of Prague, one of the world's most enchanting, storybook cities. From Castle Hill, she looked over the dark roofs of the city and the soaring church spires. In the street stood President Beneš, his head uncovered and exposed to the bright light, reviewing for nearly half a day the floats and bands of his people, marching twelve abreast in impeccable harmony. To Gellhorn, it all seemed extremely elegant and merry. The word of the day was *democracy,* emblazoned on every banner and sign. About it all there was an air of festivity. The Bakers' Union advanced down the street with breakfast rolls atop their heads; Slovak peasants danced past with colorful embellished costumes; Boy Scouts busily fixed food and ducked in and out of the smoke of a camp fire on a truck that served as a mock forest. They sang and cheered and saluted the president and the people. The talk was of freedom and of the need to fight for it. War was less than a hundred miles away at the closest border.

It was not as far from Prague to Peoria as Americans might have thought. Sooner or later, they would have to accept the fact that freedom was in danger everywhere. On a sight-seeing tour, a guide had stopped the bus at city hall and pointed out an ancient baroque clock. It dated from 1490, before the discovery of America, when Czechoslovakia was free. The country had its liberty now; it would preserve its freedom for the future, he vowed. This was a land that reminded Gellhorn of the United States: In back of the town of Troppau, small hills reminiscent of the Ozarks bent around the countryside. The parade in Prague, Gellhorn was trying to tell her readers, represented all free people. As in Spain, the citizenry were taking their stand against Fascism. If only she could open American eyes.

In March 1938, Hitler annexed Austria. In May, the Czechs partially mobilized their army. Gellhorn was there to see it: Czechoslovakia was the only European country ready to halt Hitler's advance. In August, in Prague, she was enjoying the high spirits of a people prepared to fight for their independence.

Germany surrounded half of Czechoslovakia, including its capital, Prague. A hostile Hungary on the southern frontier and an unsympathetic Poland to the north hemmed in the Czechs, whose allies, France and England, appeased Hitler with territorial concessions. Even worse, Konrad Henlein, leader of a German nationalist minority, excited by Hitler's call for *Lebensraum*—more living space for the superior German state—violently agitated for unification with Germany. Other minorities, chiefly the Magyars and the Slovaks, demanded territorial settlements and autonomy. The fragile, ethnically diverse Czech republic, created in 1918 out of the breakup of the Austro-Hungarian monarchy, felt the full pressure of the nationalism that Hitler fomented.

This is what was at stake in August 1938: Which way would the world turn? Gellhorn observed the Czechs preparing for an invasion, for air raids, for gas attacks. There were plans to evacuate children, to conserve the food supply, to conceal munitions factories from aerial bombardment—in short, to do everything possible to protect the civilian population and to strengthen the army. But the Henlein Nazis—perhaps slightly over half of the three and a half million Germans in Czechoslovakia— spoke of the country's doom: The Czechs were starving their German minority; the Czechs had willfully taken jobs that should have gone to Germans; the Czechs had thus caused the depression. Nazi radio broadcasts provoked the Sudeten Germans (Hitler's name for the German minority) by claiming they had been humiliated by the Czechs. Germany was a major power and a "great race." Czechoslovakia was a minor power and "a small Slavic race," complained the Henleinists, who saw no reason to be ruled by an inferior people—especially after Hitler's annexation of Austria.

In spite of these enormous external and internal tensions, Gellhorn saw a struggling democracy worth preserving. President Beneš had triumphed over divisiveness and helped to found a liberal democratic government. A treaty of friendship with France, Yugoslavia, and Rumania, the redistribution of lands once held by the church and the nobility, and the improvement of living conditions for the peasantry proved the country's leaders had done well. Surely the display of the people's high regard for Beneš and their military mobilization would—if nothing else—give Hitler pause and shame Czechoslovakia's allies into finally opposing German aggression.

Hemingway joined Gellhorn in Paris in September. Late summer in the city was wonderful—cool and quiet and empty like a village with friendly people, and no place in the world had trees this lovely. When Gellhorn came to write about this period in her novel *A Stricken Field* (1940), she had her heroine Mary express thoughts about her lover John that paralleled Martha's own about Ernest. In Madrid and Paris, they had done wonderfully. Why risk a marriage? Perhaps she feared the change. It meant becoming tied down and getting trapped in routine. The very nature of their relationship was founded on movement, on their being apart some of the time. Perhaps marriage could be for the periods when they were separated, when she could refer to her husband and his opinions. He became the wonderful John of *A Stricken Field* with whom she laughed and ate five times a day. She would smile at the picture of him drinking coffee on a café terrace in Paris, pausing to "hold hands" with her on a sunny day, then resuming his reading about a boxing match.

Reuniting with Hemingway in the Parisian fall (after a brief vacation in Corsica) was a guilty pleasure. Gellhorn had left Czechoslovakia to its fate, not knowing how she could be of help but still ashamed that she had the freedom to leave while her Czech friends were trapped, and sending Eleanor Roosevelt a two-thousand-word report on anti-Nazi refugees, some of which would later be incorporated in her novel. She took some comfort in supposing that Hemingway would somehow have handled it better. In *A Stricken Field,* Mary imagines turning to John to confide just how miserable she feels. If Hemingway with his knowing air often took an irritating, proprietary hold on Gellhorn's life, he also represented the one person to whom she could turn for strength. His enormously powerful ego had its positive role to play in her life. According to Bernice Kert, Martha has insisted that "real life in Paris with Ernest was in no way as lovely as the fiction." To be sure—but there is no denying that he was the inspiration for the fiction.

Pressing events in Czechoslovakia interrupted this Parisian idyll. In September 1938, Hitler demanded autonomy for the Sudetenland. Civil unrest, followed by martial law, put even more strain on the Czech state. Meetings between Hitler and Neville Chamberlain in Germany did nothing to resolve the crisis, but after appeals from Franklin Roosevelt and Benito Mussolini, an agreement was reached in Munich on September 29, 1938. Neither Czechoslovakia nor the Soviet Union (which had offered itself to Czechoslovakia as an ally) were invited to Munich. Germany was permitted to occupy the Sudetenland immediately, with plebescites to follow to determine the status of minorities in Czechoslovakia. The plebescites were never held. Although France and England promised to defend Czechoslovakia's new borders, the country had been effectively split apart and its economy ruined. Beneš, under Hitler's fierce attacks, resigned in October, realizing he had no nation left, especially after Poland and Hungary took over parts of northern and southern Czechoslovakia. A democracy that had been able to mobilize 800,000 men for war on September 3 no longer existed by October 8, the day Martha Gellhorn flew into Prague for her last visit.

From Paris on October 22, Gellhorn wrote her *Collier's* editor, Charles Colebaugh, about her efforts to contact Beneš through his protégé, Jan Masaryk. Beneš was avoiding comment on the agonizing truth that

Czechoslovakia had become a Nazi satellite. Police stopped her at the gate of Beneš's house. Although she got a message through to him, he refused to speak to members of the press. After other futile efforts, Gellhorn quit, realizing that most of Beneš's officials in the foreign office were fleeing Czechoslovakia and the concentration camps to which she was sure they would have been sent. Having obtained translations of Czech state department documents, she concluded that the British government had behaved duplicitously, withholding information from Czech officials until the very last minute as part of a carefully planned strategy of forsaking the country.

"Obituary of a Democracy," Gellhorn's article about the dismemberment of Czechoslovakia, appeared in the December 10, 1938, issue of *Collier's*. She wrote of a people who had been stunned and betrayed, of Czech soldiers returning home with rapid but awkward strides. With dejected and confused expressions, they joined their humiliated civilian counterparts in quietly watching the Czech artillery pass by. One soldier, like many others, was trying to find out what happened to his village. Was it Czech or German now? To Gellhorn, he emphasized how isolated the Czechs felt. He was sure the French and English would find themselves in the same predicament once Hitler demanded Alsace-Lorraine and other territories. Poland would also find itself alone when the führer was ready to use it as a corridor to Central Europe. All of a sudden, Czechoslovakia had been turned into a poor country. Its people, including the Sudetens, would suffer. Yet, what could the Czechs do when their allies had refused to help them?

There was talk of labor camps for the unemployed. Many Czechs were trying to leave the country, scared by reports of friends who had been intimidated or who had already vanished. The Henlein police had begun to terrorize towns, to point in the streets to the "dirty Czechs" who had opposed them before the Munich Pact. Gellhorn heard from one woman who had been struck across the face by a Henleinist and warned that all Czechs would be sent to concentration camps. Indeed, there were already reports of new camps on Czech soil at Carlsbad, Eich, and Elbogen. Czech women had been forced to scrub public buildings and military outposts while Henlein's female followers threatened and vilified them.

Gellhorn heard story after story of a people dishonored and tortured, of Czechs forced to kneel before the statue of their founding father, Tomáš Masaryk, and defame him while swearing allegiance to Hitler; of a people so ashamed, they committed suicide by poisoning themselves or throwing themselves beneath trains returning them to the Sudetenland.

She had seen an old man with his teeth and ribs kicked in, his limbs blackened and swollen from beating. He stood, in her mind, for the unbearable vision of a people degraded by Fascist terror.

Gellhorn knew her journalism was not adequate to convey the tragedy of Czechoslovakia. She wrote against deadlines and within the confines of journalistic conventions that put the focus on what she could immediately see and hear. She could absorb only so much at the speed required for filing her reports. Although her writing for *Collier's* bore the unmistakable stamp of her personality, it could not render the full force of her conviction that events in Czechoslovakia would shortly shake the whole world.

In *A Stricken Field*, Mary Douglas, a war correspondent, arrives in Czechoslovakia more than a week after the conference in Munich. The big news has already been reported, but Mary believes she is recording historic events. Like Gellhorn, she is not interested in journalism per se or in getting exclusive news items into the press. Her writing is more than a trade or a profession; it is a commitment to fighting for a better world. It has grown right out of her anger over injustice and inhumanity, and it represents a crystallization of her deepest feelings about democracy and self-determination.

The war correspondents in *A Stricken Field* are a disorderly group of heavy drinkers, faded-looking and sloppily dressed, striking poses that will eventually appear on the jackets of books advertising their memoirs. Mary's familiarity with these reporters is the result of their frequent meetings over the years on journeys to great cities and to out-of-the-way places. In these circumstances, she has developed much affection for them and has enjoyed their warm intimacy and banter. They are sometimes a pompous lot, but they have been honest with her and willing to share their experience and advice. If she has no special regard for their reporting, it is because they write less than they know and care less than they should about their subjects.

The kind of solidarity Gellhorn felt with her fellow reporters is best expressed in the scene where Mary, newly arrived in Prague, forgoes the questions she would like to ask her bored and tired colleagues. She knows they rely on her to divert them. After all, in their view she is a woman, not as well informed as they are. She does not count in the way they do. They already have the information she needs, Mary thinks, or they have little interest in the material she wants. By assuming a casual and engaging pose, she puts the men at ease.

Like Mary, Gellhorn tolerated the male prejudices of correspondents.

She could be very good-humored about their chauvinism and held her own in a man's world with no hint of defensiveness or touchiness. She enjoyed male attention, relished her femininity, and was not particularly bothered by the special category in which men might try to put her. She would do her job and enjoy herself as a woman and as a correspondent.

Gellhorn gave Mary many of her own characteristics: fine legs, a taste for beautiful clothes, high spirits, and a sharp tongue. Gellhorn has always been careful about her appearance, for it has often created a sensation, put her at the center of things, and given her the edge over colleagues without her flair. When Mary arrives well dressed and made up for a gathering of correspondents, her entrance is taken by one of them as a provocation. He treats her like a model aiming for a certain impression, that of a woman who walks in the room like a heartbreaking beauty. Rather than taking offense, she welcomes the idea of a party and suggests they go out dancing.

When Mary first greets her colleagues, one of them asks whether she has been with "old John" recently. Mary replies proudly that she has just left John, who is still in Spain and still committed to reporting the Republican side while these reporters have gone on to their next story. Indeed, to a correspondent's remark that things have settled down in Spain, she replies matter-of-factly that there is an impending battle at Ebro—the very battle in which Hemingway and *New York Times* reporter Herbert Matthews would distinguish themselves.

Although Gellhorn had scorn for the facile skills of her trade, she used them well. Her articles had the clarity and color Mary Douglas puts into her work. Like Douglas, Gellhorn collected statistics, interviewed important businessmen, politicians, professionals, and celebrities, and gave a panoramic view of the places she visited. Gellhorn was not immune to the romance of her career, but it seemed superficial to her. She felt the glamour of her role should be the least of it, especially when she reflected on how little she and her fellow correspondents really understood about the events they were covering.

The question Gellhorn put to herself in Czechoslovakia is the same question that troubles Mary in *A Stricken Field*. Given the enormity of the evil about to be perpetrated on the Czechs, what was one to do? With the Germans grabbing more territory, coal mines, industries, railroads, and people nearly every day, how could one individual make a difference? After the Munich Pact, the Czechs were a beaten people. It was impossible for them to be individuals anymore. They advanced sluggishly, unsure of their direction, waiting, feeling isolated and in despair. They had swiftly retreated into the security of silence. Prague was now a prison.

The correspondents in Prague did not dare imagine what they might do to change the course of events. Government censorship often made it impossible to file honest stories; some reporters worked for newspapers that supported the Munich Pact; other correspondents were burned out and unable to cope with the human tragedy they had witnessed. Czech police were directed to return all refugees (many of them anti-Nazis) within two days to the Sudetenland or to other parts of Germany from which they had fled. Rita, a refugee, asks Mary to help these homeless people; as a writer, perhaps she can rouse an international outcry. At the very least, her words can put pressure on England and France, which in turn might force the Czechs to withstand Hitler's orders for a few weeks and permit the refugees time to find asylum in other countries.

Although Mary agrees to Rita's proposal, she is dubious that public opinion can be a force for good, since it is a lot simpler to incite anger than it is to ask for assistance. The Nazis had already proven as much. However, Mary consents to visit the refugee houses in order to inform herself of the facts she will use to awaken public outrage. Like Gellhorn, who would send a report on the refugees to Eleanor Roosevelt, Mary is enraged and heartbroken over their plight and determined to reach people in power and to press her case.

Under the League of Nations auspices, a High Commissioner for Refugees, Sir Neill Malcolm, visited Prague for two days in early October 1938. Gellhorn was incensed to discover he had not seen any of the refugees. She accosted him at his hotel and carried on in her customary way. She banged on the table, raised her voice, and made her plea. To her amazement, he asked for her advice on a plan of action.

Gellhorn described this encounter with Malcolm in a letter written sometime in November 1938, and fictionalized the incident in *A Stricken Field.* In her letter, she gave only the barest details in a hammer-blow style that summed up the vigor with which she pursued her mission on behalf of the refugees. She suggested he see General Sirovy, a World War I hero to the Czechs and now the prime minister. Malcolm should make every effort to persuade Sirovy to suspend the expulsion order, she advised. Malcolm agreed to meet Sirovy if Gellhorn got the American minister in Prague to arrange the appointment. When she was rebuffed by the first secretary of the American legation, she telephoned Sirovy, identifying herself as Sir Neill's interpreter, and secured the appointment. Then she contacted General Faucher, who had resigned his position as head of the French Military Mission because of his disgust over his country's betrayal of Czechoslovakia. She primed Faucher to attend the meeting with Sirovy, telling Faucher about the refugees and asking him to praise Malcolm to Sirovy beforehand. In effect, Gellhorn was getting Faucher and Malcolm to act as stand-ins for the very imperial powers that should have stopped Hitler's pretensions of ruling Europe. Her hopes, however, were set too high. Sirovy could not be budged. She did not blame him, for she realized the Czechs dared not oppose Hitler without receiving much stronger backing from France and England.

Nothing could ever be the same for Gellhorn after Czechoslovakia. She had been brought up to see her fate reflected in the destiny of others. Like Mary, she would always respond positively to pleas for help, because she did not feel she was entitled by birth to "passport, job, love." Gellhorn had grown up with this feeling: Good fortune had to be somehow repaid. What you had was not yours alone; it was meant to be shared with others. The thought of living at someone else's expense and of enjoying liberties and luxuries about which others could only dream discomfited her. In the world from which she had come, private pleasure and public service were both essential to a fulfilled person. Happiness itself was not due to oneself unless it was due to others. A world in crisis had to be reflected in the agony of her own soul.

On November 3, 1938, Gellhorn and Hemingway made their final trip to Spain. It was now apparent the Loyalists would lose. This was the third winter of war, and Gellhorn's last dispatch from Spain reflected her own ebbing hopes. The International Brigades had been disbanded. No similar gesture was made on the other side. German and Italian pilots and soldiers continued to bombard Barcelona. Gellhorn was in an elegiac mood, praising the Republican army, which had matured during the war and was still in good spirits.

Gellhorn, Capa, and Matthews were among the "last ditchers," staying on after Hemingway left for New York in late November, after thousands were fleeing to the safety of France. Naturally, there was an "intense camaraderie and esprit de corps" among this small band. The constant hammering of air raids—sometimes spaced no more than fifteen minutes apart—destroyed the composure of even the most experienced correspondents. In such chaos and terror, no one managed more than a fitful few hours of sleep. One night, Capa stayed with Gellhorn in her hotel room, and they huddled together in the dark, quivering in the cold.

The Spanish Civil War would drag on for a few months into the new year. It was all but over. Nevertheless, Gellhorn tried one more plea to Franklin Roosevelt. Eleanor showed him Martha's letter: No other president in the world could lead the democratic forces. She spoke to him almost as if he were her father. Surely in this cowardly, terrified, and directionless world, there was one honorable and courageous man who could unite people by the example of his own bravery and force them to realize their responsibility to human beings less fortunate than themselves.

Franklin Roosevelt was agonizing over Spain, but the reality—as Eleanor explained in a letter to Martha—was that people did not have a clear position on Spain and were not so sure as Martha about what should be done. It was far too late to aid Spain or to convince Americans that intervention was imperative. There was nothing more for Gellhorn to do.

On December 15, Edna wrote Eleanor Roosevelt just in case she had not heard that Martha had sailed from Le Havre for the United States on December 14 and would arrive in New York on December 20. Edna was in a buoyant mood, announcing the birth of a new granddaughter. She would welcome her daughter in New York, knowing Martha would be depressed. Indeed, Martha was coming home with the feeling that England, France, and the United States had failed Spain and, as a consequence, had failed the cause of democracy itself. She doubted whether democracy could surmount this blow it had given its own values.

THE HEART OF ANOTHER

1 9 3 9 – 1 9 4 0

ellhorn spent the Christmas of 1938 in St. Louis with her family.
It was the first time in ten years she had celebrated the holiday in
this traditional way. Eleanor Roosevelt sent flowers, and Martha
felt her spirits lift. She could not ignore her sorrow over Spain and
Czechoslovakia, but it was a comfort to be among contented
people protected in their splendid geographical isolation from
European wars. She planned to complete her work for *Collier's*
and then travel south, resting and writing along the way. Then Martha
Ellis Fischel, her eighty-eight-year-old grandmother, died of a heart
attack in the early-morning hours of Sunday, January 8, and Martha
stayed in St. Louis to be with a grieving Edna.

On January 19, 1939, Gellhorn attended a formal White House dinner,
exchanging news with Eleanor Roosevelt about Spain and listening to
the latest word on the New Deal. Gellhorn urged Roosevelt to come to
the aid of Spanish Civil War veterans, to give them employment or help
edit and place their articles. The neutrality laws that kept the United
States from acting against the Fascists infuriated Gellhorn, and she let
Roosevelt know this in person and by letter.

Gellhorn did not cool off until late January, when she picked up her
mother in Washington, D.C., and drove south toward Naples, Florida.
American indifference to the suffering abroad had always angered her, yet

she began to realize that Americans were no different from others: They were forced to concentrate on their own welfare. They had precious little time for the contemplation of world affairs. Congress, on the other hand, had no such excuse, and she blamed it for American inaction.

While Gellhorn had gotten a start on writing some new fiction, she had not made much progress by early March when she joined Hemingway in Cuba. She knew she had great material for a novel about her Czechoslovak experiences, and she profited from the inspiring example of her lover, who was working diligently on *For Whom the Bell Tolls.* It depressed him to recall the good friends he had left in Spain. In spite of the hardships there, the hunger and the danger, he missed it. He had never slept better or felt more secure than when he was in Spain. He had bad dreams now; he had never had any there. The important thing, however, was to write, he kept telling himself and his friends. He had moved away from Key West, from Pauline and the constant visitors who interrupted his concentration, and settled into the Hotel Ambos Mundos in Havana, where there was no phone. He was writing by 8:30 A.M. and usually worked without interruption until 2:00 P.M. every day. After that, he kept fit by playing tennis and swimming. He was just under two hundred pounds—a very good weight for him—and feeling "happy and healthy." If he usually felt drained about midday, this was not surprising considering his enormous writing output. He had not had this kind of exhilaration or feeling of accomplishment since writing *A Farewell to Arms.* Hemingway's discipline was extraordinary. "I owe him the painstakingness of writing," Gellhorn has said of this period in their lives together.

As writers and as lovers, Gellhorn and Hemingway were never closer, yet something was missing. He always had relied on Pauline to give him an opinion on drafts of his work, to bolster him when he suspected his words were of inferior quality. Now he turned to Martha. She admired the new novel, which was dedicated to her, and found it "funny, wonderful, alive and exciting." She also had reservations. Years later, she remembered severely criticizing it, and that Hemingway nursed his injured pride by reading the novel to his ignorant hunting and fishing cronies, who gave him the unqualified approval she withheld. She had quarreled with him about his work in Spain, and she had a low opinion of the articles he had written there.

The hero of *For Whom the Bell Tolls,* Robert Jordan, is equal parts

Ernest Hemingway, Robert Merriman (leader of the Lincoln Battalion), and the author's imagination. Like Hemingway, Jordan is obsessed with his father's suicide, thinking it a shameless, selfish act. Jordan's greatness is that he dedicates himself to others. His work for the Spanish Republic, his mission to blow up a bridge so that the Fascist advance can be halted, are signs of his total involvement in humanity: "that bridge can be the point on which the future of the human race can turn," he tells himself.

Hemingway gave Robert Jordan's beloved, Maria, some of Gellhorn's physical characteristics, but he scrupulously deprived Maria of Martha's argumentativeness, her independence, and her sharp-edged humor. Maria is there to serve Jordan, to soothe her man before the big battles. Nothing like the difficulties and the intense sharing of work that distinguished Gellhorn's and Hemingway's days in Spain are reflected in the novel.

Hemingway's writing regimen was just what Gellhorn needed for herself. After several hours of work, they would spend late afternoons swimming and playing tennis. Except for splendid meals in Havana's French and Spanish restaurants, they stayed away from the city's nightlife. The hotel bothered her. He had promised to find a house for them. Instead, she was treated to a "small second-floor room" full of "fishing gear" and his "beat-up typewriter." Always a fastidious person, Gellhorn could not tolerate the mess in which Hemingway habitually seemed to thrive. She had real estate agents show her rental properties, and she found a place with interesting possibilities that was only a twenty-minute drive from Havana. It was run-down, but that was exactly the kind of project that suited her. It had only one story, a sixty-foot living room, a filthy swimming pool, a tennis court overgrown with weeds, and fifteen acres of rich farmland. It was called Finca Vigía, the site of an old watchtower, a place from which to admire a magnificent view of Havana. Hemingway took one look, said the rent (one hundred dollars a month) was too much, called the dilapidated place hopeless, and went off on a fishing trip.

Using her own money, Gellhorn went ahead, hiring painters, a carpenter, two gardeners, and a cook. Much like the narrator in her story "Luigi's House," she imagined herself making a home for her man. It was a sensuous feeling, just standing on the doorstep, looking at the garden full of "stringy dahlias," roses, and the "candelabra vines." How restful to hear the humming flies, fat and sluggish, expiring at the end of the season. The sea breezes brushing past the eucalyptus trees, the fresh-looking rock mountains arrayed against the sky, the "three mimosa trees and the old well and the rusty gate" suggested a sense of permanence absent during her hectic pursuit of war. For the moment, it was enough just to sit on the doorstep and enjoy a cigarette.

"Luigi's House" idealized the real thing. In fact, Gellhorn did not like sticking around the house, shopping, and doing errands. It seemed like drudgery compared to her journalism. Being a homebody bothered her. She feared becoming a servant to this kind of life. Nature was bewitching, she could not deny it, for it gave a degree of composure she had rarely experienced. However, would it also deprive her of ambition?

To Jane Armstrong, a State Department employee in Havana, Gellhorn complained about her new domestic role and suggested she was succumbing to the fate of women who kept house and did not write. Jane, who had typed the manuscript of *Green Hills of Africa,* and her husband, Richard, a journalist with the International News Service in Cuba, were old friends of Hemingway's, to whom Gellhorn warmed very quickly. Gellhorn became very fond of Jane's daughter, Phyllis, and engaged her to type her manuscripts, finding in Phyllis a likeness to her teenage self, throbbing with the desire to rebel, impatient to get on with her life and yet too young to know how to go about it. When Phyllis set off for a trip to New York that would include a visit to a morgue, Gellhorn suggested that Phyllis would have to get beyond the disagreeable aspects of the corpses to appreciate the vivid characters who hung around them.

Home from his fishing trip, Hemingway saw how attractive Gellhorn had made the Finca and immediately moved in, still taking care to collect his mail at the hotel. His new home proved a hospitable place to write his ever-expanding novel. His wealthy Cuban friends were impressed with Martha's concern and admiration for him, but they wondered why he had to end his marriage to Pauline. What was wrong with having a wife and a mistress? He was working so well, and Gellhorn was putting no pressure on him at all. He was making most of the decisions. When there were disagreements, he got no more than "sweet" chiding from her. His concern over Pauline's health, and his growing idealization of Hadley, his first wife, did not trouble Martha at all. As Bernice Kert has put it, "jealousy of other women was not one of her problems."

Part of Gellhorn's good mood can be attributed to the fact that she was writing fiction again. Nature in all its abundance had a soothing and stimulating effect on her. From April to August, she wrote many of the stories in *The Heart of Another* and completed *A Stricken Field.* She slowed up in mid-June, complaining about fatigue and about the grind of turning out chapters, and took time off to explore the junk shops of Havana with Jane Armstrong. Hemingway's letters during this period express his certainty about the imminence of another world war, and Gellhorn (writing to Eleanor Roosevelt) now felt such revulsion about the appeasement of Hitler that she no longer cared what happened to England or France.

This Cuban interlude was also brightened by a two-week visit from Edna Gellhorn, who arrived at 10:30 A.M. on Friday, July 21, just in time for Hemingway's birthday party. That weekend, Ernest drove Edna around the island, and she joined the happy couple for drinks and dinner in Havana. On Sunday, Martha read her mother part of *A Stricken Field* and took her to see a pelota game. Tuesday they had dinner at home and talked for hours about Spain. Edna was reading some of Ernest's fiction. On Thursday, he read part of *For Whom the Bell Tolls* to her. Then there was another wonderful weekend of swimming and reading, shopping in Havana, and dinner at home. Edna was enchanted by the splendid sunsets and moonlight. On Monday, July 31, she noted in her calendar that Martha had finished the last chapter of her novel. There had been times when Martha had felt glum and frantic about the book and the rewriting had been excruciating, but in the end she felt joy and pride and an enormous sense of relief that she had produced a solid piece of work. She had decided to go abroad again and wondered whether the English would finally have the nerve to stand up to Hitler over Poland.

On May 17, Gellhorn had written Eleanor Roosevelt that she was opposed to war. Now with the German-Russian nonaggression pact (August 1939), the complexion of events had changed. She was disturbed by the American Communist party's allegiance to the Soviet line. To her, it seemed idiotic and disloyal. The pact with Hitler was inimical to American interests. While she was no witch-hunter, and while she worried about the damage to civil liberties perpetrated by the House Committee on Un-American Activities, she agreed with Roosevelt that American Communists did not have the right to abuse freedom by serving a foreign power.

Near the end of August, Gellhorn was in New York with her completed novel. *Collier's* wanted to send her to the Soviet Union, and she began preparations to sail on September 13. She also managed to meet with

Eleanor Roosevelt and to obtain a letter from the President that might be of some help in her journey through dangerous waters and belligerent countries:

To All American Foreign Service Officers:

The bearer of this note, Miss Martha Gellhorn, is an old friend of Mrs. Roosevelt's and mine. For a period of five months or so Miss Gellhorn will visit Russia and various other countries. Her purpose is to secure material for publication by one of our weekly magazines.

I will appreciate it if you will kindly give her every assistance.

Very sincerely yours
[signed] Franklin Roosevelt

Gellhorn was pleased—as she made clear in a telegram to Eleanor Roosevelt and in a note to the President.

On September 13, during a brief stay with her mother in St. Louis, Gellhorn came down with the flu and took the advice of her doctor and of Edna to postpone the Russian trip. Ernest had driven Martha to St. Louis and dropped her off on August 27, continuing on to visit Hadley and her husband and then joining his sons at the Nordquist ranch in Wyoming. Soon Pauline arrived, having just returned from Europe. She had been writing her husband letters, mostly avoiding the subject of their estrangement. She was ill with a very bad cold, and he attended her in such a reserved, inscrutable manner that she gave up all hope of a reconciliation. Her son Patrick witnessed the final blow. He saw his mother struggle out of bed to unpack a suitcase. One of her prized Parisian suits was ruined: The wax buttons had "melted all through the fabric." Patrick was a sensitive boy, his mother's favorite. He was eager to please both of his parents, but he was at a loss as to how to console her. "She sobbed uncontrollably," Patrick later wrote Bernice Kert, and his father then decided to have a friend escort Pauline and his sons home while he phoned Martha, asking her to meet him in Billings, Montana.

From Billings, they drove in Hemingway's black Buick convertible— crammed with "sleeping bags, fishing rods, gun cases, and boxes of books"—to the Sun Valley Lodge in Idaho. The "total darkness" of the roads unnerved them, but they were unwilling to turn back. Hemingway was looking forward to his arrival at this new resort, whose owner,

Averell Harriman, appreciated the "publicity value" of the presence of a famous author, who would be photographed during his stay enjoying the mountain air and the hunting and fishing.

It was a little embarrassing at first. Lloyd Arnold, the hotel photographer, had been told Hemingway's marriage was failing. Therefore it was hard to know how to approach this new woman. Hemingway was not much help. He seemed shy, hesitant, uncomfortable, and barely audible when he introduced Gellhorn to the photographer in the dining room. She made it easy for them, however, smiling at Arnold and inviting him to join her and Hemingway. Martha and Ernest were an informal couple. He sometimes referred to her as "the Marty," and they were known to Arnold and other friends as Ernie and Marty. There seemed to be little embarrassment about the fact that Ernest was still married to Pauline. When he first met Arnold's wife, Tillie, he had Martha explain that Tillie had startled him because she resembled Pauline.

For the next six weeks, Gellhorn followed the Hemingway regimen: writing in the morning, riding, tennis, and shooting in the afternoon. Hemingway was "ecstatic." She was a quick study and plunged right into a swamp in hip-waders, even though Arnold and Hemingway had to pull her out of one mud patch. This sporting life meant little to her, but she was content to please Ernest. She learned how to shoot a shotgun. As Lloyd Arnold put it, she "responded to [Hemingway's] wishes with a firm will." To please Martha, Ernest accompanied her on horseback rides in the mountains. Although he was an experienced rider, horses did not appeal to him. He was the kind of person who made them nervous and sweaty. The couple carried wine and sandwiches in saddlebags. Everyone was impressed with her shrewdness and humor. One of the lodge's guests, Clara Spiegel, whose husband knew Hemingway from their ambulance-driving days in Italy in 1918, remembers that Martha was a "barrel of fun and sharp as a tack."

In mid-October, Gellhorn got a call from *Collier's*. Would she go to Finland? It looked as though the Russians might invade. She discussed it with Hemingway. She wrote her mother that he was selfless in these matters, wanting only what was best for her. Perhaps he could join her. If not, they would reunite in Cuba after New Year's. She needed the money, Martha confided to Edna. She was hoping to marry Ernest by the spring, and she hated to leave him. Sun Valley seemed like "paradise," but she contented herself with the idea that once married she could say to *Collier's* that she and Ernest worked together.

Both Gellhorn and Hemingway were reacting to the war that had started in Europe in September. She had always assumed they would get there to cover it. However, his letters make clear he was not at all sure what role he would play. His novel had become his all-consuming passion. When the dates were fixed for the Finnish trip, Hemingway suddenly balked, complaining "What old Indian likes to lose his squaw with a hard winter coming on?" Tillie Arnold thought it was "Martha's ambition and restlessness" that drove her to leave Hemingway. Did she really have to go, especially when "things were going well"? Gellhorn did not like making excuses or pleading lack of funds, but no one seemed to realize she had to pay her own way. She also had to admit her lust for adventure had gotten the best of her. "Tillie, I suppose you're right— but it's in my blood and I *have* to do it." To Charles Colebaugh at *Collier's,* she wrote to say she could hardly contain her excitement about the new assignment.

After reveling in his feelings of abandonment for a while, Hemingway dropped the pose and praised Gellhorn's courage to his friends. As she was about to leave, however, he could not resist saying that if he could "just get her out every day of this short week of pheasant season that's left, it might cure that itching in her feet." Martha's parting shot was to ask Tillie to keep her eye on "this big clown . . . see that he's shaved and cleaned up when you go out on the town, and to the little parties—I'm depending on *you.*" He promised to obey Tillie and to be "a good boy."

Having signed a nonaggression pact with Stalin, Hitler had been free to attack Poland on September 1. Two weeks later, the Soviet Union took Poland from the east, absorbed Estonia, Latvia, and Lithuania. Finland alone was holding out against Russian pressure. It was a democracy, and Gellhorn was eager to get there, even though it meant a hazardous journey through mined waters. It was not easy finding a ship that would carry her, but she finally booked passage on a small Dutch ship, the *Westenland,* and sailed on November 10 from Hoboken, New Jersey, with a cargo of American wheat destined for Belgium. In "Slow Boat to War," she describes food that tasted like "boiled cardboard," dead bodies buoyed up by life belts, and basketball-shaped mines bobbing on the rough sea off the coast of England. Finally, out of a fog, she sighted Belgium, as her boat, awash in the moonlight, slowly entered the Scheldt River.

Edna was naturally nervous about Martha's trip. On December 2, she sent Eleanor Roosevelt a telegram. Was there some way to find out where her daughter was? As of November 26, she had been in Antwerp. The very next day, Martha cabled her mother letting her know she had arrived safely in Helsinki on November 29, the day before the first Russian bombing raid on the city. Soon Edna was writing Eleanor Roosevelt about Martha's stirring letters from Finland. To Ernest, Martha wrote that it was reminiscent of Spain. The Finns would not follow the Czech example. They would fight. Hemingway's letters bucked her up. She thought of herself as a survivor but not the heroine he made her out to be. Their life and their work were as one, she wrote him in a "long emotional letter."

It was uncanny the way the war had started at exactly 9:00 A.M. in Helsinki. Women huddled in doorways saying nothing, showing no sign of the hysteria or anguish they had a right to express. People sought refuge in the forest, some bringing along a few belongings, others nothing at all. About it all there was the curious, stoical calm of a people determined not to be bullied by Russian might, even though they were 3 million against 180 million. Everything seemed frozen solid and the cold was horrid, but the Finns knew how to maneuver in this environment and the Russians soon found themselves trapped and unable to hit their enemy with any accuracy. Gellhorn was enormously impressed and wanted to push on to the front—even after being warned that she was in a danger zone. She had been through this kind of argument before with military men who could not believe she was ready to face any eventuality. The Finnish army was well equipped, the troops ate well, and the field headquarters she visited was notable for its tranquility and even temper. The Russian prisoners were pathetic with their tales about how Finland had attacked their country. These were inexperienced soldiers, and the Finns were shocked at how poorly prepared they were for war. They were such a contrast to Finnish troops, who were literate and well informed. The Finns knew the odds were against them, yet they would not give up their country without a fight. Finland was not about to offer itself as a gift, one of the Finnish soldiers told her.

Gellhorn had her lodgings in the Hotel Kamp, which served as headquarters for the press and as a bomb shelter. Just about everyone seemed to use the hotel: the military, diplomats, reporters, and photographers. Poorly heated because of fuel rationing, its liquor reserve slowly dwindling, the hotel still managed a booming business during the air raids.

Similarly, the city's main department store was making big sales of winter wear, such as the ugly but sensible wool stockings Gellhorn bought.

One night in December, the Russians presented the Finns with an ultimatum: Unless the Finns agreed to Russian demands, Helsinki would be bombed off the map. Frank Hayne, an assistant American military attaché to Moscow now reassigned to Helsinki for the war, noticed a lovely blonde sitting quietly at a corner table in the Kamp restaurant. He thought she might be an American. It was Gellhorn, he found out after introducing himself. Would she like to be evacuated? "Christ, yes," she answered. He was a little surprised at her directness but urged her to get her things. She was back in five minutes carrying only her pajamas and a whiskey bottle. Obviously she had been through other evacuations.

Gellhorn spent Christmas in Stockholm writing her reports on Finland and observing the Swedes agonize over how much help they should provide their neighbors. The Swedes clearly sympathized with Finland, for they realized their own precarious position: They were vulnerable to both German and Russian invasion. The question was which great power would move against them first. In "Fear Comes to Sweden," Gellhorn advised her *Collier's* readers that the Swedes believed they would eventually have to go to war, and she reported on the country's campaign for military preparedness.

Gellhorn was planning to be home shortly after New Year's, but she delayed her return long enough to travel to Paris, where she hoped to secure the release of Gustav Regler, whom she had befriended during the Spanish Civil War. In "Good Will to Men," an autobiographical story, she wrote in detail about this disheartening period, which summed up for her the demoralized state of European civilization. The story begins with Elizabeth (a correspondent much like Gellhorn) at the Dutch-Belgian frontier. It is 4:00 A.M., and she is in transit to Paris. Elizabeth and her fellow train passengers have to lug their baggage across the tracks to customs. None of the inspectors lends a hand—not even to open the heavy door for elderly people and families straining under the burden of their bundles. As the inspectors examine the baggage with filthy hands, Elizabeth realizes these are people who did not care about the destiny of others and who cannot be bothered to show the most common courtesy. The prospects for interesting the French in the fate of a German refugee are not promising.

It is a fatiguing trip. Elizabeth arrives in Paris feeling ground up and filthy. She has been done in by the foul air of the train and by an angry and despondent dullness. Paris is enchanting, however: the Champs Ely-sées looking so expansive and calm and attractive, the Arc de Triomphe appearing like a magnificent "dark ruin." Everything is quiet and snow-padded, utterly different from the ominous silence of Helsinki or Madrid. Perhaps her influential friends in government will help free Max (Regler's name in the story). They want to know about Elizabeth's assignment in Finland and about her life in America as she searches for a way to tell them about Max. They reminisce about their days in the Midi when they were young. Her French friends are preoccupied with their war, though, and have no interest in German Communists such as Max— even if he is a fine writer and an anti-Nazi. The French are interested in the French, not "foreigners." Not very "human" of them as far as Elizabeth is concerned. She is advised to return to America, where she can indulge in her humanitarianism. In retrospect, Elizabeth realizes she has not been very tactful in pleading Max's case, but she feels he is a "hostage" for herself, and it is shameful not to work for his release; just as in one of Gellhorn's letters to Eleanor Roosevelt, she feels a special responsibility for not having done more for Spain.

After Finland, Gellhorn felt peculiar. For the first time in weeks, she was not rushing to catch a boat or plane or train, or on her way to obtain a visa or military safe-conduct pass. This time there was no disaster to which to hurry, no reason to observe people with a reporter's note-taking sensibility, making inquiries and writing it all up for *Collier's*. She enjoyed the kind of life that puts Elizabeth into a "violent expensive hurry," but now Gellhorn had only Regler to think about. There was a chance he would perish of the cold in a crowded camp with no facilities for medical care or hygiene. Regler was still recovering from a near-fatal wound in his back. It seemed ironic to Gellhorn that he was always praising the beauties of Paris, the food and the culture of the French, when they had put him into a camp because he was a refugee, an exile from Germany, in possession of worthless papers issued to him by the Spanish Republic.

Regler was an idealist, having gone to fight for the Republic even after witnessing Stalin's terror in Russia. Gellhorn knew Regler was a romantic with a foolish tendency to wax eloquent about the working-class soldiers in Spain. Like Elizabeth, she saw these "heroes of the people" for what they were: taxi drivers and shoe salesman suddenly thrust into the roles of military officers trying to fight a war with inadequate preparation. Regler was an individual worth saving, however, and Gellhorn now only believed in individuals. In "Good Will to Men," Elizabeth is dismayed to learn that Tom, one of her most fervently dedicated colleagues, no longer cares what happens to men like Max. Tom is played out after twenty years of trying to awake people to the dangers of another European war. Elizabeth's last illusions are lost when she appeals to Karl, one of Max's fellow Communists in Spain. Karl supports the Hitler-Stalin pact. Karl does not say so, but it is clear that he has no interest in freeing Max, who has lately spoken critically of the Communist party. To Karl, Max is more useful as a martyr in a camp, and people like Max and Elizabeth are unreliable. Rather than following the Party's dictates, they have their own moral code. Suddenly, Elizabeth realizes that Karl never was her friend. He was only playing a role in Spain and using her so long as she was compliant with Party policy.

With Eleanor Roosevelt's help, Regler was eventually released from the camp, but Gellhorn's attitude toward the Second World War was fundamentally altered. Like Elizabeth, she no longer could see any principles at stake. It was not only a war of survival, she later wrote in *The Face of War*.

After the debacle of France, Gellhorn could not wait to get home. However, there were visa complications, problems with airflights, and bad weather. On January 2, she cabled Hemingway that she was terribly upset and sorry to disappoint him. To Eleanor Roosevelt, she wrote in support of the Finnish fight for independence. The Finns were brave and well disciplined; the Russians, sloppy and deceitful, making the ridiculous claim that Finland was somehow part of a conspiracy against the Soviet Union. Eleanor Roosevelt agreed with Gellhorn that the United States should aid Finland but stay out of the war. She read Gellhorn's letters to friends in the White House and drew attention to Martha's articles in *Collier's,* calling them, in her newspaper column, "among the finest on the war."

After a brief visit with Charles Colebaugh at *Collier's,* Gellhorn took a train from New York City en route to Cuba, writing her editor about how very, very fortunate she felt to be covering important events for *Collier's.* She hoped her writing would always get a warm reception at the magazine and that Colebaugh would excuse her long-winded and boring stories about her military adventures.

Gellhorn managed to get to Cuba to spend part of January with Hemingway. He was nursing feelings of abandonment. Although he made fun of his feelings, there was an implicit warning in the comic statement he had Martha sign. "Mrs. Martha, or Mrs. Fathouse Pig," was made to pledge that she would never abuse her prospective husband because he was a "fine and sensitive writer" who should not be deserted. She had to admit that she had provoked his anxiety during their more than two-month separation. She also had to apologize for the desolation he had experienced. She would have to do better. Finally, this agreement was to be signed with her "own free will and in [her] rightest mind and with love." The prose was childish and could be laughed off, except that Hemingway meant it. If one of her nicknames for him was "The Pig," then becoming Mrs. Pig would require a degree of fidelity she had not yet shown him.

It always took time to recuperate from travel. Gellhorn spent it figuring out her expense account for *Collier's*—always a trial for her. She had her problems with the arithmetic, and her servants had a good laugh over her struggle to present a precise record. She was feeling very much at home—although "Marta" did not appreciate everyone telling her how big and fat she looked. The comments were meant warmly, as a sign of affection and acknowledgment of her good health. No one seemed much affected by war elsewhere, and a cold day—a really big drop in temperature to sixty-eight degrees—was viewed with alarm as a record-breaking historic event. Somehow she thought she would be able to stand it all right. In fact, she was in one of her most romantic periods, extolling the beauty of her blooming mauve orchids.

January and February in Cuba were a welcome respite, especially after the Finnish winter. Writing to one of her friends, Gellhorn remarked on the beauties of the land and wondered what she had done to be so fortunate. The one discordant note was Hemingway's drinking. Writing to his editor, Maxwell Perkins, in early February, he confessed that he was taking Gellhorn to the movies to make up for his drunkenness the previous Saturday night. He had begun with absinthe, consumed an entire bottle of red dinner wine, and then switched to vodka when they went into town for a jai alai game. On top of that, he had downed several whiskey and sodas until three in the morning. Yet his ability to recover from this much liquor was impressive. He was in fine shape the next day, he wrote Perkins. To Hemingway this herculean drinking represented some necessary "counterforce" to the writing that seemed to sap all his energy.

Hemingway also had a theory he could burn the alcohol out of his system during fierce tennis matches with his pelota-player friends. Leicester Hemingway remembered visiting his brother at this time and playing tennis until they streamed with sweat. After a shower, they would gather by the pool, where Martha would join them for drinks and a swim. To Ernest's delight, she would dive in the pool and surface, laughing and reaching for a drink. "That's my mermaid. What a woman that one is," a grinning Ernest told his brother. Leicester found her "enchanting." She was full of stories about Finland, the bitter cold, and showed him the souvenirs (hunting knives) that had been presented to her. To Leicester, "Martha had real brains, beauty, and the body of a Circe."

Although Charles Colebaugh tried to entice her with more assignments for *Collier's,* she was loathe to leave Cuba—in part because of an over-whelming disgust at European appeasement. The Finns had fought bravely but lacked the aid needed from France and England. She was so furious, she suggested that leaders such as Chamberlain and Daladier should be shot. She had personal, domestic reasons for staying put. She was tired and wanted to get on with book writing.

A Stricken Field was published in March to mixed reviews. *Time* re-hearsed her interesting life—including a rather fanciful version of her job interview with Harry Hopkins, to which she took exception in a letter to Eleanor Roosevelt. The *Time* reviewer lamented that the novel's heroine, Mary Douglas, did not measure up to Martha herself. Gellhorn was irked by the comparisons and complained to Colebaugh that her work was not being evaluated as fiction. He was inclined to take the sensible view that readers would naturally see a correspondence between Mary and Martha, especially since the book jacket made much of Gell-horn's daring war dispatches and because Mary had more than a passing physical resemblance to Martha.

To Jane Armstrong, Gellhorn expressed relief after finding a few reviews that actually took her novel seriously. She hated it when her work was casually dismissed, but now she lightened her mood by suggest-ing Armstrong accompany her to town for a meal and a movie. They could act as though they were on holiday.

Despite certain irritating reviews, Gellhorn was gratified that most critics acknowledged her novel's power. She considered other kinds of writing, and wrote Colebaugh that she was afraid of being typed a war correspondent; she wanted to write on happier subjects, display her affection for America and for the things that were right about it. Colebaugh was receptive but pleaded limitations of space, the possibility of impending war, and suggested they talk about assignments when she came to New York.

On March 20, Gellhorn and Hemingway were joined in Cuba by two of his sons, Patrick and Gregory. Eight-year-old Gregory, who had had a difficult childhood, responded affectionately to Gellhorn's warmth. She was as much a playmate as a surrogate mother. In his memoir, he evoked an Edenic setting that clearly cast its spell on him:

> Mango trees lined the driveway leading up to the house, and tall royal palms grew beside the path leading down to the swimming pool in back. Flowers and bougainvillea vines bloomed all over. Hummingbirds made their tiny neat square nests in the tropical foliage, and I could watch for hours a mother sitting on her eggs, one of the most regally beautiful sights I've ever seen.

Then in April, Hemingway's oldest son, sixteen-year-old Jack, completed this new family arrangement. He had first met Martha at the premiere showing of *The Spanish Earth*. He recalled that "a gorgeous blond lady" had dashed up to him and said, "You must be Bumby; I'm Marty." He had heard of her but never dreamed how important a part of his life she would become. She was a "marvelous creature" who could say *fuck* "so naturally that it didn't sound dirty." Depending on the occasion, she could "talk like a trooper or a high-born lady." The more he got to see of her, the more natural it seemed for his father to be with her. He could sense that Ernest was about to drop Pauline.

Jack shared Gregory's admiration of the home Gellhorn had created, but he noted that to get there meant driving through the "worst slums" he had ever seen, "and the stench when we passed the tannery was not to be believed." Like Gregory, Jack held a vision of Finca that was vividly imprinted on his memory, especially the pool with its "two Grecian bath houses and the trellis-covered terrace at the western end where the step led into the water." Beside it, the tennis court, made of "crushed coral limestone, pale pink," glared in the blazing sun. Beyond the wire fence was a "stand of bamboo." A guest house, vine arbors that provided shade, gardens of papayas and assorted vegetables, the ceiba tree, and orchid plants completed the picture of this paradise. The house's large, airy rooms and high ceilings made the perfect setting for Hemingway's fine oil paintings, bullfight posters, and African trophies.

Jack liked to sleep in; so did Martha. Ernest, on the other hand, was up early even if he did not plan to work. He wrote at a big desk next to a large double bed and bookcases. Martha wrote in a "beautiful large bedroom off the east end of the living room." This is where she had her desk, and where she and Hemingway slept in a "giant double bed." Ernest had the better view. All she could see was a courtyard, where she could hear the constant cooing of white pouter pigeons.

Jack remembered that Martha was a good sport about the typical Hemingway entertainments—such as singing "old favorites" or picking up on the "current Cuban popular songs." Sooner or later, however, the boys would hear about Finland and the terrible state of the world. Patrick was the quiet one, who observed that Jack and Martha were a lot alike: "handsome young people, blonde and radiant and pleasing everyone with their charm and high spirits." Locating his feelings somewhere between Gregory's and Jack's, Patrick regarded Martha "more as a friend than as a stepmother."

After Jack left, Martha wrote his mother, telling Hadley that they had many talks about all sorts of things. She empathized with his anxiety over his college boards, remembering how awful she had found them. They were chums. She had even listened agreeably to all his talk about fishing—although she had to admit she had no experience at it and did not know the first thing about the equipment he described. She complimented Hadley on raising such a handsome son. She now felt like one of the Hemingways.

Hitler's invasion of Denmark and Norway in April and of the Low Countries in May aggravated Gellhorn. She put up wall maps and purchased a radio, not wanting to miss a single day's news, and became fascinated with the fact that they could hear about the next crisis every fifteen minutes. She wrote friends, trying to convince herself there was no reason for her to take the world's troubles on her shoulders, but she had an "itch" to know more. When the rains came, her perfect house spouted leaks and the living room ceiling collapsed, showering everything with plaster dust.

Gellhorn sent a note to Phyllis Armstrong, her typist, wishing her well on her trip to New York but warning her the city was full of loonies.

Even the President now seemed rather crazed and the newspapers were raving. It did not help Gellhorn's spirits much to have to put up with the incessant rain. It reminded her too much of a Somerset Maugham play.

As paradise disintegrated, Gellhorn gave way to raging attacks decrying the state of the world. She began to get on Hemingway's nerves. Still absorbed in his writing, he made it clear to her he did not give a damn about current affairs. She left for New York, getting there on June 22, the day France surrendered. It felt good to be a little nearer the action and then to spend a few days with her mother, where she could feel spoiled and indulged—even if the telephone was constantly ringing, and it sometimes felt as though Edna were running the whole state of Missouri from her house. Martha finished a twenty-thousand-word story, caught up on news with Eleanor Roosevelt, and questioned the First Lady about motherhood. Martha thought she must have seemed rather eccentric to the Hemingway children, but somehow she had won their confidence, and she was looking forward to seeing them again.

By the end of June, Gellhorn was back home, writing to Charles Colebaugh about a caterpillar invasion. She had observed a black and yellow one nearly half a foot long that was devouring the leaves on plants and flowers. As usual, she was very suspicious of the British and almost inclined to believe the rumors of a separate peace with Germany, so that the British and the Germans could turn on the Russians. At any rate, she had trouble envisioning a Europe permanently in German hands. That country had a genius for making war, but it would not be able to govern Europe.

In July, Gellhorn was diverted by a visit from her mother. Edna and Ernest had now become good friends. Martha believed that he loved her mother. Edna had great charm, Leicester Hemingway observed. It was more than that, however. She saw very deeply into people's characters but never intruded into their lives. She had sized up Ernest Hemingway very carefully by the time she told her daughter that she felt sorry for him. Martha was stunned—and irritated. Feel sorry for this hardy man who had been so successful? Edna did not belabor the point, but her daughter "wondered later if perhaps her mother sensed an emotional instability in Ernest that had not yet surfaced."

Edna did not allow Ernest's unreliability to bother her. For instance, there was the time when he kept her and Martha waiting while he got engrossed in telling a friend about his new novel. It was four in the afternoon, and he was supposed to meet them at two. Martha stomped into the bar, obviously beside herself with anger. "You can stand me up," she shouted, "but you can't do that to my mother." His apology did little to assuage her fury. He got up, paid his bill, and dragged himself after her. Edna thought it was funny. She was not one to show her temper. Most people marveled at the way Martha refused to coddle Ernest, but he would value her spirit only so long as she remained on his island.

The rest of Edna's trip went smoothly. There was lots of fishing, the stirring sight of a rare whale shark, flying fish, and marlin spiriting about in the water. Martha reported to Eleanor Roosevelt that Edna had gotten a beautiful tan. The war seemed so far away, but she could not help thinking about the history of her century, of the last war, and of her father, who had been given such a hard time because he was German. They had had one confrontation with a local Nazi, and Martha was surprised to see how unnerved her usually unflappable mother had become. Somehow these thoughts made her feel even more protective of Edna. After some shopping in Havana, another birthday celebration for Ernest, a Basque fiesta, sunning and swimming at the Havana Beach Club, and going to the movies, Edna left on August 20.

Somehow during the summer, Martha found time to research and write a piece on Nazis in Cuba. She had suggested to Colebaugh the rich possibilities of investigating fifth column activity: Close to two thousand aliens from Germany and German-occupied lands were in the country—a small group compared to the eighty-thousand figure alleged by Congressman Dies, the Chairman of the House Committee on Un-American Activities, whose lying (Gellhorn believed) was big enough to impress the Nazis. She had had some run-ins with local Fascists, and while she did not believe they posed an immediate threat, she made a case for documenting their operations that Colebaugh seemed to accept.

When *Collier's* rejected Gellhorn's article, indicating that the Nazi subversion was not significant enough to warrant publication, she countered by noting that there were almost eight hundred Germans and thirty thousand Spaniards in a clandestine Fascist society that American and English diplomats were monitoring carefully. She had put an enormous amount of time into the article and had called on the help of nearly every VIP on the island. Her professional prestige was at stake. The newspaper *PM* had expressed interest in her fifth column research, but if *Collier's* accepted it, she would be willing to rewrite it according to their specifications.

Colebaugh was not convinced. He regretted their misunderstanding and enclosed a check for five hundred dollars—exactly half the amount she usually received for a *Collier's* article. She accepted the check, deciding not to publish her material elsewhere (she felt it belonged to *Collier's*). She would turn over any significant material on Fascist activity to the authorities and refrain from writing about Cuba. Instead, she would bide her time, notifying Colebaugh that she thought she would be ready for an assignment sometime in November.

In early September, Gellhorn and Hemingway arrived in Sun Valley, having traveled separately from St. Louis and Key West—which seemed the wise thing to do until his divorce was granted. There had already been incidents when "absolutely lamentable females" from St. Louis had spotted her in Hemingway's company, and she did not want to embarrass her family. She had just written Clara Spiegel, saying she had hoped to marry Hemingway in Cuba, but there had been delays that had put off the ceremony until the autumn. She actually preferred going on as they were. They had had four good years, and marriage made her feel like things were closing in on her. It did not help matters that her mother had advised her not to marry Hemingway.

Just before leaving Cuba on August 23, Hemingway had also written to Spiegel, expressing his realization that with Gellhorn in Sun Valley, he would have his hands full preventing her from setting off to cover "war, pestilence, carnage and adventure." He also knew, however, that she enjoyed their trips there, especially in the off-season when fewer people spoiled the scenery. The spectacular landscape usually engendered her warmest feelings about the United States.

In Sun Valley, Gellhorn began to assemble and revise her stories for *The Heart of Another* and Hemingway corrected proofs of *For Whom the Bell Tolls*. They were joined by his three sons and got along together well—hunting, fishing, and riding. Gregory remembers having to "be careful when Marty was around." She believed it was her obligation to "enforce discipline" while he was away from his mother. She did nothing overt or heavy-handed to spoil Gregory's fun, but he knew she did not always approve of what he ordered for dinner. In her presence, he always asked for "something simple." In retrospect, he suggests she "had more primness than natural spontaneity." His overwhelming impression, however, was of a "beautiful girl. . . . Her hair was honey blond then, cut shoulder length, and she had a way of tossing it when she talked, not unlike a filly in a pasture tossing her mane." Her eyes were "warm and mischievous . . . and sparkled when she smiled." She laughed with such an absolute abandon that it could seem "sinful." He compared her skin to Ingrid Bergman's. It was "fresh and clear, with a glow of perpetual health and purity." He could talk to her about anything or feel just as comfortable saying nothing in her company. He adored the way she talked to him "like an equal," taking his opinions into account.

Both Gellhorn and Hemingway enjoyed meeting Gary Cooper and his wife, who were also Harriman's guests at Sun Valley. Hemingway wrote Max Perkins in praise of Cooper's honesty and friendliness. Gellhorn was so taken with Cooper that (according to Hemingway) she wanted Ernest to dress better and emulate Cooper's clean appearance. Short of contracting some wasting disease such as tuberculosis, Hemingway did not see how he would ever make Cooper's light weight. Even if he did, he would be stuck with the "same goddam face." Ernest did not like having his rough edges smoothed. Martha had stopped calling him "The Pig," but he did not mind tweaking her on the subject of her fastidiousness. When he started letting his hair grow, vowing not to get a haircut until his novel was completed, he was also trying to hide the beginning of baldness and to tease Martha, who liked him "well barbered."

Dorothy Parker's impressions of Gellhorn and Hemingway that October were entirely positive. She and her husband, Alan Campbell, had visited Sun Valley in mid-October, and she had written afterward to Alexander Woollcott expressing her pleasure that Gellhorn was one of his friends. It was a difficult period for Martha, Parker thought, with Pauline holding up the divorce and demanding more money from Ernest. Martha had behaved impeccably with the kids, and they had given her their confidence. Dorothy had watched Gregory and Patrick approach Martha, asking her for help in writing their mother. Martha had shown not the slightest sign of cruelty or vindictiveness. Even better was the magnificent care she was taking of Ernest. Dorothy had known him for fifteen years. She loved and revered him, but especially in his personal life and in his treatment of women he had to be called unreliable. Yet Martha would make an entertainment out of some everyday incident with Ernest that would have turned any other woman's hair white. Hemingway's response (as reported by Parker) would be solemn. His attitude was that Gellhorn knew damn well what she was getting herself into, even if it meant finding rats in her sleeping bag on one occasion.

My how gallantly Martha took this tough-guy stuff, Parker wrote Woollcott. It was on this basis that Parker believed the marriage would endure.

On about October 21, Hemingway wrote Charles Scribner about a pack trip, twenty-three miles of rough trail that was like a tonic for him. He returned to the lodge energized. Martha had taken to bed with the flu. She had the "miseries," Martha wrote Clara Spiegel, but she made no reference to her impending marriage on November 21. Instead, she was all afire to visit the Far East and was pestering Hemingway to go along. He did not expect to get much enjoyment out of going down the Burma Road, but he supposed he would get used to it—perhaps even like it—and then Martha would want to head for Keokuk, Iowa, just as he had gotten used to the Burma Road. Maybe he would grow to like Keokuk, Iowa, too, he wrote Scribner. It seemed they could never quite find the right equilibrium but were somehow hoping marriage itself would provide the solution. Martha liked the way the pack trip had calmed Ernest. He was drinking less now, and she took this as a sign of a stable future. Although she rejected his suggestion that she now write under the name of Martha Hemingway, she took no offense.

More disturbing was Edna Gellhorn's sudden visit to Sun Valley. She had come to persuade the couple not to marry. This was an extraordinary thing for Edna to do, but having already listened to her mother's reservations, Martha was not as deeply hurt as Ernest. He had profound respect for Edna and could see that while Martha would go through with the marriage, she was something less than an eager bride.

After a few weeks of denials to the press that a marriage was planned, Martha Gellhorn and Ernest Hemingway were married in Cheyenne, Wyoming, by a justice of the peace. News accounts referred to the marriage as Hemingway's third and Gellhorn's second. In St. Louis, Edna Gellhorn—who was always very open and thought nothing of reading one of Hemingway's letters to a friend—made it clear to Mary Hall that she had her reservations about the marriage: "We were all so excited about it, and Edna said, 'Well, we'll see, we'll see. Don't get too happy too soon.' She had so much wisdom. She knew all about the precariousness of everything."

The first stop for the newlyweds was New York, with Martha having to get used to a deluge of reporters. She compared her hectic life now to a "runaway elevator." She was looking forward to a meeting between Hemingway and H. G. Wells, but the encounter fizzled when Ernest showed no interest in witty conversation.

They celebrated Christmas in Cuba. Hemingway had bought the Finca, for money was no problem now. *For Whom the Bell Tolls* was an enormous success and movie rights were about to be sold. Ernest thought it was time to relax. Martha thought it was time to visit China—to fulfill a wish she had made when she was sixteen. For a short week, they would have a honeymoon at home, where a part of her wished to stay, reveling in nature—as Ernest confided to Archibald Macleish in a letter extolling her beauty, their happiness, and her last-minute desire to call off the China trip and break her contract with *Collier's*. Things had gone too far for that, Hemingway had decided, so the trip was on with no more crying and complaining about it.

Martha thought Ernest was being a good sport about the Orient and a darling at home, referring to her as Mrs. Hemingway every chance he got. Although he easily managed to get an assignment from Ralph Ingersoll, editor of *PM,* to cover the Orient, Gellhorn knew this was her show, that she was dragging him along against his will. They would also be separated for several weeks while she investigated Singapore and the Dutch Indies for *Collier's*. If he had proposed to leave her for a similar period, she would not have stood for it, she admitted to Eleanor Roosevelt. There were tricky things involved in pursuing her career while remaining a dutiful wife. Meanwhile, Hemingway boosted his ego by telling a reporter she had gone to Finland to help support his writing of *For Whom the Bell Tolls*. As Bernice Kert has put it, what bothered Martha was that "he interpreted everything in terms of himself."

Curiously, Pauline Hemingway's thoughts at this time serve as a kind of commentary on the conflicts between Ernest and Martha. She wrote his mother, Grace, about the divorce, expressing relief that it was now over. She compared the heart of another to a dark forest and thought it was a miracle that "people did anything right in this world, considering what they had to contend with." "The heart of another is a dark forest"—the very words Martha used for the epigraph to the short-story collection she handed to Maxwell Perkins shortly after the beginning of the new year.

CAREER AND

HUSBAND

1941 – 1942

15

Christmas in Cuba was lovely. Gellhorn had come to really enjoy the visits of Hemingway's children. She was also beginning to confront the conflict between having a career and a husband, she wrote Eleanor Roosevelt. She put a brave face on it all. Giving a talk to John Burroughs students during a visit to her mother in mid-January, she declared that "my husband and I are party enough to go anywhere." They had no need to join other war correspondents in their tour of China. She was amazed at herself, at how confidently she spoke about life, pointing out to students that they would have to work hard, that work was good for them, and that they should not regret growing up in a world at war. Much of history was marked by war, and as harsh as that made life seem, it was even worse to contemplate the loss of individual liberties. They ought to enjoy life as much as possible and realize how much depended on their own efforts. She was pleased with her speech and thankful for the education she had received at Burroughs. She felt something like a prophet, exhorting the students to "snap out of any defeatist attitude . . . dig into your books and prepare yourself to do a good job of making a better world." She made quite an impression on the students—this tough-talking, chain-smoking writer.

By late January, Gellhorn and Hemingway were in Los Angeles to talk with Gary Cooper and Ingrid Bergman about playing the lead roles in

For Whom the Bell Tolls. Setting off for China via Hawaii, both found February in Honolulu tiresome. There was entirely too much hospitality. He disliked the excessive politeness, all the alohas, and the flowers people kept wrapping around his neck. He was going to "cool" the next son of a bitch who touched him. Hemingway got truculent and liquored up at one literary to-do and waved Gellhorn off when she attempted to prevent his glass from being refilled. She could hardly blame him. It had not been his idea to leave the comfort of Cuba.

Gellhorn's ostensible assignment was to report on the Japanese army in action and on the Chinese defenses. In fact, she could not wait to visit the mysterious Orient, the land she had read about in Sax Rohmer and Somerset Maugham. Nothing—it turned out—was as she had imagined it. In her memoir *Travels with Myself and Another* (1978), she included her trip to China among her "horror journeys." Hemingway, on the other hand, came with no expectations and proved remarkably adaptable to an environment that struck Gellhorn as the most appalling thing she had ever experienced.

The first stop was Hong Kong, surrounded on three sides by the Japanese, home to half a million Chinese refugees, and full of color and excitement. Still in good spirits—indeed claiming she had never been more pleased in her life—Gellhorn came down with a bad throat and could not swallow. She shrugged it off, however, and busily cultivated sources, making arrangements to travel to the front. Hemingway collected an entourage wherever he went. It did not matter to him whether they were city cops or crooked Chinese businessmen and gangsters. Hemingway was a hunting man, a drinking man. Forget talk about politics or literature. Set him down with a vast liquor supply, and he would listen to the stories of the locals or entertain them with anecdotes. Gellhorn had little patience for these marathon bullshit sessions. "M. is going off to take the pulse of the nation," he would amiably inform his cronies as she crept away.

Gellhorn and Hemingway did their flying in China on the CNAC (China National Aviation Company). It was the only part of roughing it in China she really liked. The company flew freight and passengers in DC2s and 3s with steeply sloped floors, canvas chairs encased in metal frames, and toilets concealed by green curtains that provided a tiny rounded picture of the land below. There was no sophisticated instrumentation. The cabins were not pressurized. Pilots such as the redoubtable Roy Leonard always flew after dark in bad weather to elude the Japanese air force. The only amenities in these unheated planes were coarse blankets and paper bags for vomiting. Landing was never easy, since the Japanese bombed airfields. Runways had to be constantly moved and rebuilt. This was seat-of-the-pants flying, and Gellhorn loved it.

Hemingway delighted in Chinese novelties: snake wine, other local brews, delicacies, and firecrackers. He claimed the wine had healing properties and prevented baldness. He was bringing back bottles of it for his friends. He was "very disappointed" when Gellhorn demanded he stop lighting firecrackers in their room. He found a boxing partner, and there was always horse racing. So what if the Chinese cheated by applying dye to the horses? Gellhorn grew more dismayed every day at the sight of pathetic opium dens and slimy brothels. She was having her usual conscientious look at the legal system and other social institutions. People slept on the pavement. This was a hungry and feeble slave culture, with hawking and spitting on the street, a population afflicted with malaria, tuberculosis, leprosy, and cholera, roads deluged in mud, and the most primitive plumbing she had ever seen. People smelled like excrement. The overcrowding made her claustrophobic and hysterical. She had to leave at once!

Hemingway gave Gellhorn a level piece of advice. Do not suppose these people take the world as you do. He did not simply see the exploited masses. He saw people having children, setting off firecrackers, and in some measure enjoying life—even if it was not the life Martha could imagine having for herself. The point was not to behave by a set of standards to which China could not possibly measure up. In their hotel room in Shaokwan, she noticed they had only one bowl. What should be the washing procedure? Their teeth first, then their faces? The best thing to do was not wash at all, Hemingway advised her. She was crazy even to think of brushing her teeth. Through all of her grousing, he kept his aplomb, allowing himself only the occasional comment that the China adventure had been her idea. He took the trip so well that Gellhorn thought he was "heroic." He was as calm as she was frenzied. He could read, sleep, and eat without any trouble.

The usually self-possessed Gellhorn was such a mess that Hemingway could afford to quietly enjoy her predicament. One day, there was a crisis. She did not know where to relieve herself—no trees or bushes, just the mud and the "bare rice paddies." There was a latrine, some kind of bamboo monument, that could be gotten at only by climbing a flimsy ladder. From the top of the tower, excrement dropped into a "five foot tall Ali Baba jar." Looking it over, Gellhorn told Hemingway it was not for her. No one had supposed it was, he replied. Try the duck pond—a favorite of the locals—he suggested. That was worse. She began to edge up the shaky ladder when the air-raid alarm sounded. Hemingway called to her: What to do now? She was going to stay aloft, thank you very much. The planes quickly flew over and Gellhorn descended to a laughing Hemingway. What an ignominious death it would have been, he pointed out. How would he have explained her demise to a world that knew her as a dauntless journalist?

Watching a group of lepers in various stages of physical disintegration, Gellhorn suddenly remarked she had had enough. "So far," Hemingway replied, "we've still got our noses." Gellhorn found most government officials insufferable and showed little interest in the military officers. Her interpreter, Mr. Ma, spoke both Chinese and English very poorly. He had two American college degrees, loved to eat, knew nothing about military operations, and not much about anything else. Gellhorn wanted to know why a certain mountain had been burned. To free it of the tigers who ate the vegetation, Mr. Ma replied. Now they would have to look somewhere else for food, her perceptive guide pointed out. Gellhorn liked that goofy explanation: "vegetarian tigers." And the name of that tree, Mr. Ma? "Ordinary tree," the authoritative interpreter replied.

Gellhorn did her duty collecting information for *Collier's*. Her readers learned about the nine war zones, the Japanese drive to divide and conquer China, the Chinese army's lack of equipment and supplies (5 million superbly disciplined men who had no shoes), the gross underpayment of soldiers, and the hatred of the Japanese that made it virtually impossible to prevent Chinese soldiers from killing their prisoners. She and Hemingway traveled in the seventh war zone, a territory the size of Belgium, which was held by 150,000 Chinese troops.

Hemingway did the lion's share of public speaking, drinking Chinese officers under the table and in general behaving quite extraordinarily as a patriotic American sincerely concerned with giving comfort to his country's ally. He was genuinely taken with the Chinese and shared none of Gellhorn's squeamishness. She never did learn to tolerate the sound of their expectorations—they made her retch—the various burping and farting sounds they made while eating, the overflowing toilets and grimy hotel rooms covered with mashed bedbugs. As Gellhorn realized, Hemingway nailed her when he observed: "M. loves humanity but can't stand people." There was something abstract and entirely imagined about her view of the world, which was revolted when she came across life in the raw.

The Hemingways had a memorable meeting with the Generalissimo and Madame Chiang. For her *Collier's* readers, Gellhorn gave a lavishly attractive picture of the couple, including Madame's Chiang's bewitching smile, movie-star figure, luscious skin, and smooth features—even the way she applied her makeup (rouge, lipstick, and "a faint dark eye shadow") and the way her "ink-black hair" swelled "back from her forehead" and was "caught in a knot at the nape of her neck." As in all her *Collier's* reports, Gellhorn avoided expressing her political opinions. Instead, she concentrated on how hard Madame Chiang worked, getting up at six-thirty in the morning and not retiring until about midnight, and on her complete devotion to her husband's rule of China. After spending a quiet hour with him in the morning, she would answer correspondence, later receive important government officials, visit schools, hospitals, and other institutions, compare notes with her husband on an afternoon walk, and then after dinner receive guests (foreigners) and work at her desk until bedtime. Gellhorn was rather surprised when Madame Chiang suddenly asked her whether she found it difficult to be a wife. It was an "okay job," Gellhorn replied and quickly changed the subject, not wanting to compare her problems with Madame Chiang's. Gellhorn then quoted Madame Chiang's statement that she always dropped everything when her husband wanted to talk or to go for a walk. It was difficult being on call, but her "duty" was to him. In her devotion, she was "like all other women," Gellhorn commented, who found their lives interrupted by their husbands' demands, not wanting to disappoint them.

A reader of Gellhorn's *Collier's* article would never have suspected that she was intensely critical of the generalissimo and his wife. The Chiangs were not prepared to acknowledge that their government was authoritarian, and Gellhorn as their guest felt constricted by their hospitality and their position as American allies. She made Madame Chiang angry when she asked why the government did not help the lepers. A furious Gellhorn then had to sit through a lecture on Chinese civilization. Not knowing much about China when they arrived, Gellhorn and Hemingway realized only later just how much propaganda the Chiangs had spoken.

In a clandestine meeting with Chou En-lai, Gellhorn was impressed by his simple clothes and his apparent ease with Westerners. It was remarkable to her that they could share the same jokes, since Chinese humor had seemed entirely foreign to her. He was living underground, yet it appeared to her that he represented the country's future. She did not know enough to judge or to remember what he said. It was more his manner, his demeanor, that convinced her that the Communists would prevail.

Toward the end of the trip, Gellhorn contracted the "China rot," a skin disease that made her hands peel. It was not—Hemingway hoped— the first sign that her nose would fall off. The remedy was an application of foul-smelling ointment. Her hands were then covered with gloves to prevent the spread of the disease. Hemingway preferred to keep "up-wind" of her. Yet he had been such a good sport all along, she felt immensely grateful to him. They were in Rangoon and the heat was intense. Hemingway behaved like a "beached whale" and Gellhorn had trouble breathing. She put out her hand to touch him, to express her gratitude. "Take your filthy hands off me!" he shouted. They watched each other in "shocked silence." Was this how their "horror journey" was to end? They rolled on the cool marble floor, "laughing in [their] separate pools of sweat."

Gellhorn's *Collier's* pieces on China had one simple message: The Chinese would endure. It did not matter that the Japanese controlled much of the country. The Chinese could take any amount of suffering and hardship. After nine hours of riding horses, with nothing to eat or drink, Gellhorn was fatigued. Her Chinese companions, on the other hand, seemed as fresh as ever. She and Hemingway visited a thousand-acre airfield the Chinese had built in a hundred days without machinery. Later, in St. Louis, Hemingway showed a reporter a picture of 75,000 Chinese working on this airfield, "mixing concrete by wading in it and tromping the gravel in, like peasants crushing grapes with their bare feet to make wine." They would outlast foreign conquerors. "In the long run," Gellhorn told her Chinese interpreter, "I'd hate to be Japanese."

Hemingway returned to the United States via Hong Kong, writing to Max Perkins, on April 29, that he had enjoyed his time at the Chinese front, even though it had been a strenuous expedition. For the most part, he and Martha had pursued separate news stories, although she admitted borrowing (with Hemingway's sanction) some of the intelligence he had gathered on the Ch'eng-tu airfield. When he used the material for his own story, a *Collier's* editor accused him of competing with Gellhorn. A nettled Hemingway wrote the editor to say the magazine had made out handsomely with him along as messenger boy, fumigator, and travel agent.

Gellhorn, Hemingway told Perkins, wanted to give up reporting and come home. She had commitments to fulfill, however. She made brief stops in Java and Singapore, reporting on military installations for *Collier's*. In Java, she was impressed with Dutch competence and humanity. Java lay directly in the path of Japanese expansion and was a rich storehouse of oil, tin, rubber, sugar, quinine, and other essential war materials. The Dutch had mobilized their small army of white men, made elaborate plans to destroy much of the infrastructure should the Japanese invade, and had used the native population in a humane, efficient way that boded well for their survival. Indeed, there was much skepticism about an invasion, for the thinking was that the Japanese would follow the German example of conducting a "war of nerves," intimidating their neighbors without actually taking on the risks of a full-scale war.

In a very lively piece, Gellhorn could not get over the unreality of Singapore; it was its own movie, abounding in colorful types and sights. On the streets, she saw rickshas and Rolls-Royces, dance halls and country clubs, and English military men who were the kind of caricatures favored by Hollywood. Every luxury was available, but the vast majority of the Chinese population lived in dire poverty. The contrast was stupendous. She was especially delighted with the down-to-earth Australians. When an English press officer advised her to downplay the democratic spirit of the Aussies, she balked. Well, he guessed that "as a layman" she "would not understand." The English thought the Aussies were "poor stuff" indeed, calling each other by their first names and not saluting. Gellhorn pointed out that the press officer had been a "layman" and a reporter, and she did not see how his new position qualified him to speak as a "military man." He was, in her opinion, just a snob. She believed that sooner or later it would be the lower classes, the rank and file, the democratic Americans and Aussies who would be bailing out the high-living British merchants and officer class. To her delight, her article caused considerable anger in the British community. She was no follower of Marx, but she had once confided to Eleanor Roosevelt her belief that Marx had been absolutely right in his analysis of the class system. When Gellhorn later found an article defending her in a Singapore newspaper, she sent it on to Colebaugh, saying it had stimulated a respect for her work that she had not experienced in years.

Landing in San Francisco on May 28, 1941, Gellhorn cried with "relief and gratitude" at the sight of the Golden Gate Bridge and thought she could not have survived the trip without Hemingway's stalwart companionship for most of it. She was not happy with the way she looked and so took a few hours to shop before boarding a plane for Los Angeles. She also predicted in a San Francisco *Chronicle* interview that there would be no war between Japan and the United States, for the Japanese were in no position to continue their invasion of China and take on another enemy.

After a brief visit with her mother in St. Louis, she met Hemingway in New York and traveled with him for a debriefing session in Washington, D. C., before preparing for another Cuban summer. Colonel John W. Thomason at the Office of Naval Intelligence was impressed with her report on the inadequacy of British defenses in Singapore.

During that summer, the Hemingways specialized in improvised late suppers and Sunday pool parties. They invited guests from the American embassy, who could see how disorganized Ernest was—even if he was a genial host. Martha liked eating late and sleeping in, but keeping things straightened up was a full-time job. Ernest's vile-smelling tomcats roamed everywhere—including on the dining room table. The servants were inept. She had to show them how to cook, yet she knew nothing about preparing meals. Tensions that might have built up were relieved by visits from Ernest's sons and Edna Gellhorn. Edna especially enjoyed the "goggle fishing"—catching two tuna by herself—going to movies and dinners, and the pelota players. On Monday, August 11, Edna recorded in her diary that Martha had won a pigeon shoot.

Martha confided to Jane Armstrong that Hemingway had been contemplating an autobiography, but it made him feel affected. She had advised him to think of it as a journal and to get on with it. The timing was not right, however, and he abandoned the idea. Phyllis Armstrong's recent marriage provoked Gellhorn's rather resigned and not very enthusiastic comment to Jane on the institution: People often married at an early age with mixed results. One could learn a lot from marriage and, on the whole, it was probably more orderly to marry than simply live together.

Martha was doing her best not to think of the war. On August 23, she wrote to H. G. Wells concerning his written declaration of the "Rights of Man": "a definite and vigorous reassertion of individual rights" in the face of the vastly increasing centralized power of governments. She was neither a scientist nor an abstract thinker, she told Wells. All she really wanted to do was read and write fiction. His declaration struck her as far more hopeful than she could ever be. She did not like the style of the document. There was nothing memorable about it; the prose was not inspiring. It was entirely too vague, she disingenuously suggested, for plain homebodies such as her. It was also a puzzle to her as to how he and his group proposed to safeguard the rights about which they declaimed. Yet she could not help offering advice on how to rewrite it. In a subsequent letter, she apologized for her harshness and pointed out that Wells and his associates were trying to construct a model of conduct, while she was intent on declarations of war. But then what did he expect when he asked the opinion of a woman who wrote fiction?

The Heart of Another was published in the fall, at a time when Gellhorn and Hemingway were enjoying a healthy holiday in Sun Valley. She was improving her marksmanship and feeling very mellow about the reception of her stories. This was the first book of hers that seemed to have real depth, she thought, and she was very pleased with it. The book was far from perfect, but she felt there were four good stories in it that gave promise of better work to come. She had simply tried to write about people—not to purvey a message or a particular point of view. It did not matter much that reviewers exaggerated Ernest's influence upon her style. "Pure Hemingway—romantic under a surface of hardness" is the way one critic put it. Every writer in America had been influenced by Hemingway in some way, Gellhorn suggested to Eleanor Roosevelt, who replied that she thought one story reminded her of Hemingway, but that several others closely resembled Gellhorn's correspondence. "Luigi's House" was Roosevelt's favorite, for it deeply probed the human psyche.

There was a strong autobiographical element in the collection. The stories were set in Cuba, Finland, Germany, Spain, and France and read like a virtual map of Gellhorn's own itinerary. "Luigi's House" was particularly close to the bone, since it followed the fanatical desire of a fastidious woman to make her home a special, comfortable place for her husband, who is returning from the Spanish Civil War. In her efforts to spruce up the place, she has to dislodge Luigi, a peasant who has lived a rather decrepit existence taking care of the vines on the property. She cannot understand why he so fiercely resents her improvements, and he is incapable of telling her he fears her ultimate aim is to throw him off the land. Her confident manner is so unsettling that the man finally hangs himself. It is as if Gellhorn had been writing a cautionary tale for herself, pointing out the consequences of her mania for improving the world.

What seemed "better" for her was not necessarily what others desired. It was a hard lesson to learn, and one that Hemingway had tried to present in China.

"November Afternoon" grew out of days Gellhorn and Hemingway had spent in France in 1938, when he was still weighing his commitment to Pauline against his romantic interludes with Martha. The story's couple walk along a river canal. The woman comments on the pleasant, settled life people have on barges. The man asks a workman what he is fishing. The woman soaks in the lovely smell of the water and the leaves. The man concentrates on the fish. He walks quickly and away from his companion, alone with his thoughts. Sensing she is snubbed, she follows him without haste, reflecting on her "unreal problems," the problems the rich have with their relationships—not the genuine problems such as catching fish, worrying about cargo on a barge, or getting the washing done. She is fed up with the passions of her heart. His steady aloofness turns her frustration into anger over their predicament. Why did they have to make life so complicated? Yet why should she shoulder the blame when he was the one who would not settle down? The man feels torn in many directions, obligated to others, and concerned that he should not hurt or disappoint them. The couple eventually returns to the city after failing to find a country place for the weekend, and the woman fears she has driven him away from her. The characters in the story are not named and the male character's responsibilities are not identified, but the precarious state of the woman's feelings—her wish to know where she stands in her man's life—are evocative of the ambiguous position Gellhorn found herself in, one that not even marriage to Hemingway could clarify.

Several stories in *The Heart of Another* have a female narrator or center of consciousness cut off from others by her impregnable self-sufficiency. It is not that Gellhorn or her female alter egos cannot feel for others; rather, her accomplished women lack a certain susceptibility. They do not have the openness to experience that Hemingway recommended. Except in "Luigi's House," there is, in the words of one reviewer, no "driving force or emotional center" in the stories.

There was an air about Gellhorn, a way she had of arrogating the atmosphere to herself, that could be imperious and off-putting when it was not comical. During a Sun Valley–Grand Canyon vacation with Ernest in December, she stopped at a Navaho trading post in a dusty little town. Martha, "blond and chic, stood at the counter." In what Ernest remembered as her "best Bryn Mawr manner," she called out rather haughtily, "Have you any beads? I want to see some beads." Bent over a display case near her was an aged Indian. Out of his pocket, he extracted one bead no bigger than a pinhead. "Here bead," the ancient one said, gravely offering it to Martha. "Now you see bead."

Gellhorn and Hemingway were in a bar outside Tucson, Arizona, when they heard the news of Pearl Harbor. Hemingway was angry at the destruction of the American fleet. Gellhorn longed for a European assignment, even though she believed just as strongly that she and Hemingway should retire to Cuba and work on their fiction. In a letter to Charles Scribner, Hemingway reported her contentedness. He was still very much taken with her beauty and reassured by her eagerness to get back to Cuba. On December 12, he wrote Scribner from San Antonio about a wonderful tour of Indian country. He had never seen Martha look lovelier or more cheerful.

In January 1942, the Hemingways were madly figuring out their income taxes. Hemingway was having trouble with the records of his China trip, and Gellhorn wondered whether *Collier's* could send him her expense accounts, which were the same as his—except for the money he spent buying his buddies beer. She was having a tough time getting ready to cover the war, poring over technical manuals and other texts. It was like being in college again. However, she was making some progress, and she presented quite a picture, bent over contour maps and reading up on arms and tactics.

In February 1942, Gellhorn wrote Eleanor Roosevelt, declaring her need to report the war, but women were not being allowed in combat zones. Gellhorn could do nothing about her sex, but she would be willing to become a man if that were possible. For the time being, she preferred staying at home, especially since she believed the war would last a long time. She was shooting pigeons with some of the old sportsmen and was amused at how politely they treated her, always saying something courteous when she missed her target.

Except for brief visits to St. Louis, Florida, and Mexico City, the Cuban idyll continued. Gellhorn's days were filled with much happiness, and she was playing the devoted wife, but she was uneasy at the thought of so much human suffering abroad. The war news made her feel the prospects had never been bleaker. She hated to think what would happen if the Russian offensive was not a success. It bothered her that there did not seem to be enough people to oppose an increasingly cruel world, which was building up a reservoir of malice. Was there any way to harmlessly dilute the German race, which itself was bent on exterminating the Poles and the Jews? Hemingway's personal solution was to work even harder at his writing. He had a discipline and a talent far greater than hers, Gellhorn confided to Mrs. Roosevelt.

Gellhorn's letters to Roosevelt are full of expressions of love and concern for a First Lady who was selfless and indefatigable in her efforts to help others—as Gellhorn observed in a newsreel featuring Mrs. Roosevelt with a little girl who had paralysis. At the same time, Gellhorn was profoundly moved by her own mother, who was laboring harder than ever in the League of Women Voters to spread the idea of democracy all over the country. Such examples of dedication tempered the long passages in Gellhorn's letters that were filled with despair and anger over the failure of the democracies to oppose Fascism. She had little faith in government institutions and in the American foreign service, and she wrote Mrs. Roosevelt constantly about individual cases of Spanish refugees and others who were being persecuted for their political beliefs. Edna Gellhorn and Eleanor Roosevelt, in Martha's opinion, came from a generation more admirable than her own. They had an incredible capacity to make people feel accepted and worthwhile.

In late April, Gellhorn wrote Patrick Hemingway, describing a bird shoot his father had won the day before, the playful kittens at home, her busy gardening and writing while recovering from fish poisoning that had laid her low for ten days. Her pleasures, however, were tempered by the island's isolation from the theater of events. When her fellow correspondent Virginia Cowles had visited in February, Gellhorn was tremendously excited to hear her news, to relive their days in Spain, and to listen to Cowles's accounts of her various trips. Cowles had seemingly been everywhere, and Gellhorn obviously missed traveling with this courageous woman who had become so incisive and intrepid in her years of covering wars. Cowles was one of several friends from Gellhorn's Spanish days that kept her in good cheer and sustained her belief in human dignity.

Everything was entirely too lax in this "Latin, Catholic, tropical, leisurely, unstable, sinful and corrupt country" that her husband had taken to his heart. It was not enough for her to carouse with Loyalist refugees, and there was no intellectual life of which to speak. She sent Hemingway loving letters when she was away. They missed each other terribly. They still had good times together, sometimes roaring with laughter, but she noticed he indulged his anger more often. Anything might happen when he was in a rage. He might throw glasses, shoot out a window, hurt or embarrass his guests. Gellhorn feared for her family crystal and bought cheap glasses for him to hurl during his tantrums. If he seemed a genius, he also appeared to be half-mad.

Gellhorn was aghast at how little Hemingway cared about his appearance and hygiene. He seemed to think it was manly to be dirty. He took his revenge years later when he told A. E. Hotchner:

> She liked everything sanitary. Her father was a doctor so she made our house look as much like a hospital as possible. No animal heads, no matter how beautiful, because they were unsanitary. Her *Time* friends all came down to the "Finca," dressed in pressed flannels, to play impeccable, pity-pat tennis. My pelota pals also played, but they played rough. They would jump into the pool all sweated and without showering because they said only fairies took showers. . . . That began the friction between Miss Martha and me—my pelota friends dirtying up her *Time* pals!

It was getting to the point where she could no longer josh him out of his bad moods. On a June visit, Gregory was shocked to hear his father tell Martha: "I'll show you, you conceited bitch. They'll be reading my stuff long after the worms have finished with you." He was incensed when she refused to take his German submarine hunting seriously. He tried to convince her he was performing important intelligence work. After all, German subs had sunk ships off the East Coast of the United States, in the Gulf of Mexico, and off the coast of South America. All she could discern, however, was that he was having a fine time cruising the sea with his cronies. It was a big fantasy of his to think he was helping the war effort.

Gregory Hemingway remembered his father's sub-chasing activities and Martha's scorn for them. Ernest's plan was to turn his forty-foot boat, the *Pilar,* into a "sub-destroyer." Deploying two men equipped with submachine guns in the bow and two with BARS (Browning automatic rifles) and hand grenades, in the stern, Hemingway was somehow going to steer his boat next to a sub. Then "a pair of over-the-hill jai alai players with more guts than brains would heave The Bomb ['a huge explosive device, shaped like a coffin, with handles on each end'] into the open hatch

of the conning tower." And that would be the end of the sub. "What
if The Bomb misses, Ernest?" Martha wanted to know. The conning
tower of a sub was higher than the bridge of the *Pilar* and the hatch
measured only thirty inches across. The chances were that the bomb
would bounce around, blow up, and drive the conning tower into the
stranded *Pilar*. Then the sub would pull away and use its six-inch deck
gun to "blow the *Pilar* right out of the water." Not giving Ernest a
moment to reply, Martha said, "Kitten, you need a vacation." She suggested he write the article he had promised to do on the way the Chinese
watered the human feces they sold to truck farmers. "Don't you think
I know the realities of war?" Ernest countered. He reminded her of the
237 or 238 pieces of shrapnel that had been taken out of his leg in World
War I. "Love, this time, if that bomb misses, they won't find two hundred
thirty-eight pieces of *you,*" Martha retorted. Well, too late to stop the
project now, Ernest declared. The crew was all set to go and "terribly
excited" about their mission. He went on to praise his crew, singling out
one to praise his loyalty, if not his intelligence. "Yes," Martha said, "I
think his uncle went down on the *Titanic.*" This was a doomed enterprise,
and she was not going to let her husband have the last word on it.

They were now doing things to hurt each other, and some of their
friends were taking sides. As William Walton has put it, "I know Martha
Gellhorn well. It takes two to tango, you know. Martha was a wicked,
wild bitch. Oh, the joint cruelties." Based on a story in *The Heart of
Another,* on her frequent fights with Ernest, and on her flirtations with
other men, Leicester Hemingway accused Martha of infidelity. Gellhorn's
story "Portrait of a Lady" concerns Ann Maynard, a newspaper reporter
covering her first war who makes love to a Finnish aviator in his hotel
room. Compared to Maynard's rich, idle, empty life, the aviator's keen
concentration on war seems meaningful and intense. While the aviator
does not reject her advances, he finds her seduction of him contemptible.
Maynard's handsome husband is fifteen years her senior. Their marriage
is one of wealth and beauty, and each is at liberty to live unencumbered.
While this arrangement is agreeable, it leaves Ann Maynard rather at a
loss. What is the point of her life? This is not a question Gellhorn had
to confront, but it was a state of mind with which she could empathize.
She hated the feeling of being useless, of having no aspiration in life, and
she was attracted to selfless men dedicated to causes bigger than themselves.

The story hardly proves Gellhorn was unfaithful, but it reflects a worldliness about marriage and sex that would have shocked Leicester, who hero-worshiped his brother and never understood why Gellhorn stood up to him. Leicester was not alone, however, in witnessing her familiarity with other men. Ernest referred to one of her favorites, Felix Areitio, a Basque jai alai player, as "my rival." Much later he would write to Bernard Berenson claiming that she had betrayed him. Gellhorn repudiated these stories, but her carefree behavior provoked them. She liked to play tennis with Areitio, who was handsome enough to be a movie star. They were openly affectionate with each other. She thought nothing of jumping into his arms after tennis so he could "carry her up to the house." Was this an affair? The very obviousness of it suggested to one of Hemingway's friends, Mario Menocal, Jr., that Gellhorn was indiscreet but not unfaithful. Robert Joyce, an American diplomat who frequently visited the Finca, rejects the idea that she was promiscuous: "*Where* in Cuba could she have had a secret affair? They lived in a village twelve miles from Havana. And when either of them came into town they were immediately recognized as distinguished *Americans,* which they were in Cuba." If Hemingway had actually believed his wife was making love to Areitio, he would have "killed him," his son Jack asserts.

As Jeffrey Meyers has suggested, Gellhorn's *The Heart of Another* may be the most persuasive evidence of her fidelity to Hemingway—or at least of her unwillingness to abandon it for Areitio. Her opinion of Hemingway's pelota-playing pals was never very high. In "Night Before Easter," she even names the handsome pelota player Felix. The female narrator mentions their tennis games, the bond they share because of the war in Spain, the pleasure she has in talking with him, admiring his mouth, the way he smiles. When she dances with him, however, he senses her reserve. The movements are all there, but they are inhibited. No real intimacy, it is clear, can develop between them. He knows there are special rules for her, and he pays for the women with whom he has sex.

Cuba was a corrupting life for both Gellhorn and Hemingway. His vaunted discipline had been disintegrating in the past few months. He could not summon the energy or the concentration to write. She wrote but had little faith in the result. Her new novel had a Caribbean setting, and she was not certain she knew these people well enough, she confessed to Eleanor Roosevelt. Somehow she had to ground herself more completely in the lives of others. Then it came to her that she should do a series of stories on the West Coast, adopting the guise of a munitions worker. She was ready to set off in a cheap dress to find work whenever

Collier's gave her a destination. She was palling around with a manicurist and going to dances with soldiers. Hemingway scoffed at the idea that a Bryn Mawr girl could pass herself off as working class. And how would things work out if she had to wait weeks just to get into a war plant? On reflection, she had to admit her confidence was shaken. Soon she was practically asking Colebaugh to call the whole thing off, even though she admitted that it still held exciting possibilities for her.

A Caribbean trip seemed a more promising project. This was a defense area but not a war zone, so she should be able to obtain the appropriate travel documents. On June 11, just a day after expressing her misgivings about munitions work, she wrote Colebaugh again, explaining the inquiries she had made about Caribbean travel. She was going to think through this trip carefully, no more brainstorms, she assured her editor. On June 19, he replied, relieving her of the working-girl assignment and confessing that he, too, had wondered about how she had planned to disguise her accent—speak ungrammatically and hope to be taken for a foreigner? He was much more interested in setting up her Caribbean itinerary. Maybe she would get lucky and spot a submarine base—if such things existed there. She replied on June 25, asking him to get her passport validated for every part of the Caribbean, since there was no telling what she might turn up in her journey, and she was mad to be off, feeling crazy in the tropical heat that always undid white men in Somerset Maugham's fiction.

Gellhorn wrote Mrs. Roosevelt that she was cavorting with joy to be going on a trip. The best thing of all was to be a great writer, but that took a certain genius that could not be acquired. Superb journalism, on the other hand, was a simpler matter—a product of hard work and travel, not inspiration. She loved the kind of life in which she could put everything she needed in a suitcase. She hated housekeeping and felt reassured by Hemingway's rapport with his children: They would be fine with their father teaching them about boating and hunting and telling them the most marvelous stories and jokes. He was also busy editing a book of war writing. She was leaving, in other words, without a sense of guilt.

Gellhorn was prepared to write about exotic, out-of-the-way places, headhunters—whatever was bizarre. She had had it with being a respectable homeowner and felt more like a pirate, promising to bring Colebaugh a submarine as a memento. The stories about submarines near Cuba had become quite ludicrous—such as the one about four Cuban women who had been abducted from a yacht and held hostage by the submariners until their men had been dispatched to town to bring back provisions for the sub.

On July 16, her credentials from *Collier's* and other documents arrived. One item identified her as Martha Hemingway. That was all right, she wrote Colebaugh, but there should be no confusion. Her articles were signed Martha Gellhorn. It was too late to cultivate another name for herself. In a few days, she would be flying off on another *Collier's* assignment, secretly hoping she would actually spot a German sub. Hemingway was not the only one indulging fantasies in this first summer of the U.S. involvement in the war.

LIANA

1942 – 1944

16

Port-au-Prince, Haiti, July 20, 1942: Gellhorn wrote Hemingway about how rested and content she felt. The heat was suffocating, but she had always liked it hot, preferred "traveling light," and loved the spontaneity of not knowing what each day would bring. As a journalist, her primary mission was to observe; she could not imagine herself actually in charge of things. She had neither the bravery nor the hope to think of herself as the governor of an island such as Haiti, she confided in a letter to Mrs. Roosevelt. To watch the Haitians take charge of their land was a pleasure, and in the process they seemed to have acquired more respect from the whites.

August 9: Puerto Rico's poverty troubled Gellhorn. People were so badly off, they looked upon enlistment in the army as a kind of "health cure." At least men got good food and had jobs worth doing. Her piece on Puerto Rico really masked her main objective, however, which was to soak up the Caribbean atmosphere for her novel and to play the explorer of unknown lands. As long as she was absorbed in her note taking—examining but not analyzing what she saw—she was happy.

These kinds of trips kept Gellhorn jolly and agile. It was better to feel young than to be wise. She had no ambition to be another Jane Austen. She had chucked her Proust after several futile attempts to read him. She was getting along famously, having been recognized as the wife of the

175

"grande escritor." She confessed uneasiness about benefiting from his name and felt relieved when "an Austrian refugee waiter" asked her to sign his copy of *A Stricken Field.*

Hemingway did not understand why Gellhorn had to fret about such things. Why could she not just be a happy member of Papa's family? He had not wanted her to take the Caribbean trip and wrote his first wife, Hadley, about how much he disliked living alone. However, he was very worried about finances and concerned that Gellhorn make what she could. Although he was earning an enormous income from the sales of *For Whom the Bell Tolls,* federal taxes were taking most of it—or so it seemed to a man who exaggerated his money troubles and resented his rich ex-wife Pauline for insisting on the five hundred dollars he sent her every month. Gellhorn, he felt, was ignorant about money. She was great at scrimping on the little things and then would splurge on big items. She was not looking ahead to that time when she would be older and writing books would not be so easy, especially if she was planning to write seriously. He had an irritating "Papa knows best" attitude—considering the fact that Gellhorn was the one trying to finish a novel, not him.

As on all her trips from home, the farther away Gellhorn got from Hemingway, the more she missed him. She grew frantic when his letters and cables did not reach her. She worried that he had rejected her and wrote with relief on August 2 when his mail got through to her and she knew for sure he still loved her. It was as if she could only imagine herself his when she was on the move. Hemingway on the fly was fine. It was the everyday intemperance of his life that ground her down. Any kind of permanently settled life bored her. Right now, for example, she was behaving like some Huck Finn of the sea, an innocent abroad dreaming of picking up survivors from torpedoed ships, finding caches of enemy provisions for submarines or clandestine radio transmitters.

The very names of the Caribbean islands conjured up delicious visions of charting new territory. She was positively "chirpy" when a motorboat deposited her on Tortola after a four-hour drenching ride in the rain. With not much more than one dusty street and a bunch of weathered shacks, there was nothing to hold her there. She promptly made arrangements with Carlton de Castro, the local lady-killer and owner of a potato boat, to take her on a cruise around the islands. Cruise was not exactly the word for it, since Carlton's thirty-foot sloop, the *Pilot,* was about as unglamorous as she could get. It had a hold for potatoes and a single sail that looked like a "patchwork quilt." It had no equipment—certainly no instrumentation—and the dinghy attached to it was so full of holes, it would have sunk just as soon as it took on passengers. If Hemingway went off on his nonsense wartime trips, at least the *Pilar* was well provisioned. Here Gellhorn was in her shorts, shirt, and sandals with Carlton and his disheveled crew of two setting off in hurricane season to see the islands. She was quite a sight scrunched up in the dinghy, lying on her hatch-cover mattress, her umbrella stuck out for protection from the sun, and ducking every time the boom swung over her. A passing boat full of Carlton's friends inquired as to his cargo. "De lady," he replied to their amused shrieks.

Rarely sick at sea, Gellhorn was immobilized by a steady queasiness. The boat pitched and rolled in peculiar ways that kept her off balance. The crew's cooking of fish and onions nauseated her. After two full days at sea, she was praying for a sub to appear and put her out of her misery. Eventually, they made it to Anguilla, with Gellhorn marking the extent of their adventures: They had seen "three hurrycane birds and four flying fish." Along the way, she had lost her umbrella and watched her skin redden and blister. What could the natives have made out of this shabby figure in soiled clothes and knotted hair, with pimpled and dried-out skin?

Farther on, she made it to Saint Martin, where she swam naked in the sea and felt she was recapturing her youthful, unencumbered days. Saint Barts, on the other hand, was an ugly, arid island. She could not wait to leave—although she did meet three interesting figures who became the prototypes for the main characters in *Liana*. One was Jean, a young "boat bum" using up a modest inheritance, who felt stranded and altogether too safe on this serene shore. He yearned to enlist in the Free French but felt fettered by a witch's voodoo charm, which was especially effective since she was his lover. Although Gellhorn advised against his believing in such superstitious nonsense, he seemed genuinely fearful. The witch turned out to be a lovely mulatto with the feline grace of a jungle cat—a cat-woman who distrusted Gellhorn and would not eat with her. Another French-man, middle-aged and subdued, regretted his marriage to a black woman, claiming he had succumbed to the stupor of the island: Miscegenation had ruined these people and had produced moronic children who were impossible to teach. What was the point, anyway? he wondered. How could they use an education on Saint Barts? Out of these three characters, Gellhorn would produce a triangle that evoked powerful feelings about race, education, politics, and sex. All three characters would be magnificently transformed to reflect the tensions and contradictions of their environment.

The Caribbean trip raised interesting questions about culture. It was fascinating for Gellhorn to see how each island took on the customs of its European rulers and how the Europeans seemed largely oblivious to this phenomenon, preferring to maintain the fiction that the races were separate, that the mingling of minds and bodies did not result in profound consequences for humanity. Gellhorn was enchanted by these handsome people of mixed blood.

It was a curious thing for her to be alone on this trip and to meet so many people whose lives implicitly raised questions about a sense of belonging and identity. She had her own need to belong, to be a wife, to share her interest in humanity with others, yet she so enjoyed being a loner. She was somewhat surprised that along the way she acquired a cat, caring for it like a child and feeling guilty when the rough sea voyages sickened it. She even made an impassioned speech for the animal at Saint Kitts, which prohibited the importation of cats and dogs, and succeeded in bringing it along.

It is not possible to improve upon Gellhorn's account of her Caribbean adventures in *Travels with Myself and Another:* her encounters with natives, whom she describes as lubricated with reeking coconut butter, and who squeezed and stroked her to the accompaniment of raucous laughter; a bizarre white couple who lived in a crude cabin, praising a life of sin and deploring the craziness of contemporary life; and her protest against a village incident in which a woman's screams convinced her some horrible torture had commenced. Hustled out of the village by her guide, whom she preferred to call Mr. Slicker—because of his sunglasses, red bow tie, crumpled hat and suit, and oily manner—it took her years to realize (with a friend's help) that she had probably intruded on a childbirth. All in all, the trip was really quite ridiculous. Charles Colebaugh, her editor at *Collier's,* circulated her reports to the staff. They were worth a "good giggle" and convinced her editors they were right to remain where they were. No sensible person would have set out on such a sojourn. The absurdity of it did not escape Hemingway, who wrote to his friend Evan Shipman that if Gellhorn succeeded in getting sunk along with her sailors, *Collier's* might consider doubling the fee they usually paid for her articles. On second thought, he proposed that perhaps the magazine would ask him to write a piece in homage to her.

* * *

By late September, Gellhorn was home in Cuba. In spite of the strain in her marriage, she relished her days with Hemingway and their collection of ducks, dogs, cats, chickens, lovebirds, and pigeons. He wrote Patrick about Martha and Gregory going out into the "back country" and running into big coveys of quails. She began a draft of *Liana* and finished three articles for *Collier's,* which she delivered to New York in person in early October.

Gellhorn had had a heartbreaking time editing the articles. She had done as much as she could, and Colebaugh or his staff would have to do the rest. There was so much funny and exciting stuff she had sweated mightily to get that was left out: stories about the lives of French escaped convicts serving in de Gaulle's army, prison life, natives panning for gold, and Moravian missionaries. It had also taken a while to recover from the trip. She spent days in bed like a complacent dullard, but how she prized her memories of the merry people she had met—people not bothered by war but serving out the sentence of time and bearing up so well with loneliness. She was itching to get to New York and Washington, and Hemingway said she deserved the trip. She wrote asking Colebaugh for news about the United States' entry into the war and warning him to be prepared for her questions.

Gellhorn arrived in New York in early October for a two-week stay, nursing a fever and a broken wrist (the effects of her Caribbean trip), and writing Hemingway that she felt "like a dying cow, but am *very happy.*" She was in touch with Patrick, who felt rather imprisoned in the Canterbury School in New Milford, Connecticut. On October 21, she spoke to Sarah Lawrence students, urging them to "live and write—but mainly, live. . . . In order to write you must live in your time. You were born in the period of a huge war which will influence all your thinking, living and writing." Most important, she said, was the cultivation of an objective point of view, which was possible only through "writing all the time." It was necessary to practice with sentences as if they were "muscular exercises." Described as "handsome, smartly-dressed, soft-voiced," Gellhorn spoke of how difficult it was to write good fiction. Journalism provided you with facts. In fiction, you were on your own, having somehow to develop your own characters and achieve the compression required of a fine short story. On the other hand, the freedom to invent was wonderful. Mentioning her own days covering the morgue and the ladies' clubs for the Albany *Times Union,* she suggested journalism made for a good writing apprenticeship so long as the writer did not spend too much time on newspaper work, which tended to produce clichés because of the large demand for copy. In speaking about the literature of World War II, she predicted it would not be as pessimistic as the writing of World War I. For one thing, writers were not beginning with the high hopes that characterized the earlier generation. Women, she maintained, had a special role to play, to remind men what they were fighting for, and to be the "guardians of liberty and of the four freedoms."

From New York, Gellhorn flew to Washington, D. C., for several days at the White House. In talks with both Eleanor and Franklin Roosevelt, she heard the latest news and pressed upon them her own political concerns. When Eleanor left for a trip to Great Britain, and Franklin left the White House for the weekend, Gellhorn spent her time in Lincoln's bed trying to recover from a cold. After seeing a doctor for a physical, getting a good haircut at Elizabeth Arden, buying a few things for Hemingway, dining and lunching with the Roosevelts and with Colebaugh, Gellhorn was overcome with longing for the Finca. What she really wanted, though, was to have Hemingway to herself, suggesting to him that only a divorce would keep them lovers. Yet she had already asked two Spanish friends to visit her home in January.

By early November, Gellhorn was back home for what Hemingway sarcastically called "a spot of domesticity." She wrote Patrick on November 7 about his impending Christmas trip, trying to cheer him after he had learned his headmaster would not permit him to visit the Finca for Thanksgiving. She told him about hunting, the animals, the looming hurricane weather—the things he would find most interesting. Each Hemingway cat had a personality Gellhorn meticulously described. There was also a new butler, a vast improvement over the unreliable, slovenly Luis. She was hoping the household staff would perk up and be of some use around the holidays. On the twenty-eighth, she wrote to say the other cats had picked up Thruster's pissing habit and now the Finca smelled like a zoo. The only good news was that she had a new gardener who seemed competent. She felt she was not doing very well on the team shoots Hemingway organized—a fact confirmed by Winston Guest a day earlier when he wrote Patrick to report that he had shot fifty-three birds, Ernest fifty-four, and Martha twelve.

Gellhorn's mind was on writing, not on the sports and sub chasing that filled her husband's days. She was relieved when he turned over this war work to Gustavo Durán, a Loyalist refugee known for his impressive military record. Durán and his wife, Bonte, came to live at the Finca. Gellhorn's respect for his war record did not mitigate her dislike for his wife, whom she found dull. She came to resent their presence at precisely the time she craved the privacy to complete her novel. Bonte found Martha arrogant. When she asked Martha whether she could borrow a copy of *Moll Flanders,* Martha replied, "Don't you think it's a bit heavy for you?" Spotting a flower on Bonte's dress, Martha remarked: "Darling, I didn't tell you it was a costume party. You really do dress like a Cuban." Durán complained to Ernest, who explained that Martha did not like any woman "except her mother." When Bonte tried to placate Martha with a manicure set, Martha smirked and said, "Now I don't have to go into Havana for my toenails." Ernest felt responsible for the disturbances in his wife's writing life and turned hostile toward Durán when he realized the Spaniard had nothing but contempt for the *Pilar*'s sub-hunting expeditions. Durán found more important work to do at the American embassy. Then one night, an embassy driver carelessly sounded his horn under Martha's window. Her sleep interrupted at five in the morning, she could not write the next day. "I don't know who your friends were last night, but I would have shot them if I could," Hemingway roared at Durán. Martha contributed her own snide dismissal to Bonte: "I hear your husband has ulcers. Don't you think you ought to get him to bed earlier? I think Gustavo is able to pay for his own hotel." It was the culmination of several incidents that led to the departure of the Duráns and the destruction of what little domestic harmony was left at the Finca.

The battles with the Duráns were just another facet of the war between Gellhorn and Hemingway. The more she wanted to retreat into her private, literary world, the more he seemed to want an audience of admirers. It was as if he were turning himself inside out. Where he was once the writer affecting a public personality, he was now a celebrity pretending to be a writer. Rather than creating new works of fiction, he was lying and exaggerating his personal exploits. Even his close friends were treated to preposterous accounts of his life, as though they were fans or members of the press. He had always been prone to mythologizing his experience, but Gellhorn saw his hyperbole as outright lying. Extravagant gestures and lavish displays were his style. One night in Havana, she had to tolerate a public rebuke when he felt she had not been generous with her Christmas presents to the servants. She could hardly have merited this treatment from him—which included his leaving her stranded while he drove away in his Lincoln—since his own attitude toward servants was "feudal." On another evening, she insisted on driving her drunken husband home. He gave her the back of his hand across the face.

Slowing down to ten miles an hour, she decided to drive his beloved Lincoln "through a ditch and into a tree, leaving him there and walking back home." She could not bear to be on the *Pilar* with him. At the first port of call, she would often hire a car to take her home. How could he waste himself this way when there was a war about which he should be writing? She nagged him all the time about it.

Ostensibly, Gellhorn's novel had nothing to do with her and Hemingway. It was about a woman of color who was kept housebound by her white husband. Liana gradually awakens to a sense of the world when she is taught to read by a French schoolmaster. Winston Guest, one of Hemingway's submarine-hunting buddies, remembered Ernest reading the novel in manuscript, making corrections and suggestions. Guest read parts of it. He thought the book was really about how Ernest was keeping Martha incarcerated in Cuba. It was "very gallant, very honorable of Ernest" to help improve the book, Guest thought. He portrays Martha as something of a monster:

I'll never forget Martha asking me what I thought of her choice of a husband. She explained to me that she'd picked Ernest because of his ability as a writer and possible remuneration from books. And I thought to myself, what a tough, mercenary bitch to discuss her husband with me, someone she hardly knew. She didn't imply that she loved him at all. She implied to me that she married him as a practical matter; it might help her improve her writing.

Gellhorn has characterized Guest's memory as "rubbish." She pointed out that she has never profited from the Hemingway name, never allowed him to support her, and that her career was well established before she met him. On the other hand, it must be said that she did feel she had much to learn from Hemingway and received attention from the press and from reviewers because she was married to him. If she never permitted him to pay her way, it is clear he never offered. Gellhorn has admitted that if Hemingway had ever suggested sharing his money with her, she would not have felt compelled to take so many assignments as a war correspondent. In retrospect, Guest has exaggerated and blackened Gellhorn's feelings about Hemingway, and Gellhorn has simplified and sanitized hers.

Somehow Gellhorn continued to write, even though living with Hemingway was like sorting through wreckage from the Blitz, she wrote Alexander Woollcott on December 14. Much of the nastiness she had shown the Duráns was undoubtedly connected to her anxieties about writing fiction. She said as much to Woollcott; any obstacle set in the way of her writing still put her in a rage. She complained that nothing happened in Cuba, but the country was as lovely as ever. She was tired, but it was the wonderful kind of fatigue that resulted from writing well.

As soon as Patrick and Gregory arrived for Christmas, Gellhorn left, arriving in St. Louis on December 27 to be with her mother. Once again, she wrote Hemingway telling him how much she missed him. American censors had seized her unfinished novel in Miami, and with nothing in particular to do, she was addressing him as her "darling, housebroken cobra." Three days later, she sent him a typed three-page letter reflecting sadly on the past. She was going to proceed with her manuscript, which had just turned up. She was also reading Dostoyevski's letters to his wife. She assured Hemingway she would be home soon.

Bad weather delayed Gellhorn's journey to Cuba and she returned to St. Louis from Chicago. She wrote her husband to tell him she could not possibly get to Cuba by January 12, the departure date for another of his sub-hunting expeditions. At the moment, her primary concern was her mother's disappointment at her departure. Gellhorn knew she had a book to finish but wondered whether she was a "real writer." Edna seemed more important than writing fiction. The only people Martha really loved were Ernest and her mother, she told him in a passionate letter. She felt suicidal when she contemplated the thought that he might suffer some misfortune while she was away. They had a wonderful life and so much to be thankful for—although she had to admit the last year had been awful. She had ended her December letter to Woollcott asking him to buy a candle for her. Now she told Ernest she had gone to a church and lit a candle for him and his boys. Away from home, her powerfully protective instincts were aroused.

From January to June of 1943, Gellhorn labored over *Liana* in Cuba. Hemingway enjoyed reading the chapters as she completed them, "like in the good old days when there were good magazines and good installments." As she wrote in her letters to Patrick, the work left her apprehensive and exhausted. When she was not writing, she was repairing the house, dickering over prices, and keeping careful accounts for Hemingway of her expenses. When she was through, the Finca had a retiled floor, a reconditioned roof and tennis court, repainted walls, new electrical wiring, new furniture, and trees. The household staff had to bear up under her campaign of improvements. She had even redeemed some of Ernest's old lottery tickets for sixty dollars. When he returned from two months at sea on the *Pilar,* he might actually appreciate the neat, clean, and spacious place she had created. She had even put herself out by entertaining the pelota players with a fiesta, at which they all got terribly drunk. Still bound to him as a fellow writer, she sent a letter deploring her superficial talent. She was not at all sure she had the fire to produce first-rate fiction. She desperately needed his support. She loved him, and she needed his love, for she was a competent woman suffering from lack of confidence.

On June 27, Gellhorn was astonished to find she had finished *Liana.* She asked Jane and Bob Joyce from the embassy to come over for a swim. She was exhilarated that night and could not stop talking. At five in the morning, she awakened asking herself whether the novel was any good. Was she deceiving herself? The last two weeks had been her best period as a writer, even though she was constantly tired and got a stomachache from smoking forty cigarettes a day. She steeled herself to the possibility that she might have to rewrite her work. How much better *Liana* was than *What Mad Pursuit,* she confided to Hemingway. Somehow this novel roused memories of her meager existence in Paris in the thirties, and she longed to be young again, to cancel things—the house, her reputation, her experience, all of it in exchange for the girl she once was. In what had now become a theme for her, she wrote her husband that she wished they could start over again. She detested being sensible and cautious, dependable and settled. He craved marriage; she loved the role of misfit, of the wanderer. She knew he would not like this letter, this yearning for youth and its lack of attachments, but what kind of marriage was it if she could not speak to him of her profoundest emotions?

The first week of Hemingway's return to the Finca was splendid. Husband and wife were merry and tender with each other. Edna's presence, as always, calmed tempers. They all admired Martha's household improvements. She assumed Ernest would begin writing again. "You're the writer in the family now, Marty," he declared. According to Gregory, his father meant it. "Marty was flattered at first, then amazed, and finally disgusted," Gregory recalls. It was one thing to encourage her literary ambitions; it was quite another to watch him retire at the age of forty-four. He praised her writing and expressed contentment with being her editor. "Let's give Marty a chance. She deserves one," he would say, adopting a domineering, condescending tone. When Martha got word from *Collier's* that she would be sent to London in the fall, all she could think of was that Ernest should get a similar assignment. He hung back, loathe to give up his Cuban comforts. The fights between them started again.

Fred Field, an old friend of Martha and Edna, visited the Finca and witnessed some "strange evenings" with the Hemingways. He did not know Hemingway, but he admired his work. Things started off with heavy drinking. Soon Ernest ran out of ice. He called for one of the servants. No answer. He shouted. No servants appeared. Enraged, he screamed. Field found such scenes distasteful and was tempted to tell this son of a bitch Hemingway to stop "browbeating servants." Field would just as soon have gotten the ice himself. Martha rushed in, however, and quietly got a servant to supply the ice. Most of two evenings were spent listening to Ernest's monologues on cloud formations and machine guns. Field was spared Ernest's baiting of Martha. Hemingway's son Gregory saw it, though, and was embarrassed to admit he thought she was usually right.

For a long time, Gellhorn had tried to overlook the fact that their sexual life was a failure. One of her friends has suggested that her "interest in sex was more literary than personal, that she was more excited by Hemingway the writer than by Hemingway the man, that ambition rather than passion had inspired her marriage." If so, his dwindling literary powers meant her commitment to him had attenuated. He never lost his physical appetite for her, but he was callous about her feelings. Making love only aggravated their estrangement, he later confessed to Gregory.

Gellhorn had had Hemingway's male cats sterilized while he was away on the *Pilar* and claimed that she was merely preventing the kind of inbreeding that led to deformity and blindness. Hemingway's Cuban friends believed she had taken her revenge, performing "a symbolic castration of her husband." Deeply offended and enraged, he complained bitterly that "she cut my cats!"

As Gellhorn was leaving the Finca on September 20, novel in hand, she encountered Dr. José Luis Herrera Sotolongo, who had attended her and Hemingway since their days in Spain. "I'm leaving for Europe and I won't come back to the *beast,*" she told Sotolongo. When he asked Ernest for an explanation, the only word he received was that "She's from St. Louis, Missouri." For Hemingway, that comment put Gellhorn in her place. He knew it would have rankled her to hear it.

Gellhorn bided her time in New York, making corrections in *Liana* for Scribner's, waiting for her visa, having a jacket photo taken in Central Park. Max Perkins was very high on her novel and promised that it would head the publisher's list in 1944. Movie producers and Book of the Month Club were interested, and she hoped she could send Hemingway some money to ease his financial concerns. She wrote him a self-abasing letter: He had only to say the word, and she was his. She wanted him to tell her what to do. But how convinced could he be when she was in New York and he was at the Finca? Spending some time in Connecticut with her brother Alfred, she was flooded with memories of Hemingway and recalled for him their days along the Loing Canal in France, the setting for "November Afternoon," her story in *The Heart of Another*.

"November Afternoon" encapsulates the on-again, off-again feelings Martha and Ernest had for each other. The story suggests just how difficult it was for these two very independent people to make a life together. *Liana* expresses even more strongly the deeply buried feelings that Gellhorn vented only after Hemingway's repeated attacks. In his conflicts with her, he liked to refer to "the great unending battle between men and women." This phrase could easily have been used as *Liana*'s epigraph.

In *Liana,* Marc Royer, a wealthy white businessman on a Caribbean island, marries a mulatto and changes her name from Liana to Julie. At the same time, he is in love with his dead brother's widow, Marie, a middle-aged white woman who is as elusive and independent as Liana is available and dependent. Yet Liana rebels when she realizes Royer simply wants her as a sexual possession. She has been thrilled at the promise of becoming a white man's wife, visited by white ladies, and dressed in European clothing. While Royer supplies her with finery, he keeps her at home, and she receives no company. She locks her bedroom door and refuses his advances, for she knows he also beds Marie. Enamored of her own beauty and having some sense of self-worth, Liana is bitter about her fate.

Royer is a man who is frustrated by women. Marie, for example, is indifferent to his visits and not at all concerned by her lack of good looks. She enjoys sex, but she does not let it rule her emotions. Royer is angered not to own women as he owns his business and much of the town. Liana's race simply makes it easier for him to indulge his craving for ownership. If he cannot possess Marie, he will find a way to bind Liana to him. His sense of sex is allied to his sense of power: The point is to be the dominant partner in all transactions. Liana figures it out for herself: "she was something he had bought for use when he could not have what he loved."

Royer is only really comfortable in the company of men, drinking with them and exchanging stories, but his marriage to Liana and his great wealth isolate him. This is why he conceives a plan to relieve Liana's boredom and provide himself with a male companion. He pays Pierre Vauclain, the French schoolteacher, to give Liana lessons in reading. Not only does Liana learn quickly, she begins to develop a mind of her own. She reads novels and begins to identify with the characters. She becomes interested in war news and what is happening in Vauclain's beloved France. Suddenly, it is Liana's conscience and not the shape of the island that determines her view of things. She presses Royer to show her precisely where France is on the map. In short, she begins to locate her own feelings.

Vauclain, a sensitive teacher, opens up the world to Liana. They become friends and are accused of being lovers. The very accusation prompts in them an awareness that their intimacy has been sensual as well as intellectual. Then they become lovers. Royer's discovery of the affair turns him against Liana, not Vauclain, for women have always thwarted Royer. He has coveted Vauclain's friendship all along and persuades the Frenchman that he must abandon Liana so that he can fulfill his desire to serve in the Free French army. Vauclain has been unhappy on the island, and Liana—in spite of his passion for her—is not enough to deter him from his thoughts of home. Accepting Royer's offer to help him return to France, Vauclain abandons Liana, who has long since concluded that the island is too small for her. She must find a world commensurate with her maturity. Abandoned by her lover, ostracized by the island, repulsed by Royer, she commits suicide.

This is Gellhorn's only feminist book, in which issues of race and sex are paramount—indeed, they are identical—since it is the subjugation of human beings that is at stake. Like Liana, who must answer to Royer's "Julie," Gellhorn was asked to answer to the Hemingway name. For her work, she never used her husband's name, but in private letters she was "Mrs. E. Hemingway" or "Martha Hemingway."

Men behaved as if it was their world. What gave men the right to decide? This was a question Gellhorn had never asked in so many words. In *Liana,* every page is suffused with feminist questions: Why is it that women must stay at home? Why must they be sequestered from the action? Why should a woman's imagination be seen as second rate, a product only of the emotions and not of the intellect? What is the evidence supporting the treatment of women as inferiors? Why should men be allowed to rule as the superior sex? Gellhorn was not writing a tract; such questions are implicit in the narrative. As one critic of *Liana* puts it, "there is a truth of observation in the studies of Liana herself and of Marc . . . the keen feeling for atmosphere, emotional as well as environmental."

Liana did not become a Book of the Month selection, nor did it become a motion picture. However, some of the reviews were very fine. Diana Trilling pointed to a "perfect blending of intellectual and emotional pitch." Mark Schorer was impressed with Gellhorn's handling of the two men, who "come to understand, almost to love, each other." It is the utter exclusiveness of this male world that causes Liana's total breakdown. Reviewers noted a certain weakness in characterization, in Gellhorn's tendency to draw her figures a little too sharply and simply. Her work did not quite have that circumspect sophistication of the finest fiction, but it was an extraordinary performance. Gellhorn seemed to find herself all at once in the composition of this book. It could not have escaped Hemingway: She had written herself out of his life.

1943 — 1945

17

Octtober 29, 1943: "Having a fine, brainless time," Gellhorn wrote Hemingway from Estoril on her way to cover the war. She had had some fun dancing with an airline crew during a four-day layover. She was in London by November 3, staying at the Dorchester, breakfasting with Virginia Cowles, waiting to get her official credentials as a war correspondent, and reporting to Hemingway that she was getting special treatment because she was his wife. How fine it would be if he would give up his phony and foolish Cuban life and join her.

Gellhorn's first *Collier's* assignment was spent covering RAF bomber pilots, thousands of whom left on missions in the moonlight, flying toward the fortified French coast, ten-thousand-foot mountain peaks, and miserable winter weather. It was exhausting, hazardous duty performed by gallant men, who called their work "a piece of cake." She found it an enormous relief to be among them and no longer on the sidelines. The English amazed her. Just a few short years ago, she had been outraged by their stolid attitude, when they seemed impervious to the devastating war that was about to be visited upon them. Now their self-confidence ensured that they would not surrender. Bomber pilots had to spend long hours waiting for assignment, yet their nerves never broke. They could sit in the mess at teatime reading and behaving like obedient schoolchildren. After all the planes had safely returned from a night mission, there was only the briefest understated exchange of words between the pilots and their group captain, who politely asked about their trip as though they had come back from a casual outing.

It was characteristic of Gellhorn to become interested in London's poor children, the cockneys who worked forty-eight-hour weeks for an average pay of eight dollars. By the time they were fourteen, they were supporting families who had sent their older men to war. They were a rugged, spirited, and clever lot, meeting in their own clubs to jitterbug, asking Gellhorn whether she knew movie stars such as Humphrey Bogart. Few of them had any illusions about the war; they expected their lives to be just as hard when peace came. However, they enjoyed arguing about whether the war would bring changes to their lives. They were proud and patriotic but had little sense of what the war was about—other than that the Germans had started it. These children numbered some 2 million, Gellhorn pointed out to her *Collier's* readers, and they were more vital to the survival of England than they realized.

In spite of a bad cold, Gellhorn trudged through badly bombed neighborhoods and felt stimulated by these energetic people. Everywhere she went, she was struck by how warmly Hemingway's writing was received. She felt she had become attached to a "mythical" being. She wrote urging him to send her more cables, telling him she had his pictures on her desk and was talking about him all the time. Yet he seemed so distant now and not quite real. She was, of course, wooing him, coaxing him to come over where she said absolutely everyone felt he should be. His replies made it clear he would have none of it.

Interviewing three Poles in London, Gellhorn began to get firsthand reports of Nazi atrocities. Jews had been forced to dig their own graves and were publicly executed. Old people, Jews, and the disabled were packed (130 to a cattle car) and sent to concentration camps to die. A ten-foot wall had been built around the Warsaw ghetto. More than a half million Jews were incarcerated, deprived of work and access to other parts of the city. Laughing German soldiers watched starving Jews struggling for the bits of bread tossed into the street. Shooting parties took aim at whatever Jew happened to be in sight. Corpses were left in the streets covered with newspaper and picked up later. Slave laborers were given barely enough food to survive and often had to work in wooden shoes with no underwear or socks. Their diet consisted of meager amounts of potatoes, vegetables or soup, and bread. Diseases such as typhus and tuberculosis were spreading. Poland was a cemetery. Already two-thirds of Poland's Jewish population (two and a half million people) had been exterminated. The Nazis planned to make Poland "German forever."

As hopeless as it seemed, Poland had not given up. Close to 100,000 children in Warsaw were attending underground schools. Teachers were paid, textbooks were printed, and students were educated on every level, including instruction in the creation of explosive devices for sabotage. There was, in fact, a clandestine government with meetings in shops and German factories, even though the penalty for such activities was death. As Gellhorn learned these things from Polish escapees, she marveled at their composure. As with the RAF pilots, she saw the toll on their lives registered in weary eyes that had witnessed too much.

Interviewing Dutch refugees in London, Gellhorn reported further signs of resistance to the Nazis. Prisoners in solitary confinement in German jails used heating pipes to communicate with each other; cars commandeered by Germans were sabotaged by putting sand in the oil; and a general strike in Amsterdam protested the deportation of 160,000 Jews from Holland. She highlighted instances of Dutch heroism and Nazi brutality: A boy caught talking along the heating pipes had had his eardrums pierced; the Dutch offered Jews places to sit on public vehicles and hid Jews, even though the punishment for aiding them was death. Like the Poles, the Dutch had a thriving underground press, in spite of the fact that the Nazis were quite deliberately depriving the Dutch of their leaders.

As she had done in Spain, Gellhorn visited military hospitals and did not flinch from reporting the gruesome consequences of war—severely burned and scarred men with unrecognizable faces. It was hard to say how old they were because their features had been destroyed. Only by their eyes and their voices could she sense their feelings. Most of the wounded men stayed a minimum of two months and some much longer, submitting to excruciating operations aimed at restoring their features. The doctors had done wonders and the men's morale was very high. The men were encouraged to travel in pairs to London to get used to their new faces and to meet the gaze of others without self-consciousness, but nothing could quite still the anxieties of men whose wives, parents, and friends broke under the strain of such disfigurement. She noticed these men made a "joke of disaster," and she implied that many of them had the strength to overcome the tragedy war had made of their lives.

Though Gellhorn continued with her assignments, her cold had developed into an infection and other ailments she could not shake. Her weakened spirit seeped into her letters to Hemingway. She was not prepared to return to Cuba and still hoped he would join her in London—if not to do his own work, then for a vacation. When she could not budge him, she followed up with a long letter on December 12, 1943, marshaling all her arguments: He was *the* writer to cover the war; no one else could write as brilliantly about its significance—indeed, his very career was at stake, not to mention their marriage. He was making a profound error, and she regretted not being able to share the war with him. He would be the eyes for both of them. She followed up with all sorts of suggestions as to how he could get his accreditation as a war correspondent.

The very next day, four letters from Hemingway arrived announcing his absolute opposition to leaving Cuba. Gellhorn tried very hard not to feel disappointed. She could not resist saying once more that he was making a mistake, but she promised not to hound him about the war anymore. Instead, she wrote in self-justification, explaining that she was acting upon her most profound convictions. She was the kind of writer who had to see things for herself; she could not merely make them up like a Jane Austen or the Brontë sisters. All she could say was that she had to honor her convictions as well as his; otherwise, he would be stuck with a woman who had no faith in herself. She did not think he would really be content with her if she sat at home surrounded by a high stone wall.

Hemingway was not so sure. On December 25, 1943, he wrote Archibald MacLeish about how forlorn he felt without Gellhorn. He was passionately in love with her and terrified as to what he would do if he lost her. Yet he was also spending time in Havana's bars talking like a cowboy who would soon saddle up, ride after his woman, and "kick her ass good." Stay home or go to military school—those were the alternatives, he said. Letters in which she called him her "own" had not swayed him, especially when she admitted Cuba had become unreal to her. She had been out reporting on an English village, observing children wearing outgrown clothes and old men walking in cracked shoes, amidst the roar of Spitfires overhead and to the east. Meat was rationed, the village's young men were off to the war, houses were in disrepair, but everyone made light of the hardship in comparison to what their brave soldiers had to endure. When Gellhorn thought of Cuba now, she dreaded it. She apologized to Hemingway, but she could not resist comparing Cuba to being "strangled by those beautiful tropical flowers that can swallow cows!"

February 1944: Gellhorn was driving in an army jeep through the windy hills of Italy. First it snowed, then it hailed as the French driver tried to negotiate the narrow, curving roads. Up ahead, the Germans held the higher mountains. To the right and left were Poles and Americans. She had come north from Naples, passing every sort of military vehicle, trying not to get stuck behind the long convoys that rumbled like herding elephants. Tents flanked the roadside, with men shaving and overhauling their vehicles. Houses looked sliced apart. Roofs were ripped off; homes were now reduced to rubble. Telephone wiring wound its way everywhere like the tendrils of exotic jungle plants. She could see children using old telephone wire to swing on and women doing their washing at an ancient stone trough. The pounding of the batteries, when she got near enough, created a pressure she could relieve only by opening her mouth and breathing hard. It was grim work prying Germans out of the rocky sides of cliffs. In a field hospital, she spoke with two French soldiers who had been repairing a telephone line. One had had his leg virtually severed by a shell, and the other—blinded in one eye—stopped his friend's bleeding by making a tourniquet of telephone wire. He then had to cut off his friend's leg, since it was attached only by skin and tendons. The blinded man refused all treatment until his friend got attention. It was ghastly for the French: poor food, bitter cold, no opportunities to relax, and no replacements. As Italian refugees swarmed the roads, the French soldiers showed no sympathy, remembering their own refugees. The French fought on, giving the lie to people who said France was finished.

Gellhorn's writing captured the feel of slippery, obstacle-strewn roads, where her jeep hit things before Burton (her driver) could see them. A windshield would crack, Gellhorn's and Burton's heads would snap back, their knees smashing the dashboard. "I ain't had so much fun since the hogs ate my little brother," Burton exclaimed after they had a moment to react to the jolt. She captured the exhilaration, the camaraderie, and the exaggeration of war, but also its incomprehensibility. American GIs did not hate Germans. In fact, they respected them as soldiers who dug in and refused to give up territory. This nettled Gellhorn, who wanted to see more anti-German fervor, but how could she dispute with men who were doing the fighting holed up on cold, barren mountainsides. Their feelings would have been different if they were dug in on their own land, they told her. The dispatches from Italy showed Gellhorn at her best. As Hemingway declared in the March 4, 1944, issue of *Collier's:* "The things that happen to her people really happen, and you feel it as though it were you and you were there." Despite this tribute, he sent her cables asking "ARE YOU A WAR CORRESPONDENT OR WIFE IN MY BED?"

On February 27—just before leaving Italy—Gellhorn and other correspondents were shot at near a river crossing on the outskirts of Cassino. It had been her idea to go there and, according to correspondent William H. Stoneman, "in a weak moment we volunteered to go along with her and check up on the situation." At one point, they had to make a sharp right turn and "dash across a short stretch of road into a shelter of cliffs on the other side." For more than a half mile, the correspondents were "under direct observation by the Germans." It was, unquestionably, a "hot spot." Suddenly, the Germans started shooting and Gellhorn "hit a nice deep ditch at the same second" the other correspondents did. After fifteen minutes of shooting, they ran across the road and took a jeep, flying around turns with shells dropping beside them. Somehow they managed to get out unscathed. Unabashed, Gellhorn wondered aloud why they did not advance on Cassino. "Let her go on wondering," Stoneman concluded.

On a brief visit to the North African front and to Morocco, Gellhorn's friend Lady Diana Cooper had her dazzle André Gide for a day. Jack Hemingway, on leave from the army, remembers staying for the weekend at a "beautiful villa in the hills above Algiers," where Lady Diana's husband was installed as ambassador to the new French government. Jack had presented Gellhorn as adding "more than a touch of glamour" to a gathering graced by Lady Diana, "one of the great beauties of her time." In company that included Randolph Churchill, Sir Winston's son, "Marty was in good form, though she scarcely mentioned Papa," Jack concluded.

In March, Gellhorn returned home to Cuba to have it out with her husband. She had had a long, tiring flight from Tangiers, couped up in the ice-cold innards of a bomber with some sick soldiers, but right from the start Hemingway was at her. He would not let her sleep. He raged that all she craved was "excitement and danger." She must be crazy. Where was her sense of obligation to home and husband? In Gellhorn's view, her true "crime really was to have been at war when he had not."

The curious thing is that he finally gave in: Okay, she wanted him at war. Then not only would he be there, he would take the choicest assignments and be her fiercest competitor. His first ploy was to contact *Collier's*. Their offer to make him their frontline correspondent meant that her access to combat zones would be restricted. According to U. S. Press Corps rules, a magazine could have only one correspondent in combat areas. It was a mean thing to do, since he had his pick of numerous offers from newspapers and magazines.

In April, the quarreling continued in New York. Hemingway was certain he would be killed, and he would have Gellhorn to thank for it. He hoped she was satisfied. "My father was always much more frightened of getting killed than Marty," Patrick Hemingway has said. "He felt that he was entitled to stay behind, living in a place that he liked, and enjoying himself." Gellhorn told Hemingway bluntly that his behavior was destroying her love for him. When she asked him to use his influence to arrange a flight with him to Europe, he replied "Oh no, I couldn't do that. They only fly men." As a result, she embarked on May 13, the only passenger on a freighter carrying explosives and no lifeboats. For two weeks, she lived under blackout regulations, the ship zigzagging through murky, freezing, and foggy waters trying to avoid collisions with other vessels. After this long and dangerous trip, she learned that Beatrice Lillie and Gertrude Lawrence had both accompanied Hemingway on his plane to Europe.

Gellhorn was in no mood to hear about Hemingway's accident when she docked in Liverpool on May 27. Reporters explained that he had been involved in a car crash after an all-night party. He had been thrown against a windshield, gashing his scalp and sustaining a concussion. She was angry and contemptuous of such antics in wartime; they might be common, but they deserved nothing but scorn. She checked into the Dorchester, next to the room Hemingway had reserved for its "safe angle." At the hospital she found him lying in bed, a huge figure lounging with his hands behind his busted head. With bandages wound around his scalp in a kind of turban, holding forth like a sultan, and surrounded by his cronies, he was disgusting. She saw champagne and whiskey bottles under the bed. This was a sick man's room? He showed not the slightest concern about her frightful trip. She was indignant. This was it, she told him. Their marriage was over. She was through with it and she would regard herself as free from now on. All his taunts, his intimidation, his lying and bragging—it had all come to an end for her. He was profoundly shocked and hurt at how cold and offended she seemed. She had the nerve not only to criticize his carousing but to demean his reputation as a warrior. "Never had a WAC shot out from under him," was his joke of a reply. She did not find him funny, although she had actually laughed at him and walked out, switching to a "wonderfully exposed" room at the Dorchester—a considerable distance from his "safe angle."

On May 29, Hemingway was out of the hospital and determined to make Gellhorn's life miserable. He got her on the phone and invited her to dinner. When she arrived at his room, he opened the door to expose his nakedness and feigned an attack on her as she retreated weeping angrily. Ira Wolfert, a fellow correspondent, persuaded him to apologize, and on the phone he got her to agree to meet him at her room. Before they got there, however, he spotted Mary Welsh, whom he was already courting, and left Wolfert to escort Gellhorn to dinner.

Both Hemingway and Gellhorn used an uncomfortable Leicester Hemingway to deliver notes back and forth. When Ernest was not aggressive about their separation, he was mournful. "She only came to see me twice while I was laid up and hurting. . . . What a way for a wife to be," he complained to his brother. According to Leicester, Ernest still respected Gellhorn's professionalism and spoke of her important assignment in the "Mediterranean theater of operations." As chief of correspondents, he tried to operate in a businesslike manner—even when it came to approving her expenses. "He's worse than the government," Gellhorn told Leicester when she wanted him to intercede on her behalf.

D Day: Like the rest of the press corps, Gellhorn was told in a morning briefing in London of the Allied invasion just hours after it had begun. An English press officer had stood up to announce, "In five seconds the first communique will be given to the world. You may leave. Go!" She ran out, like the rest of the press, to send a cable, then had trouble convincing the driver of her car that the invasion had begun. He was a volunteer, and he was sure they would have called him. It was a quiet, wintry, overcast day that seemed a universe away from the Normandy beaches. Gellhorn watched a man vacuuming the carpet of Westminster Cathedral and groups of American soldiers sight-seeing before she drove out of the city into the shiny green and calm countryside, passing village schoolgirls and mothers pushing baby carriages.

Hemingway, as a frontline correspondent, had been taken aboard landing craft, where he could observe troops wading ashore. His dispatch for *Collier's* emphasized the danger and the confusion of battle. Like the other "36-foot coffin-shaped steel boats," his "took solid green sheets of water that fell on the helmeted heads of the troops packed shoulder to shoulder in the stiff, awkward, uncomfortable, lonely companionship of men going to a battle." Although he never actually got ashore, Hemingway began his dispatch by referring to how "we took Fox Green beach" on June 6. He was in the line of fire and described "the concussion and report" of shells that hit "men's helmets. It struck your near ear like a punch with a heavy, dry glove." He portrayed himself as a strategist, studying and memorizing maps, advising soldiers on how to approach the beach, responding to questions about their position, using his field glasses to analyze the action, pointing out danger zones where inactive and then burning Allied tanks indicated concentrations of German firepower. Sometimes the soldiers called him Hemingway, sometimes Mr. Hemingway, reflecting his somewhat ambiguous position among the men actually fighting. If his behavior exceeded the conventional restrictions put on correspondents, it also fell short of active duty.

Determined not to miss this historic event, Gellhorn hid in the bathroom of a hospital ship that was scheduled to cross the Channel at daybreak, June 7. The ship seemed "painfully white" to her, an easy enemy target. The Geneva Convention forbid firing at hospital ships, but who could tell for sure aboard this vessel that did not have a single gun? As the ship made its way through a lane cleared of mines, she heard that two previous ships had hit mines anyway—although the damage was slight and there were no wounded soldiers aboard.

Just as Gellhorn sighted the coast of France, she was overwhelmed by the size of the invasion forces and by the strategic minds that had deployed more ships than she could have imagined. Destroyers, battleships, and transports converged to present the picture of a "floating city of huge vessels anchored before the green cliffs of Normandy." Smaller craft seemed to sport about in the water, but the distant gunfire reminded her of the treacherous sea full of mines and submerged tanks. Drowned bodies drifted past her. Barrage balloons "bounced" in the strong wind above the giant ships to the accompaniment of dance music coming from a radio on the beach. With planes buzzing out of sight high overhead, mines exploding, troops pounding out of barges onto the shore, and tanks clanging into action, Gellhorn saw the most impressive orchestration of war ever attempted.

As the ship moved in toward the French beaches, water ambulances were lowered slowly into the water to avoid mines. It was strenuous for the stretcher-bearers, whose hands quickly became covered with blisters from carrying the wounded from the shore to ambulances to the ship and down the twisting stairs to the hospital wards. Four doctors and fourteen orderlies were assigned to take care of four hundred men on a trip that lasted twenty-nine hours without a break. Operations went on all night long, as did examinations, transfusions, wound dressing, and countless other medical procedures. Only one man died, and he had seemed gone even before he was brought to the ship.

Acting as a nurse herself, Gellhorn distributed water, food, medication, and cigarettes, and carried urinals. After dark on June 7, she snuck ashore with the stretcher-bearers. On the Normandy beachhead, she maneuvered her way around mine fields and barbed wire. Having done everything through official channels, Hemingway found himself confined to watching the action from landing craft. He was angry at Gellhorn for actually getting ashore, and even tried to deny that she did, claiming she could not have done so because she did not have the proper papers. In fact, she had shown more initiative than he had, and he would never forgive her for it.

Gellhorn thought the wounded men were impressive, talking and joking among themselves when she was sure they were near collapse. Many had not eaten for two days, but they always behaved like professional soldiers. German soldiers were treated as well as the Americans, although the Germans were arrogant and complained loudly. The American hospital crew did not pause during an air raid, even when she could sense the anxiety of wounded soldiers who were immobilized during the attack. When the ship returned to England, she was struck again by the black American ambulance companies doing their job quickly and competently.

In London, Gellhorn noted the theatrical way a German officer carried himself, "with his hands on his hips, registering scorn and indifference." One American soldier marveled at the sight of this German who seemed ready for a movie set. A captured German doctor assured a British officer that the invasion was the Allies' final desperate act. It was fascinating to watch how tenderly black American GIs carried these "Aryans" on stretchers, never commenting on how defeated this "master race" now looked, for most of the Germans were scrawny and in poor health. No one really sympathized with the enemy, but it was a poignant experience watching a Jewish doctor attend the wounded carefully and wisely. The doctor found it difficult to treat the Germans because they were making so much noise. He asked Gellhorn to tell them to keep quiet so he could hear his patients. Very courteously, she relayed the doctor's message to one of them, who thundered, *"Ruhig."* The absolute silence after the command made her feel as though she were in the Third Reich. She and the doctor exchanged expressions of "contempt and despair," as if in recognition of the fact that these Germans knew only how to give or take orders. There was "nothing in between." They seemed like a different species of human being.

Gellhorn sent Hemingway a note saying she was happy he had returned from Normandy safely. She was departing for Italy to follow the war rather than stay in a London hotel. The implication was clear. Her passive husband preferred to receive the attentions of his admirers at his hotel—as she had seen firsthand. When she returned to the Dorchester, she discovered him in her room with a girl. He also entertained himself by writing "acidulous marginalia" on her note.

Gellhorn's plans to see the war seemed to go awry when she was arrested by the United States Army's PR office for not having the proper credentials. She had gotten to Normandy when she was supposed to have confined herself to areas outside of the combat zone. She was sentenced to confinement at an American nurses' training camp outside London and was told she could fly with the nurses when they were ready to set up a base hospital in France. Gellhorn tolerated this discipline for a day, then hoisted herself over a wire fence, bummed a ride to a military airfield, and got an unauthorized flight to Naples, telling the pilot a sob story about missing her fiancé in Italy.

In Italy, Gellhorn was entirely on her own: "no papers, no travel orders, no PX rights, nothing. I was a gypsy in that war in order to report it," she later told Bernice Kert. While Hemingway played soldier and big brother to younger correspondents, exaggerating his military exploits and holding back some of his best material from *Collier's,* Gellhorn threw herself into the lives of the French, the Italians, the Poles, and the Americans who fought and coped with the war. Having no myth of herself to maintain, her reports surpassed his in concreteness, sensitivity, and intelligence. Harold Acton, who reviewed correspondents' cables in the censorship office at the Hotel Scribe, singled out Gellhorn's as "the best written and most vivid of the articles submitted" to him.

Hemingway's imagination was not deeply stirred by the Second

World War. He identified only with the Americans, the French, and the Italians, and with his memories of the Europe he had known during World War I. He liked nothing better than to be out gathering intelligence from underground groups. He occupied himself with the day-to-day tactics of war and praised the manly qualities of army-officer buddies such as Buck Lanham in letters to his new love, Mary Welsh. Gellhorn, on the other hand, was already assessing the fate of Europe after the war and reporting on developments that argued an anxious peace, if not a cold war. In July, she traveled with a squadron of Poles who called themselves the Carpathian Lancers, because they had fled Poland through the Carpathian Mountains. They had not seen Poland in five years. Assembled in 1941 as a cavalry regiment in Syria, they fought in the Middle East and the Western desert. In Egypt, they had distinguished themselves in armored cars at Tobruk and El Alamein. For almost a year, they had outlasted the intense heat of Iraq, protecting oil fields. By January 1944, they were in Italy, taking Cassino by May. They had now progressed two hundred miles up the Adriatic, having to contend for every stretch of road, battling a magnificently trained enemy.

At the moment, there was a lull in the fighting. It was a nearly perfect day. Gellhorn decided to join the soldiers for a swim. The trouble was the mines. Well, if you let such obstacles get in your way, life would become hopeless. So, like a troop of Balinese dancers, they daintily trod over a wrecked bridge, careful not to disturb the split-up railroad ties. Down the road on the other side of the bridge, Gellhorn pushed on with a companion who agreed they should walk together, since it would not be fair for just one of them to be blown up. As they swam, they could observe the Germans getting shelled. What if the enemy broke their way? The best thing to do, they thought, was to stay in the water.

The main theme of her dispatch on the Carpathian Lancers was their fear that after the war Poland would fall under Russian domination. The Soviet Union would never let go of the Polish territory it already held. After all, Stalin had invaded from the east just after Hitler had entered Poland from the west. Many of the Lancers had family members imprisoned in the Soviet Union, and no Pole could forget that his country had been dominated by foreign powers for more than two hundred years. Gellhorn tried to console them. Surely the Russians would have to respect Poland's autonomy. They would have to honor the sacrifices the Poles had made to fight the Germans. Sounding very much like Mary Douglas in *A Stricken Field,* Gellhorn knew she was expressing her Americanness, "the optimism of those who are forever safe." She realized she had no right to lecture them when Americans had come nowhere near the tragedy Poland had experienced.

Collier's did not print Gellhorn's piece on the Lancers. In *The Face of War,* she speculates that her article damaged the reputation of the Soviet Union, whose standing was then at an all-time high in the United States. She voiced no direct attack on Russian intentions—indeed, she was hopeful the Poles would be treated magnanimously—but her words were disturbing, for they raised difficult questions about what the world would look like after the war. This was also one of her most personal articles, for it reflected one of the joys she took from life: discovering new places and people. Poles intrigued her. She could no longer say there was such a thing as a Polish type. Because they were all so different, she found them fascinating. Each one had a unique story to tell: about escape via the Jewish underground, or fleeing the country on the Trans-Siberian railroad to Japan. Some of them had been slave laborers in German and Russian concentration camps. It was here in Italy that her love affair with Poland began. It would become one of her special concerns after the war.

From the Italian coast, Gellhorn followed the Eighth Army to Florence. Under German attack, the Americans were attempting not only to defend the city but to preserve its art treasures. For Gellhorn, this was a most telling point. The Americans could have shelled the city and turned it into a battlefield, thus shortening the time it took to drive out the Germans. Instead, the Eighth Army had chosen a more difficult and laborious route and respected the rights of the Committee of Liberation, which had formed before the Allies arrived in Florence.

Gellhorn prevailed on a British officer to take her out in an armored car to meet with partisans. She was impressed by very young men, constantly on the move, daring and resourceful in capturing weapons from the Germans. They fought well—now that they had a cause worth fighting for—and had lost a third of their men, wounded and dead, in ten days of intense warfare. She was awed by the unruffled, elegant Florentines, who coped so well with hunger, with the lack of drinking water and fuel, and with enemies both in and outside their city.

Staying with the Eighth Army in its historic advance across Italy, Gellhorn was anxious to impress her readers not just with military feats but with the implications for humanity of these victories. The Eighth Army seemed to include nearly everyone: Poles, Canadians, South Africans (black and white), Indians, New Zealanders, Englishmen, Scots, and Irishmen. Somehow in this babel of languages—including numerous dialects of English—the soldiers understood each other. It amused her that this polyglot army got along so well. They had become "neighborly men."

Hemingway had spent much of August participating in the battle for Paris. He made much of his exploits accompanying French guerilla fighters out gathering intelligence on "German tank movements, gun positions, and antiaircraft emplacements, the strength of German troops and their disposition." It was Hemingway on patrol, addressed by a guerilla force as Captain and joking about his failure to advance in rank because he could not "read or write." He intimated there were things he knew that were not "publishable at this time."

Among his camp followers, Hemingway said he had gone to war to see his wife and claimed that "whenever he showed up, she ran away from him." He had been deeply mortified by her walking out on him, and he was beginning to build an ego-soothing story that grew outrageously in the postwar years. He talked like a man pursued by a conniving woman, a man who had finally wised up: "When I got to know Marty, I knew she collected things. She collected brick-a-brac, oriental rugs, paintings; and it took me some time to realize that I was part of the collection. She collected me." On September 15, he wrote his son Patrick that he had not had a letter from Martha since June. She was a "Prima-Donna," he assured his son, who had callously refused to do anything for him after the accident, treating him worse than a dog, even though he was suffering from a terrible head wound. What a blunder he had made with her. He hated to give up such a beautiful woman, especially one who could write so well and who they had taken such pains with on their hunting trips, but she was different from the woman he had married. All Hemingway could think to do was to accuse Gellhorn of selfishness and coldness and to condescend to her—dismissing her like a bad bet on a racehorse.

After the Italian campaign, Gellhorn sped south through France, now occupied by both Germans and Allies, with a machine-gun escort of three madcap companions. In between assignments, she met with Hemingway in Paris and, according to her, he "*insisted* that I have dinner with him; I did think we could talk about divorce. Instead he had a band of his young soldier pals from 'his' regiment and in front of them insulted and mocked me throughout dinner. They were miserable and slowly left and when I could, I got up from the banquette seat where I'd been hemmed in and fled."

Gellhorn told Robert Capa that Hemingway had become furious when she had brought up the subject of divorce. She had wrecked his life; he was certain to die in battle, leave his children fatherless, and she was the cause of it all. If she talked any more about a divorce, he would shoot her. She was crying in her room at four in the morning when Capa found her. Did she know about Mary Welsh? Capa asked. Why not call the Ritz and ask for her? When the call was put through, Hemingway answered. "Tell him you want a divorce," Capa coached her. Shaking all over, she did so. Hemingway started swearing. "Tell him that you know all about him and Mary Welsh and that he *must* give you a divorce." She did so, and more of Hemingway's swearing followed. Now it was clear he would have to cooperate.

In spite of the turmoil in her personal life, Gellhorn filed one of her best dispatches for *Collier's.* Called "The Wounds of Paris," it took readers on a tour of the torture cells of the city. In underground tunnels, the Germans had inflicted on the civil populace every kind of agony imaginable. Huge brick ovens, five feet wide and ten feet high, were fired. Then a prisoner was put into a metal-lined plain wooden box and lowered from hooks in the ceiling onto the ovens. People were literally burned alive in these five-foot-high boxes. You could not stand up in them; instead, you tried to relieve the scorching of your feet by leaning against the red-hot metal siding. Sometimes the torture would cease, a person would be released for medical treatment and questioning, or returned to the box if answers were not forthcoming. Other devices stretched and broke bodies; still others electrified or drowned prisoners. Praying for mercy, people had scrawled messages to their families or to the resistance, affirming their beliefs and calling for revenge. "The Wounds of Paris" was an unflinching piece of reporting. As Gellhorn said in conclusion, it was vital to understand it all, to visualize the terror because of the way it had devastated the city's people. This was very different from the almost jaunty "I took Paris" pieces Hemingway was filing. Leicester Hemingway made the mistake of showing a "memorable" dispatch—probably "The Wounds of Paris"—to his brother, thinking he would be pleased and acknowledge the quality of the writing. Instead, he growled, "There will be a damn sight more to come. She can't seem to realize what's going on."

Yet it was Gellhorn who was on the move, reporting on the Allies' October invasion of Holland. She wrote about Nijmegen, a small town that had become a strategic area for opposing armies. After a month of shelling, the place looked like a natural disaster. Now the Dutch were cleaning up, identifying collaborators who had done business with the Germans and fathered their children. There would be punishment for these traitors, but not the torture practiced by the Nazis. The Dutch were a decent people who had tried to hide Jews, to prevent their certain destruction in the gas ovens of concentration camps. Over half a million Dutch men had been sent to Germany as slave laborers, and the country's intellectual leaders had been murdered.

Everything had changed, beginning on September 17 when three airborne divisions had parachuted into Holland. The 82nd Airborne was led by General James Gavin, only thirty-seven and eager to have the daring of his men documented in war dispatches. Gellhorn was one of three correspondents brought from Paris to cover the action. She soon became attached to the men and their commanding officer. They had made history by parachuting into Sicily and Salerno, and they were among the first soldiers to hit the beaches of Normandy. That several Lincoln Brigade veterans were among the 82nd Airborne endeared it all the more to her. These men had withstood seven German counterattacks on Nijmegen. They had battled without respite or replacements and had never retreated from enemy fire.

There was much to admire in James Gavin, who had enlisted in the army at age seventeen, earned a place at West Point, and risen to the rank of lieutenant general. He was, in Gellhorn's estimation, virtually the ideal soldier, one who had a sense of history, fought alongside his men, and showed unusual courage and creativity. He was tough and demanding, but he fostered initiative and individuality and would protect his soldiers when they got into trouble. While training them in the States, he had stood up to a superior officer who had wanted to discipline a paratrooper for having had "sexual intercourse with a young lady on the lawn of the courthouse in Phenix City" (outside Fort Benning, Georgia). When Gavin was asked what the punishment should be, he replied, "In view of the fact that that young man will be asked to give his life for his country in the next few months, I suggest we give him a medal." The bond between Gavin and his men was extraordinary—as Gellhorn tried to illustrate by noting that he was called "General Jim" and that men saluted him as though they were shaking his hand. They liked the "cocky way" he wore his hat, and it was evident to her that they were "fiercely proud" of their fighting record under him.

Gavin led his men by jumping out of the lead plane. He slept with them on the ground and criticized his fellow officers for removing themselves from the action. He believed a general should be at the battle and get the "odor of it in his nostrils," and he had little patience for grand strategists and "set piece" tacticians who stood still collecting forces. He preferred the aggressiveness of Patton to the plodding cautiousness of Montgomery.

It was Gavin who had brilliantly and courageously devised the plan that had taken intact the Nijmegen bridge, a huge modern structure that had explosives cemented into it, Germans hiding underneath it, and machine-gun nests, artillery, and mortar fire trained on every access route. Tall and thin, with a charming Irish face, he was dignified but not pompous. Gavin recalls being just as impressed with Gellhorn's intelligence and writing talent. He liked her independence and the thorough way she analyzed problems. She was very quick of tongue and perceptive. There was clearly a special rapport between Gellhorn and Gavin, and after the war, rumors of a romance would reach Hemingway. In the meantime, she introduced Gavin to Robert Capa and the correspondent Charles Collingwood, and the four of them became close friends.

On November 3, Gellhorn had written Hemingway suggesting the time had come to resolve things. She had her future to think about, and he had Mary to consider. They should be frank with each other, she argued, and not tie themselves up in silly arguments. She suggested it would be better all around if he simply let her go. That it was tough for him to face reality is apparent in the elaborately false letter he wrote to his son Patrick a few weeks later, claiming that as soon as he had dropped her, she had "wanted [him] back very much." He was tired of war and of chasing his wife, the "Duchess." They did not quarrel any longer, but he was not going to be lonely anymore and put up with a wife who worried about their competing for stories in the same war zone. He was going to find a woman who would be loyal to him and allow him to be "the writer of the family."

By early December, Gellhorn was on her way back to France, headed toward Toulouse, when her car dived over a sixteen-foot embankment. She escaped with a broken rib and bruises. However, she thought she might be reaching a point of no return. In an anguished letter to her *Collier's* editor, she described her exhaustion. She wondered whether she needed a rest or really wanted to run away. She feared the war had completely depleted her, and she despaired of her recovery. Her writing seemed inadequate to the enormity of the horror she had witnessed. How could she imbue others with the indignation she felt over the atrocities she had reported? She had seen pictures of two bodies dug up with gouged-out eyes, the victims of gestapo terror. An escapee from a German extermination camp told her everything: 2,700 people a day were gassed and burned; everyone in the camp had their arms tattooed with numbers and their bodies shaved; Jews were forced to shovel the bodies of other Jews into the ovens. The stench of burning flesh permeated everything and made people retch. She had not spared herself in witnessing the worst of which human beings were capable, but somehow these last incidents had shocked her into an uncharacteristically emotional lament. What kind of civilization had created this insanity, and was there anyone who could stop this vicious infection from spreading?

At Toulouse, Gellhorn managed to visit a French concentration camp, where refugees from the Spanish Civil War had been languishing for nearly six years. Many Republican soldiers and their families had been moved as many as six times from camp to camp. Men had untreated, unhealed wounds; some had been beaten; one child affected a toughness, the result of many hardships, but still wept when he was asked about his father. These were people without a country, sleeping on straw in frigid cement huts. Perhaps half a million Spaniards had fled to France after Franco's victory. Some seven thousand had become slave laborers for the Germans; others had been put in the camps; still others had become part of the Maquis (the Resistance). The Spanish Maquis had sabotaged 400 rail lines, 58 locomotives, 35 railway bridges, 150 telephone lines, 20 factories, and 15 coal mines. Somehow, even with poor military equipment, they had managed to capture three tanks. In southern France, without the assistance of Allied troops, they had liberated at least seventeen towns. What Gellhorn wanted to say, and what she very much had to believe, was that after the horrible defeat in Spain, after years in the camps, these Spaniards had endured and their spirits were sound.

On December 16, the Germans launched a surprise attack in the Belgian Ardennes and broke through the American front. General Gavin's 82nd Airborne was called in to force a corridor for the rescue of four American divisions. Stationed in nearby city of Luxembourg, Gellhorn was invited by Colonel John Ruggles to spend Christmas Eve and the next day with

Honolulu, January, 1941: Hemingway disliked the excessive politeness, all the alohas, and the flowers that people kept wrapping around his neck. He pledged to "cool" the next son of a bitch who touched him. (*John Fitzgerald Kennedy Library*)

Hemingway got truculent and liquored up at one literary to-do in Honolulu and waved off Gellhorn when she attempted to prevent his glass from being refilled. (*John Fitzgerald Kennedy Library*)

China, 1941: Gellhorn did her duty collecting information for *Collier's*. Her readers learned about the nine war zones, the Japanese drive to divide and conquer China, and the Chinese army's lack of equipment and supplies. She and Hemingway traveled in the seventh war zone, a territory the size of Belgium held by 150,000 Chinese troops. (*John Fitzgerald Kennedy Library*)

Hemingway was a hunting man, a drinking man. Forget talk about politics or literature. "M. is going off to take the pulse of the nation," he would amiably inform his cronies as she crept away. (*John Fitzgerald Kennedy Library*)

In Cuba, Hemingway and his friends would gather by the pool, where Martha would join them for drinks and a swim. To Ernest's delight, she would dive in the pool and surface laughing and reaching for a drink. "That's my mermaid," a grinning Ernest told his brother Leicester. (*John Fitzgerald Kennedy Library*)

Gellhorn beside the edge of the pool at the Finca Vigia. (*John Fitzgerald Kennedy Library*)

December, 1942: Gellhorn complained that nothing happened in Cuba, but the country was as lovely as ever. Later she could not resist comparing Cuba to being "strangled by those beautiful tropical flowers that can swallow cows!" (*John Fitzgerald Kennedy Library*)

From January to June 1943, Gellhorn labored over *Liana*. Hemingway enjoyed reading the chapters as she completed them, "like in the good old days when there were good magazines and good installments." (*John Fitzgerald Kennedy Library*)

High living in New York City. (*UPI/Bettmann Newsphotos*)

April 1944, New York City: Despite appearances, the quarreling continued in New York. Hemingway was certain he would be killed reporting on the war, and he would have Gellhorn to thank for it. Gellhorn bluntly told Hemingway that his behavior was destroying her love for him. (*John Fitzgerald Kennedy Library*)

September 18, 1944: Hemingway and Colonel C. T. Lanham at the Siegfried Line with a captured German 88. Remembering his meeting with Gellhorn, Lanham declared, "She was a bitch from start to finish." (*Princeton University Library*)

Gellhorn during her "golden years" after the war—on her own, uncommitted, ready for romance, but on her terms. (*Franklin Delano Roosevelt Library*)

Merry Xmas
Happy New Year
from
Sandy and Martha

He was perfect: sturdy looking, affectionate, and fearless. His features—"wide green-brown eyes, the mouth, the button nose, the square hands, the strong little chin"—all seemed to bear her out. The boy's name was Sandro, but he would always be Sandy to her. (*Franklin Delano Roosevelt Library*)

By May of 1951, Gellhorn had a suitor—Dr. David Gurewitsch—a close friend of Eleanor Roosevelt. He was forty-eight years old and Roosevelt (at sixty-three) doted on him. (*Franklin Delano Roosevelt Library*)

T. S. Matthews at his editors desk at Time Inc. Gellhorn thought he had the chiseled, austere features of a founding father. (*UPI/Bettmann Newsphotos*)

Gellhorn and Jouvenel would remain close friends for the rest of his life, Jouvenel becoming a steadfast supporter of her books and writing admiring articles in the French press such as "Avec Martha Gellhorn, Collaboratrice du President Roosevelt." (*Éditions Robert Laffont*)

Gellhorn pictures herself as part of a "global fellowship" of people fighting for the well-being of the earth and of its most vulnerable citizens. (*Ginger Sharp*, Lansing State Journal)

the 22nd Infantry, where Hemingway was stationed. Ruggles knew nothing about the couple's estrangement and mistakenly thought he was preparing a pleasant surprise. In effect, she was on her husband's turf at a time when he was still making it difficult to discuss their divorce. Well briefed by his buddy Hemingway, the commanding officer, Colonel Buck Lanham, took an instant dislike to Gellhorn:

> She was a bitch from start to finish and every member of my staff who met her—and most did—thought so, too. I turned over my room to her and went out and slept in this icy trailer, and almost froze to death when I did get to sleep that night. You never had a thank-you, you never had anything from her. They hated her guts. She was rude, just plain country rude. I was sitting next to her in the jeep. I always let Hemingway ride in the front seat next to the driver. She went on in French thinking I couldn't understand it. Well, I'd gone to school at the Sorbonne in Paris in the 1930s, so I could speak French somewhat. She'd taken on what Hemingway always called "a big Christmas counterattack." He gave her hell and really made her just shrivel up when he turned on her and said: "Now you've gotten through with all the privacies in your life speaking in French, it might interest you to know that Buck speaks better French than you do!" That shut her up.

It never occurred to Lanham to wonder why Hemingway had let Gellhorn go on in French if what she said was supposed to be private between them. So close in attitude to Hemingway, Lanham could not see the situation was a setup. It might have been Lanham's habit to seat Hemingway in front, but it struck her as an act of "supreme arrogance." Hemingway did other things to demean her—such as using his private nickname for her, "Mooky," in public, accusing her of an affair with a Polish officer, and telling her (in another of his preposterous statements) that "she had now been as close to the real front lines as she was ever likely to be." Years later in an interview with Dennis Brian, Gellhorn admitted, "I'm sure that every word of Buck Lanham's is absolutely true." She had behaved badly and felt embarrassed and powerless in the midst of what Hemingway called "his" division. As in his letters to his son Patrick, Hemingway felt he had to build a case against Gellhorn, showing his friends and family how unworthy she was not only of him but of them, as well.

If Hemingway took some satisfaction in humbling Gellhorn, he could not extinguish her competitive instincts. As Lanham was driving them on dangerous roads that might at any moment be strafed by fighter planes, they caught sight of a V2 vapor trail. Stopping to watch it, Gellhorn noted the time and place and turned to Hemingway, saying, "Remember this, Ernest. . . . That V2 is my story, not yours." Incidents like this egged him on to find other ways of disconcerting her.

On New Year's Eve, Hemingway's friend Bill Walton met Gellhorn for the first time and liked this "tall girl with honey colored hair and well-fitting slacks." She had the elegance and bearing of a "fine race horse," he recalled many years later, and he was pleased when she accepted his dinner invitation. When Walton got back to his room, Hemingway was waiting for him, listened to his friend's account of Gellhorn, and announced (with a grin) he would join them for dinner. Hemingway loudly harangued Gellhorn—Walton's efforts to soft-peddle the conversation notwithstanding. The back and forth was like a hotly contested tennis match—although Walton remembers Gellhorn behaving well "under the circumstances." Back in his room, Walton chided Hemingway for his boorish behavior. "You can't hunt an elephant with a bow and arrow," Hemingway replied. As if to complete his ridiculous big-game metaphor, he appropriated a chambermaid's bucket for a helmet and her mop for a lance and paraded down the hall in his long underwear in a mock assault on Gellhorn's room. Behind her locked door, she dismissed him, simply saying, "Go away, you drunk." After such incidents, Hemingway would sometimes apologize. "I feel the way a man would feel who had spat upon the Holy Grail," he remarked. It was too late to impress her, however.

On New Year's Day, Gellhorn traveled along the road to Bastogne, seeing piles of dead Germans clumped together. Thunderbolts, the American dive bombers, swooped down on the enemy. The planes got so close to the ground, they left her breathless and thinking they would surely crash. At one point, before her visit, the 101st Airborne had been encircled by a German force outnumbering it four to one, yet the Americans had held on through intense bombing and shelling and now seemed incredibly chipper about it, never conceding the gravity of their position. Strafed by two planes, Gellhorn and a companion took off for the front, thinking it could be no more dangerous than their present situation. This was a confusing period, when U.S. planes sometimes attacked American troops on the ground and the disposition of certain infantry units could not be immediately determined. The Germans were still capable of fighting tank battles, and she was turned away at one section of road where as many as thirty German tanks were reported on the attack. Reluctantly, she left these gallant soldiers and made her way to the farmhouse headquarters of a tank commander, observing the way everyone instinctively ducked when a shell landed some distance away on the road. In spite of the continuing combat, she knew that the Battle of the Bulge (called that because of the bulge created within Allied territory when the Germans counterattacked) was over. She took the rest of the day off, imagining herself among the millions who were disgusted with war, and went sledding with a dozen Luxembourg children.

The Thunderbolts—Gellhorn called them "snarling bulldog planes"—fascinated her. She wanted to know what it felt like to fly in them. After so many grueling assignments and disheartening dispatches, she found a way to relieve her tension by writing almost a comical report about her ride in a Black Widow night fighter over Germany. Titled by *Collier's* "Night Life in the Sky" and reprinted as "The Black Widow" in *The Face of War,* the piece begins with an army major advising her not to fly: The planes are tempting targets and are just as likely to come under friendly fire as enemy fire. Of course, she ignores him. As she puts on each piece of gear—pants, boots, jacket—her breathing becomes harder. Then there is the cumbersome oxygen mask that is not exactly designed for "ladies." With gloves in hand, packing a parachute, and suffocating in her mask, she is deemed ready for flight. The trouble is she can hardly move. She keeps getting dragged down when she intends to stand up—the result of the hefty parachute attached to her bottom. It is so cold she feels like burying herself in her own clothes, but it is a marvelous-looking aircraft: Its "two long tails and the long narrow wings" remind her of a "delicate, deadly, dragonfly." Just after she receives complicated directions about bailing out, the plane seems to hurtle into the sky without actually taking off. A veteran of unpressurized, bad-weather flying in China, she is still stunned by the few seconds it takes the Black Widow to jump from 11,000 to 22,000 feet. It feels like being pressed into some huge iron machine. The pressure is viselike; her stomach seems apparently attached to her backbone. She would welcome any change now—just so she could catch her breath. The cold has made her nose run, and the drainage freezes on her face. She has barely enough presence of mind to hear the pilot pointing out a fiery V2 rocket. Then her plane becomes the target of enemy flak and takes acrobatic, evasive maneuvers before landing. In the pilot's view, it has been a dull trip. Gellhorn could only marvel at men who took these missions (two or three a night) with such aplomb. "Night Life in the Sky," was presented as a kind of lark, the *Collier's* lead caption noting that its "girl correspondent sat on a wobbly crate and flew over Germany looking for enemy planes at night. . . . They didn't down any Germans, but otherwise that's routine life for the Black Widow pilots."

After it was clear that the German counteroffensive had failed, Gellhorn flew from Luxembourg to London. In March, at the Hotel Dorchester, she saw Hemingway for the last time. He had come to say he was planning to divorce her in Cuba. This was the easiest way, since they were both residents there. She made no demands. His proposal was a convenience, since the last thing she wanted to do was leave the war for weeks of residence in Reno. She had taken to her bed with the flu, and his visit was brief. He promised to attend to her affairs as though they were his own. She wanted her passport "changed back to Gellhorn. I wanted above all to be free of him and his name; and step out of the whole picture fast," she later told Bernice Kert. Not yet realizing her integral role in the Hemingway myth, she badly underestimated its hold on her. Getting rid of him would prove to be an impossible task.

POINT OF
NO RETURN

1945–1948

18

From London in April, Gellhorn returned to the war in Germany. Like the soldiers she followed in the 82nd Airborne, she was tired of the fighting and hardly bucked up by awards ceremonies that honored bravery. Acts of heroism had to be remembered, of course, especially in these fatiguing last days of the conflict. On a featureless street, cluttered with toppled telephone wires and the ruins of buildings, she witnessed a weary General Gavin pin the Silver Star on six men, bloodied, grimy, and battle worn, who stared stonily and quietly ahead before moving off to find places to sleep. In their faces, she read the lost lives of their comrades in campaigns going all the way back to Africa.

Gellhorn was disgusted with the Germans. Facing an American army of occupation, no one would admit to having been a Nazi. Indeed, everyone seemed to have a story about hiding Jews: "all God's chillun hid Jews" she sarcastically commented. The Germans seemed to her to have suffered little. They led neat, disciplined lives and spoke in terms of which they thought Americans would approve. When asked what form of government they now desired, democracy was the answer. Gellhorn thought she got a more candid reply from a group of women who said they did not care *who* was in charge so long as they prospered. This confirmed her suspicions that Germans were authoritarian and liked to give and to take orders.

211

Like other correspondents, Gellhorn was keen to report on the Red Army, now meeting up with the Americans for the first time in Germany. She crossed the Elbe to the Russian side. It ought to be a simple thing to stroll over and talk with some of the Allies, she reasoned. Instead, she met with guardedness. While individual Russian soldiers and support personnel were friendly enough, she had trouble with the people in command. To one military officer, she peevishly pointed out that their correspondents had moved quite freely on the American side, while she had met with all sorts of restrictions and petty obstacles. Finally, like a great tidal wave, the Russians were loosed onto the American side, crossing over the pontoon bridge on the Elbe in their antique wagons drawn by ragged but powerful horses, as if they had come right out of some motion-picture epic. In its sheer size, in the density of men and women and material, this display of strength reminded her of the Russian resistance to Napoleon. This did not look like a modern army; it moved like a natural force the Germans must have regretted meeting. The American soldiers were impressed. She reported one GI as saying, "I used to think we were rugged . . . until I saw these Russkis. Boy, they're really rugged, I mean."

Gellhorn's perceptions of the Russians impressed General Gavin. She realized the Soviet Union would not release its hold on Eastern Europe. There was something very crude in the mentality of this military power, which was not the awesome fighting force Gavin had been expecting. It was huge but antiquated, relying on horses and wagons and suffering from inadequate medical supplies. Stalin was liquidating Russian soldiers returning from German prison camps or imprisoning them in Siberia. Democracy had no meaning for this dictator, and Gellhorn realized this immediately, disabusing her colleagues of their sentimental notions about "Uncle Joe" and what a progressive force for good Communism was. Gellhorn had great skepticism about governments, including her own. She was not about to romanticize a secretive and devious dictator.

The day Germany surrendered, May 7, 1945, Gellhorn was at Dachau. The camp's survivors seen through the electrified fence on a sunny day appeared as skeletal figures examining themselves for lice. They all looked the same, ageless and featureless. In this place of plague and death, it was hard to make out the countenances of these bony, shriveled, tortured people. Many of them had been subjects in experiments: deprived of oxygen to measure how long pilots could survive at high altitudes; submerged in freezing water to study the effects of prolonged exposure to extremes of temperature; injected with malaria to determine whether a vaccine could be developed for German soldiers. Others had been castrated or sterilized. Gellhorn described these atrocities in detail, quoting a Polish doctor who found them incomprehensible. He was enraged but also mortified that the human race could be capable of such things.

Gellhorn found no relief in her tour of Dachau. When she could no longer listen to the stories, her only recourse was to visit other sights: torture chambers that were no larger than telephone booths; stifling, overcrowded barracks where starving inmates struggled for a bit of sleeping room; the gas chambers, where she was advised to cover her nose with a handkerchief because of the stacked-up dead bodies the Germans had not had a chance to burn. Some inmates had died of their own joy when they were liberated; others had perished hysterically eating the food that had finally been made available to them; some had died on the fences rushing to their deliverers. Hearing the news at Dachau of victory in Europe made it a symbol for Gellhorn. Ultimately, the war was about places such as this. Victory had to mean the abolition of all Dachaus once and for all.

Dachau marked a divide in the world's experience and in Gellhorn's own. There had been nothing quite like it in human experience—as she would try to make clear in *Point of No Return,* a war novel she would soon begin to write. The war had set her adrift. Back in London, she wandered the streets wondering what to do next. She bought a house, badly in need of repair, as a gesture toward her new peacetime life, but she found it difficult to stay put. Her immediate plans, she wrote Hemingway on May 27, were to spend the summer with her mother and then to cover the war in the Pacific or return to Europe. Her letter was kind and conciliatory. In a lot of ways, the war was over. She had heard the good news that Hemingway's son Jack had been released from a prisoner-of-war camp, and she wanted Ernest to know how well she had been treated by his military friends when she had visited Nuremberg. Walter Winchell had announced their separation on a radio broadcast, but there had been no big uproar about it. She hoped Hemingway would take care of the divorce soon; she wanted to resolve things. She wished him well with his writing and conveyed her warm regards for Patrick and Gregory. She was feeling well and in a good, almost tender mood, signing off with his pet name for her, Mook.

In an undated reply he never sent, Hemingway was gracious, giving Gellhorn some details about his sons, including Jack's imprisonment, and remarking that both of them spoke about her warmly. Hemingway remembered their final meeting at the Dorchester fondly, assuring her that he had told columnists the story they had agreed on in London. He had been full of praise for her, and she should have no fear of embarrassment. He saw no reason why they should not have the same friends. He had had a friendly exchange of letters with Edna and Martha's brother Walter. Mary Welsh was with him, and he did not hesitate to tell Martha about her, comparing Mary's recent accident to Martha's jeep mishap. Martha was not to worry about her things; everything was packed and put away in a closet and aired out from time to time. He wished her well on a play she was writing with Virginia Cowles about war correspondents. He preferred not to start divorce proceedings just yet. He was finding it difficult to write in the aftermath of the war but vowed he would try as a doubtful compensation for everything they had lost. He even offered to share the Finca with Martha and her mother. This was a long, rambling, and somewhat repetitive letter, and it was the last time he would express his love for Martha in a straightforward, uncritical fashion.

At various times, Hemingway wrote Buck Lanham comparing Martha's behavior in Spain to that during the Second World War. In Spain, she had lived with him on a truck, sleeping on a double mattress covered with canvas, and she could rival any woman of the time for coping with these appalling conditions. He admitted giving her trouble there and cited *The Fifth Column* as evidence of his dislike for her. Yet he had grown to love her intensely. Of course, he had steered her away from the major battles, yet it was brave of her to stick it out through the siege of Madrid. She had been in peril when the Fascists launched their drive to the sea and during the Loyalist defense of the Ebro. In fact, as he began to think about it, he admired her courage during the retreats in the grim winding-down days of the war. She had taken it all in good spirits, and he loved her for her beauty and reliability. Buck should not think that her spoiled and selfish behavior in the later war reflected the way she had always been. In setting the record straight, he could not resist putting her down by averting to a meeting he had had with her in Paris, where he claimed to have torn her apart in front of her friends, told her he was in love with another woman, and pointed out she would never die in war because she carefully avoided the danger zones.

When Lanham and his wife, Pete, arrived on September 22 for a visit at the Finca, Pete quickly sized up Hemingway as a man who loathed women. She had made the mistake of disagreeing with his view of coexistence with Russia, even suggesting that his arguments sounded like capitulation to her. Jumping to his feet, red-faced and blazing, he was about to throw his wineglass right into her face, but something in her disapproving countenance checked his violence. Pete had to listen to stories about Hemingway's mother, whom he characterized as an over-bearing nag who had provoked his father to suicide. Martha was also in disfavor. He exaggerated the consequences of his automobile accident in London, claimed he was in mortal danger, and that Martha—located at a cocktail party—had told the surgeon he could do whatever he wanted. Hemingway said it had been of no consequence to her. Later, the surgeon, according to Hemingway, advised him to get rid of his wife as soon as possible. Pete realized that these were the only two women who had defied him, and she was not sympathetic when Ernest complained that Martha was demanding the return of the flat silver, a gift from Edna, who had also written him a "tactful letter" about it. Pete politely suggested he would not want to keep items that had Martha's monogram on them. He hardly seemed to hear her, preferring his own discourse on how Pauline had snatched him from Hadley, and that when Pauline objected to Martha's similar maneuver, he had replied that "those who live by the sword must die by the sword."

Mary Welsh felt uncomfortable surrounded by Martha's things at the Finca. On Martha's enormous desk, Mary set up some family photographs and was amazed when Ernest "muttered something about [her] trying to 'clip' him." Surely she could surround herself with things that belonged to her, especially since in his study he kept "a handsome framed photo-graph of Martha." His excuse was that his children adored Martha. She had labored to make their stays in Cuba pleasant. Mary was not persuaded and wrote him a note: "I cannot help wondering whether or not you kept pictures of Pauline around for the sake of the children, when Marty was here." Eventually, with Mary's prodding, he put Martha's things in storage and allowed Mary to have furniture designed to her specifications.

In late July, Gellhorn accompanied American troops home in a C-54, trying to cheer the wounded and impressed that they never complained about their pain or boasted about their military exploits. As grim as the war had been, it was difficult to let go of it. They had become used to fighting and almost desperate to prolong the feeling of solidarity. Everyone had had an important job to do, and now they wondered about what to do with the rest of their lives. This was a generation that had been cut off from home and was worried about how it would adjust to peace.

On July 24 in New York City, the Associated Press quoted Gellhorn's plea on behalf of "one hundred and fifty thousand Spanish Republican refugees in metropolitan France." At a press conference, she described her visits to French concentration camps and pointed out that the Spanish Maquis had "liberated southwestern France without assistance" but "were still without a country and remain unfed." The French, unfortunately, did not have the means to adequately care for these "neglected outcasts."

Staying only briefly with Edna in St. Louis, Gellhorn announced to the press on July 27 that Hemingway would be divorcing her in the fall. She had no "matrimonial plans," and was preparing to leave for Japan in August. Within two weeks, she heard over the radio about the bombings of Hiroshima and Nagasaki. The reports troubled her. How could two bombs take out two entire cities? She wanted to know what other people thought and so she took to interviewing lower-middle-class St. Louisans, going door-to-door to question half-dressed husbands and wives about their reactions. They were uncomfortable about the bombs but relieved that the war had been shortened.

On November 22, 1945—just one day after her fifth wedding anniversary—newspapers announced "Martha Gellhorn Sued For Divorce." In a petition filed in Havana, Hemingway charged her with abandonment. In affidavits accompanying the divorce suit, he described their married life as "peaceful and uneventful" until his departure for London in 1944. As one newspaper account put it, "Mrs. Hemingway subsequently informed him she had decided to continue her writing independently." For part of the fall and winter of 1946, Gellhorn returned to London—its dilapidated condition a welcome, familiar environment for a displaced war correspondent. Somehow she and Virginia Cowles worked on their play, *Love Goes to Press,* in between trips to ruined Berlin, where the 82nd Airborne was stationed, and to Portugal and France, where she drafted her war novel.

In January and February, Hemingway wrote Buck Lanham about

Gellhorn's letters of complaint from Europe. Although she had once loved him, now even a sober Hemingway disgusted her. She wanted a social life; he wanted to stay home. She also wanted the freedom to rove as a reporter. He suspected that her letters were actually a ploy to get him back. Even if he shaped up (so Hemingway told Lanham) and stopped drinking and gambling while perfecting his manners and sensitivity, it would not be enough, for he believed she persisted in attacking him for thoughts he neither held nor implied. In short, this was an impossible woman who wanted everything to run smoothly all the time.

A final war-reporting assignment beckoned Gellhorn to Java in February 1946. As she would later say of Vietnam, Java represented a new kind of war. This was an anticolonial conflict: the Indonesians against the Dutch. The Europeans blamed the war on the Japanese occupation and on Indonesian extremists—nationalists who had taken advantage of the Japanese antiwhite campaign to proclaim "Asia for Asiatics." In retrospect, Gellhorn regarded U.S. support of Doctor Soekarno [sic], a corrupt Asian dictator, as prophetic of the many hideous mistakes Americans would make in Asia. She saw the ghastly results of Japanese forced labor on people who looked as if they had come out of Dachau; she was amused at the Indonesian penchant for sloganeering that in English sounded quite comical: "WE WANT TO REIGN OURSELVES; HOSPITALITY FOR EVERYONE"; she faced the usual problems of censorship and prohibitions against visiting certain military camps. Dutch prisoners were not beaten or tortured but simply left to die in abysmal detention centers. She distrusted Soekarno and his oratorical powers. He reminded her of Hitler and his hold over German youth. On the historical importance of Java, however, she was clear: It signaled the end of European domination of Asia. Gellhorn was frustrated at what she thought was the impracticality of Indonesians, but she let Johnny, a cheerful Indonesian poet, have the last word on developments in Asia. When she asked him how his people would govern the country, he replied that they would allow the Dutch to remain and help out.

The war in Java did not engage Gellhorn's most profound sympathies; war itself had lost its potency as an event she had to witness. Driving in a jeep with two English officers through the jungles of Java and worrying whether they would be ambushed or hit a mine, she joined them in expressing an absolute weariness with war. It no longer seemed to matter who did what to whom. It was at this moment she vowed she would go to the wars no more.

In May, Gellhorn returned to the States and spent a week driving through the Catskills and the Poconos with Edna, leaving St. Louis on June 15 to attend the premiere of her play in London. On June 18, *Love Goes to Press* by Martha Gellhorn and Virginia Cowles opened to generally enthusiastic reviews. Gellhorn has called it a "frivolous play." Initial reports in American newspapers of the play's reception praised its humor and liveliness. It is set on the Italian front, and it focuses on the romances and rivalries of war correspondents. The two female heroines, Annabelle and Jane, bear some resemblance to Gellhorn and Cowles. They are good-looking, brave, and competent women who know how to get stories and how to manipulate military officers. The male correspondents, on the other hand, are competitive and covetous of each other's work and quite willing to steal a story or a woman if the opportunity presents itself.

Many of the lines in the play sounded like Hemingway, who had written sketches involving two women war correspondents during his wartime stay in London, referring to their loose morals and unethical behavior. It is not hard to imagine that Hemingway had Gellhorn in mind in his description of Janet Rolfe, an elegant blonde, walking with a bold strut, knowing what a good backside she has as her luscious highlighted hair swings heavily just above her nearly perfect shoulders.

In *Love Goes to Press,* Hemingway's variety of bitterness is played for comic effect. The male correspondents distrust women and accuse them of not working hard for their stories and relying on their looks. Any decent woman, one male correspondent argues, would be at home. The maternal Annabelle is out to save the world and is angry about the restrictions put on her in battle zones, but she can switch in mid-sentence to complimenting Jane on her hair. Annabelle prides herself on her fashions and knowing how to dress for war. Obviously, Gellhorn and Cowles are getting in their licks, but the play also suggests the wish— especially strong in England at the time—not to dwell (not yet, at least) on just how debilitating six years of war had been.

* * *

In November, Gellhorn was at Nuremberg. The first paragraphs of her report skewered each Nazi on trial with telling details—Göring's forced smile, Ribbentrop's rigid posture, Keitel's stony, cheap-looking façade—so that evil took on a familiar, concrete visage. She wanted her readers to see these men as individuals and not to dismiss the horror of Nazism as an abstraction. They should be held responsible; the world should know Nuremberg was a rare historical event, a tribunal aimed at reaffirming international law. She felt the tremendous dignity of the judges. They were exhausted by the incredible burden of having considered these cases slowly and carefully. She felt they were the voice of history, establishing the principle that nations, like individuals, were responsible for crimes against humanity. The Germans had waged total war, and they had instituted their evil as an enormous enterprise. Two-thirds of European Jewry had been murdered. Death had become a "mass industry." The judges had documents and months of testimony that had been scrupulously examined for accuracy.

If Gellhorn took great pains to demonstrate the sincerity and justness of the Nuremberg trials, it was because they were dismissed in Germany as simply one of the prerogatives of the victors. Along with other correspondents, she had spent time talking with a young German soldier who could only think in patriotic terms. Germany went to war because England was preparing to attack it, he said. Then why did the Germans attack Polish and English cities first? the correspondents asked. He had no answer but was sure his government had good reason. He abandoned his claim that the deaths in the concentration camps were exaggerated, that in fact the Jews were put in camps for their own safety, when he sensed how poorly his rationalizations were being received. All right, he admitted, it was an error to kill Jews, but after all, they were not genuine workers, and he had observed the devious way they handled money. He still had fond memories of the Hitler Youth and seemed confused when his words obviously failed to impress his listeners.

The next day, verdicts were handed down at Nuremberg. If the guilty were punished, no sentences could be severe enough to fit the enormity of the crimes. The Nuremberg trials, Gellhorn implied, were the *least* that could be done to affirm basic human rights. She had no illusions about the trials. They guaranteed nothing for the future; they simply expressed the faith that an international body of law might check the combined malevolence, avarice, and stupidity of any state.

In December, Gellhorn attended the peace conference in Paris. Twenty-one countries had convened to discuss conditions in the postwar world. It was depressing. The delegates insulted one another and talked only in terms of national self-interest. Idealists were regarded as fools. She could already see the world being divided between the great powers, the United States and the Soviet Union. The world wanted peace but it had been poisoned by war. Her own view was that people, not governments, could promote peace. The peace conference was never meant to resolve problems; it served only as a forum for public expressions of national policy. Nations had given each other notice. There was not much here in Paris to engage an individual's interest.

Gellhorn's memory of New Year's Eve 1946 summed up the feeling she had of being suspended between the war years and the undefinable years to come. At the Chelsea Arts Ball in Albert Hall, she came dressed as a gypsy. It was an unruly affair that encouraged a lot of romantic playfulness. There she met her Polish friends, the Carpathian Lancers, dressed up in chef's outfits, and got drunk and danced all night. These were her people—refugees from the war and from concentration camps who wound up as door-to-door salesmen, housekeepers, and cooks. In the banter, the empty jesting, and foolery, Gellhorn pondered her own fate.

In St. Louis, on January 1, 1947, Edna Gellhorn noted on her calendar that the critics had closed *Love Goes to Press.* The play's raillery offended New York reviewers, who expected the subject of the war to be treated more seriously. They did not see much wit in the jokes or much point in the plot. The play vanished from Broadway in four days. More disturbing was Edna's suggestion that Martha was turning into an expatriate. The word had a rather shabby, decadent connotation to Martha, so she decided to sell her English house and return to her country in the spring of 1947.

It was characteristic of Martha not to settle down somewhere but, rather, to take Edna on a trip by car up and down the Eastern Seaboard, reporting on what she saw for *The New Republic.* From May 17 to 20, Edna and Martha vacationed with James Gavin at Myrtle, North Carolina. Then they visited Black Mountain College and headed over the Great Smoky Mountains to Maryville, South Carolina, and down to Atlanta. In June, they toured New Jersey, Pennsylvania, and Maryland. What struck Martha was how immutable everything looked, as if the United States had changed places with war-ravaged Europe and had become the "Old World." It was impossible to believe that sites such as Gettysburg would ever see another war. On flawless highways, they stopped at neat Howard Johnson restaurants and ordered the plentiful, tasty—if unvarying—food. Martha seemed intrigued by middle-class matrons, eating in small groups, driving their two-tone sedans, dressing nondescriptly, looking out of heavy eyeglasses just below their fancy, dinky hats, and devouring their meals slowly and carefully. Somehow they lacked character.

Except for blacks, who looked like the Polish slave laborers of Germany and whose voices were enchanting, the country seemed complacent. It was hard to believe in the politicians' claims that Americans feared for their security as the result of internal subversion and foreign aggression. Martha visited a division of soldiers stationed in South Carolina, where she was glad to see Americans who still thought of Europe, of towns such as Nijmegen that had been smashed by the war. However, it was disturbing to hear from veterans that neighbors now looked upon them as fools for having fought in Europe.

After a July break in Cuernavaca, where Martha worked on her novel and Edna enjoyed the local market, they explored more of the American South. In Charlotte, North Carolina, Martha was amused at a convention of "Does," a female offshoot of the Elks. They seemed fantastic to her—like another race or a third sex. These conventions were the equivalent of fiestas. Although Americans were known for their industriousness, she had never seen a people more dedicated to their leisure and she predicted that someday masses of people would come from abroad to watch how Americans took their pleasure. Traveling in the South meant never being alone; there was always some loudspeaker, sign, or advertisement promoting the consumption of something such as the soft drinks she referred to as "colored, sweetened horror." She was charmed by the Southern expression "Come back," and curious that so many Southerners spoke English as if they were still having trouble getting the hang of it.

Back at Black Mountain College, Martha reveled in the liveliness and intellectuality of its students. They formed a genuine learning community that reminded her of European students gathering in cafés to discuss the big issues and argue over culture and society. Black Mountain students showed none of the conformism she deplored in their fellow Americans. At Tuskegee, she thought it was splendid that black students had a place of their own, apart from white domination, so that they could function as truly proud and independent people. She knew, however, that after graduation these black students would have a tough time coping with a culture that had not attained their maturity.

Gellhorn had no particular message to convey about the country, except for her impression that it seemed unreal because it was so magnificently untouched by the tragedies of world war. She concluded by wondering how Americans could be shown the devastating history of other countries. She found it frightening for one nation to be so fortunate. It behooved Americans to help others. Her country might be vulnerable precisely because it had suffered so little.

Washington, D. C., seemed the right place for an American wanting to replant her roots, so in September 1947, Gellhorn rented a Georgetown house from a wartime colleague. She remembered Georgetown as calm and attractive, with compact brick residences. Her first priority was her novel, but she could not ignore the hearings held by the House Committee on Un-American Activities. In "Cry Shame," an article for *The New Republic,* she excoriated the committee, calling it the "Un-Americans" and pointing out that its victims had no right of cross-examination and could not call witnesses or make a statement. The committee was interested only in exposing people it had deemed to be Communists. She watched the committee attack Hanns Eisler, a composer, because he had applied for membership in the German Communist party. It did not matter that he had never paid dues, never attended meetings, or that (in Gellhorn's view) he probably was similar to many people in the 1930s who felt desperate about the state of society, wanted to make some sort of statement, and then changed their minds, not taking their initial commitment at all seriously. Eisler was also suspect because he had visited the Soviet Union before the Second World War—but, Gellhorn pointed out, so had many people in days when a person could book a trip to the Soviet Union as easily as one to France or Italy. The committee completely overlooked the fact that between 1933 and 1939 the Soviet Union was much admired as a staunch anti-Fascist power. In short, the committee had no sense of history at all, and everything was interpreted in terms of current Cold War ideology.

The object of the hearings was not justice but intimidation. Indirectly the committee's real target was the New Deal. It could not attack Eleanor Roosevelt directly, Gellhorn suggested, so it went after easier targets, foreigners, like Eisler, who had come to America in 1940. While the committee infuriated Gellhorn, she knew that compared to what had happened in Europe this was a minor tyranny designed to intimidate the small fry. However, that was the insidious consequence of the hearings. Normal, decent men with families would be afraid to speak frankly: The committee was suppressing free speech.

It disturbed Gellhorn that the press did not call the committee to account. Why was there no outcry against undemocratic tactics that reminded her of Fascist Germany? Why were there no congressmen condemning the committee? When others did not speak up, she appeared shrill. Feeling ashamed for her fellow Americans, she took yellow roses to Eisler's wife on the day they left the country. In November, she visited the Hollywood Ten, scriptwriters, directors, and a producer accused of subverting their movies with Communist propaganda. To their Washington hotel, she came to share her outrage with them. She even broadcast an attack on the committee, noting later that her words on a local radio station had been hasty and emotional, an impotent effort at preserving liberty. Altogether, Gellhorn spent about four months in Washington and then a brief period of solitude in rural Florida, retreating further and further into her novel as her disgust with current affairs deepened.

When "Cry Shame" appeared in the October 6, 1947, issue of *The New Republic,* Hemingway wrote Charlie Scribner expressing his approval: "She is at her best when angry or moved to pity." She was "at her worst when dealing with daily life or, say, more or less natural life without runnings away or atrocities." War had spoiled her by feeding her vanity. She seemed to regard it as a "sort of very highly organised tribute to her own beauty and charm in which, unfortunately, people were killed and wounded." He wondered whether she would have continued as a correspondent if her earnings had not been tax free, or if war ceased to be the big drama "in which there was a satanic enemy fought by Our Side." Sounding very much like the carping men in *Love Goes to Press,* he charged her with luxuriating in war, reveling in the "hospitality of the Generals" and taking advantage of her expense account. He claimed she was upset about her assignment to a nursing outfit during the Normandy invasion because she could not go over to France on "a glamour basis." He remembered her writing about the beauties of Rome when "we were not yet out of the hedgerows in Normandy." Even while he was insisting he wished her well and that her *New Republic* piece reflected her strong convictions, he had distasteful memories of "the smell of the beauty lotions, face packs etc. in that Hotel at Luxembourg, the last time I saw her on the Continent. . . ."

Hemingway was warming up for the attack he would make on Gellhorn's character a few years later in *Across the River and into the Trees,* where he would emphasize her mean-spirited competitiveness. He wrote Lillian Ross that he had to let Gellhorn *"almost* win [at tennis] for her to be happy. If you *let* her win she became insufferable. You had to let her win sometimes insufferable or not." She was a good player, he admitted, and "quite handsome to watch. But was lead-footed." She hated people watching her and her game would deteriorate. She was much better when she could play alone with him or with the Basques, who praised her "Bryn Mawr serve . . . built her up and made her shine."

When Buck Lanham wrote Hemingway about rumors that Gellhorn was going to marry James Gavin, Hemingway replied on November 17 with nasty descriptions of Gellhorn's sexual parts. Paul Johnson reports that Hemingway later wrote a poem, "To Martha Gellhorn's Vagina," that he would recite to his lovers. From the tone of Lanham's letters, Hemingway suspected Gellhorn of spreading damaging stories against him, so he was counterattacking and reminding Lanham of their encounter with Gellhorn during Christmas 1944, when (Hemingway claimed) he had rejected her, saying his one devout wish was to see her dead and to be allowed the opportunity to refuse to speak at her funeral. He claimed that she had written him letters trying to get him back, saying her love for him was stronger than ever, but he had flatly told her there would be no second chance.

Hemingway regarded James Gavin as the hero Gellhorn had always wanted and failed to get in Hemingway himself. He thought Gavin would get a bad bargain, but military heroes were often not very smart off the battlefield. Yet Hemingway contended Gellhorn had been able to fool him, so he had to give her credit. If she had revamped herself once to catch him, maybe she could do it again to get Gavin.

A week later, Hemingway's mood had shifted from all-out attack to a condescending interpretation of Gellhorn's need to snare Gavin. After all, Hemingway had kicked her out, so she had to marry a finer, more courageous man, good-looking, highly decorated, and (on the evidence of *Infantry Journal*) a good writer.

For six months, Hemingway had been building up his case against Gellhorn—much of which seems to have been stimulated by a letter from his publisher. In June 1947, Hemingway had written Charlie Scribner, asking for a report about Gellhorn and remarking that he had a new housemaid named Martha whom he enjoyed ordering around. He figured his ex-wife must be forlorn without a war about which to write. Scribner replied with news on Gellhorn's novel, anticipating the reactions of several male reviewers who marveled at the novel's "masculinity." How could a woman know men's minds so well; how could she know so much about combat? the publisher wondered. Scribner foolishly thought, however, that Gellhorn should play up the wartime romances in her novel. The last third troubled him—all that grim stuff about Dachau. Maxwell Perkins had already talked her out of what he deemed to be a depressing title, *Point of No Return,* in favor of *The Wine of Astonishment,* taken from a biblical prayer for healing a land broken by war.

Obviously disturbed over the advance praise accorded Gellhorn's war novel, Hemingway conducted a campaign against her that reached epic proportions (at least in his own mind). He cut off communication with her, refusing to answer her letters, and letting her know through a third party that he would ship the possessions for which she had asked. In the meantime, he was stuck with paying storage on the rest of her furniture. He rehearsed all his favorite charges about her never having seen real battle and he got so worked up, he imagined hunting her down as though she were big game. He was sure her war novel would not make any money.

Hemingway was pleased when he learned that Gavin had married a twenty-three-year-old girl just as Gellhorn was turning forty. Hemingway let Lanham know that he was angry about a rude letter Martha had supposedly written Mary. He had decided to continue his policy of not answering any of her letters. She was already complaining to friends about his uncooperativeness, and he had written advising them to tell her he was so mad that they were afraid to approach him. When he was not sneering at her German heritage, he was engaging in anti-Semitic slurs at her expense. He knocked a recent story of hers that appeared in *The Atlantic Monthly* and hoped her writing would continue to deteriorate.

Hemingway got so steamed about Gellhorn's war novel, he wrote her a letter he did not send. He jeered at the book jacket's description of her war experience and claimed she had trespassed on the territory he and Buck Lanham had covered during the Battle of the Bulge. He was still rankled over their Christmas jeep ride when he had tried to compliment her by saying she had seen almost as much war as he had, and she had claimed to have seen more—unless he was counting World War I. Coming from a thrice-divorced man, his cutting words about her failures with Jouvenel, himself, and Gavin were pretty lame.

As Jeffrey Meyers has suggested, Hemingway's separation from Gellhorn was the most "traumatic" of his married life. None of his other wives had shown such a strong will or an intellect and imagination that matched his own. Hemingway's letters to Lanham reveal that he regarded Gellhorn as a competitor. When she published a story in *The Lady's Home Companion,* he took that as a sign of her decline as a writer, working now only for the money. He felt abused and victimized by Martha and had to accuse her of conniving ambition in order to salvage his pride. He was used to hurting women. It was a new and devastating experience to have a woman walk out on him and publish a war novel before he was ready with his own.

In spite of Hemingway's claims that Gellhorn poached on his war preserve, the setting of her novel is not in Hürtgenwald—where he and Lanham were stationed—but Luxembourg. *The Wine of Astonishment* takes place during the last winter of the war. After the Normandy invasion, the Allies had driven the Germans back across the borders of several countries. The war was clearly won, yet the Germans fought on, reluctantly giving ground. The battle would not be over until they were thrown back over the Rhine. During a lull in the fighting, weary American soldiers begin to speculate that the "krauts" are all played out. Lieutenant Colonel John Dawson Smithers, commander of the 277th Infantry of the Twentieth Division, a conscientious soldier admired by his men, begins—as they do—to think about the coming peace. His life has been transformed by leading men into combat. He is no longer a small-town salesman from Georgia and he wonders how he can possibly go back to his prewar career, where his lack of class and clout showed, where he hungered after but did not dare approach the town's most desirable women. They were out of reach—too rich, too conscious of society to have anything to do with him.

Smithers has the prejudices of a small-town Southerner and reacts with distaste when he learns that his new jeep driver is Jacob Levy, a Jew. There are no Jews in his outfit. Yet Levy proves to be a regular guy, reliable in combat, a good driver, discreet, and absolutely loyal to Smithers. To Smithers's mind, Levy is no different from his other good men. In other words, Levy does not behave like a Jew.

Although Smithers remains a major character in the novel, attention quickly shifts to Levy, who senses what it would mean if he was typecast as the "Jewboy." As he puts it to himself, "a Jew had to earn being left alone." In effect, this means suppressing any acknowledgment of his Jewishness—a tactic he long ago learned from his father, a shop owner who always advised his son not to associate with many Jews. In short, Levy knows little about what it might mean to be a Jew. In fact, he does not know much more than Smithers.

Both Smithers and Levy find women to love. Dorothy, a Red Cross volunteer, is a sophisticated, war-weary woman who disconcerts Smithers with her forwardness and her seeming lack of vulnerability. He wants a woman to lean on him and to look up to him. She is a gratifying woman to be with, since her type is only attracted to officers. He could not have had this kind of woman in Georgia. Kathe, a Luxembourg girl, delights Levy because she is so submissive and so eager to please him. He has no trouble fitting her into his dreams of a shack in the Smokies where he can live on his own off the land. When she asks him his name, however, he panics and tells the Catholic girl he is John Dawson Smithers. Shocked at just how much of a liability his Jewishness is, Levy is still not prepared to see how he has never been willing to acknowledge his true identity.

Gellhorn makes a point of how elegant, even princely, Levy can look. He can easily pass for a Gentile, although he has never explicitly thought in such terms. This handsome and graceful man, whose appearance is admired by men and women, fantasizes the circumstances in which he will tell Kathe about his real name and background. Like Smithers, Levy contemplates somehow acknowledging his origins while dreaming of transcending them.

Levy is from St. Louis, and the people in the Luxembourg restaurant where he meets Kathe remind him of Germans back home. There are no scenes set in St. Louis, and not much is made of Levy's St. Louis background—leaving a certain vagueness in his character reminiscent of Gellhorn's own vague St. Louis German-Jewishness, a Jewishness never acknowledged. Half the novel hovers over Smithers and Levy, over their uneasy lack of fulfillment and grandiose plans for the future, and over the stagnant front, where the soldiers have nearly convinced themselves the Germans are about to give up. Gellhorn's pacing is exquisite. She captures both the boredom and the anxiety of a stalled infantry campaign, the camaraderie of combat soldiers, and their private daydreams. Her narrative's smooth, engrossing surface is pricked by subtle hints of trouble to come. With the sudden unpredictable onset of war itself, her novel explodes with action:

Then with a suddenness the High Command could never quite explain, the Germans attacked this tissue paper front. The weather went over to their side and a thick dripping cloud settled low above the trees. It was iron cold and snow began to fall, as if to order. The Germans attacked through the snow, the pine forests, across the rivers and over the dumpy hills. Nothing like this had been seen; it was no counter-attack. They seemed driven by a final and furious hope. The front broke.

The rhythm of this passage—the precise reporting of weather and terrain, the feeling that nature (at least momentarily) was on the Germans' side, the sheer crazed quality of the enemy's drive, and the sense of confused defenses snapping—rivals Gellhorn's best reports on the war.

The sudden summons to combat is also what changes Jacob Levy's life, making him the novel's focus. Watching his best friends being maimed and killed by the German thrust, he realizes he has not given the war serious attention. If the Germans continue their penetration, they will retake Luxembourg city, where Kathe lives. Suddenly Levy feels he has a very personal stake in the war. What happens to her and what happens to his buddies is now of overwhelming importance, for he has a share in their fate. Similarly, Dorothy has become Smithers's symbol for everything he has earned to set him apart from his small-town self. Losing her in Luxembourg would mean a retreat to the background he has overcome.

Slowly, the Americans gain back lost ground. Levy and his fellow soldiers overrun German towns, do some looting, and begin to see how Germans have lived. They visit a doctor's home and imagine his family life as similar to their own until they see pictures of him in an SS uniform—a family man and a murderer, they realize. For Levy, the profound shock comes at Dachau, where he follows much the same route Gellhorn took. Heinrich, an inmate for twelve years, recounts in a matter-of-fact voice the tortures and mass extermination. For Heinrich, this has become an everyday reality. For Levy, it is the recognition of a destiny that could have been his own—simply because he was a Jew. The families he sees at Dachau could have been his own. Although he had been vaguely aware of the extermination of the Jews, he never knew the extent of it, never identified with their humanity. Indeed, he realizes that he did not take any of it seriously. His whole life had been built on the illusion that if he behaved like everyone else, he would survive and even prosper. But what about all these Jews leading normal lives? They had died simply because they were Jews. The Germans had acted as though they had a right to rule everyone.

Back in his jeep after visiting Dachau, Levy sees a group of Germans in the middle of a wide road, not moving at the sound of his horn, acting just as if they own the world. He runs them down and crashes into a tree. He recognizes his action as murder. He also views it as a symbolic act. He has finally accepted his Jewishness. The novel ends with the suggestion that Levy will be let off with a suspended sentence for involuntary manslaughter. More troubling to Smithers is the depth of Levy's emotions. He did not know how his driver felt about being Jewish. Levy, of course, did not know himself. Unlike Smithers, he does not try to rationalize his action, but he is, in a way, reconciled to humanity when he learns that not all the inmates of Dachau were Jewish. Having thought himself doomed, having given up any hope of a postwar life, he begins again to hope, reinterpreting his murder of the Germans as an act of solidarity with all people, not just his own people.

Gellhorn had poured her intense hatred of Germans into the novel. She had also chosen a hero typical of the American blindness she decried. Americans had not felt they had a personal stake in the war. The concentration camps and the battles had not been on home ground. Americans knew they were returning to an undefiled country. Only by reaching a point of no return, by seeing his world shattered, is Levy able to empathize with the lot of humankind.

Is this what Americans needed: some kind of overwhelming disaster to make them see their place in world history and accept responsibility for others? In spite of herself, Gellhorn's novel was the work of an expatriate. Like Smithers and Levy, she had seen years of war that made her wonder what was left for her at home. She had tried living in the United States for less than a year, then she returned to her rented house in Mexico. She never again would worry about living most of her life abroad. She had reached a point of no return. Her native land was large, well-off, and secure. It could attend to itself.

Part Four

... WITH NO CONFLICT TO CONFRONT

EXCEPT THE ONE WITHIN HERSELF.

... LOVED HUMANITY BUT PEOPLE

MADE HER NERVOUS.

... HER LAST HURRAH.

... RIGHT ON....

THE HONEYED PEACE

1948 – 1953

19

Martha Gellhorn's four years in Mexico were her "private golden age." She rarely read a newspaper. Except for a brief trip to Israel in the spring of 1949, she avoided war zones. Even there, what interested her most was not the fighting but the immense courage of a people surrounded by hostile Arab powers. Riding in jeeps to reconnoiter desert airfields and gun emplacements gave her that familiar chilled feeling. She was impressed with how all Israelis—young and old, male and female—were mobilized in the defense of their modern nation on ancient ground. Women were just as vulnerable as men: An Israeli major and his female second-in-command had been shot from behind and killed on the same route Gellhorn had traveled shortly before. Her highly partisan report from Israel was never printed, and she returned to Mexico from her fleeting attendance at war, declaring "a separate peace." More inclined to turn on music than a news broadcast, Gellhorn had to get word of the onset of war in Korea via a neighbor's telephone call.

The Lowest Trees Have Tops, a novel published in 1967, captures much of the joy she experienced in Mexico. The weather was a wonder: half a year of drought, half a year of nightly rain, every day aglow with sun. Or as Gellhorn put it in a story published in 1952, the climate instilled an elemental sense of enchantment in spite of one's troubles. Mexico was

233

a poor country, yet in its gleaming atmosphere, poverty did not seem so painful. The scale of village life was most appealing. From a café, Gellhorn could watch craftsmen, merchants, and begging children on the square. Like the narrator of her novel, she was moved by the handsome slim Indians. They might hang out in grungy bars, but she did not have to go to such places. She could create her own home, associating with other foreign residents in a comfortable, unchanging environment. It was as though they were all "preserved in amber."

It was an enchanting way to live, allowing herself to succumb to the spell of the seasons. Toward the end of the dry months, the foreign residents tired of the heat, chafed each other, developed imaginary illnesses, and fantasized about getting away to Europe. Like the trees, everyone seemed to sag in this land of dried-up gardens and dust, but she loved this climate, in which people could indulge their peculiarities and take long siestas when life became too much of a trial for them. After the evening rain, the land seemed reborn the next morning, smelling fresh and shining. In *The Lowest Trees Have Tops,* she captured the delight of feeling the earth sprouting around her—exotic trees blooming in hues of orange and red, plants in luscious pinks and lavenders, snow-white flowers and purple morning glories enveloping everything in a riot of color. Lawns and gardens were perfect green arbors. Residents who had left for the season returned with news from foreign parts; suddenly everyone perked up with gossip and visits to one another.

Through her heroine, Susanna, in *The Lowest Trees Have Tops,* Gellhorn offered a glimpse of what it was like to enjoy these days: sunning in the afternoons on the lawn, gazing in reverie at the sky, imagining herself a world explorer, a renowned scientist, or a celebrated, fashionable woman. The "real world" seemed far off, full of strife and devastation, while in Mexico, history had stopped, apparently absorbed into the warm, radiant air. After the rainy season, in October, the nights were clear and studded with the moon and the stars; the days were unclouded, pure blue and gold. In *The Lowest Trees Have Tops,* Gellhorn called it the "sober season," when Mexico's foreign residents take stock of themselves and each other, feeling that perhaps something should be done to better themselves.

Mexico was beguiling because Gellhorn could make her life from scratch. People often talked about freedom and being left in peace, she wrote her mother, but she actually had it: the great challenge of facing each day afresh, with nearly total liberty to do as she wished. There were no wars, no political controversies, no jockeying for position, authority, or prestige; she could concentrate on her own feelings.

The Lowest Trees Have Tops is dedicated to Edna Gellhorn "in memory of the golden Mexico years." Edna visited Martha in Cuernavaca often, and Martha wrote her mother long, loving letters filled with the details of her domestic life and the delight she took in the natural splendor of the country. If only she could keep it all beautiful for herself and preserve it from the developments that were sure to spoil everything.

It was quite easy for Gellhorn to get her life in order now; all she had to do was close her door for peace to reign. If she had any worry, it was whether her mother would find the accommodations pleasant and comfortable. If the view from Martha's rented house was not spectacular, she now knew about many more places they could visit. She was living quite modestly—she wanted her mother to know—but she hoped Edna would find things sufficiently pleasant, nevertheless.

Martha enjoyed planning her life as though it were a military campaign. She had a strategy that depended on the sale of stories to popular magazines. A home in Mexico would serve as her base, from which she planned trips to Europe, especially to Italy, where she would investigate the plight of children made homeless by the war. She had ambitious plans not only for a book but for the children she wanted to bring home with her and educate—sending them to a local school and perhaps supplementing their studies herself until they were ten or twelve. She was anxious to get on with it. Four years after the break with Hemingway, she felt that time was passing rapidly and she was merely getting by.

In the summer of 1949, Gellhorn was in Rome reporting on a country buoyantly recovering from war and yet neglectful of its orphaned children, who were sequestered from the amiable façade of daily life, collecting cigarette butts and begging in the streets, suffering from tuberculosis and undernourishment, wasting away in dull, authoritarian orphanages, and terrorized by their memories of the war. It was hot, she was feeling fat (having gained ten pounds), old, and tired as she desperately searched for a child she could somehow spirit through the Italian bureaucracy and take back with her to Mexico. To most Italians, her quest seemed quixotic, the vagary of a wealthy American. She already had had one heartbroken failure in her effort to adopt an illegitimate five-year-old boy whose mother would not give him up.

In Venice, Gellhorn met "Miss Pauline"—as Hemingway put it in a letter to Charlie Scribner. His war novel, which would be published the next year, was set in Italy, and he complained about "two god-damned ex-wives in Venice now queering my pitch." He suspected they were "spreading horrid tales; Miss Martha's inventions are fairly lurid." He doubted they could do him "much harm. . . . That is pretty much my town; or it was. And I loved both of those women." For the moment, he seemed to think of them as a team—perhaps because Pauline had written him about how devoted Martha was to his children. He thought she might be "pumping them for material." He warned Scribner that if Martha published a book about Venice before Scribner published his book, he would "turn in my suit. You can really count on this. Seriously. And double seriously." When Gregory reported to his father about seeing Martha in Venice, Ernest took some satisfaction in the report that she seemed less ambitious and was content to write formula fiction. Her trouble, Hemingway speculated, was trying to compete with major writers. He could not let her go, telling his friends what he thought of her in unprintable anti-Semitic language and threatening to dump her remaining things into the sea.

In *Across the River and into the Trees* (1950), Gellhorn appears only faintly disguised as Robert Cantwell's estranged third wife, an aggressive journalist, a sort of mean Dorothy Bridges: "She had more ambition than Napoleon and about the talent of the average High School Valedictorian." Cantwell's wife marries him only to "advance herself in Army circles." She is too "conceited" to feel sad about the breakup of their marriage, especially since getting a good story—even if she has to steal it from her husband—is her primary concern. Cantwell claims that if they were to have another run-in, "I'd look straight through her to show her how dead she was." Other passages on the way Cantwell's ex-wife sleeps and on her inability to provide him with a child are unmistakable hits at Gellhorn. Hemingway had interpreted her refusal to try to have a child as a rejection of him in favor of her career. Certainly this was a consideration for her, for she told a friend after the war, "There's no need to have a child when you can buy one. That's what I did."

Hemingway admitted to Buck Lanham that his depiction of Cantwell's ex-wife was a direct and brutal attack on Gellhorn, and he imagined that she was going to lose a lot of sleep over what he had done to her inflated reputation as a war correspondent. Charlie Scribner worried over Hemingway's libeling her. Should Gellhorn raise objections, she better be prepared to fight it out with him was Hemingway's pugnacious reply.

* * *

Few of Gellhorn's friends shared her enthusiasm for adoption. They wondered how she could be sure of the child's background, and they felt she was certain to suffer over the sacrifice of her freedom. A single woman should not take on such an overwhelming commitment, they told her. And why did it have to be an Italian child? Because she felt closest to Italian children in the war. She had seen them shifting through the rubble of Naples, terrorized and injured by land mines and bombs. Peace meant somehow healing the wounds of maimed and homeless children. Martha took one of her mother's friends, Anna Lord Straus, on a tour of the milk stations set up for orphans. Writing to Edna afterward, Straus was moved by the sight of Martha's weary yet dogged persistence: sitting on the side of a dusty road with a flat tire while her companions fled to the bus. Straus was collecting information on the plight of Italian children, and Martha had provided the facts for demonstrating why Americans had to help. Martha knew the odds were against a single parent, especially one who depended on an uncertain income from writing. Yet what were these worries worth next to the obvious need these children had for loving, caring parents? Better to have one parent than none at all.

Gellhorn had the help of an Italian attorney while she doggedly made her tours of orphanages. When she reached Florence, the weather seemed even worse than that of Rome: The breeze felt as though it were coming from a hair dryer; her dress stuck to her with sweat. Finally, however, in an orphanage teeming with unusually active children, noisy, rowdy, and "comfortably dirty," she found her boy, "a blond fatty" in a flour sack, lying on his back, "counting his toes." He appeared to be blissfully by himself in the contentious crowd of children. She extended her hand and he watched her with affable curiosity. Then he took her hand, holding it while they exchanged smiles. Soon they were beaming at each other. He was fifteen months old, and as far as she was concerned, he was perfect: sturdy-looking, affectionate, and fearless. His features—"wide green-brown eyes, the mouth, the button nose, the square hands, the strong little chin"—all seemed to bear her out.

The boy's name was Sandro, but he would always be Sandy to her. He had almost starved before being brought to the orphanage from a nearby village in the hills. She spent a week playing with him, delighted to see his interest in every little thing, even weeds and pebbles. It took more than two months of paperwork and negotiations and the assistance of Eleanor Roosevelt, the American ambassador to Italy, the Italian ambassador to Mexico, and the Bishop of Missouri for her to get her boy. Then there were hurried preparations for the trip to New York, with Gellhorn going through a crash course in motherhood offered by an Italian nurse. When it was time to depart, Sandy had bronchitis, then measles, and Gellhorn got the flu. Furiously reading books on child care, she was terrified every time her child cried. Was he dying? Was he getting enough to eat?

Finally, amid a heap of luggage and baby-care equipment, mother and son took off on their plane for New York. Diapering Sandy while flying over the Alps was Gellhorn's supreme test. She was clumsy and could not find the right balance between being firm and gentle with him, and she was irritated to discover the stewardesses were no help at all. Surely her fumbling treatment of Sandy would wreck him for life, she thought. When he slept, and she had time to consider her predicament, it seemed that her war experiences were never anything so tough as motherhood. Mothers were now uncelebrated heroes to her. The plane terrified a teething Sandy, who cried and slept his way home in the strange, dark, tunnellike environment of the aircraft.

In New York, a pale, exhausted, sobbing Sandy (his diapers slipping and his clothes on backward) and his mother (her hair and clothing gunked up with baby food and medicine) stared dully at the immigration officials. She was told they could not stay in New York. Much to Gellhorn's chagrin, Sandy was treated as an alien, and the few days she spent at her brother Alfred's home in Englewood Cliffs, New Jersey, were exasperating. Concerned for Sandy's health (she had him examined at a nearby medical center), pacing with him until the early hours of the morning, she felt out of place in a family with five children who regarded caring for a baby as a rather routine matter. Hearing everyone speak English confused Sandy, but when Edna saw he had double-jointed thumbs, she assured Martha he was going to be an adaptable child. The plane trip to Mexico was easier, with helpful stewardesses and a child who had stopped teething.

It had taken Gellhorn eight months to find her baby. Now they were home. She realized that much of her fantasy about finding a child was ridiculous, but there he was: soundly asleep, his head in her lap, his feet on her feet. They would be happy forever in a modest white house surrounded by a walled garden and tall velvety trees. This would be Sandy's quiet kingdom, where he would trudge around the garden making speeches to himself in his own secret language, friendly and confident with the neighbors and the natives, and delighted by the movement of the birds, bees, and busses that passed by his house. Gellhorn watched him bloom like a flower, at peace with himself. She felt as though he had adopted her.

At Christmas in 1950, Bill Walton—still friends with Hemingway—visited Gellhorn. He had just come from the Finca, where Gellhorn had written him. Hemingway had recognized her handwriting while he was checking the morning mail and hectored Walton for two days about being Gellhorn's agent, spying on him. It was quite a charge to make, considering that Hemingway had used Scribner's to gather intelligence on Gellhorn. She left the publisher when she discovered reports on her work were being forwarded to him. Many years later, she told Bernice Kert that she had no curiosity about Hemingway after she left him. When she saw items on him in the gossip columns, she was embarrassed for him and chagrined that she had been his wife—although this did not stop her from making cutting remarks about Mary Hemingway.

Walton took Hemingway's badgering good-naturedly and maintained his right to get mail from anyone he like. He pointed out that Gellhorn would find it funny that even her handwriting could arouse fury in her ex-husband. It was at about this time that she received a haphazardly packaged shipment of damaged crystal and china from Cuba.

Gellhorn was fascinated at the comical progress Sandy was making with English and Spanish vocabulary. He had a nurse who bathed him and took care of many of his essential needs, and he did not appreciate it when his mama tried to take over, for he regarded her as part of his play time. He liked crawling all over her and practicing faces. Although he was a strapping kid and almost two years old, she went into a frenzy at any sign of sickness and studied her child-care books. By the end of February, Sandy had started nursery school, coming home with new crayons, which he proudly used on the walls to show his mama he was working.

Tied down to a very domestic existence in Mexico, Gellhorn kept in touch with friends through her letters and enjoyed occasional visits from Dorothy Parker and others. She had struck up a correspondence with Bernard Berenson, who wanted to know about her years with Hemingway. She acknowledged her ex-husband's genius but deplored his decline into the self-serving and egotistical writing that brought him, no doubt, a fine income. Men in general did not interest her just then, and she had never gotten along very well with them. She wanted to be left alone and to enjoy Sandy. Occasionally she felt nostalgic about the past and her flaming youth, when she witnessed riots and strikes and wars with no sense of caution or responsibility and with hardly a thought about where she would get her next meal.

When Gellhorn had decided on her year's trial residence in Mexico, she had written her mother that she doubted she would ever marry again. She was not forsaking men, and she looked forward to romances, but it would be hard to adapt to another's ways. She did not say so, but it was also evident that the men she would now allow into her life would have to accede to her terms. She wanted no part of another Hemingway.

By May of 1951, Gellhorn had a suitor—Dr. David Gurewitsch—a close friend of Eleanor Roosevelt. He was forty-eight years old and Roosevelt (at sixty-six) doted on him. He was extraordinarily charming. Women sensed immediately that he took them seriously, and they were drawn to him. He was "slim, elegant, and smiled shyly," and knew how to take hold of a woman, gaze at her deeply, kiss her hand, and initiate an intimate conversation. He was a sympathetic listener, and he was irresistible. Gurewitsch was also remarkably like the attractive males Gellhorn was creating in her fiction of this period: a cultivated European cut off from his homeland but making his way admirably in a new world.

Gurewitsch was born in 1902 of Russian parents. His Jewish father was a mystic and philosopher who had surrendered his life by submerging himself in a Swiss lake (to be at one with the elements). His mother was a powerful doctor with "psychic healing gifts." Gurewitsch spent his youth in Russia, leaving at the time of the revolution for Berlin. There, while pursuing his medical studies, he became romantically involved with actresses in the new film industry. A young Zionist, he left Germany during Hitler's rise to power and worked as a doctor in a Jerusalem hospital before coming to the United States in 1934, where he studied pathology at Mt. Sinai Hospital in New York City. On his way to the States, Gurewitsch had met an attractive Scottish woman, Nemone Balfour, and fell in love. Soon he was having second thoughts about Nemone, but he made good on his promise to marry her, heeding his mother's injunction: "Gentlemen do not walk out on such pledges." Nemone suffered from depressions, however, and Gurewitsch from his susceptibility to the charms of other women. Nemone had given birth to a child, Grania, in 1940. By the time Gurewitsch met Gellhorn, sometime in 1950, he was seriously thinking of divorcing his wife.

Gellhorn has described Gurewitsch as a kind of son on whom Roosevelt could spend all her concern. Roosevelt worried about his diet, his tendency to overwork, his career; indeed, everything concerning him became her obsession. Joseph Lash has intimated that Roosevelt's attachment to Gurewitsch was something more than a mother's love for her son. Gellhorn has bridled at the very idea, threatening to throttle anyone who suggests a Roosevelt-Gurewitsch love affair, but Roosevelt's letters reveal that for a brief, uncomfortable period, Roosevelt found herself competing for Gurewitsch's love with a much younger and much more physically attractive woman.

Roosevelt craved Gurewitsch's company. She found his psychological insights compelling and shared his feelings about an unhappy childhood. She wrote many letters inviting him to stay at Hyde Park or proposing trips they could take together. "I would be broken hearted to miss hearing your voice!" she wrote. She had to be assured by his letters that she was "not really far away from your thoughts at least." She followed his travels with intensity, saying in one letter that she "could almost see the scene around you." She had been "drawn" to him at their first meeting and had "taken him into [her] heart." Being with him was a "joy," she would begin to say and then break off—perhaps not knowing how to continue, not daring to say much more. She hated to leave him and be "beyond the reach of your voice," and she wanted to know "what beauty you look out on." There was no doubt Gurewitsch was her special man—so much so that Lash has admitted having been jealous of him—for Gurewitsch was the object of Roosevelt's "constant thought and love." She would imagine intimate scenes between them, in which they sat alone by a fire and talked. As Lash put it, Roosevelt's letters to Gurewitsch "vibrated with the delighted discovery that she still could love and communication with him had a special sweetness."

Gurewitsch was attentive to Roosevelt and usually signed his letters "Your David." He valued her interest: "You have done nothing but giving and I nothing but accepting and still I am not ashamed, not even shy about it, just grateful and much closer." She was gratified by his expressions of devotion, but he was never attentive enough to suit her. She would rarely chide him about it, but she was clearly disappointed that he did not spend more time with her. She acknowledged the disparity in their ages more than once, yet hoped her very maturity would help to guide him "over the rough spots that come in all lives." She encouraged him to "lean" on and "cling" to her.

Lash has suggested that Roosevelt could keep her equilibrium so long as Gurewitsch remained married to Nemone. Roosevelt could advise him about his troubled married life—"a state not altogether unpleasant to the altruist in love"—without having to worry about other women. She always knew when there was a new woman in Gurewitsch's life, but so far none of them had had sufficient allure to pose a threat to her. This changed when Gurewitsch met Gellhorn. Roosevelt—still very fond of Gellhorn—was incredibly generous considering the circumstances, even forwarding to Gurewitsch letters Gellhorn had written to her and which Roosevelt felt he would like to see. These letters had compliments for him, and Roosevelt found herself (at first) abetting a romance about which she had profound misgivings. Gurewitsch responded to Roosevelt by thanking her for the letters and proposing they visit Gellhorn in Mexico: "I feel a little shy reading the adjectives she [Martha] puts behind my name but it would be wonderful if we could go down there together?!"

Roosevelt knew only too well that Gurewitsch would be the perfect man to listen to Gellhorn's troubles, to help her when she got depressed. Roosevelt wanted him to confide in her and to tell her about the weekends he was now spending in Mexico. She needed reassurance that he still wanted to be with her. By the middle of July 1951, she was alarmed at how devoted to Gellhorn Gurewitsch had become. Roosevelt wrote Gurewitsch that she was unhappy. His first priority, as she saw it, was to straighten out his feelings toward Nemone. He had to decide whether or not he was going to divorce her. Anything less would not be "worthy" of him. Then, without mentioning Gellhorn by name, Roosevelt noted that "because a woman offers to go on a holiday with you and you want to find out if you can stop thinking of Nemone does not to me seem good enough." This was a very painful moment for Eleanor Roosevelt. She was making every effort to distance herself from her personal feelings about Gellhorn and to elevate her comments to a point of principle. Gurewitsch had not said, she observed, that he was in love. He had not said he "wanted to be sure . . . if this was a real and deep love." Rather, he seemed to want to go off for a casual "three weeks holiday. . . . Well, one may forget a night now and then but 3 weeks of constant companionship either is very good or no good it seems to me." She was really straining to get him to make a forthright declaration of his feelings.

Roosevelt admitted that she was thinking not only of Gurewitsch but of herself:

> I realize I cannot give you what a young woman can but till you are fairly sure of what you want, do you really want what you are now planning? It worries me for you and I think just now the care and love that it would be a joy to me to give might make you happier with yourself in making your final decision.
>
> I do not want to interfere in your life for of course I have no right to do so but I do not want you to do something you regret. May God help and bless you.

There it was: Better he should lean on the older woman than cling to the younger one. Roosevelt was so wrought up at this juncture that she had to add a postscript: "Perhaps one basic thing that bothers me is that you are letting an offer of this kind be made *to you* rather than making it yourself *to a woman* because you really love her." Never for an instant would Roosevelt commit herself to a word about Gellhorn's aggressiveness, but it would not have been difficult for Gurewitsch to read between the lines, even though Roosevelt kept the focus on him, on his tendency to allow women to chase him. She felt he was "spoiled by pursuit and . . . perhaps too sensitive to go out and get what you really want."

Clearly, Roosevelt was using this extraordinary letter to temper Gurewitsch's excitement about Gellhorn. Referring again to her years of experience, Eleanor Roosevelt suggested that in the long run happy marriages developed "when the man shows his desire to the woman and she responds fully and happily." Gurewitsch, in short, was too passive; he was allowing himself to be led by a strong woman. As Lash has pointed out, however, Roosevelt "underestimated the strength of the sexual drive." With a full head of passion, Gurewitsch could not be content with the consoling sentiments Roosevelt used to conclude her postscript: "Even at your age, tho' some physical satisfaction is essential, you must be even surer of mental interests and sympathetic understanding which will lead to complete and happy companionship."

These last words summed up what it meant to be Mrs. Roosevelt. She was a famous authority figure whom her male confidants had trouble calling by her first name. Even to Gellhorn, she was always Mrs. R. As one of Lash's friends said to him, "How do you sleep with a woman you call Mrs. Roosevelt?" Even Gurewitsch, "an old hand at paying court to older women," always addressed her in person and in his letters as Mrs.

Roosevelt. As Mrs. Roosevelt, she would not want to have been regarded as Gellhorn's rival, yet that is what the situation amounted to, since Roosevelt insisted that Gurewitsch mattered to her more than anyone else. In September 1951, she wrote him:

David dearest,

This is a birthday letter whenever you read it. I fear it will not be a happy day this year but I will be thinking of you *every* day and wishing you greater happiness in the future than in the past. I shall be deeply sad when you go away but if you are happy I shall be glad for you. Remember always please that wherever I am open arms await you. My home *anywhere* is yours when you need it whether you are alone or whether you want to bring those you love. If you forget this I will never see you and that would leave me bereft. I cherish every moment we are together these last days that I am here for I realize that there may not be many more. You know I think that I would rather be with you than with anyone else, whether we are alone or whether I am just watching you from afar. I am grateful to have known you and hope that we may keep close even though you establish a new life far away.

God bless you and keep you and bring you satisfaction and happiness in your life, that is my daily prayer.

I wish I did not have to be away these coming weeks.

All my love David, dearest friend, and happy days to you always.

E.R.

Lash has noted "an undercurrent of desperation in Eleanor's birthday letter." She was trying to prevent David from leaving the country and settling in Cuernavaca with Martha. He had overcome a serious illness and had worked hard to establish a thriving New York practice. Now to give it all up seemed senseless to Roosevelt.

Eleanor Roosevelt could not understand why Gellhorn did not join Gurewitsch in New York. It was a sign to her that Gellhorn did not really love him and that she was not ready to commit herself to another marriage. Some years later, she confided to a close friend her astonishment at Gellhorn's selfishness. Roosevelt felt that as a writer Gellhorn could live anywhere, whereas Gurewitsch, who had been a stateless person most of his life, was taking enormous risks. In Roosevelt's view, if a woman really loved a man, she should be willing to make sacrifices so that they could be together.

In November 1951, Roosevelt prefaced her most pointed criticism to date by observing she did not want Gurewitsch "hurt," but she had to say "marriages are two way streets and when they are happy women must be willing to adjust. *Both* must love." Gurewitsch had made his decision, however: spending a month in Mexico after deciding to divorce his wife. His move may have been speeded by Gellhorn's jitters. If Roosevelt was not sure of Gellhorn's love for Gurewitsch, it was now clear to Gurewitsch how much Gellhorn wanted him with her. Roosevelt seemed resigned, perhaps even relieved to have the struggle for Gurewitsch over:

> Marty will be alright now you are with her. Your plans for the fellowship in Mexico sound very good and I think it is wise to keep some ties to the hospital and your courses until all is settled and you are sure what you want to do.

From Mexico, Gurewitsch wrote Roosevelt what a "wonderful rest from tension" the country was. Sounding like Gellhorn in one of her recuperative periods, he remarked, "I'm trying not to think, at least for a short time."

Now that he was in Mexico, Gurewitsch seemed to pull up a bit. "Cannot commit myself to an expression of how I feel, not even to you—I imagine this is because I do not know myself." Gellhorn's assertiveness seemed to be getting the better of him—although he was quick to assure Roosevelt that "Martha understands that her gift and her inclination to make plans have to be held back just a little at the moment." Roosevelt saw Gurewitsch as a divided person, torn apart by his feelings for Gellhorn, his wife, and his daughter, whom he had not yet told about the divorce. Wisely, Gellhorn backed off, provoking Roosevelt to remark, "I'm glad Martha is happy and easy, that is the way she can help you best." Into December, Gurewitsch was still fretting. He was a treating two patients and giving well-received lectures, but he was apprehensive about "starting life here."

By Christmas of 1951, Gurewitsch was wavering—over Mexico, over Gellhorn. Although she claimed she was in "no hurry," he observed, in Lash's words, "a willfulness that comes from having been desired by many men." She had an irrepressible energy—that was part of her appeal—but her high-strung temperament would inevitably lead to conflicts. She was, frankly, a little more than he cared to handle. The most telling sign of his change of attitude was his presence at Roosevelt's side during the holidays.

All through this period, Gellhorn and Roosevelt exchanged the briefest of messages, even though Gellhorn was accustomed to writing long typewritten letters that Roosevelt lovingly answered. "I wrote Marty . . . and thanked her for her Xmas wire and said little else," noted Roosevelt in a letter to Gurewitsch that worried over his indecisiveness. Both women wished to avoid framing the issue between themselves. When Roosevelt learned Gellhorn would not be visiting her in the spring of 1952, she promptly invited Gurewitsch to stay with her.

Finally, no longer willing to wait for Gurewitsch to make up his mind, Gellhorn resolved things by writing Roosevelt. She announced that she was unwilling to accompany Gurewitsch and Roosevelt on a trip they were planning to take to Israel and the Middle East. She declared that her romance with Gurewitsch was over. He lacked for nothing except her, yet this was hardly a tragedy, since she had noticed the lessening of his interest. Gellhorn indicated he no longer needed her, and that Roosevelt should persuade him to see it this way. Roosevelt was obviously relieved but apparently made no reply to this astonishing letter.

The dalliance with David Gurewitsch was indicative of Gellhorn's unsettled, even flighty state of mind. Upon first arriving in Mexico, she had written her mother confessing that she was not ready to commit herself to serious fiction. After one of their long Mexican walks, Edna Gellhorn noted on her calendar for August 3, 1951, that Martha had made up her mind to write a novel. In fact, she would not publish another novel until 1961. Instead, she produced bits and pieces, good stories and bad stories, and fairly superficial journalism and travel features. Although Roosevelt did not say so, the Gellhorn of this period was a disappointment. Roosevelt could not have found much to admire in trite *Saturday Evening Post* stories such as "Lonely Lady," about a beautiful woman who dies unloved, or in travel pieces with inane titles such as "Everybody's Happy on Capri," which extolled a life of ease "without fuss." For Gellhorn, an article on Washington socialite Perle Mesta, "Party Girl in Paradise," or "Strange Daughter," a simpleminded story with a Mexican locale, helped pay the rent. This kind of writing was not meant to be taken seriously. Still, it seemed like a corruption of her talent that was mitigated only by her more significant reports on American soldiers in England, education at Eton, and the British mood during the early Cold War years. However, even these pieces did not merit inclusion in her collection of peacetime journalism, *The View from the Ground.* When Hemingway saw the piece on Perle Mesta, he could not resist writing

Buck Lanham, asking him to convey to Mesta his apology for having married a kook.

The Honeyed Peace (1953), mostly a selection of Gellhorn's best fiction since 1948, finally brought her out of this creative trough. The title of the volume has an ironic thrust, for her stories reveal a postwar world that has soured even as its survivors try to convince themselves of their good fortune. They are people who have lost faith but cannot quite abandon their convictions. If there is honor in this rather grim, gray world, it derives from deeply felt emotions—such as Evangeline's unshakable love for Renaud, her French collaborationist lover in the title story. Gellhorn showed remarkable sympathy for Evangeline, who is a gossip more interested in fashion than in politics. Evangeline's devotion to Renaud is shown to advantage against the political opportunism of the French, who behave as though they had not colluded with the Germans.

Evangeline's friends worry about her sanity should Renaud come to harm in prison, and Anne wonders "if any man ever felt for any woman as Evangeline did for Renaud: did any man ever die of fear for a woman?" Like Gellhorn, Anne has never had such an overwhelming feeling for a man and wonders what she has missed. When it is announced that Renaud has committed suicide, Anne thinks of how Evangeline's whole world is destroyed. The story is a surprising tribute to romantic love and not just an ironic counterpoint to Longfellow's sentimental poem.

The Honeyed Peace is full of female characters who read like echoes of Gellhorn's past. Lily Cameron in "Week End at Grimsby" is well traveled, having lived since the war in an Italian villa, a Paris flat, a London house, and a New York hotel suite. She has even been to China. Homeless and practically stateless, she verges toward self-pity but brings herself up short, revolting against a picture of herself as a "female Flying Dutchman or Wandering Jew." She has been to war and shown a stylish competence. Like Anne in "The Honeyed Peace," Cameron cannot forget the war and cannot help contrasting the straightened circumstances of her Polish émigré friends in Great Britain with their heroic behavior in the Italian campaign. For Cameron, her best days were spent with these crazy Poles, when she knew exactly what she wanted. It had been a time to treasure the joys of day-by-day existence. Now her Polish friends live in Grimsby, which is as grim as it sounds, and she has to force herself to see its grayness as a thing of beauty these Poles have come to accept as their new home.

Divorced immediately after the war, Cameron's feelings are close to Gellhorn's. Her life now has no definition, and the peace seems ugly—as ugly as the thick, stocky legs of her Polish friend's girl, as ugly as the fiftyish newly married couple Cameron observes on a train, happily unaware of a grotesqueness that should have consigned them to a "solitary life in a cellar." Cameron speaks for the side of Gellhorn that cannot forget the war, the side that Hemingway claimed was now in trouble because there was no war to fight. Cameron's problem is that she perceives these gallant soldiers in peacetime as being no more than shadows of themselves, working and living in circumstances beneath the bravery that should have been rewarded with a better future. The Poles, however, see it another way. They have made a new world—nothing like the one of their native land, of their ancestral estates—but one in which they have found love and labor that is satisfying, if not ennobling. The triumph of this story is that Gellhorn was able to see these Poles from their point of view as well as her own.

One of the stories in *The Honeyed Peace,* "A Psychiatrist of One's Own," suggests how Hemingway continued to dog Gellhorn. He knew of her correspondence with Berenson and had begun his own, initially presenting himself as a chastened ex-husband who wanted to set the record straight, expressing the hope that Gellhorn was happy and acknowledging that she had spoken harshly about him. That was understandable, but he cautioned Berenson not to believe too much of it. It was difficult to find the truth behind a marital breakup. Hemingway would not claim his version was trustworthy. He had been unwise to be impressed by her ambition and good looks. Berenson's renown as an art collector and critic prompted Hemingway to gibe at Gellhorn's lack of taste, her ignorance of the arts, and her romantic view of war and its trappings, while recounting his own faults and praising her command of French. He felt that his guilt over leaving Pauline and the children had contributed to his unhappiness with Gellhorn and had led to his drunkenness. The sight of her always moved him, and he was envious of her friendship with Berenson, telling him he was not to speak about what Hemingway had told him.

During an interview with Robert Manning in 1954, Hemingway showed off his collection of Gellhorn photographs and exclaimed, "There's my beautiful Martha. Isn't she beautiful?" Manning thought she would be pleased to hear of Hemingway's admiration, but her only comment was, "That son of a bitch!" She did not want to be anybody's "beautiful Martha"—least of all this braggart who acted as if he still owned her.

"A Psychiatrist of One's Own" differs from Hemingway's fictional representations of his marriage. Gellhorn describes Matthew Hendricks, a good-looking American novelist in his forties who has lived all over the world, including the Caribbean and Montana. His story is an excruciating prediction of Hemingway's decline and a warning Gellhorn gave herself to be wary of the kind of writer's life that is self-isolating and irresponsible. Hendricks wakes up in Paris one day and finds he cannot write. Until now, he has gone from novel to novel, from one success to another. Writing has been a daily occupation, and his stories have flowed effortlessly. He has not had much contact with reality. His wife has arranged everything around his writing schedule. All he has had to do is write. The irony is that this freedom from daily cares, family responsibilities, and social and political concerns has resulted in a monumental writer's block. Suddenly, nothing he tries to put on the page seems worth saying. He does not understand why this is so and blames his inability to concentrate on external disturbances such as the weather or the quality of the household help.

The unreality of Hendricks's writer's world has been developing for some time and has arisen out of the very conditions that he thinks have made him happy. He likes climates where there are no seasons. He finds the rain in Paris distasteful. Although he is not conscious of it, the change in the weather is a sign of changes in his own life. He leaves home, moves from hotel to hotel, considers an affair, but nothing works. He has lost his conviction as a writer, his pride in his "discipline and skill." He has been hallucinating, and at odd times he has been visited by a figment of his imagination, a psychiatrist, whom he calls Dr. Raumwitz. The psychiatrist silently observes Hendricks and refuses to engage him in discussion. Hendricks's hallucinations continue even after his wife arranges for his treatment by a psychiatrist. For Hendricks, only his invented psychiatrist will do. He resists treatment and flatters himself that somehow he and Raumwitz are co-conspirators. And so they are. For together, they constitute the writer's dialogue with himself, a dialogue that is impervious to influences outside of itself.

In effect, this is what had happened to Hemingway. From the time of their days in Cuba, Gellhorn had seen him wall himself off from others. Hemingway was not as physically isolated as Hendricks, to be sure, but he was giving way to the mentality of a writer who interpreted everything in terms of his imagination, who refused his wife's efforts to engage him in the war and in the importance of world events. Hemingway's strength was his imagination and discipline, but those qualities in themselves were not enough to sustain a writing career. Those qualities, left to feed on themselves, destroyed the writer and, ultimately, the man.

This was a restless time for Gellhorn. As Jacqueline Orsagh has suggested, *The Honeyed Peace* is permeated with a tension the author had trouble resolving, provoked by her guilt in having survived the war. She was adrift, with no conflict to confront except the one within herself.

OPEN MARRIAGE

1952 – 1962

20

Sandy was reaching school age. His mother had some choices to make. When she had first conceived her scheme of adopting and educating Italian children, she had had doubts about the wisdom of placing them in Mexican schools. On a trip to Italy in the summer of 1952, she found a large farm less than a half hour from Rome, where she and Sandy could quietly live. She liked the idea of his growing up on the land with animals, far away from the atom-bomb culture of the United States. He was ready for a Montessori-type kindergarten and could bicycle there himself every day. It was a safe, peaceful environment where she could write and indulge her current love affair with Rome.

On April 10, 1953, Edna arrived in Rome for a visit with Martha and Sandy. They dined at the home of the Irwin Shaws, took trips to the zoo, ate picnic lunches, shopped in Naples, toured museums, saw Pompeii, and boarded the boat to Capri and relaxed, enjoying the magnificent scenery until it rained and Sandy got tonsillitis. Edna—always helpful and easy to please—contented herself with shopping, reading to Sandy, and amusing him. Trips to Florence to see Bernard Berenson and to Rome and more picnics filled out Edna's days until she left in midsummer.

It was not long before Martha's Italian period, like her Mexican interlude, filtered into her fiction. The last story in *The Honeyed Peace,*

251

"Venus Ascendant," is a novella-length study that suggests her maturing interest in the clash of cultures. Enrico Chiaretti, a married, well-to-do professional man takes an amorous interest in Moira, a single English-woman. He finds her lack of purpose in life repugnant and her complacency infuriating, yet at the same time he feels challenged to arouse her passion and to violate her imperviousness. Her English "correctness" taunts him. He vows to "train and explore this unformed creature." He plies her with good food, charming entertainment, and gradually makes her feel that she is the center of his universe. She responds to him with a fierce sensuality that has never before been provoked. What amazes him is how quickly she forsakes her virtue. He attributes this capitulation to her Protestantism, since good Italian girls do not abandon their chastity without much agony, anxiety, crying fits, loss of sleep, indecision, and crisis in their religious convictions.

Chiaretti does not appreciate that Moira takes him to be her kind of gentleman. Given their intimacy, she presumes he can have only one thing in mind: marriage. She cannot imagine what his life is like: a complex balance of wife, profession, social life, lovers, tête-à-têtes for tea and drinks. He does not regard Moira as his responsibility. When she learns that he has a wife, he remarks with bland disingenuousness that he has never made a secret of his marriage and he is surprised she did not know of it. He faults Moira's English relatives in Rome, thinking they surely must know she has become a kept woman. In fact, they accept her silly story about staying out late to help an old woman write her autobiography. Chiaretti feels offended and ridiculous and suspects that the English have fooled him. To complicate the misunderstandings, Moira feels abused because she has been deceived by Chiaretti and is nudged out of her cousin's home when her cousin no longer wants Moira to chaperon her children. Chiaretti is forced to spell out the facts of life for Moira. He can neither marry her nor keep her. He is too well known in Rome to set her up in her own apartment. Moira's belief in herself, in her place in life, is shaken. Yet the story ends with her maintaining a façade of control, leaving for England after six months in Italy to attend her sick mother, and putting on a good show, remarking, "Frightfully bad luck. But I mustn't complain, not after I've had this lovely long holiday."

With "Venus Ascendant," *The Honeyed Peace* ends on a deeply ironic note. Trying to keep her English cool, Moira only succeeds in having her cousin think she is unfeeling and inhuman. This is quite a judgment on a woman whose emotional turmoil has left her devastated and near panic. This story's concentration on male/female relationships, on the conflicts within a woman, and on the tragic/comic misunderstandings of its English and Italian characters reveals a growing sophistication with regard to Gellhorn's point of view. In "Venus Ascendant," characters exhibit an independence and an ability to interact that distinguishes her best postwar fiction.

Italian worldliness and cynicism had their appeal for Gellhorn, who found Americans too cheerfully innocent and the English insufferably smug. However, the kind of elaborate deviousness and chiseling that were characteristic of Italian society troubled her. There was a smallness in the way Italians treated her, and she accused them of hiding their heartlessness with charm. To her friend Martha Symington, she remarked, "You know what got me in Italy. It's the little cheating that they do. If they just wouldn't cheat you just a little *every time!*" It irritated her. "A big cheat," Symington observes, would not have bothered her nearly as much. Sooner or later—as Gellhorn herself realizes—she would fall out of love with a place. Italy was no exception. She could drop it like a love affair, with no repercussions but plenty of fond souvenirs.

A July 1953 encounter in Yugoslavia with David Gurewitsch (traveling with Mrs. Roosevelt) brought back a passion Gellhorn thought she had relinquished. Seeing Gurewitsch again confirmed her belief that he was the love of her life. Although they had not seen each other in over a year, the pain of having lost him was almost more than she could bear. Instantaneously, they resumed their relationship, even as she realized she would never be willing to marry him and live tied down to New York. This meeting, however, also lifted the harsh, melancholy feeling she had experienced when they parted and which had been partly responsible for her wanting to leave Mexico. Now she could accept the fact that she still loved him but would never live with him. It was this need for reconciliation with the past that Hemingway had denied her. He had blocked all avenues to the good memories she would have liked to have kept of their time together. To Mrs. Roosevelt, Gellhorn admitted she could not mention Gurewitsch for fear that she would cry. It would take a long time to get over him. She sensed the awkwardness between herself and Mrs. Roosevelt and wanted to convey to her how sad she felt about it and vowed she would never speak of it again.

* * *

Gellhorn spent much of 1953 in London, her postwar base from which she would "roam freely and return"—rather like an "open marriage." Having recovered from the devastation of war, the city was comfortable and at ease, and she took her time walking in it and meditating on the next phase of her life. She had been seeing Tom Matthews, whom she had known since her days at *The New Republic*. He had recently retired from the editorship of *Time*. He was fifty-three, wealthy, elegant, and an Anglophile looking to retire in England to write the books he had postponed working on for far too long. He was a poet, though Gellhorn doubted his gift and was worried that he was entirely too conventional and scholarly for her taste. He had the chisled, austere features of a founding father. He was fiercely determined to marry her, and was assisted by Sandy's equally persistent demand for a father. Matthews was impeccably tailored and had exquisite manners. She was tempted by him, but she was also scared and keeping their relationship a secret. She did not feel the passion she had had for Gurewitsch. It was just as well, however, since she could not imagine living with such intensity day to day.

Matthews had kept abreast of Gellhorn's career and was at *Time* when Ralph Ingersoll thought of hiring her. Later, when Matthews became managing editor, he asked one of his staff members, Content Peckham, what she thought of his employing Gellhorn at *Time*. He particularly wanted to know how she would be accepted by the other writers. Peckham (now Mrs. Joseph Cowan) was in a tough spot and framed a noncommittal reply, trying to be as fair as she could. She pointed out that there would be resentment among some of the researchers who wanted an opportunity to write, but she thought they would behave themselves, and she left it at that, hoping she had gotten herself off the hook. Although Peckham had been in Gellhorn's Bryn Mawr class, the two women hardly knew each other. However, Peckham did remember an incident in which she took an instant dislike to her classmate. It was during freshmen week in the fall of 1926:

> We were all sitting on the floor—sort of in a circle—and getting ready to elect temporary class officers. There were several groups that came from large girls' schools, so they were all sort of ganging up. And this dame was marching around in the center of the circle saying, "Don't

you think so and so"—one of the St. Louis girls—"would be good?"
And I thought, Who in the name of heaven does she think she is? She
was electioneering as though she were Lee Atwater. And grandstanding
at the same time. I also got the feeling that she thought she would be
much better than so and so.

Matthews did not hire Gellhorn, but Peckham and others at *Time* were
aware that he was courting her.

Still, it was something of a shock to many of Matthews's friends when
he married Gellhorn in London on February 4, 1954. She was nothing
like his first wife, Julie Cuyler, who had died of cancer in 1949. Julie had
had remarkable "presence." She had been a lady in the most gracious sense
of the word. Lovely to look at, nicely boned, with a beautiful voice and
impeccable manners, she had charmed her husband's acquaintances and
friends. As Matthews later described her in his memoir *Jacks or Better,*
Julie was "small, dark, pretty and completely feminine" with an "inherent
sweetness." Martha, on the other hand, seemed big-boned, "a swinging,
rather masculine kind of gal," as Peckham puts it. (Gellhorn had once
described herself to Berenson as equal parts male and female.) Julie had
been thoroughly at home in her husband's world and comfortable with
herself. She had exuded a sense of security with her surroundings that was
markedly absent in most of Martha's contacts with Tom's friends. Martha
had a bravado that seemed suspect. It looked like the ploy of someone
out of her element.

A close friend of Matthews recalls that "we all got the general impression that Martha wanted to be in charge." She was not interested in Tom's
old friends in Princeton, in Newport, or at *Time* and did not want to
be viewed as part of their circle. In fact, she was disgusted by his social
connections and his house in Newport, presided over by his stuffy father,
the Episcopal bishop of New Jersey. In the early months of the marriage,
however, they were quite happy to be in each other's company, and
Sandy was ecstatic to have a daddy. He was growing up sturdily and
would soon be sent to school in Switzerland. As she had predicted to
Berenson before her marriage, Gellhorn tired easily of family life but was
grateful that her husband took a sympathetic view.

When Gellhorn learned that Hemingway was about to visit Berenson in
the spring of 1954, she cut loose with comments on his inept writing,

pointing out how grandiose and snide he had become. She said that if she went to visit Berenson, he must assure her that her ex-husband would be nowhere near. She did not want to feel his "hot jungle breath" on her neck. As a rival for Berenson's affections, she was most curious to hear from him how he took to Hemingway.

Hemingway did not manage a visit to Berenson but wrote him, veering from rehearsing his stories about Gellhorn's ambition and how she had made a fool of him to wishing her well in a marriage to a rich man with a reputation for being "extremely nice." When one of her more sentimental stories, "The Smell of Lilies," appeared in a national magazine, he could not resist ridiculing it, however. Filling in the margins of the story with annotations, he complained of boredom at the clichés and inserted biographical asides. Next to a description of a female character who always wore a belt "clinched tight around her middle, always looking wonderful, unexpected, young," he remarked that this was one of Gellhorn's favorite habits, which was spoiled by her tendency to apply too much makeup. On another sentence—"The rocketing hope was gone from her eyes, clouded over with a milky strange fixed look, ready to be fear"—he circled the word *milky,* and dryly observed that Gellhorn had never learned how to use adjectives. He had begun his criticism of the story by pointing out that Gellhorn had used his line "Nothing ever happens to the brave" as an epigraph for *What Mad Pursuit.* He regretted the line but derided Gellhorn—not known for bravery—for quoting him. Did Berenson know the plot of *What Mad Pursuit*? Hemingway wanted to know. It was the story of a girl who had mistaken a case of crabs for syphilis. It made Hemingway melancholy to think of it. He concluded by observing what a terrible writer Gellhorn had become.

Gellhorn and Matthews spent part of the summer of 1954 in New York. Establishing a pattern that would hold for the entire marriage, she saw many of her friends (such as Leonard Bernstein and his family) separately. Later in the summer, she and Matthews visited Edna, whom Matthews adored, and then they split up—Tom going to Princeton to visit old friends and Martha and Edna taking a vacation together at the Delaware Water Gap. Later, at a party in New York for the newlyweds, Martha ignored Tom's friends and spent her time with Robert Capa's brother, Cornell. On other occasions, she could be downright rude. "She didn't suffer fools, and she had a wider category of who she thought were fools than most people have," suggests one of Matthews's colleagues, who was so incensed he thought of sending Tom a wire that said, "When you get back to England, your friends will still be here." Over the years, Matthews's friends never knew what kind of reception they might get from Gellhorn. As one of them recalls: "She was very moody. If you were coming for a visit, it would be agreed that the four of you would be having dinner. Then you'd get there and find out she'd gone, and you wouldn't even see her."

Few of Matthews's intimates and acquaintances ever got close enough to Gellhorn to understand why he became so enamored of her. To be sure, they appeared a handsome—even awesome—couple to Stanley Flink, a young writer at *Life* who remembers what an urbane, attractive pair they made at parties. Matthews was tall, trim, and athletic—an excellent tennis player who had no trouble keeping up with his active wife. She looked crisp and intellectually interesting. Although they were both born in the Midwest, their speech had a cultivated mid-Atlantic accent that made it impossible to identify them with any particular region. Their conversation was very bright, very witty. They had a special gift for knowing how to entertain each other.

For Matthews, Gellhorn represented something he thought he always wanted. Marrying her would fulfill a certain ambition, a need that had nagged him all his life. He had always wanted to be his own man. He had been born a clergyman's only son in Cincinnati at the turn of the century. Educated together with his sister at home, he grew up a guilt-ridden, timid boy, learning to be "afraid—not only afraid of outsiders and of the outside world but most of all afraid of being judged and found wanting." He had never measured up to his father's standards, but he had remained his mother's "dearest hope." In a poem published during his marriage to Gellhorn, Matthews put it starkly: "We loved my mother and we feared my father." Gloom seemed to pervade his childhood. The city was dirty and other children were menacing. His private tutor seemed a Dickensian blackguard who banished Matthews to a dark closet for fifteen terrifying minutes a day.

Like Gellhorn, Matthews traveled abroad at an early age. He developed a fondness for England and for poetry, but he lacked her confidence and outgoing nature. At school, he behaved like a "shy and pious misfit." Not until he attended Princeton and met Schuyler Jackson, a brilliant undergraduate poet, did Matthews find an outlet for his "adolescent bitterness." Jackson spoke with such force and quickness, he bowled Matthews over, convincing him of poetry's superiority over all other forms of writing, and of the poet's unique place in the literary world. Poetry was "the essence, the distillation of writing itself." Long after Jackson failed his mission to be a great poet, Matthews worshiped him and the very idea of the archetypal writer who was above all pettiness, aloof, creating his own standards and excellences.

With Jackson aiming so high, it was perhaps inevitable that Matthews's own trajectory was set much lower. He never was certain of the value of his own verse—writing to Allen Tate, in January 1942, that he did not regard himself as a significant poet. Matthews had a good ear and his lines scanned well, but by his own account his poems were rather sentimental and self-pitying. Julie Cuyler, with whom he had already fallen in love, called his poetry "morbid." It could not have helped matters when Matthews's class voted him "Worst poet," and Jackson "Most brilliant." A "slow developer in every way," subject to "black depressions," and "lengthy sullen silences," Matthews was grateful to Jackson for sticking with him and often pulling him out of his gloom.

When Matthews began reviewing books for *The New Republic* in 1925, he had a taste of what it might be like to be an independent literary man, if not a great poet. Max Gissen, who worked for Matthews at *Time,* believes that Matthews in the 1920s was the leading book reviewer, an independent critic with a unique style. Edmund Wilson, who had encouraged and advised Matthews, was terribly disappointed when his protégé joined *Time* in 1929 as one of its anonymous editors. In Wilson's book, *Time* was not "respectable journalism." He bluntly told Matthews "*Time* is dirty. . . . And it's getting dirtier." He never spoke to Matthews again.

Initially, the switch from *The New Republic* to *Time* did not seem like such a momentous change to Matthews. After all, at both publications he was reviewing books, not engaging in the "great writing" to which he aspired. It soon became obvious to him that he had become a company man, however. He deplored the way *Time* made every writer conform to the absurd phrases and epithets in its style book. As he told an interviewer years later, he did not have much respect for the magazine. The staff was not well educated; there were certainly no literary stars— just arrogant Ivy Leaguers who did not know nearly as much as they thought. In his own eyes, this was shameful—this air of self-importance *Time* assumed in its lectures to the public on self-improvement.

Yet Matthews endured twenty-four years of what he came to call his "servitude" at *Time.* He had enough money. He did not have to work.

But what were his options? He had no style of his own—so he thought—and he rationalized his years at *Time* by declaring he would make it "respectable . . . if not serious." He saw to it that the books section reviewed more poetry. Max Gissen recalls that Matthews was particularly tough on clichés, stopping everything to call in a young writer for a sharp lecture, circling the offending phrase and demanding that the culprit never do it again.

Matthews had the bearing, the manners, and the backbone of a gentleman. When there were arguments between himself and *Time* owner Henry Luce, more often than not it was Luce who would back down. Matthews was also a man of principle and was outraged when he discovered that Robert Fitzgerald, his colleague at *Time,* was trying to convert Julie, an Episcopalian, to Catholicism. "There are only two or three points that separate us from the Catholics, but those two or three points I consider terribly important," Matthews told Gissen, who thought of him as quite rigid. Matthews should have struck out on his own, Gissen suggests, because in going to *Time* Matthews compromised his integrity.

Something in Matthews's makeup made him submit to Henry Luce's regime even as he rebelled against the corporate tyrant. Early in life, he had been taught that "higher authorities exist, and that they are to be respected and obeyed." True, he had defied, evaded, and challenged the authorities, but in the end he "never doubted that those authorities exist and reign." Better to be Luce's "disloyal, unloving" subject than not to be a subject at all. Full autonomy, for Matthews, was inconceivable.

Gissen saw what this meant when he accompanied Matthews for a weekend visit to his father at the Matthews's huge Newport mansion. It was 1953, and Matthews's wife, Julie, had been dead for over three years. Each morning in a chapel on the grounds of the house, a devout Matthews prayed for her. He had gone to pieces when she died; he was the type of man who could not live without a woman. Gissen thought of him as the hero of a Graham Greene novel: a compassionate, sincere man—indeed a man of religious convictions. Matthews was tortured by the fact that he was praying for Julie yet seeing another woman. He had been unfaithful to her while she was alive, and in her last months of suffering she had taken on a saintly glow that had profoundly moved him. Among her last words to him had been "Love God."

The god in Newport was Matthews' eighty-four-year-old father. "I am fifty-four years old and he still scares me to death," Matthews confided to Gissen. Nothing could be said to contradict the elder Matthews, and there was nothing that could be said that the father did not contradict, disapprove of, or improve upon in his authoritarian manner. Gissen saw that the father had totally dominated the son.

Although Matthews never knew how to break away from his father's authority, he managed to leave Luce when *Time* produced a scurrilous attack on his college classmate and friend Adlai Stevenson. Matthews knew virtually nothing about politics, Gissen observes. Matthews once recalled being present for a "skull session" of Stevenson's advisers. At one point, Stevenson turned to Matthews for his opinion. "I think you should declare war on Ohio," Matthews replied by way of demonstrating how utterly out of his element politics were. However, *Time* had produced a cover story after Stevenson's nomination in 1952 that was so malignant, Matthews personally edited the entire piece, taking it away from an editor whom he referred to as a "vulture in human form and a son-of-a-bitch unworthy of the name." Thereafter, Matthews was not allowed to edit political pieces. He felt he had no choice but to resign.

The departure from *Time* signaled Matthews' disaffection with his country. "This is not my day in America," he announced in *Name and Address*. His reason was the same as Gellhorn's: McCarthyism. America had become obsessed with national security and with the "Communist threat. . . . The United States has become an exclusive society. Our demagogues now orate about *preserving* America's liberties, not attaining them." The "fancied moral superiority of America" disgusted him and seemed almost as repugnant as "the outspoken German claim to be the master race." In her calendar for March 1954, Edna Gellhorn confided her fear that in the current climate she doubted that the Bill of Rights could be approved by the Congress.

Some of Matthews's friends believe that Gellhorn had much to do with his angry rejection of America. The truth is she encouraged his lifelong tendency to reject American vulgarity. He had a temperament that was at least as fastidious as hers. If he now spoke with some violence on the subject of American crassness, it was because of all those years he had kept himself in check. Unlike Gellhorn, he had not gone off on his own in desperate search of a style and way of life befitting a writer. Except for brief leaves of absence, he had remained in Princeton, commuting to New York City, while she had trusted her own instincts and had always lived by her own authority.

With the death of his wife and his departure from *Time,* Matthews quickly fell under Gellhorn's spell. He liked women and felt comfortable with them. Strong women did not intimidate him. Indeed, he sought them out and became a part of their circle—as he had with Laura Riding in the 1930s until she married his beloved friend Schuyler Jackson. However, Riding had not been sexually attractive to Matthews, who seemed to crave women who combined a certain allure with authority. Matthews's success with women was due, in part, to his diffidence. It was endearing—and amusing to Max Gissen, who spoke to an interviewer about how retiring Matthews was with women. He adored women and could be foolish about them. If a woman was good-looking, she could get away with almost anything.

As with Gurewitsch, Gellhorn found the sympathetic, urbane, good-looking man irresistible. He let her make plans. He gave her room. She would pursue her career, travel—have all the things an ambitious, restless woman wanted. He was amused and fascinated by their differences: by her need to control things; by his capitulation to fate; by her lively reactions to life's possibilities; by his intense acceptance of "doom." He had money. They would live comfortably. He had his own writing to do, but he did not look upon her as a competitor. It would be a congenial life, with Matthews providing a soothing sense of security that the high-strung Gellhorn deeply appreciated. As one of Gellhorn's friends put it, Matthews had the subtle intelligence and the exquisite delicacy to calm Gellhorn without her even realizing it.

For much of his career, Matthews felt at though he had been on a treadmill. He had not paid enough attention to where he was going. He had no heroic account to give of himself. He had said nothing memorable. The best he could offer was that he had "put my best foot forward. I made a leg." Gellhorn gave him quite a kick, with her penchant for taking on the world—reporting for the *Times* of London in September 1954 about the Senate hearings investigating Joseph McCarthy and noting that no one had the nerve to censure McCarthyism itself. Outrage in a beautiful woman could be very appealing. Matthews got her access to Adlai Stevenson, to whom she could vent her feelings about Israel, the Gaza strip, and Arab refugees. Not caring passionately about politics himself, Matthews was nevertheless swept up, for a time, in Gellhorn's activities.

At the outset, marrying Matthews seemed to entail no great compromise for Gellhorn. They both wanted to live in England. He had raised his own family (four grown sons) and would be sympathetic about Sandy's needs (by coincidence, he had a son named Sandy), and he delighted in Edna's periodic visits to them in England. She would dine with her daughter's friends, take Sandy on various excursions (when he was home from private school in Switzerland), shop, watch her son-in-law play tennis, and accompany Martha and Tom on short sight-seeing trips on the Continent.

In Martha's trashy, well-paying fiction (read her *Collier's* story "The Good Husband") and in her journalism, she developed considerable fondness for marriage and other domestic institutions. This was her most settled period. She practically doted on the calm, articulate, and sensible English electoral system. Even when charges of treason were leveled against government officials, she praised Parliament for its sane, good-humored discussion of the matter. It seemed wonderfully refreshing to observe the English steadfastly refuse to give way to anything like American hysteria about Communism. There was to be no McCarthyism in England. So taken was she with British fairness and democracy that she did not for a moment question whether the country had been perhaps a bit too complacent about men such as Burgess and Maclean who, after all, turned out to be spies.

Trips to Israel and Poland reflected the undercurrent of Gellhorn's temperament. They were tantamount to sabbaticals from family life and from her burdensome house in England. She craved periods when she could be off on her own, and Matthews indulged her in these moods. Yet she missed him terribly, marveling at how bound she felt to him and surprised at her sense of incompleteness—a new experience for a woman who reveled in solitary travel.

England was peace and comfort and civility when she wanted those things, but Israel was a bold pioneer society and Poland a heroic, irrepressible state. Both countries reminded her of what the war had been about. The Poles and the Jews both had been threatened with complete extermination. Now Israel gallantly faced hostile Arab multitudes; Poland still refused to give up its quest for independence even after centuries of foreign domination. The Israelis had a sincerity and oneness of purpose that the first Americans must have had. It was no larger than New Jersey, Gellhorn pointed out in an article in *The New Republic;* Israel was a kind of melting pot of peoples, and, curiously, a more secure society because its people spoke each other's languages. The romantic strain in the Polish character charmed Gellhorn, who loved the hand kissing and impeccable old-world manners of the men, young and old. She was now past fifty, and yet she had no trouble associating with Polish youth. Nearly thirty years earlier, she had felt at home with French students; now the sophisticated Polish students and their "lion-hearted gaiety" thrilled her. These were rugged people who had not given up thinking for themselves. Americans, on the other hand, had become stuck in a "fear neurosis," as she later came to call it. Communists, labor organizers, and various social protestors had always been branded subversive by an insecure society. She had no patience with this brand of anti-Communism—not when the Poles had a real, external enemy to confront.

Gellhorn had long since tired of explaining to her friends why she lived abroad, but she took one more humorous stab at it in an article for *Harper's Magazine.* In earlier pieces, she had mentioned her delight in the clarity of English public speech. Now she remarked on her fondness for the stately language of the London *Times.* The paper's soberness soothed her mornings and helped her prepare for the day. Like so much else in English life, the newspaper created no fuss. It used to be that she hated the gray, rainy weather. Now she was grateful to slop around with the rest of the population in old clothes and rain gear. It so eased the mind not to worry about fashion, said this most fashionable of women. It would have been truer for her to have said that just then it suited her fancy to hear the English compliment her on an ensemble she had worn "four years running."

Gellhorn did not minimize the inconveniences of London life. For example, the English had never gotten "the hang of central heating." Her furnace had exploded more than once, and the electrical system seemed to date from Edison's day. The plumbing was none too good (causing the ceiling to fall) and the shops were none too efficient in filling her orders for things such as writing paper and food. However, she made it all sound pleasantly *daft*— an English word she treasured. The English had quaint terms for this survivable incompetence, such as *muddling through.*

The English could be wildly eccentric, and no one seemed to take particular notice: "So he's getting married again? His fifth, is it? Well, well, never say die." Through the years, Gellhorn had derived much pleasure from her dear friend Lady Diana Cooper, whose incredible variety of ailments and propensity for expecting the worst had not prevented her from savoring a long, successful life. After one of Lady Diana's trips, Gellhorn wrote her:

> If I hadn't heard you were safely back at Chantilly, I would be frantic for fear you were dead as a smelt. . . . Have all the pains and anguishes gone? Was it anything like the year you decided your heart was weak

or the year you had cancer? It's awful to enjoy your ailments as much as I do, but they've always been so wonderful, so fatal and so sad that I cannot help liking them.

Gellhorn believed the English ignored eccentricity out of politeness. She had never known a more varied vocabulary of graciousness. The "background music of life in London" was this "chorus of please, thank you, may I, would you, so sorry, how kind of you, no trouble at all," and so on. To her delight, Sandy had picked up this behavior, adding the word *please* to his mother's order "Go to bed now, darling." London was restful and cozy, and the large number of English expressions Gellhorn quoted in her article and would use in her collection of stories *Two by Two* suggest how completely she was able to immerse herself in English life.

Two by Two is dedicated "To Tom, With Love." It is Gellhorn's most carefully constructed collection of stories. Each one is about a marriage and takes for its theme a phrase from the marriage vows: "For Better or Worse," "For Richer for Poorer," "In Sickness and in Health," "Till Death Us Do Part." As in "Venus Ascendant," these stories reveal a mature Gellhorn, the expatriate shrewdly assessing the Italians, the English, the French, the Americans, and other nationalities. While she is sympathetic to her characters, the ironic stance of the well-traveled observer pervades her stories.

In "For Better or Worse," Kitty, an American woman, devotes her whole life to her Italian husband, Andrea. The heir of a large estate, Andrea feels useless—a captive of his inheritance who must patiently await his father's relinquishment of authority and endure the German occupation of his country. Then the Americans arrive and Andrea offers himself as an interpreter, abandons his estate for a tour of duty with the U. S. Army, and returns home as "Andy"—a new man planning a new life for himself and Kitty in Montana. At first, Kitty is frightened by this change of character, then she sees that her very devotion to Andrea has abetted his passivity and she welcomes his transformation. And then she dreads the return of his fatalism as he becomes mired once again in the postwar conditions of his estate.

As in all the stories of *Two by Two,* love itself is not enough. What counts is how that love is expressed in different temperaments and in different circumstances. Gellhorn is not a determinist; people are capable of changing their lives, but these changes are accomplished at great cost. Kitty's kind of unqualified love both debilitates and invigorates Andrea, and that is the paradox of their marriage, a paradox she has grown to appreciate but is powerless to resolve.

"For Better or Worse" reveals how the themes of Matthews's life entered Gellhorn's creative work. She did not use him as a character or herself as a narrator, but the portrait of Andrea, tied to an ancestral home, dominated by his authoritarian father, dogged by his sense of doom, recalls Matthews's old-world mentality. At any earlier age, Gellhorn would surely have had less patience and interest in the fatalistic aristocrat of her story, but now the pull of home, family, and tradition had more of a place in her imagination. She could actually see it: How a son would feel bound to the role history had cast for him. Like Matthews, Andrea yearns for a great change in his life, seems on the verge of making it, and then mournfully acknowledges it is too late for him to become a new man. As Matthews would later write in *Jacks or Better:* "I quit my job in New York twenty-one years ago and went to live in England, 'to learn to write'—but it was too late or I was too lazy."

"For Better or Worse" has a romantic, yearning quality that barely escapes sentimentality. By contrast, "For Richer for Poorer" is refreshingly astringent, with lots of sharp dialogue. The story concentrates on Rose Answell, an ambitious women who schemes to make her pliable husband, Ian, a cabinet minister. She has a great love of position and no love for Ian after he realizes his marriage and family life have been a sham. She abandons him as soon as she sees he is serious about retiring to farming. Much of the story's interest comes from observing Rose's maneuvers in England's high social and political life and in her dealing with ladies whose "beauty was a public service." They are "elegant, serene . . . able and sportingly willing to please," and find Rose's conniving progress to the top beyond what their conventions will allow. Gellhorn conveyed their feelings through the tone of their dialogue— as she did with Rose, whose coldheartedness needs no explanation after this cutting exchange with Ian:

> "I thought Chloe was looking a treat," Ian said.
> "Oh, did you? I thought she seemed rather haggard. And she never varies, does she? I find that tiddily talk quite exasperating in the long run."

Sensible and funny and generous, Ian thought, what more could anyone be? But there was something more and better, and he did not know exactly what it was.

"She's a very good friend."

"Oh, Ian, what a *pointless* thing to say."

Gellhorn avoided melodrama in her depiction of Rose by showing how Ian and other men have allowed themselves to be manipulated by her. When Ian realizes Rose is all ambition, he leaves her, and she easily switches to another man whose credentials for the cabinet she can brighten.

"For Richer for Poorer" is set in a highly polished world of surfaces that Gellhorn knew well from her friendships with Lady Diana Cooper and Virginia Cowles. The story begins with Lady Harriet Adderford frowning at "the exquisite curve of her mouth" in a mirror. She is unhappy about her lipstick. The seemingly trivial detail is precisely the point of Gellhorn's art: Ladies and gentlemen in this society build their reputations by attention to esthetic details, to form and fashion. Rose Answell irritates Lady Harriet primarily because of her style, which reflects aspirations that threaten to upset polite society.

"In Sickness and in Health" is the least satisfying story in *Two by Two*. It is a rather maudlin study of a man who cannot bring himself to leave his childlike wife, a woman who has suffered over many years with a heart condition so severe the couple has not been able to make love. Originally published as "The Smell of Lilies" in *The Atlantic Monthly*, its excessive emotionality is uncomfortably close in spirit to Gellhorn's commercial stories, but it does provide a counterbalancing tone to the piquancy of "For Richer for Poorer."

"Till Death Us Do Part" is the most haunting episode of *Two by Two*. Based in part on Robert Capa, who died in 1954 photographing the war in Indochina, the story demonstrates Gellhorn's most complex treatment of autobiographical material. A world-famous photographer, Bara, as Capa is called in the story, has had one true love in his life and, in turn, is loved by a woman who regards him as her one true love. Helen Richards cannot have him—not all of him—because he has never stopped loving Suzy, his unfaithful yet ideal soul mate. Suzy, also a photographer, has died in Spain just as Capa's beloved, Gerda, did.

The first part of "Till Death Us Do Part" is about Bara's death and Helen's attempts to cope with it, to understand her attraction to him, and his inability fully to reciprocate her love. The second part constitutes the testimony of Lep, Bara's closest male friend, who explains to Marushka (Martha) Bara's life in terms of her own. Marushka is the pet name Lep and Bara have for correspondent Mary Hallett, who amuses them because of her anger. She is "angry to pop," Lep reports to Bara, in describing her reaction to the extreme casualties sustained by Allied soldiers invading Italy. In her fondness for Poles, in her obvious happiness in war and sharing the men's vulnerability, Hallett is a dead ringer for Gellhorn.

Marushka and Bara see each other only for brief periods of time, yet Bara calls her my "sister *and* brother," since she reflects both his male and female sides. Capa was Gellhorn's twin. Both were noncombatants, aggressive on their assignments, willing to risk their lives to witness war, yet not wholly a part of the action. Capa never pretended—as Hemingway did—to be a soldier or an intelligence agent. Capa's pictures and Gellhorn's dispatches were important, but they never overrated their celebrity or influence and never made themselves the main event.

There is something childish in Marushka's discontent with the world which recalls Gellhorn's. Marushka often behaves like a frantic child who sees the world collapsing on her head. It amuses Bara that she should take human suffering so personally. Who could live with the weight of the world always present on one's shoulders? No wonder they often find themselves on opposite sides of the street, furious with each other. How can he take seriously a woman who is always so serious about the world's fate? How can she take seriously a man who seems to take nothing seriously? In his view, the world will never change, but she insists on progress and deliverance. She has this "major tic" about injustice and does not understand that injustice is not an aberration but something built into the very nature of things. To him, it seems futile and foolish to be constantly hectoring the world to reform itself.

Gellhorn knew how well Capa understood her. In "Till Death Us Do Part," this realization became Bara's observation that "Marushka loved humanity . . . but people made her nervous." There it was, in a nutshell. Her view of things was so enormous. She had been taught to embrace the world on such a large scale that individuals, sooner or later, bored or irritated her. How could she make a life with one man when there was the whole world to think of? For Capa, as for Bara, the premise to begin with was that the world was lost. Know that, and perhaps you could enjoy yourself, find love, and be contented with your friends. For Bara, there is almost something insane about Marushka's badgering people to come to the immediate aid of others. Certainly Hemingway had felt this pressure to take on the world and resented never really having Gellhorn to himself.

Capa thrived on his disagreements with Gellhorn. Capa's quarrel with Gellhorn, like Bara's with Marushka, was a family spat. They never stopped talking to or amusing each other, and their politics were the same even when they disagreed on the ultimate effectiveness of politics. She admired his winning personality. He was a likable fellow and a healer. He brought people together and accomplished a kind of social comity, whereas for all her grand plans, she actually produced—to use Marushka's word—"nothing." Bara is deeply worried when Marushka's visits to concentration camps destroy her faith in human perfectibility. When she no longer expresses her anger, he is unnerved, for he has always counted on the energy of her outrage as fuel for his own accommodation with life's disappointments. To a large extent, they survived on their memories of Spain. As Lep puts it, Spain is the "home" of Marushka's heart. It is where "everyone was poor and friends," fighting passionately for "the rights and dignity of man."

Although Gellhorn had resolved to cover war no more, it was with her all the time. She had found nothing to take its place, and she felt compelled to come to terms with her war correspondent's experience. The result was *The Face of War,* a collection of her *Collier's* dispatches with an introduction and autobiographical glosses on her decades of war reporting. Although she has always tried to maintain complete separation between her work and her life, between her career and interest in her personality, *The Face of War,* in fact, proves these aspects of her life are inseparable, for its introduction begins with an autobiographical statement about her youthful belief in the "perfectibility of man, and in progress," which journalism as a "guiding light" would support. Looking back upon it, she felt her pride in her professional prowess was "absurd." As in *The Honeyed Peace,* she expressed some guilt in surviving the wars, calling herself "a special type of war profiteer." She still professed the educational function of journalism, but she no longer believed it had much to do with making the world a better place. It was important to keep the record straight. Carefully done, journalism was a "form of honorable behavior."

The advent of nuclear weapons had convinced Gellhorn of the ultimate idiocy of all wars. The world now had the power to destroy itself and perhaps only the memory and imagination of other wars could prevent it from annihilating the future. *The Face of War* earned her the best reviews of her career. In *The New York Times,* Herbert Mitgang called it a "brilliant anti-war book that is as fresh as if written for this morning." In *The New Statesman,* Nigel Nicolson called her "one of the best correspondents whom the War produced." Like Mitgang, he was impressed with the immediacy of her reports. They seemed to write themselves. He found a curious contradiction in her condemnation of war, however. He noted how intensely she identified with the Spanish cause, the nobility she found in the Finns and in the Chinese who fought to repel invaders. He was responding, in fact, to her own contradictions (she used this word about herself in the introduction), which friends had pondered for years. "Martha was always talking pacifism and couldn't wait to get to the frontline trenches," one of her friends recalls, "it was absolutely a scream." As Emily Norcross observes:

> The thing that stunned me in our early adulthood when she started writing seriously and I was still quite a close friend of hers was that she was *vehemently* a pacifist and yet she kept writing passionately about war. I thought it was just cuckoo and terribly funny.

Many years after the Spanish Civil War, Martha Love Symington met Gellhorn in Spain and listened to her memories of war: "Well, when I was here before, they were shooting in the streets, and I was in the trenches." Gellhorn made it all seem "very dramatic, *very dramatic,*" to her friend.

Each year with Matthews and family proved to be more of a strain. Gellhorn did not get along with his children especially well, and she hated holiday gatherings, the exchanging of presents, and entertaining people— which was a peculiar torture for her. It was some relief to travel in Europe, visit friends in France and Mexico, and labor away at her writing, but it was all so correct and so predictable. What she lacked was that sense of creating a life for herself. She knew she was a trial for both her son Sandy and Tom, that she had turned them into nomads like herself.

In May of 1959, Martha traveled through Spain looking for a "rentable castle." Although she had made several quick visits to her mother (sometimes with Sandy and Tom), it had been ten years since she had taken a close look at her native land. Matthews proposed an American tour and a jointly authored book that would assess the changes he had begun to note in his autobiography *Name and Address,* a draft of which Edna had read in July of 1958, along with *The Honeyed Peace.* Not much interested in co-authorship or in the United States, Martha brightened up when Tom suggested they take her mother along on their ride across the country. Edna was agreeable so long as the couple started their trip by visiting St. Louis.

Matthews arrived in New York a few days before Gellhorn and met her at Idlewild (now Kennedy) Airport. She detested New York, and the airport did nothing to improve her mood when she found she had to lug her heavy suitcase through customs by herself. It was enough to "kill an ox," she remarked to Tom before having to negotiate her way through an electronic door. Somehow the mechanism baffled her and she stopped in mid-stride, almost getting caught in the closing automatic doors. "Well, I never! What a thing," she exclaimed in an accent that had a distinctly British intonation.

St. Louis was always a bother for Martha. Why did people have cocktail parties at five-thirty and not eat dinner until nine-thirty? Why did restaurants serve twenty-ounce steaks and advertise their weight on the menu? She could not understand why Tom bought Mexican jumping beans (currently in vogue). What were they for? she asked. "For company," he replied. Chewing gum was everywhere, like the plague, she noted, as she pulled some off her sweater. They went to see Liberace one evening and were at a loss as to what to say about him. "He plays the piano very nicely," Edna remarked with characteristic geniality.

Tom adored Edna. She had a gift for finding what was good in everything. He thought her devotion to St. Louis was splendid. He even liked St. Louis—much to Martha's irritation. He conceded the city's looks were none too appealing, but he liked the quiet, tree-lined streets and private neighborhoods closed off by gateways. In his estimation, it was a congenial place with a history of tolerance that might be explained by its commingling of the French and the German refugees who had fled the failed revolutions of 1848.

Martha was not impressed with Tom's liking St. Louis, but her friends were. He seemed like such a sensible person, sincere in his attachment to the city. They could see he was devoted to Edna and respectful of Martha.

Emily Norcross observed that Tom was very taken with Martha's charm and wit and "terrific sense of fun. He was authentic, a gentleman in every sense of the word." His interest in the city and in Edna would survive his marriage to Martha. Each year after Edna's death in 1970, he sent a thousand-dollar check in her memory to the United Nations Association, one of her favorite causes.

Even though Martha could hardly share Tom's affection for St. Louis, their time together there was pleasant enough, and friends saw no sign of the acrimony that would soon ruin the marriage. William Julius Polk took Martha and Tom to a new development in St. Louis around Olive Street, called Gaslight Square. It was an unpretentious area filled with old antique shops—not the posh kind but rather run-down, even junky, places where one could find some real bargains. The area had the air of a village green. People could wander about until midnight. Polk took Martha and Tom to a bar-nightclub called The Crystal Palace. It was a glittery place filled with wonderful chandeliers and other glassworks from the collection of a family of artisans who had come to St. Louis at the turn of the century. Their sons had built The Crystal Palace, which featured Mike Nichols, Elaine May, the Smothers Brothers, Hildegarde, Bobby Short, and other outstanding performers. The next day, Martha called Polk to say they had had such a good time that they almost had thought of returning to America to live. This was not really a serious possibility, but Polk was awfully pleased, given Martha's usual contempt for the city.

Gaslight Square delighted Martha because it preserved some of the older character of a city that was prone to tear down everything in the name of progress. As far as she was concerned, no one had a sense of history. She visited private schools and branded the children "over-privileged poops and phlegmatic doughheads." She did not understand why they did not speak in sentences, and she got into arguments with students and college professors over her condemnation of American education. It was her impression that they felt it was un-American to ask so many questions and to criticize American institutions. She was suspicious of all the people who kept telling her how happy they were. "What about all the overworked psychiatrists and the loony bins? Anyhow, happiness, that's no way for grown-up people to talk," she pointed out to Matthews. She was put out by the signs of conformism, the emphasis on having well-adjusted children. "It makes me very nervous. I'd hate to be adjusted, and I think it's an awful thing to do to children," she concluded.

"I saw one St. Louis, M. saw another," Matthews admits in *O My America*. Their feelings coincided only when they observed Edna address a meeting of the League of Women Voters. He liked her speech. She was spontaneous, "forthright and funny without trying to be, and she never faltered. We all woke up and felt warm and alive again." Martha had another good moment when she agreed with a museum guard about some objectionable modern pictures. Usually, however, she felt like a foreigner.

The three of them crossed the country from Denver to Seattle to Portland (where Edna visited with Stanley Pennell), to several parts of California, Arizona, New Mexico, Texas, and Florida. From time to time, Martha would give vent to heated generalizations—a sign of her Germanic blood, she thought. Martha stated that American women, for example, were hardly better than "Arab females" in the way they obeyed their husbands. Edna "sighed, lightly." American women were chauffeurs for their children, cooks, and housekeepers and spent the rest of the time building up their husband's egos. "If I had to work as hard as most of the women I see, and notably the young women, I'd go into a decline," Martha asserted. "Yes," Edna remarked, keeping her voice neutral. Even worse, what time American woman had to themselves was wasted on shopping sprees, Martha claimed in a lengthy monologue. "Oh, my child," Edna interjected in the space between her daughter's long speeches. Martha wanted to know what her mother meant by the expression. "I was thinking about generalizations," Edna replied. "And how difficult they are." Martha was forced to concede the idiocy of all generalizations and to cease her tirade.

Lots of things were new and amusing to this Europeanized couple—such as motels and drive-in movie theaters. They were saddened and outraged by how much of the natural beauty of the West had been destroyed. Most of the Indians they saw were a sorry group of human beings who lived in dingy surroundings or looked just like other Americans. Conversation was often difficult as soon as Gellhorn and Matthews announced they lived in England. Americans could not imagine why other Americans would want to live abroad. San Francisco was still a pleasure—cleaner than most cities and more visually interesting. Los Angeles's traffic and urban sprawl were appalling, and Hollywood served only as a brief entertainment. It was Edna's idea to travel to the Southwest, where they enjoyed good solid food, more interesting Indians, and better conversation. Even here, however, Martha was distrustful of Texans who talked up Dallas as though they were trying to convert themselves. She had a hankering to see what she called "the pea-brained, talkative South" she and Edna had explored in the late 1940s.

Florida had changed greatly, having gone through the "development" Martha detested in other places. Military installations and motels so broke up the landscape that it looked "explosive." When they finally found a quiet place that resembled the vanishing past of ten years earlier, they stayed two happy weeks, viewing a dazzling, expansive Gulf from their "screened-in balcony." It was time to call an end to their journey.

Matthews wanted to believe that the steady, thoughtful, and sensitive Edna was representative of some deeper truth that belied the junked-up spectacle that was now the United States. Martha had little sympathy for her husband's worry over what it meant to be an American. He reminded her of Henry James. Gellhorn only wanted to get back to London and to writing fiction. Her novel *His Own Man* demonstrated that her imagination had taken a sharp turn away from her native land. As one of the novel's reviewers commented, it gave the reader "the essence of Paris" by concentrating on the smug, comfortable career of Ben Eckhardt, a perpetual student in Chinese history who drops his French-American lover for a wealthy Englishwoman, who slowly corrupts him and deprives him of his vaunted independence.

His Own Man is one of Gellhorn's most tightly constructed novels, full of sardonic humor and cold, worldly wisdom on the subject of the sexes and marriage. As in *Pretty Tales for Tired People,* over and over again her male and female characters circle around the issue of commitment to each other. There are well married, happy couples in her fiction, but they are a rarity and serve only as fixed points in an unstable marital universe, where the most urbane couples take lovers and treat marriage as a form of convenience, as a necessary—even comfortable—institution but seldom as a permanently romantic or inviolable union. As Gellhorn admitted to an interviewer, with *Pretty Tales for Tired People,* she had picked a title that made trouble for her: "Half my friends seemed to take it as a personal insult, and even the favorable reviewers in the United States seemed to think I was being unpleasantly frivolous or plain obscure."

The fiction of these years is not without compassion for married life, but there is a bitterness in it that seems personal—as one interviewer (mentioning Gellhorn's divorces) pointed out. Gellhorn was startled: "I never thought of the stories like that. Now you mention it, I suppose they all are about divorces."

Much of Gellhorn's imaginative work in the late 1950s and early 1960s is about couples who go wrong. What went wrong with her and Matthews? In a word, she was "a traveler in life," a term that Jessica de Camberges applies to Ben Eckhardt after he abandons her. He is from Milwaukee, but it might as well be St. Louis. He is the type of person Gellhorn knew well, because in some ways he was herself. Speaking of Milwaukee, Ben explains, "I had a perfectly okay time, living the way everyone I knew lived, but it ran on rails. I couldn't see anything in it." Ben tires of women because he tires of having things expected of him. He has trouble staying put and feels trapped.

Years later, Gellhorn would make snide, dismissive comments on a marriage that was dull, absurd, and futile. She felt as if she was in retirement and obviously resented Eleanor Roosevelt's assumption that she lacked for nothing, that she was fine because she had a husband to look after her. She felt inauthentic in a marriage to a wealthy man and ensconced in a magnificent residence.

Gellhorn complained that Roosevelt had become less of a factor in her life. The truth was that Roosevelt could not understand her. In Gellhorn's reluctance to leave Mexico to be with Gurewitsch, there had been a selfishness that Roosevelt could not abide. Roosevelt rarely gossiped, but on one occasion she was so incensed by Gellhorn's comments about Sandy that she shared the letter with close friends who knew Gellhorn well. "When you finish it, throw it away," she told them. She had saved many of Gellhorn's letters, but the egotism of this one appalled her. Roosevelt's reaction was remarkable, for "Once Mrs. Roosevelt loved you, she always loved you," as one of her intimate friends put it. She was an utterly constant and loyal friend.

Gellhorn and Matthews would not divorce until 1963, but she was already eyeing a life alone in Africa in 1962. When Mary Hall visited her in London, Gellhorn admitted she was having trouble remaining at home. She wanted to be off. Her period of English domesticity was drawing to a close. If Matthews delighted in Gellhorn's "terrific sense of fun," it was also a trial to find out how much it would take to amuse her. England was now his home. He was not that fond of sight-seeing and running off to the ends of the world. He admired Gellhorn's reporting on the Eichmann trial, on Israel, and on Poland, but the marriage was not working. His friends saw increasing signs of his impatience with her. Never disposed to like her, they saw in her a woman who could no longer control her man. Matthews reached a point where he no longer felt he could stand being ruled by her whims and enthusiasms. He longed for something more solid, more permanent. To live a life by phases—first in one place, then another—was not to his taste. Gellhorn had given real evidence of settling down in London, but in fact she treated it and her marriage in an open-ended fashion. To Matthews, Gellhorn lacked gravity.

Matthews thought too seriously of himself and of marriage to go on in Gellhorn's way. He had been born in a generation that regarded itself as "the hope of the world" and then had felt defeated by all he and his generation had not accomplished. His residence in England had marked a new beginning. For a time, he and Gellhorn were able to believe they had gotten through to the peace and happiness of a life together and the hard work of writing books, but a sense of finality and emptiness overcame Matthews. Doom pervades his autobiography *Jacks or Better.* It had to weigh heavily on Gellhorn, who was not about to sit still for such melancholy and self-pity. They were united in castigating a world that was polluting and tearing itself apart, but only Matthews would write in such mournful terms about a "collapsing civilization."

Even as Gellhorn was fretting over what terrible shape the world was in, she was lauding the importance of the private conscience, of the Europeans who had defied the Nazis and helped the Jews, of the Poles who stoutly maintained their individualism in a totalitarian system—and expecting great things from the Kennedy administration. Africa would be another Mexico—although she could not foresee that this next self-indulgent interlude would be interrupted by a new kind of war that once again would plunge her into the fate of humanity—this time leading to a writer's block that would last nearly half a decade.

AFRICA AND A NEW KIND OF WAR

1960–1966

21

Gellhorn spent the spring of 1960 in Poland. She could no longer abide London. Life there now seemed too easy. In Poland a few years earlier, she had concentrated on politics. The subject inevitably arose again, but this time her focus was on the culture. As inept and destructive as the Communist regime was, it had fostered education and tolerated culture. All over Poland, she discovered theatrical companies and an interest in the arts that astonished her. In one hideous Silesian mining town, she found a theater performing Arthur Miller's *A View from the Bridge.* Having just toured America, she was certain one could not find anything comparable in, say, Alton, Illinois. The Polish government did not deserve much credit; rather, it did not dare to suppress the Polish public's demand for high art.

Poles yearned for a look at the West. It delighted them to think there were people like Gellhorn free to travel just about anywhere. It pained her to see how little contact they had with the outside world. Consequently, she used her own money to endow what she called "the Polish Fun Fellowship," which was to be used by a Pole to visit as many museums in France or Italy as the time limitations on a Polish passport would allow. For some reason, the Polish government acceded to this wacky plan, and the first "Fun Fellow" lived up to her hopes, but the government subverted her intentions by sending a second who was its own loyal adherent.

A year later, Gellhorn was reporting on Arab refugees in the Middle East. She had always had a strong bias in favor of Israel, but she had gone to the region to visit several refugee camps, to see how people lived and to hear them describe their feelings about themselves and Israel. She did not claim to be reporting on a representative sampling of refugees, but she found their responses to her questions so uniform that she could not resist generalizing from her experience. Her writing abounds with clear, vivid descriptions of the refugees she met. There is no doubt that she tried to engage herself with their problems, but everywhere she was met with the same attitude: Israel should not exist. It should be driven into the sea. She listened to wild reports of massacres supposedly perpetrated by merciless Israelis. That Israel had won two wars meant nothing. Israel should be forced to give up everything, even though the refugees had made it clear that if the Arab nations had been victorious, the Israelis would have been massacred. Finally, Gellhorn lost her temper and shouted terrible things about Israel's right of conquest and its historic claim to Palestine. In the end, she could not identify with the refugees because they were unable to identify with others. They pitied only themselves and had shown no mercy toward others.

In May and June of 1961, Gellhorn collected her information on Arab refugees and attended the Eichmann trial in Israel. She was incensed by world opinion that ignored the moral and historic importance of bringing to justice a man who had been in charge of robbing humanity of 6 million lives. She was full of admiration for the Israeli judges who proceeded in a coherent, orderly fashion with profound respect for "rules of evidence." She was fascinated with Eichmann, with the way he tried to minimize his role in the Nazi bureaucracy of extermination. In his glass booth, he sat virtually impassive, giving spectators little to observe other than a taut mouth and a small tic beneath his left eye, better prepared than his attorney and voluble on the intricacies of his job. He was, in Gellhorn's estimation, "the greatest organization man of all time," identifying absolutely with the Nazi state, doing what he was told, and justifying the most heinous crimes by deferring the consideration of all moral issues to the nation's leader.

Gellhorn wondered whether postwar Germany had managed to surmount the legacy of Nazism. Her trip there in the early winter of 1962 was not reassuring. She felt uncomfortable about German obedience to authority and about the closed climate that made it difficult to discuss ideas. Many students she met seemed to think it was unpatriotic to criticize their government. It was a relief, however, to see that the younger generation rejected militarism and appeared to have no attraction to the dress and paraphernalia of war that Hitler had exploited so successfully. Yet these young men and women did not seem to understand the purpose of the Nuremberg trials and treated them merely as a national humiliation. Similarly, the import of the Eichmann trial was lost upon them, and she deplored their inability to empathize with the plight of others.

German women bothered Gellhorn. She called them the "Arab women of the West." Their submission to authority was even greater than what she had observed and deplored in American women a few years earlier. In general, Germans had little notion of civil liberties, and Gellhorn doubted their capacity to create a genuine democracy.

An underlying theme pervaded Gellhorn's writing during this period. Like her mother, she cared deeply about being a good citizen, about taking responsibility for one's own actions and calling one's government to account when it failed to serve the public welfare. Citizens had an obligation to be aware of more than themselves. They had to know about the greater part they played in community and world affairs. This was, in large part, why she wrote. As she explained in a letter to President Kennedy, since World War II the United States had lost its purpose and failed to understand the tenor of history. With Kennedy's election, the country seemed to have revived.

Kennedy was the first American President since Roosevelt to stir Gellhorn's imagination. She had met the President and his wife and had confided to James Gavin (still one of her close friends) her fondness for them. She had very personal reasons for feeling grateful to the new President, for he had used his influence to obtain American citizenship for twelve-year-old Sandy. With Kennedy's support, Senator Stuart Symington of Missouri had introduced a bill in the Senate that waived residence requirements for the child, who had spent his school years in Switzerland and his vacations in the United States. Gellhorn had written Symington that Sandy "adores America and calls himself American." At his Swiss school, he had fought with a classmate who claimed the United States "would not admit Italians."

Sandy was Gellhorn's hope for the future. She wanted him to have a cultivated background, to speak several languages, and to attend Harvard. Kennedy, a Harvard man, represented her highest hopes for her country, and she took it as her personal mission to defend his administration. In

November 1961, she was outraged over a newspaper item concerning a Dallas publisher who attacked Kennedy's foreign policy. She did not like this kind of jingoism and wrote the President to say that millions of people were on his side and approved of his diplomatic efforts.

In the first three years of the new decade, Gellhorn traveled for business and pleasure to France, England, Spain, Italy, Israel, Germany, Mexico, Switzerland, and Africa, with brief stopovers in New York and St. Louis, where she would sometimes leave Sandy in the care of her relatives. If her son was to understand her world, he would certainly have to know languages and get used to shuttling across continents. He had a formidable mother with high expectations. She was easily disappointed in people and places and impatient with conventional arrangements and expectations. What if he did not want to be as adventurous and independent as Gellhorn herself was at an early age? His mother's brand of self-reliance was a heavy burden for a child to bear. As in so many other families, tensions between mother and son inevitably developed as he matured and as she realized that he had a nature quite different from her own. Sandy was in boarding school, just entering his teenage years, when his mother took off for Africa in late January 1962, embarking on a new phase of her life at the age of fifty-five.

The plan was to traverse Africa from west to east. Judging by her own account, Gellhorn set off with less knowledge of the continent than one might acquire from reading a few entries in a standard encyclopedia. Her doctor thought her trip was sheer lunacy and injected her with every kind of antitoxin he could think of, since he was sure she would be brought down by one of the continent's exotic diseases. For a three-month trip, she packed a suitcase with a hot-water bottle, wool clothing, cotton dresses, a few pairs of dress shoes, a big straw hat, and a cosmetics case with drugs. She knew no one in Africa. Books by Jane Austen and William Shirer and some paperback thrillers were her only company.

Gellhorn departed from London on January 23, 1962, still suffering the consequences of her shots. She found in Douala, Cameroon, exactly what is described in *The Columbia Encyclopedia:* "swamps and dense, tropical rain forests" with one of the wettest climates in the world, not the golden land she had conjured in her imagination. In the early morning hours of January 24, she staggered off the airplane into the stifling heat, feeling drained after so many hours of sleepless flight. The thought of her hot-water bottle made her laugh loudly. Her fellow passengers gaped and retreated from this obviously unbalanced traveler.

From the start, Gellhorn felt harassed and inconvenienced. How was it that Isak Dinesen had written about Africa so composedly? Gellhorn wondered. She felt sweaty, greasy, swollen, and infected. Throughout her nineteen days in Africa, various parts of her body would blow up. In this distended state, she traveled Cameroon acutely conscious of how her white skin made her stick out and dismayed that she was "literally nauseated by the smell of the blacks." Was it the climate or the lack of soap (an expensive commodity) that accounted for an odor that seemed to be a mix of urine and perspiration? she wondered. Gellhorn was ashamed of herself, of the damage she had done to her convictions about "human brotherhood."

She felt there were many differences that created a barrier between whites and Africans. The Europeans she met—several Frenchmen and a Czech couple, for example—had considerable rapport with Africans but admitted their affinity had its limits. The African's sense of time (or lack thereof) and inexperience with Western notions of technology and government made it virtually impossible to effect a genuine human exchange of ideas and emotions. It did not matter how long the whites might spend in Africa, there was a mystery the colonizers, merchants, diplomats, and other European officials had not been able to fathom. To Gellhorn, European claims of having brought civilization and religion to the continent were the sheerest nonsense. Christianity had not been practiced very well in the West, and who had the right to say that Europeans were justified in tampering with African culture? No white had any warrant for feeling superior to an African, she felt. There was much evidence of what the whites would call African incompetence, but what else could be expected when Africans were held to Western standards, if a young African boy had to deal with complex machinery that an American child grew up taking for granted? Nevertheless, Gellhorn had to rein in her impatience when an African official (who may not have been able to read) turned her passport every which way for long, laborious minutes.

Every day, Gellhorn was confronted with the strangeness of things, with jungle tom-toms beating out their sinister rhythm just as in the movies; with visits to leper colonies, where she observed people without noses and with limbs worn away by the disease dancing and cavorting. She felt a little better about her sickening reactions when she heard that Africans thought whites had a revolting smell—something akin to rotting corpses.

Gellhorn's aim was to escape civilization. No wonder she was disconcerted to find it was not so easy to relinquish her civilized habits and blend into the natural surroundings—even though she had not come to hunt game or to be taken on guided tours. She craved the adventure of finding out things for herself and wanted to be surprised, to be daring without courting real danger. Given this contradictory set of expectations, it was probably inevitable that she would be caught in a terrifying situation.

On the morning of February 1, she was in a stew about her two guides, who had shown up late. Their tardiness meant she would miss the elephants arriving for their morning bath. Although she had been assured that she could rely on Ali and Ibrahim, she had her doubts. They seemed to know little about the habitat, and she distrusted the exaggerated way they took note of such things as elephant droppings, the position of twigs, and the wind direction. They were putting on a good show, but did they really know what they were doing? A tree crashed and Ali did a little dance. By the sound of it, Gellhorn knew a lion was near. Ali seemed at a loss as to how to figure out where it was. Didn't *he* know? she asked herself. Suddenly, she realized just how incompetent he really was. Less than sixty feet away stood a silent elephant herd, which was precisely what she had wanted to avoid. It was no part of her plan to confront, on the ground, and accompanied by an incompetent guide, the wild beasts of the jungle. She just managed to steal a retreat without riling up the female elephants protecting their babies.

Gellhorn kept getting into these scrapes because she refused to take anything like a conventional tour of Africa. She constantly made mistakes with her African guides and never learned how to treat them properly, yet the Westerners she met had little practical advice to offer other than their conviction that a woman should not be out alone traveling in Africa. West African hotels were wretched, the roads were ruinous, and the African women, Gellhorn thought, were treated wretchedly—useful for sex and begetting children but not much else. There was a certain horrid fascination in observing African customs such as barbers shaving the insides of their customer's nostrils with a sharp knife, and she was startled by a Frenchman who ordered an African waiter to bring a new tablecloth before he served drinks. It had never occurred to her to make such a request. She had come to see Africa on its terms.

East Africa was more like it: weather like Cuernavaca and wonderful game parks where she could indulge her main interest, nature watching. She wanted a driver and translator so she would be free to enjoy the view and to question the natives. When the prissy, dainty-looking Joshua offered his services, she overrode her instinctive doubts and hired him, for she was eager to be off to the real Africa (the one of her dreams) and scornful of celebrities such as Robert Ruark and Kirk Douglas who were setting off from Nairobi on their white-hunter safaris.

Joshua turned out to be a pious and priggish city boy. He could not drive but would not admit it, conning Gellhorn into taking the wheel with a number of excuses: He could show her the way better if she drove; his license was not good in certain countries; the authorities would be hard on him if he had an accident; he would be better than she at watching for holes in the road from the passenger's side of the Land-Rover. It was not long before she realized that she was giving him a free ride, that his Swahili was barely serviceable, and that he had never been out of Nairobi and was useless as a guide. Gellhorn spent much of her time cajoling, threatening, ridiculing, amusing, and comforting Joshua, or, as she wryly puts it, he made a man out of her.

What prevented Gellhorn from jettisoning Joshua? It was her comic inability to relinquish her illusions. She wanted to believe him. She wanted to think she could reach an accommodation with this African, and he had his endearing moments. When they observed the elegance of giraffes, huge and glossy with long eyelashes, Joshua remarked, "Oh, *nice,*" and laughed, making Gellhorn realize she was showing him his country for the first time. These were the times Africa approximated the fairy tale she was trying to live. More often, she got stuck in the middle of nowhere, realizing her maps offered nothing more than a guess as to how to get around this continent.

Bitten by tsetse flies, stuck in the mud, having to cross flooded areas in an aged Land-Rover that took four hands to put it into four-wheel drive, Gellhorn was constantly having to order the whining Joshua to *"buck up."* He was more fussy and fastidious than she—expressing re-pugnance with his handkerchief over his nose at the Ugandans who sweated "dirty." When she upbraided him, he would sulk and play the "offended damsel" and make her out to be the bully. Even so, she had gloriously happy days watching African animals in their natural envi-ronment. She thought it charming that one of her European hosts had a garden regularly visited by hippos who munched on her flowers and seemed to like them even better with the pepper the gardener thought might put them off.

Things did not improve after Gellhorn managed to foist Joshua off on a white couple traveling to Nairobi. Her Land-Rover had to be pulled out of a stream after it had gotten stuck on a rock, and her wonderful day of swimming on the African coast turned wretched when she returned to her hotel with a massive sunburn. This last disaster made her wonder whether she would ever grow up. Apparently she lacked the "mechanism" that prevented adults from making fools of themselves. Yet Africa gave off glimpses of itself as the land of her "heart's desire." In ten months' time, she would return for thirteen years of intermittent residence.

In late May 1962, Martha, Tom, and Edna were in Cancún, staying at a wonderful hotel on the beach, visiting Corfu, and driving to Paleocastrizza, where Edna was deeply impressed by the conjunction of the cliffs, the mountains, the sea, and the monastery. Then in early June, Tom departed for London, and Martha and Edna took a flight to Geneva to pick up Sandy. Martha, Sandy, and Edna joined Tom in London for the rest of June, but by July 5, Tom and Edna were on the *Queen Mary* sailing for the States. Martha remained with Sandy in London until they left for Italy in August. It was a typical schedule for Martha and was reflective of her restlessness—of her need to be alone with Sandy, or alone with Edna, or apart from Tom, who from now on would visit Edna alone. While Tom was visiting Edna in March 1963, Martha was spending the month in Kenya. In April, Martha and Sandy spent his spring break from school in St. Louis. Then he returned to Switzerland and she spent several days in New York.

One of Gellhorn's New York appointments, on April 30, 1963, was with Carlos Baker, Hemingway's authorized biographer. Hemingway had died a suicide on July 2, 1961, and she had refrained from any public comment on his death. Privately, she expressed her belief that the Mayo Clinic had made "terrible mistakes" in its treatment of his depression, and that his wife, Mary, had compounded the problem by not having him institutionalized. Her opinion was shared by Hemingway's son Patrick, with whom she had kept in close touch, and by several other Hemingway intimates—although they agreed with Gellhorn's view that the last thing Hemingway would have wanted was to be put into a mental institution.

Gellhorn was touchy about the part she had played in Hemingway's life. The interview at the Hotel Gladstone was brief, and she later refused any further cooperation, forbidding Baker to thank her for her help. Writing several years later to Jacqueline Orsagh, Baker described Gellhorn in her mid-fifties, still slim and tall, her blond hair graying. She had a bold, open face, and a manner of speaking that was distinctively British.

Baker had made a conscientious effort to investigate Gellhorn's career, to read her books, and to give her an opportunity to comment on drafts of chapters that dealt with her Hemingway years. Perhaps it was inevitable that with Hemingway as the focus, Gellhorn came out looking (in an early draft) like little more than the great author's appendage. Needless to say, she was deeply offended.

In Chapter 41 of his biography, entitled "Capital of the World," Baker had started out describing January 1937 this way: "Hemingway spent two weeks in New York, prosecuting his love affair with Martha Gellhorn by long distance telephone." In her copy of the chapter, Gellhorn underlined her objection to "love affair" and commented that at this point their interest in each other was purely literary. She had admired Hemingway's writing; he had been trying to help hers. They had shared an interest in the Spanish Civil War, but she had considered herself far better informed and committed to the cause than he. In a similar vein, Baker wrote of Pauline, who "did not yet fully appreciate the threat to her marriage posed by Ernest's growing infatuation with Martha Gellhorn, who was soon to follow Hemingway on the *Ile de France.*" Gellhorn underlined "growing infatuation" and "soon to follow Hemingway," recapitulating her own political history in Germany and her anti-Fascism. At that time, she had been her own person, writing a novel, concerned about her mother after her father's recent death. She would have gone to Spain regardless of what Hemingway had done. She could not deny that he had found her attractive, but she was not his follower, and she had always made her own way.

Baker was relying, in part, on information from Sidney Franklin, who adored Hemingway and hated Gellhorn. On almost every count, Gellhorn contradicted Franklin, and her view was corroborated by Herbert Matthews, who also read and annotated Baker's drafts. Franklin claimed to have eased Gellhorn's way into Spain. It was a lie, and she resented the implication that she was a helpless female. She became so incensed that she cursed Franklin's lies in the margins of Baker's manuscript.

Gellhorn insisted that during their first days in Spain she and Hemingway had been careful not to appear in public as lovers. She was amazed at a description of her as a "sleek woman with a fair halo of hair." She had not been that thin. It must have been the contrast with Hemingway that made her seem so. About an intimate scene where Baker had her in bed with Hemingway, who was trying to think of words that captured the sound of shelling, she commented that the biographer had it all wrong; they had not shared the same bed.

In Baker's early draft, Hemingway had secured permission for Gellhorn to visit forward command posts. This was nonsense, she pointed out. She had accompanied Hemingway and Matthews wherever she liked and had needed no special authorization. Often she had been entirely on her own. Baker could have known this much, she argued, from reading her own journalism. Finding still other inaccuracies, she railed at the necessity of going over the chapter.

In Baker's draft, Hemingway seemed to glide with ease from one episode to another with no recognition, for example, that Gellhorn was the one who worked hard to get a showing for *The Spanish Earth* at the White House. Over and over, Baker left Gellhorn out of important battle scenes in which the intrepid Hemingway appeared. Repeatedly, Gellhorn would insert her name, finally wondering whether the biographer was interested in her presence. She hated being typed, circled the biographer's reference to her as Hemingway's "paramour," and asked him whether that expression was necessary.

The interview with Baker at the end of April 1963 was especially irritating to Gellhorn because her own life had been at least as adventurous as Hemingway's, and she was about to return to Africa to act out her fantasy of pioneering in Kenya. By the fall of 1963, she had located a rather crude and run-down house and set about fixing it up just as she had done many years earlier with the Finca in Cuba. This setting, however, was more exotic, more challenging, frustrating and frightening. She had never done battle before with jungle creatures creeping along her interior walls or taking up residence beneath her dining table, or dodging a black mamba snake, jabbing at it with sticks, or whacking away at a tarantula with a rolled-up magazine.

As in her Mexican interlude, Gellhorn had retreated to Africa to get away from civilization as she knew it—even if she raged against the inconveniences of her disheveled household and the incompetence of workmen. She wanted exposure to a rougher-edged world, but brought along two skeptical Spanish servants to provide some of the comforts of home. While the Spaniards complained of the proximity of wildlife, Gellhorn reveled at the noise monkeys made on her roof. If incidents such as a bat invasion terrified her, if she was bad-tempered a lot of the time, she also developed peculiar passions for things such as tree pruning and indulged her penchant for "goggling" at the underwater sea life so abundant and so near her coastal residence.

Gellhorn traveled to the Serengeti hoping to satiate her craving for African wildlife. For her, it was "an irreplaceable art museum of creation," the size of Connecticut. African politics interested her as well, for she was always keenly sympathetic to people who were trying something new. Tanganyika, for example, was an "African New Frontier." She had high hopes for President Nyerere, who had guided his country to independence without violence. He was the leader of a compassionate people. She had her doubts about the applicability of twentieth-century Western ideas to the country. Not having trained themselves to live by the clock, Africans seemed to lack the "time sense" Westerners took for granted, and she feared they would be able to only half-educate themselves by Western standards, resulting in considerable damage to everything that was sound in their own culture. She could not be against education, but the country's entrance into the modern world would be rough going.

Gellhorn's African adventure was interrupted by her need to return to England for divorce proceedings. On June 23, 1964, one of Edna's English friends wrote her concerning Martha's apprehensions about testifying in court. This seemed unnecessary and humiliating, but at least the ordeal was coming to an end, and Martha's future would be secured by the divorce agreement, so that she would be free to write and not worry about her income. As it turned out, Martha was relieved to get a hearing from a accommodating judge who made it possible for her to return, happily, to Africa.

Until February 1965, Africa worked its magic, but it could not continue so because of Martha's frequent visits to Edna in St. Louis. Edna was well into her eighties and her health was beginning to fail. Always, she had been able to join Martha in Mexico and other hideaways, but a strenuous trip to Africa was unthinkable.

By the autumn of 1965, Vietnam was an everyday event on television screens. Unlike her attitude toward Korea, Gellhorn could not now avoid the face of a war that had such an immediate presence in American homes.

Her opposition to the war was instantaneous, the very idea of napalming poor villagers appalled her. Yet the enormity of this atrocity and of her anger at it made her turn away and fasten on, of all things, St. Louis. Spending so much time in the city provoked her to probe the underground life that thrived beneath its placidity. By concentrating on something local, she might have a manageable subject about which to write.

In "Spiral to a Gun," Gellhorn's beat is the St. Louis criminal courts. She got to know a detective and observed some cops and judges in action. Although she was disgusted with the prevalent racism, and with the way the legal system tended to operate against the poor, her piece is suffused with an affection for both the accused and their prosecutors. She was delighted to hear a judge call a special assistant circuit attorney "Buster" during a break in a trial. If much of the law-enforcement community fastened on the capture and punishment of the guilty, she was encouraged to find a sturdy minority of them who also believed in rehabilitation and work to remedy the injustices of the legal system.

Gellhorn turned a keen eye on the individuals who ran the courts. As a group, they looked a certain way that confirmed the choices they had made: Aging deputy sheriffs with potbellies, they created a brisk, determined atmosphere that made it difficult for the accused to speak up, to relax in a court environment that was so different from the situations in which crimes were committed. For most of the accused, the court setting was so overwhelming, they did not protest the harsh sentences that often were imposed. Although Gellhorn deplored the injustice of it, she showed remarkably little rancor toward these legal officials. Rather, she saw them as men who deeply believed in their work, even though they were taking advantage of people whose lives had spiraled downward since youth. Most of the accused were bewildered, not very intelligent people who had committed crimes of passion with handguns that were too readily available. Their stories were grotesque accidents: A man made a threatening gesture toward his pocket (in fact, he was unarmed) and was shot by another man (or perhaps a woman, since in this case the circumstances were confusing). Gellhorn had written about a similar group with the same feeling in *The Trouble I've Seen;* these were people who did not know how to take care of themselves, let alone defend themselves from each other or from society.

The point of Gellhorn's brief foray into the criminal-justice system was to learn more about the society she had forsaken. She pitied these people. They lacked education and common sense. Without the wit to evade the snare of circumstances, they were pathetic, but she never lost sight of them as human beings and wrote riveting courtroom scenes in which they revealed great love for each other and strong friendships—admirable virtues that were not often seen in the upper classes. Some of the accused had an unspoiled elegance and grace, like a lovely black woman with a "Nefertiti neck."

"Spiral to a Gun" was written in February 1966 on the Caribbean island of Bonaire, where Gellhorn had retreated in disgust at an America exterminating Vietnamese in a racist war that was reminiscent of what had been done to blacks. Gunning people down, as far as she was concerned, had become the American way. "Spiral to a Gun" ends with a plea for gun control. For Gellhorn, Vietnam was the surest sign that her country had given way to lawlessness.

For five months, Gellhorn remained in the Caribbean, retreating into her memories of Mexico and writing a novel, *The Lowest Trees Have Tops.* It was a glorious time. There had been far too many books she had failed to produce, and traces of them were to be found all over the world. This time it would be different. She was grateful to get Janet Flanner's encouraging letter about her writing. Earlier, Gellhorn had written Flanner to congratulate her on receiving a literary award. Flanner's support was welcome because Gellhorn had been depressed about the reception of her work and doubted she had been able to communicate what she felt.

The new novel's title and its epigraph were taken from a work by Sir Edward Dyer:

Seas have their source, and so have shallow springs;
Love is love, in beggars as in kings.

Gellhorn was angered by the way ideology and geopolitical arguments had deprived people of their humanity. They were categorized as "Commies" or "niggers." Yet she had seen people in St. Louis courtrooms accused of heinous crimes who still behaved like human beings, and not like monsters or crime statistics. Her novel makes the same point: No matter how deep or shallow, how high or how low, humanity is one, capable of love.

The Lowest Trees Have Tops is about Tule, a village in which exiles and expatriates from Europe, the United States, and elsewhere have found a way of tolerating and even appreciating their differences as human beings. It is presided over by the loving spirit of Susanna. Like Gellhorn, she has her prejudices and people she does not like, but her sense of community is catholic. She is outraged when Honorable, Freddy Wingart, one of her aged fellow residents, plays upon his friends' sympathy by falsely announcing he has a fatal illness, yet she does not ostracize him, for she recognizes the very idea of death threatens Tule's craving for continuity.

Although Susanna shows some of Gellhorn's penchant for moralizing, she does not impose her views on others. Indeed, much of Susanna's energy is spent opposing American visitors who try to get the community of foreign residents to conform to an ideological line and to expel anyone who does not have the right politics or manners. Even the contingent of Americans who are victims of McCarthyism and who have just arrived in Mexico (in 1954) are not given much sympathy in this anti-American novel, for they exhibit all the smugness and provinciality that Gellhorn always detested in her compatriots. These refugees from political persecution show little interest in the foreign community, even though it contains its share of political exiles such as Zaza, who dresses in widow's weeds for Poland. Most of the Americans in this novel are in mourning for no one. They lack any sort of empathy for others.

The Lowest Trees Have Tops is the only Gellhorn novel written in justification of her expatriate life. Abe Amadeo, an earnest young painter who has lost a leg in the war, leaves Sarah Kent and her beautiful son because his art calls him to New York. The American refugees from McCarthyism counsel him that great art flourishes only when it is nourished by its native roots. He must immerse himself in his own time and place, absorb the wealth of his culture, or he will become a lost soul, his inspiration attenuated. Susanna counters with the examples of James, Conrad, Eliot, and Joyce—not exactly stay-at-homes. For Susanna, as for Gellhorn, most forms of nationalism are rubbish.

Tule represents a marriage of foreign sensibilities, and *The Lowest Trees Have Tops* conforms to the pattern of a classic romantic comedy, with Raquel de Castana (a Spanish aristocrat with Communist principles) taking Bartolo, a pudgy Indian silversmith, for her husband. Mexico, a land of Aztec gods and Christian festivals, is the perfect setting for Gellhorn's attack on provinciality and prejudice. Each character is wonderfully fleshed out, so that Raquel, for example, is more earth mother than Communist and full of contradictions. If we look closely at human behavior, Gellhorn implies, we see no ideological consistency and very little threat to the commonweal.

It had been easy to set *The Lowest Trees Have Tops* at the end of the Korean War, a time when Gellhorn had been most removed from daily headlines. Yet the novel's harping on American intolerance for other nationalities and races had as its subtext Vietnam, for it was in this period, during a brief visit to New York, that she made herself most unpopular by suggesting she and her friends who protested Vietnam would in the future be known as "good Americans," just as people talked of "good Germans" who protested Fascism.

Having completed *The Lowest Trees Have Tops* by the summer of 1966, Gellhorn looked for some way to get a job covering the war in Vietnam. She had no contacts and was considered too old for a war that was being covered like a "sports event," with reports of "kill ratios" and "body counts." Her aim was to report what the war had done to Vietnamese civilians, and no newspaper, except the *Guardian* in Britain, thought this a newsworthy subject. Out of her brief stay in August to September 1966, Gellhorn produced six newspaper articles of enormous power, originality, and unity, which the *Guardian* reprinted in booklet form. In retrospect, she admits to having censored herself—the reality was far grimmer than she could write—but her very restraint (in part the result of not wanting to be accused of writing Communist propaganda) makes the articles magnificent examples of tightly controlled, evocative reportage.

What made Vietnam a new kind of war? It was not so much a war of strategic objectives, of territory to be captured, as it was of winning "the hearts and minds of the *people* of South Vietnam." This is how an U.S. Government briefing document put it, and Gellhorn's first report began by citing this apparently humane statement. The trouble was, American bombing of the country was indiscriminate. Countless civilians died in the American effort to kill the Vietcong. While military casualty figures were acidulously reported, civilian wounded went unrecorded, she noted. How could the hearts and minds of a people be won if their daily dying made no impact on the Vietnamese or American governments? And why was it that the richest South Vietnamese *never* visited the hospitals and never attended the wounded and the dying? The well-off had no conscience, a nun in one hospital told Gellhorn.

Although millions of dollars were sent from the United States to help Vietnamese civilians, little of it reached the people. Civilians were afraid to criticize their government; the politicians and the military were thinking only in terms of ideology, of Vietnam as a "second Spain," the advance battleground for World War III. Self-proclaimed anti-Communists were reaping a fortune in Saigon. The overstaffed war commands of the South Vietnamese and the Americans concentrated their firepower on ridding the countryside of Vietcong—a nationwide search-and-destroy mission that was pushing the peasants off of their land. While the Vietcong had been accused of assassinating somewhere between 6,000 and 13,000 village officials, American bombing had killed and displaced hundreds of thousands of villagers. American propaganda exaggerated the menace of the Vietcong (after all, millions of peasants remained on their land and grew their crops with no evident fear of Communists) and falsely extolled the strength of the South Vietnamese.

An air of unreality pervaded virtually all aspects of the war, including the reporting done by several hundred correspondents—almost none of whom thought to cover the civilian tragedy. While it has often been said that Vietnam was the most reported war ever, and that its daily presence on television helped move the American people toward opposing the war, Gellhorn reminded her readers that famous pictures like the one of a naked girl sheathed in napalm fire running down a road appeared rather late in the war. Most graphic reports about the way napalm melted human flesh were not published. Only Gellhorn's tamest pieces appeared in *The Ladies' Home Journal* and the St. Louis *Post-Dispatch,* but they provided relentless eyewitness accounts of human suffering: the abominably dirty hospitals served often by only one doctor and nurse, with patients (usually two to one narrow cot or bed on boards) being cared for mostly by their homeless families, with bathrooms overflowing with human excrement, with at best one meal a day, with children looking out at Gellhorn with maimed and lopsided faces, with missing limbs and eyes. This eyewitness testimony was so overpowering that she was the only correspondent to be put on a South Vietnamese blacklist. After just this one brief trip, she was never able to get a return visa to Vietnam. And no wonder. How many readers of the *Ladies' Home Journal* would forget her descriptions of children who looked at her with agony and confusion? Could her readers deny the testimony of Americans such as a photographer, a housewife from New Jersey, and a physician who spoke over and over again of how "grossly careless" the American military had been with its bombs? This was a war of sheer terror, and the hospitals were full of women and children who had gone insane. These were crimes against humanity. What had happened to the principles of Nuremberg? Gellhorn asked.

Spending the spring of 1967 in St. Louis, Gellhorn wrote a piece comparing the war in Vietnam to Lyndon Johnson's War on Poverty. She quoted his election-year statements that insisted Vietnam was not a war American boys should have to fight. Yet Vietnam and the obsession with Communism had eclipsed the fight to help the poor. By one estimate, it was costing $400,000 to kill a *"single"* enemy. The total budget of just under $4 billion for nonmilitary aid to Vietnam equaled the amount spent on the War on Poverty in a country fifty-seven times larger than Vietnam. The bureaucratic definition of poverty and the inadequately funded domestic programs were evidence to Gellhorn of a country that was deficient in insight and mercy. As she noted much later in a postscript on her Vietnam reporting, more bombs were dropped on Vietnam than on "all theaters of war by all air forces in World War II." The Vietnam bombings were not the "surgical strikes" they were touted as. Even worse to Gellhorn was the fact that for all the retrospectives and movies on Vietnam, little had been done to show the war as the Vietnamese experienced it. As a result, the impression had been created that Americans suffered most from the war, she concluded.

For Gellhorn, Vietnam was another Spain—in the sense that she believed its people had a right to determine their own destiny instead of becoming proxies for superpower battles. She identified with their quest to settle things on their own, and her reports are filled with admiration for the beauty of the Vietnamese people. They had a gentleness and refinement that profoundly impressed her. Compared to their diminutive elegance, "we are overweight, unlovely giants," she wrote. It was not just an excess of feeling that made her also write that if she were a generation younger, she would have gone to Vietnam and "joined the Vietcong."

HOPE AGAINST HOPE

1967 – 1972

n 1967, a new edition of *The Face of War* appeared that included Gellhorn's six Vietnam reports for the *Guardian* and her commentary on them. She could not get over the sight of American streets "bombed by poverty" and the massacre of Vietnam. Driving her through a city slum, listening to her excoriate the government for spending over $2 billion a month while allowing its own cities to deteriorate, a plaintive taxi driver summed up the public paralysis and hurt: He could not believe his own nation had done "wrong." This bewildered man was a world away from the proud army major in Vietnam who showed Gellhorn color photographs of his kills. These dead Vietnamese were Vietcong—he was sure of it. Why not stick their heads on poles to encourage others? she asked him in disgust.

By the late 1960s, Gellhorn saw encouraging signs of massive public protest against not only the war but against Cold War politics. She had attended a protest meeting in which the young and middle-aged, black and white, got together to review the history of Vietnam, to call for peace, and to demand a decrease in defense spending in favor of investment in social welfare. Julian Bond was the star speaker. Twice he had been refused his elected seat in the Georgia legislature because of his opposition to Vietnam. She was impressed by his slim, elegant "Negro" looks, his quiet articulation of the issues, and the total integration of the

293

audience, which was inspired by his fortitude and wisdom. It seemed as though public opinion had swung Gellhorn's way when the audience rose to applaud Bond's concluding sentence: "It's not our job to make the world safe for democracy, but to make American democracy safe for the world."

Never an all-out pacifist, Gellhorn—like many Americans—was exhilarated by Israel's victory in the Six Day War. Nasser had vowed to destroy Israel and announced on May 30, 1967, that Egypt, Jordan, Syria, and Lebanon had armies that were prepared to invade their enemy. In addition, he boasted that Iraq, Algeria, Kuwait, and Sudan— indeed the whole Arab world—had declared its opposition to Israel's existence. As far as he was concerned, a state of war had been in effect since 1948. The next day, Cairo radio broadcast this chant: "Slaughter, Slaughter, Slaughter."

According to Gellhorn, Israel had less than 50,000 soldiers, including its reservists. The four principal Arab powers had three times as many tanks and planes. While Israeli territory was a mere 8,000 square miles, the Arabs controlled 677,000 square miles. It was 46,100,000 Arabs in Egypt, Jordan, Syria, and Lebanon against 2,300,000 Jews and 350,000 Israeli Arabs. These were the figures Gellhorn counted up. Yet in six days, Israel had vanquished its enemies with a minimal loss of civilian life (less than two hundred casualties). She was not exaggerating when she called this victory an "unparalleled military achievement."

Gellhorn did not arrive in Israel until June 10, the fifth day of the war. In the Sinai, where much of the fighting took place, she observed the rotting, stinking bodies of Egyptian soldiers, mounds of mines, abandoned gun lines pointing at Israel, and burned-out tanks. Flies swarmed over bodies that resembled bunches of rags and moved onto the living, darting into eyes and mouths dried out from the heat and the glaring sun. In the midst of this carnage, she met the reservists, the "citizen army" of Israel—young men and women who already were being sent home just days after victory. There seemed to be almost no sense of hierarchy, for everyone addressed one another on a first-name basis. Officers wore no insignia and there was no saluting. Everyone seemed to know his or her job, so there were few orders issued. It was a unique army because of its lack of uniformity and regimentation. Men wore beards, mustaches, sideburns, ducktails, and just about any kind of khaki clothing served as a uniform. Gellhorn was especially struck by two female soldiers wearing "soft black ballet slippers." They were radio operators in the Signal Corps.

This was a democratic and humane army that had stopped returning Egyptian prisoners of war when they observed them being shot by their own army. Gellhorn was amazed to find a virtual absence of personal animosity toward Arabs, even though Arab propaganda had been producing Nazi images of Jews as fat and swarthy with great hook noses and dribbling lips. She was familiar with this revolting portraiture from her trips to refugee camps in 1961. Surveying the Golan Heights, from which the Arabs had shelled Israeli villages for eighteen years, Gellhorn reaffirmed her conviction that Israelis had been fighting for their very existence.

After the first days of victory, Gellhorn was dismayed to see how quickly support for Israel evaporated. It was treated like just another occupying power and not like a small nation that had brought off something akin to a biblical miracle: the victory of David over Goliath. Her mission in her Six Day War articles was to show how careful Israel had been in minimizing civilian losses, for Arab propaganda was already alleging atrocities in areas she had visited that had actually sustained minimal damage. She tried to sit calmly and listen to Arab charges that Bethlehem had been constantly bombed. She could see it was not so, and she could find only one incident in the entire war where Israel had dropped ten or fifteen small bombs on a Syrian town holding troops. This was not like Vietnam; this was a battle of armies incurring very few civilian casualties, but the Arab peoples had been taught to hate Israel and to imagine their defeat in terms of human massacres. Gellhorn reported that King Hussein had urged them to murder all Jews, even if it meant attacking them with bare hands, nails, and teeth. She was not unsympathetic to the plight of Arab refugees, but they were not as destitute as the term *refugee* might imply. Indeed, some of them were prosperous businessmen. She called for a census of the refugee camps and a realistic effort to relocate the displaced that was not predicated on Israel's destruction. After all, she argued, there were at least 35 million refugees worldwide, not counting the Arabs, and many of them had quietly and courageously created new homes and careers. Gellhorn's support for Israel never wavered. On a national scale, Israelis were pioneering a way of life she envied and tried to emulate.

* * *

For thirteen years, beginning with her first trip in 1962, Gellhorn lived a part of each year in Africa, and this is where she returned after her stint in Israel, still worried over Vietnam and writing her ailing mother anguished letters. On June 8, 1968, Martha wrote Edna that she was in Nairobi the day the radio announced that Bobby Kennedy had been shot. In shock and horror, she lashed out at a land that made it so convenient for criminals to arm themselves. Less than five years after John Kennedy had been assassinated, the United States had sunk to a such a level of lawlessness that it made a mockery of hope everywhere.

As usual, Martha was full of complaints about the Africans and Asians who were building her new house. Between the thievery and the incompetence, she was going mad. Actually, she made it seem quite funny, as she wrote from her shell of a house with no roof or floor and unfinished walls that had been improperly measured. She was sending Sandy encyclopedic letters in New York trying to convince him that he was not going to die in Vietnam. (Sandy had been a student at Columbia for a while before being drafted.)

The previous month Edna had taken a bad fall, breaking her hip, and was expected to stay in the hospital for at least three weeks recovering from surgery. She had been released early, however, prompting Tom Matthews (who wrote and visited her frequently) to send her a cheerful letter about outwitting pessimistic physicians. For many, many people, Edna had been a beacon, a source of assurance and a touchstone. She had a freshness that delighted everyone who knew her. Her growing frailty was frightening to Martha, especially at a time when Sandy was going through such a rough patch. He had been a puzzle to many people, including Tom Matthews, who was going to write him in New York at the address Edna had provided. Tom had heard from Diana Cooper that Sandy might be sent to Vietnam. There was something unpredictable about Sandy. He had not had an easy childhood, and his adolescence had been made all the harder by weight problems, which his mother found hard to bear.

Two or three times a week, Martha would write her mother lively letters talking up her domestic troubles (such as the delivery of a gas-fueled icebox that was so dented its door would not close). There were also observations on a delicate-looking family of antelopes that would surely eat everything in the vegetable and flower garden she was getting ready to plant, and on a new typewriter that lumbered along tearing up paper.

By June 20, Martha was back in London, sorrowing over Edna's sad notes. Martha had those feelings, too. She wished she was with Edna—if only to hold her hand and to watch inane television programs. At the moment, London was unbelievably sunny. Martha's professional plans were at a standstill, however. Not being able to get back to Vietnam had induced a writer's block.

Things looked as if they might pick up for Sandy. By July 12, he had gotten a discharge and no longer faced the prospect of serving in Vietnam. He was sharing Martha's new London flat with her. She loved her new digs but as usual was upset about her disorderly and incompetent household help and workmen.

Ten days later, Sandy was off to explore Europe. At twenty-two he had barely gotten over his adolescence, Martha thought, but now he would have to start making his own choices. As for her, she announced she was taking cooking lessons, although she was ready to drop everything if her mother needed her. Subsequent letters were filled with comments on her adventures in the kitchen. She was getting instruction on how to cook fancy meals but hoped she would be good enough to do some plain cooking, buffet-style, for her friends. The whole cooking episode had richly comic, not to mention ironic, reverberations—considering the fact that her grandmother had run classes in cooking for the children of the poor generations earlier.

On August 9, Martha wrote her mother a long, reminiscing letter. She had been tacking up family photos in her bedroom and had found a lovely portrait of Edna holding her head high in a beautiful and elegant fashion. Martha thought her childhood pictures always made her out to be a scold or a protester, the most serious and irritated of the Gellhorn children. All this talk of family made her think of Sandy, who had had no real home in his teen years. She felt some guilt about this and regretted to say her real preference was to live by herself. The truth was, she loved no one but Edna. In a subsequent letter, Martha quoted Felicia Bernstein (Leonard's wife), who had visited Edna often and who had written that knowing Edna had made her life better, that Edna's love for her was a boon and made her proud.

In January 1969, at the Paris peace talks, Gellhorn reported on Madame Binh, one of the North Vietnamese negotiators, a slight, diminutive, weary, but indomitable woman who demonstrated exactly why the

United States had not been able to prevail in Vietnam. This frail, modest figure had a belief in her cause and an endurance that would outlast all foreign invaders. She had been imprisoned, tortured, separated from her family, and bombed, but nothing had deterred her fight for independence. Most remarkably, she revealed no hatred for Americans, and she could conceive of being on good terms with them just as she was now on good terms with the French, Vietnam's former European masters.

Similarly, Gellhorn was amazed at the exuberant, polite, and gentle nature of the young American protesters who had gone to Washington to demonstrate against Nixon's expanding the war into Cambodia. This was after Kent State, where students had been shot simply because they were dissenters. These young people in Washington were well organized. They picked up after themselves and were generous with each other, determined to make the system work for them. Gellhorn found something liberating in their joyful laughter, in the "Fuck Nixon" chant, soon replaced by the more rhythmic "Fuck you, Agnew." Even a cop was prompted to compliment a young girl on her smile. This was the generation of youth John F. Kennedy might have understood and valued, she concluded.

Having been away from the country so long, Gellhorn never imagined so many thousands of young people could assemble at such a good-natured and serious event. It was not an America she could have dreamed up and certainly not the country she had thought of so contemptuously during her African and English years.

Vietnam was an agony that coincided with the pain of Edna Gellhorn's death on September 24, 1970. Martha had made frequent trips home in the last few years of her mother's life—usually refusing to see her friends but occasionally making an exception for Mary Hall, who was worried about the possibility of her son being sent to Vietnam, or for Martha Love Symington, who helped to protect Martha's privacy. "I'm here to see my mother," Martha would announce as a way of declining most social invitations. She would often stay with Symington, using her own key to come and go as she pleased. She also resented the claims people made on Edna's time, but then Edna was far more giving in her daily associations with people than her daughter ever could be. Martha had never had much use for St. Louis, anyway. "The reason I talk so much when I'm in St. Louis is that everybody's so boring. I'm the only interesting person here, so I might as well talk and listen to myself," she told Mary Hall on one of their long walks together. The St. Louisans Martha really cared for were people such as William Julius Polk and Martha Love Symington, people with "great character," Mary Hall observes.

On Martha's last visit to her mother, Symington remembers, Martha told Symington that she was leaving the next day. "My mother is definitely going to die, and I don't want to be here when she dies. I want to remember her as she was." Symington thought this very strange. She told Martha: "I think you must stay if you think your mother's going to die. You have a responsibility." Martha replied, "I'll leave my brothers to do that." In fact, her brother Walter's wife, Kitty, took care of most of the funeral arrangements, as she had taken care of many things for Edna through the years. Martha was "skipping out before the real nitty-gritty happened," Symington observes. She remembers Martha standing on the staircase in her home, predicting the very day her mother would die. After her mother's death, she called Symington to ask what day she had said Edna would die. When Symington told her, a heartbroken Martha kept saying, "I knew it. I knew it. I knew it."

Martha's absence at the time of her mother's death and memorial service troubled many of her St. Louis friends and acquaintances. "I think I'd want to be right there when the person I loved made that passage," Mary Hall suggests. Martha's absence seemed less than courageous for a woman who had always shown so much fortitude. One of Edna's close friends doubts that Martha could have lived through the memorial service. "I don't think anybody could have said what she thought should be said," remarks Mrs. Aaron Fischer, who spoke at Edna's service. In one of Martha's last letters to her mother, she made a veiled reference to some family tensions, and remarks she made about her family to close friends suggest how impossible it would have been for her to share her grief with anyone.

The years between Edna's death in 1970 and 1975 were a very bad period. Martha was not inactive. In fact, she traveled as much as ever, with trips to Africa, Turkey, Greece, the Soviet Union, Denmark, Holland, Sweden, Italy, Switzerland, Yugoslavia, France, Costa Rica, and Malta. But to what purpose? It was as though a "paralysis" brought on by an interminable war had "gripped" her mind.

In 1960, when Gellhorn had felt useless in London and constrained by her settled, married life, she had taken off for Poland, searching there for a sense of solidarity, of a society on the move and in tune with itself. Israel, where she spent part of 1971, was another source of strength for her—although what she found this time did not result in the book she thought would develop from her journey.

By the Red Sea, Gellhorn encountered a group of traveling hippies high on hash. They were inarticulate and apolitical, a disorganized group for whom travel was simply "great, beautiful, heavy." They lectured her on smoking cigarettes but otherwise barely noticed her. She tried to tell them she had tried pot once and that it had induced a terrifying stupor. Besides doping themselves up, their main occupation seemed to be humping each other under blankets on the beach. Gellhorn could not get over how dull the young women were. They behaved like docile females stroking male egos. In her youth, she had set off to see the world with not much more than a knapsack, but her travels had never resembled this kind of drugged and filthy group wandering. Her idea of travel had always been to get to some place that mattered. Traveling was meant to give a sense of direction, to demarcate the world she could observe and about which she could write.

By the time Professor A. S. Knowles wrote Gellhorn on February 29, 1972, about his interest in Hemingway, she had developed a new enthusiasm—the work of Russian dissident, Nadezhda Mandelstam, the wife of a great poet—and had little patience for his query. Knowles was seeking information about Hemingway's trip with Gellhorn to China in 1941 in order to confirm certain conclusions for a literary article he was writing. He felt she would have the most accurate account of a flight that had resulted in a forced landing. He wished to put some questions to her, either in a letter or in person at her convenience.

Gellhorn replied from London on April 13, explaining air travel in China was rough, but there were no forced landings. Flying had been thrilling there, but Hemingway's claims were unfounded, and she finished off by doubting the China episode was very important in Hemingway's life. Knowles wrote back on April 24, explaining that Malcolm Cowley had told him about a dangerous flight in China that, according to Hemingway, had "for the first time since 1917" cured him of his "fear of death." Knowles was tracing a pattern in Hemingway's fiction after *For Whom the Bell Tolls,* in which autobiographical characters were struggling with how to deal with aging and death. Perhaps the anecdote was evidence of a change in Hemingway's work, Knowles suggested.

On May 3, an exasperated Gellhorn wrote back pointing out the preposterous details in the forced-landing story. Solzhenitsyn, Osip Mandelstam—these writers were real heroes. She was preparing for a Moscow trip to see Nadezhda Mandelstam. Her book *Hope Against Hope* had profundity in every line and was an example of genuine courage. Gellhorn would be willing to see Knowles if he would talk to her about the students he taught and about the McGovern campaign.

Knowles visited Gellhorn on May 22 at her flat in Cadogan Square. At sixty-four, she was still slim, blond, and attractive in a Bryn Mawr kind of way, and she clearly knew it. She managed to be both patronizing and coquettish toward him. They talked for about an hour and a half over drinks. It was obvious to Knowles that Gellhorn deeply resented Hemingway. He was a fraud with an inflated reputation. His fame had obscured hers. She was mainly famous as his third wife—a dirty trick. Yes, his early work had merit, but *For Whom the Bell Tolls* was a phony book describing guerilla fighting that had not occurred in the Spanish Civil War. Only once does Knowles remember her relenting, when she admitted Hemingway had a certain flair. She told a story of their flying on a transport plane in China that hit an air pocket and took a terrific plunge, sending everyone sprawling. Hemingway had been about to take a slug of gin in his Dixie cup just before the plunge. When the plane stopped falling, the rest of them, scared out of their wits, started pulling themselves together, only to find him, unshaken, swallowing his gin and grinning, saying proudly, "Didn't spill a drop!" She admitted that this gave them all a laugh and helped them get over their fright. She would later recount this incident in *Travels with Myself and Another,* but to Knowles her story did not seem a confirmation of Hemingway's favorite maxim of "grace under pressure," but only as certain "boyish bravado that Hemingway could manage on occasion."

Knowles could tell that Gellhorn thought less of him for not knowing about Nadezhda Mandelstam. Gellhorn was "very anti-American, outraged by the war in Vietnam" and active in antinuclear demonstrations. She was polite throughout her meeting with Knowles, but he got the distinct impression that she thought his interest in Hemingway was "foolish" and his "lack of political activism incomprehensible." Knowles felt—perhaps because of the way she phrased her letter of invitation to him—that she wanted to flirt as well as have him join in her denunciation of American imperialism. Instead, here was an eager academic who had gone to see her not for the value of her own career, or for her opinions, or for her attractiveness, but to use her as a resource for some Hemingway research. In retrospect, he acknowledges his visit must have been trying for her.

On July 3, 1972, with much foreboding, Gellhorn set off to meet the great author of *Hope Against Hope.* When a book moved her, Gellhorn was in the habit of sending off an admiring letter to the author. In this case, the admiring letter led to correspondence that eventuated in Mandelstam's inviting Gellhorn for a visit. The invitee felt morally obligated to a writer in her seventies who had so effectively shown what it was like to live day to day in a horrifying authoritarian society. How could Gellhorn refuse a writer who had such a quick, sharp style?

The trip was worse than Gellhorn's first journey in Africa. In heavy clothing, she sweated her entire week in the Soviet Union, not having believed the weather reports that had put the temperature in the nineties. Rather than accept as a matter of course that traveling in a secretive, rigidly controlled, and backward society would be inconvenient, Gellhorn chafed at everything: the laborious process of changing money, broken elevators, the lack of a city telephone directory, restaurants with dirty tablecloths and inedible food, and dour public manners. She missed London, where just recently a bus-ticket inspector had given back her ticket and said, "Thank you, my blossom." There was little civility in Moscow, taxis drove recklessly, and she felt the pressure of a state that snooped on its citizens relentlessly. In some sense, she knew it would be like this for her and had come only for Mandelstam.

That, too, was a disappointment. Mandelstam held court in her apartment every day, where a famished Gellhorn had trouble following chaotic conversations and grabbing the morsels of greasy fried mushrooms, strawberries, tomatoes, and cucumbers that were passed around at intervals. It unnerved her to hear Mandelstam talk of possibly leaving Moscow for London. Gellhorn could see her future: One of constant attendance on this great woman—doing her bidding. Then it occurred to her that all this talk of living abroad was a diversion, meant by Mandelstam to rile up her friends. The final disillusionment came in an argument about Vietnam, when Gellhorn found that Mandelstam and her friends supported Nixon. Gellhorn blew up. She had spent six years of her life opposing the war, she told them, and accused them of not being able to identify with other people's anguish. These Russians did not seem to know that the war was the most appalling event in her country's history.

In Africa, at least, there was the consolation of nature. Moscow, by contrast, was hideous. In *Travels with Myself and Another,* Gellhorn calls the architecture "Stalin-Gothic." Her only good word was for the Moscow subway—although it puzzled her as to why this one example of magnificence (marble arches, brilliant mosaics, and murals) should have been put underground. The landscape was reminiscent of the Midwest's dullest parts. The city was ill-lit and shapeless. She had taken a plunge into the "Squalor Society" that stared incredulously at her painted toe-nails while she rode the subway. Russians were sadly lacking in the panache she had always enjoyed in Poland. She became paranoid, fearing she would never get out of this "claustrophobic prison-land." E. M. Forster had been right, she observed: Democracy deserved its two cheers.

Gellhorn decided to campaign for George McGovern. In Cambridge, Massachusetts, she drove about with a bullhorn in a voter-registration drive. One friend of hers thought she sounded apocalyptic, like one of the gods exhorting the people to realize the end was nigh. Yet she rang doorbells and stood on street corners distributing McGovern buttons just like any other volunteer.

Martha Kessler was a volunteer working at the McGovern headquarters in New York City, which was stashed in a crummy old brownstone in the East Thirties, when Martha Gellhorn walked in, dressed in stylish slacks and looking nowhere near her sixty-four years. From her doctoral work on the Spanish Civil War, Kessler knew about Gellhorn and older McGovern workers who had been active in New York Democratic party politics recognized the Gellhorn name and were pleased that someone of her importance had arrived and could be shown off to the staff. Kessler was working in the speaker's bureau and remembers Gellhorn being very concerned about getting the right people to make speeches on McGovern's behalf. Many of the big names already sensed that he did not have a chance of getting elected, so everyone was very pleased that Gellhorn was so willing to help, especially since she had none of the haughty manner of a star. She had only a few days in New York, and she wanted to put them to good use, which meant doing the typical drudgery of political campaigning—calling people, stuffing envelopes, and so on.

Approaching the age when many people think of retirement, Gellhorn still wanted to be in the thick of it. With the prospect of another four years of Richard Nixon, she did what she could to change history. It seemed to her to be her last chance to do so, and to feel part of a country that had disappointed her so often. James Gavin, whose own view of things had been greatly influenced by hers, called it her "last hurrah."

NEVER GIVE UP

1972 – 1988

23

With the failure of the McGovern campaign, James Gavin was sure Gellhorn had given up America for good. She kept her hand in, though, writing in December 1972 to *The New York Times* attacking Nixon's "peace with honor" policy and his political and financial support of the South Vietnamese dictator Thieu. She pointed out that during the deadlocked Paris peace talks more Vietnamese villages were being tragically bombed each day. By July 1974, she was back stateside awaiting the impeachment of Richard Nixon. She wanted to see him tried, so that the record of criminality—as in the Nuremberg and Eichmann trials—would constitute a precedent for succeeding generations. She was disappointed when Nixon resigned, for it was an action that forestalled the public examination of this sorry episode in American history.

Gellhorn resumed writing when the Vietnam War ended. In her own words, it was like being released from prison and walking out into a suddenly expansive world. Two books, a collection of African stories and a travel memoir, were produced rapidly between 1975 and 1977. *Travels with Myself and Another* was written, appropriately enough, all over the world. Much of *The Weather in Africa,* on the other hand, was drafted in her London flat. She preserved her large, bright, austere sitting room for answering friends' letters. In her attic room, she donned her casual clothing, seated herself at a level table, and pounded out her stories on a manual typewriter. When she needed inspiration, she could always gaze out through the short, wide window or at the picture of her mother. In this unheated room, with only an electric heater to take out the dampness, she wrote as much as fourteen hours a day, with several drafts going into the wastebasket.

In *Travels with Myself and Another,* Gellhorn confessed her frustration at never getting close enough to Africa. She thought that if she had had an African occupation, if she had been a botanist or a farmer, she might have come to some fuller understanding of the continent. She might have been thinking of Beryl Markham, whom she visited in the early 1970s in Markham's sturdy "settler" furnishings. Like Gellhorn, Markham still had a glamorous physical presence and clothing.

In *The Weather in Africa,* three interlinked novellas—"On the Mountain," "In the Highlands," and "By the Sea"—Gellhorn achieved an identification with a land that had eluded her in her daily experience of it. In "On the Mountain," Bob and Dorothy Jenkins build a hotel on Mount Kilimanjaro, where they rear their two daughters, plain Mary Ann and the family beauty, Jane. Although Bob and Dorothy think of their hotel as a family legacy, both Mary Ann and Jane live for some years abroad in the United States and Europe. When the daughters return home unmarried, the tacit understanding is that they will take over the running of the hotel. Mary Ann has improved herself by her two years in Cleveland. She now dresses and makes herself up carefully, but she loves Africa as much as her parents do and treats the Africans in her charge with remarkable sensitivity.

These white hotel owners are vestiges of a colonial mentality that has gradually made its peace with African rule. Mary Ann takes it for granted that the hotel will remain at the sufferance of the Africans and that she must run her business in a way that accommodates the new rulers. Jane, on the other hand, is a racist. She is contemptuous of everything African and is shocked that her parents allow Africans to stay at the hotel. Neither the political nor the cultural realities of the new Africa make the slightest inroads on her sensibility. She has been reared as a spoiled child expecting to get her way, and she naturally assumes all Africans are there to serve her. Even with Mary Ann, Jane is condescending and contemptuous.

In this new Africa, whites are isolated and entirely thrown back upon themselves if they do not reach an accommodation with Africans. In Jane's case, her air of superiority is fatal to her. She has returned home from Europe after failures in both her singing career and her love life. Nothing in the African environment interests her until she petulantly tries to hurt her parents by turning her attention to Paul Nbaigu, a minor African bureaucrat who regularly stays at the hotel. Nbaigu is handsome and composed, an educated man who in his own way is as proud as Jane. For a long time, she has needed a man and has denied that need. The sexual attraction between her and Paul overcomes her. She has erotic dreams about him and cannot stop herself from going to his room, where she finds he has been waiting for her.

Even as they make love, as Jane finds her craving for Paul is unquenchable, she expresses her distaste for all things African. Mortally insulted, this proud man determines to humble this white woman and succeeds by slowly withdrawing his sexual favors and making her beg for more. Paul is a manifestation of Jane's wish to be dominated, to feel her life completed by the act of sex, for nothing else has given her a moment's fulfillment. Nothing has proven satisfactory for a woman who has been taught to believe the world revolves around her. Having no grip on reality, Jane slips wildly into her orgasmic coupling with Paul, dreading yet welcoming this all-enveloping attraction that has been apparent since their first meeting.

Mary Ann, on the other hand, has always tried to take the world on its own terms and has not supposed that it would shape itself to her desires. Africa, she concludes, is where she feels most at home with herself. The environs of Cleveland produce a heavy depression, and she cannot abide the huge polluted lake, the slums, the dull suburbs and countryside. It is no accident that Mary Ann falls in love with an English botanist who comes to study African plants. If her pregnancy also puts her into trouble, she does not break down—as Jane does. Indeed, she finds a way of spiriting Jane away from the hotel before the scandal of Jane's affair becomes known to her parents. Then Mary Ann accepts her lover's offer of marriage, realizing how happily he welcomes the prospect of having a child.

As Victoria Glendinning suggested in her review of *The Weather in Africa,* the book is about the "inner and outer weather of Africa," and it presents a narrative that itself is a projection of what it feels like to live there. One senses how solid Mary Ann's life is, for example, her enjoyment of her botanical trips, filled with wild fig trees and other exotic plants and high-banked streams with "water creaming around the boulders and over smooth brown pebbles." These trips are entrancing—especially in contrast to Jane's hothouse passion.

The dominant theme of *The Weather in Africa* is this quest to be at one with the land, and Gellhorn's most distasteful characters are precisely those people who blindly deny the land and its people. In "In the Highlands," Ian Paynter, an English bachelor who has lost his family after surviving five years in a prisoner-of-war camp, comes to Africa to build his dream farm, only to see it almost ruined by the interference of an Englishwoman, who has maneuvered him into marriage—seeking security but not Africa, not a farm, and certainly not Ian's affection and loyalty to the Africans who work for him. Ian feels so strongly attached to the African farm that it becomes his life. He adopts an African child, investing in her many of the same feelings of protectiveness and gratitude that Gellhorn felt when she adopted Sandy. Almost like a male alter ego to Gellhorn, Ian goes it alone, furnishing his home and improving his farm at a maddening pace that startles onlookers. Africa becomes, as it once was for Gellhorn, the land that is his heart's desire. For Gellhorn, there were moments when it was enough to survey Africa from the height of her home and lose herself in the quiet immensity of the view. For Ian also the panorama of Africa from the top of his farm is in itself a fulfilling, self-contained universe, incredibly fresh and clear, lush and many-leveled, soaring into a southern mountain range and dropping down into a northern cover of woods. Ian manages eventually to get rid of his craven and manipulative wife and to resume the luxurious sense of freedom his residence in Africa has given him.

"By the Sea," the third novella, is the tourist's Africa, the coastline kingdom of hotels, crowds, and pollution that Gellhorn deplored in *Travels with Myself and Another*. Mrs. Jamieson, on vacation to forget her failed marriage and the death of her young son, takes a car trip to get away from civilization, to observe some of the native species. Suddenly, she is involved in an accident. Her car has run over a black child. Naturally, she identifies with the black child's mother. Isolated in her hotel room, grieving over this misfortune, she is visited by a hotel employee who tries to extort money from her by exploiting her sense of guilt. Her hysterical response is to throw herself from the balcony, an act of despair that is heightened by the story's closing line, which laments that this unfortunate woman should have come to Africa.

* * *

Much of Gellhorn's writing in the 1970s and 1980s took the form of reminiscence, as she revisited old haunts and took up old themes in new settings. In early 1976, she traveled to Spain to witness the end of Franco's rule. Arriving just after his death, she was glad to see that in spite of Franco's tyranny, a whole new generation of people had grown up ready to establish a democratic state. The army and the police, the interrogations and the torture, had been relentless, and yet Spain seemed less divided now and more capable of democratic change. She was surprised to see, in one instance, how well a Communist and a priest got along. In spite of censorship and bans on public demonstrations, the ideals of Republican Spain had not perished. Fascism in Europe had finally fallen.

Gellhorn had a limit of six thousand words for her piece on Spain for *New York* magazine. It grew to 150 pages before she finally edited it to thirty. The writing and rewriting never did entirely please her. She was completing a circle that had begun with her first war-correspondent article in 1937, but the most she could manage by way of a reunion with that period were brief meetings with men who had fought on the Republic's side.

At Christmas 1976, Gellhorn investigated lives of the unemployed, a population the British government did its best to keep her from seeing. It had been simpler, she remarked, to contact protestors in the Soviet Union and in Spain. Welfare regulations, she found, were nearly impossible to decipher and the amount given was disgracefully low in spite of government propaganda that made it seem as if the unemployed were coddled. As in her Depression-era reports, she found the poor amazingly resourceful, honest, and even cheerful. When an angry Gellhorn persisted in asking questions of a hostile bureaucrat, she was told all information was protected by the Official Secrets Act.

It might have been this encounter that led Gellhorn to request information about herself under the Freedom of Information Act. What she got back from Washington were pages of blacked-out lines. Where there was something to read, it was based on information supplied by agents spying on her. One of her *New Republic* articles on the House Committee on Un-American Activities had been clipped, with the notation: "She tells the people to rise up and overthrow the government." These were snoops who did not even understand English, she concluded.

The FBI had been on Gellhorn's trail ever since she had urged a group of unemployed men in Idaho to raise a ruckus about a corrupt contractor. She had been fired from her federal job and yet supported by the Roosevelts. It was a different country then—as she pointed out to Emily

Williams, who interviewed Gellhorn about the Roosevelts at the St. Moritz Hotel in New York City on February 20, 1980. Against a background of muffled street noises, a very polished, English-accented, and somewhat husky-voiced Gellhorn vented her wrath at a recent book by Doris Faber, *The Life of Lorena Hickok, Eleanor Roosevelt's Friend.* Other than stopping occasionally to light a cigarette, Gellhorn's lashed out at the vulgarity and stupidity of Faber's book. Faber's offense was to have suggested a sexual relationship between Roosevelt and Hickok. This was a contemptible thing to even think, let alone publish, Gellhorn exclaimed. The country did not deserve Mrs. Roosevelt, she opined, and it was contemptible for not knowing how to respect its distinguished figures. It had never been a very cultivated country, but the Roosevelts had given it some style. Why did Faber's book even have to be reviewed? Gellhorn asked. Mrs. Roosevelt would write warm letters about hugging you, but that hardly justified the suggestion of sexual intimacy. The curious thing is that Gellhorn went out of her way to prove how physically unattractive Hickok was: a huge, ugly woman. Hickok had had an immature emotional life, and Gellhorn could not imagine that anyone had ever taken much notice of this dull person except Mrs. Roosevelt—although a letter from Gellhorn to Hickok (dated January 7, 1935) addresses Hickok warmly and praises her writing. One of the reasons it had been worth returning to the United States and working for the New Deal was that Gellhorn had found Hickok in the thick of it. She regarded Hickok as a welcome new friend and was immensely pleased. Gellhorn's letter is itself a bit girlish. Other references in the Roosevelt archive also suggest a degree of friendship with Hickok that Gellhorn has apparently wished to forget.

The St. Moritz Hotel interview about the Roosevelts gave evidence of a certain crankiness and fastidiousness on Gellhorn's part. In October 1975, Gellhorn had written an article for the London *Times,* confessing to immobilizing rage attacks, which she compensated for by practicing excessive politeness in her public dealings with people. She thought the society as a whole was feeling more frustrated and giving way to its anger about traffic jams, terrorism, and all of the other anxiety-producing maladies of modern life.

Gellhorn has always been angry at the world for not getting things straight, but in recent years she had become apoplectic about what she called the "apocryphiars": falsifiers of history who build themselves up or denigrate their famous subjects. Are apocryphiars acting out of resentment? she asked. Are they trying to secure a better place in history, or has their conceit gotten the best of them? Her mission, she announced in the *Paris Review* (Spring 1981), was to admonish the apocryphiars and instruct future historians. Her immediate targets were Stephen Spender and Lillian Hellman, both of whom (in her view) had claimed important relationships with Hemingway that the facts did not support.

As in her St. Moritz Hotel interview, Gellhorn put absolute trust in what she remembered and in what she took to be the facts—although, like most people, she is capable of romanticizing her past, as is evident from a comparison between her letters written to Stan Pennell in 1931 describing a glum cross-country trip and her article published in 1985 extolling the gaiety of it all. She distrusted Spender's words because his Hemingway did not speak like the man she had intimately known, and she could not imagine Hemingway confiding in Spender, a mere acquaintance. She denied Spender's story about the lunch he had had with her and Hemingway, and she was offended because Spender reported Hemingway as saying that he regarded his participation in the Spanish Civil War as a test of his courage. Gellhorn thought this demeaned Hemingway, who was selflessly devoted to the cause of the Spanish Republic. However off Spender might have been in his recollections, he was surely right to reply that what Gellhorn really objected to was the emotional coloring he had given to events. On the one hand, she was literal-minded about facts—as if each person did not perforce shape them to his or her personality. On the other hand, she seemed oblivious of her own Hemingwayesque style. Spender remembered the "banter between Hemingway and her in the style of dialogue in Hemingway's early novels, in which she addressed him sometimes as 'Hem' and other times as 'Hemingstein.' " What is more, Spender pointed out, her article on apocryphying was written in the same manner. Indeed, her article is riddled with her ex-husband's tough-guy, swaggering, and patronizing idiom: "Built-in falsehood, children, is bad," Gellhorn started off her article in fair imitation of Papa.

Lillian Hellman was a much better target—although Gellhorn's literal-mindedness weakened her argument here, as well. Hellman made a large point in her memoirs of not vouching for the dates she gave. They were only approximations and could easily have been off by a year or more. So when Gellhorn demonstrated that Hellman could not have been in certain places at certain dates, she had really demonstrated very little. Her more telling point was that in some cases—as in Hellman's travel itinerary for 1937—there were so many internal inconsistencies that it would have been impossible for Hellman to have been in all the places she claimed to have visited. She caught Hellman on such things as her reading the proofs of *To Have and Have Not* in Spain. Hemingway had actually read them before leaving for the war. Hemingway and Gellhorn could not have stood on their balcony in Madrid watching the fireworks from bombing (as Hellman claimed), since the bombs in Spain did not give off light.

Gellhorn was hilarious in her summary and critique of Hellman's "firsthand" description of an air raid. Though Hellman had children screaming and women running, Gellhorn recalled how impressively quiet Spaniards had been in dangerous situations. Was the policeman who pushed Hellman under a bench for protection during an air-raid an "imbecile"? Gellhorn asked. What kind of shelter was afforded by a park bench? This could not have been Hellman's attempt at humor, could it? Gellhorn wanted to know.

Of Hellman's description of a plane dropping down and setting loose a bomb that "slowly floated . . . like a round gift-wrapped package," Gellhorn remarked that the planes over Madrid flew at a "prudent height," were not dive-bombers, and that the bombs did come one at a time floating "like an auk's egg, or a gift-wrapped package." Gellhorn's fundamental point—that virtually all of Hellman's descriptions were self-serving and self-aggrandizing—was not only sound, it was crushing. At the most, Hellman had spent three weeks in Spain. In Gellhorn's memory of their brief meetings, she had been a grumpy, sullen presence and no match for her splendid companion Dorothy Parker, who had shown none of Hellman's conceit. Gellhorn considered most of Hellman's scenes in her memoirs between herself and Hemingway to have been sheer inventions, especially the one in which Hemingway complimented Hellman on her courage, saying she had "cojones" after all. "In my opinion," Gellhorn concluded, "Miss H. has the *cojones* of a brass monkey."

Behind Gellhorn's attack on Hellman was the suspicion that Hellman was not only a liar but mentally unstable. She warned Dorothy Parker's biographer, Marion Meade, not to trust a word Hellman had to say on Parker, for Hellman was probably incapable of telling the truth. Gellhorn wrote to me to say that Hellman was cruel and false to Parker, proceeding to elaborate the conviction that Hellman could not have been a true friend to any woman because she was unattractive. Of course, Gellhorn conceded there were ugly women such as Golda Meir and Mrs. Roosevelt who had been endearing, but these were only major exceptions to the theory. Gellhorn obviously resented having to spend time denouncing liars, but her anger had driven her to it.

December 1981: For some time, Richard Whelan had been trying to get Gellhorn to agree to an interview for a biography he was writing about Robert Capa. She had been ill, but at the last minute consented to a meeting just a few hours before he was scheduled to leave England. Martial law had just been declared in Poland. When he arrived at her London flat, he was greeted by a Gellhorn dressed entirely in black who announced quite dramatically that she was in mourning for Polish liberty. Throughout their interview, he remembers her phone ringing with calls from editors responding to her requests for an assignment to cover events in Poland. She was quite relaxed and spoke in that rich cultivated voice of the expatriate, a woman of impeccable breeding and manners, smoking and drinking and commenting to Whelan that the smoking and drinking had been so much a part of her generation that it was too late to quit now. Her flat was sparsely decorated in a Danish Modern motif and had an open, tasteful air to it. For both Gellhorn and Whelan, this seemed to be a most enjoyable interview. After all, Capa was a man she had dearly loved.

Bernice Kert had a much more difficult time of it. The very concept of her book on Hemingway's women was enough to set Gellhorn on edge. Although Gellhorn agreed to be interviewed, Kert had had trouble setting a date for their meeting. When she left for Europe, she still was not sure she would actually get to meet her subject. As with Whelan, however, she was eventually granted an audience. Although she came prepared with questions Gellhorn answered, most of their meeting consisted of Gellhorn's monologue. Kert had to make several "pacts" with her, including one that stipulated she could not write about Gellhorn's life before meeting Hemingway, except as it seemed to relate to her career. Kert was pleased at how frankly and passionately her subject spoke, making her book much richer than it otherwise would have been, but it was a tense interview. Kert knew that over the years Gellhorn had become increasingly volatile. When one of Gellhorn's Bryn Mawr classmates was asked to describe her at college, she replied, "Not quite so angry as she is today."

Kert produced a most sympathetic and engaging portrait, yet Gellhorn was not pleased and even threatened legal action at one point. It bothered Gellhorn that someone had come along and written up parts of her life with Hemingway that had not been previously known. Now the book would be quoted by others. It was like losing control of part of her life. That this was inevitable—given the enormous interest in Hemingway— did not console her. Emotionally, she could not concede what she knew rationally to be the case.

After her own experience with Gellhorn, Kert was not entirely unsympathetic (as she would have been as a woman) to Hemingway, due to the fact that she realized what it must have been like to have this conscience focused on him all the time. There was a kind of Prussian heaviness in Gellhorn that held people to a strict accounting and made them squirm.

Coming along a few years after Kert, Jeffrey Meyers did not let unanswered letters and phone calls deter him from interviewing Gellhorn. He "went round to her flat in Cadogan Square, wrote a letter reminding her that we had corresponded about Wyndham Lewis' portrait of her mother, and left it with the porter to slide under her door." Gellhorn was impressed by his "dogged enterprise" and "agreed to talk for an hour and a half." Gellhorn was still "tall and blond, with a good figure, soft skin, and sharp tongue," but Meyers had to put up with her suspicions about his work and her claim that she would get "stomach pains" if she discussed Hemingway. Yet Meyers was rewarded with her compulsive pouring out of "venom about [Hemingway's] habits and abusive behavior."

For Gellhorn, it was aggravating to be hounded about Hemingway when she had spent so much of her life on other things, when she had continued her engagement with politics and society, when she was eager at seventy-four to spend a summer in Lebanon and frustrated because "nobody would send" her, thinking she would be killed or taken hostage. At seventy-five, she visited El Salvador. It was a part of the world about which she knew nothing, but she felt it was her duty as a citizen to find out. She never could abide people who claimed out of laziness or cowardice that there was nothing they could do about their government. The United States had become involved in Central America, and she thought it would be shameful of her not to confront her country's invasive presence in other lands.

Gellhorn found San Salvador, the capital of El Salvador, one of the most terrifying places she had ever visited. In Spain, cities had been bombarded and she had been in danger, but the threat was external, and she had been able to tell from which direction it was coming. In San

Salvador, terror was indiscriminate and internal. There was no knowing where or when the death squads would strike. Two American advisers had been shot dead in a hotel garden restaurant, an American reporter had disappeared, Archbishop Romero had been killed at the altar during a mass, and people on the streets were silent, grim, and in a hurry. As in Vietnam, the rich Salvadorans isolated themselves from the populace, while the army was filled with the poor. Her briefings at the U.S. Embassy were all too reminiscent of Vietnam in their fatuous confidence in America's ability to interfere in the internal affairs of a small country. The Salvadoran government had been brutal, with atrocious human-rights records; and in the guise of killing guerrillas, war was waged on the civilian population. The government practiced torture that was worse than what the gestapo had perfected in Europe.

Nicaragua, on the other hand, had a popularly elected government defending itself against the Contra terror raids. Gellhorn could see that the Sandinista leaders had made several blunders and were disorganized, but she did not believe for a minute that they were the Communist thugs President Reagan claimed. Compared to the Salvadoran regime, the Nicaraguan government had significant rapport with its people. Gellhorn could see as much in the interviews she conducted and in the tone and temper of daily life. Although businessman feared government interference and takeover, Gellhorn pointed out that much of the economy was still in private hands. She could not find examples of the Communist tyranny Reagan attacked. The fact was, Nicaragua was not subservient to U.S. interests; that is what really bothered the President. If loyalty to U.S. policy was the test, then where was the moral distinction to be made between the Soviet Union invading Hungary and Czechoslovakia and the United States invading Nicaragua? Gellhorn asked.

The policies of the Reagan and Thatcher administrations in the 1980s appalled Gellhorn. She supported independent organizations, such as Amnesty International, that investigated and recorded the hideous increase in the practice of torture all over the world. The latest edition of *The Face of War* (1988) concludes with a passionate argument against the madness of stockpiling nuclear weapons. Chernobyl, Gellhorn observed, ought to be the definitive warning of nuclear disaster. Large parts of the Soviet Union and of Europe had been contaminated, including her beloved Wales, where for some years she has kept a cottage.

* * *

On her way to Nicaragua in 1986, Gellhorn decided to visit Cuba for the first time in forty-one years. She was impressed with the cleanliness of the people. They were better dressed and nourished than the Cubans she remembered from her days with Hemingway. She was surprised to see so many black Cubans and then realized that her memories of Cuba were of a country that practiced its own forms of segregation. Now Castro had made all forms of discrimination illegal. At first, it was disconcerting to be constantly addressed by her first name, but this was also a new style mandated by the revolution, and she soon got used to it and to the use of the intimate form of address in Spanish. When the weather turned bad, she had to give up hopes of what she had really come for: snorkeling. Instead, she toured the island seeing things she had never bothered to visit when she had lived there. There was much evidence that Cuba was a poor country: crowded buses, unpainted cement in shopping areas, the lack of certain consumer goods such as good clothing, and atrocious food in the restaurants—but it was wonderful to see how much equality there now was between men and women. Having been in many police states, Gellhorn was sure Cuba was not one of them. These people were not marked by fear. They were not suspicious of foreigners; indeed, they were eager to meet her and learn about her life abroad. Yet the country did have political prisoners, and it was certainly not a democracy. She cited Amnesty International figures to show torture had been practiced in Cuba and that it disgraced the revolution.

Gellhorn made her obligatory visit to the house in which she and Hemingway had lived. It was now a museum. She recognized the furniture she had had made to order by the local carpenter and was amused by the later addition of stuffed animal heads on the walls. She left quickly, feeling depressed, remembering how elated she had been on her first visit and how empty it all seemed when she had left for good. Cuba as she saw it now was a much more decent country for the majority of people than it was in her time. This collectivist state would not do for someone as crustily independent as herself, but it was a vast improvement over "feudal" Cuba. In her view, Castro's revolution, whatever its faults, posed no threat to the United States.

Much of Gellhorn's writing in recent years has been dedicated to showing the inhuman results of domestic and foreign policy in Britain and in the United States. In early 1984, she visited the courageous women of Greenham Common, who have protested the presence of nuclear weapons on their land. Putting up with primitive, makeshift shelters, enduring police harassment, and absolutely dedicated to a better future free of nuclear poison, these women reminded Gellhorn of the suffragettes of her mother's generation. These were the women Gellhorn had always taken for granted, yet they were the ones who had provided her with the choices and the liberty she enjoyed. The women of Greenham Common were engaged in nothing less than trying to secure the future of a planet that could easily blow itself up. In their determined nonviolence, these women were worthy of the memory of Gandhi. They had been beaten up by furious men and vilified by Thatcher's government, yet they refused to leave their camps. Their courage thrilled Gellhorn. She was amazed at their good humor and told them so. It was because they believed in what they were doing, one of them replied. Gellhorn was now too old to spend a freezing night on Greenham Common and announced to the women by way of tribute that they were now a "fact of history." It was a revealing phrase for a woman who had been raised to believe in public demonstrations of conviction, a woman virtually born with a protest sign in her hand.

At the end of 1984, Gellhorn visited the Welsh miners, whose strike Margaret Thatcher would eventually break. The Prime Minister's goal, Gellhorn was sure, was to privatize the mines. All the government cared about were profits, even though its supply of coal—not to mention its hardworking coal miners—was one of its most precious assets. By breaking the strike, Thatcher was also mounting an assault on the working class. Thatcher's victory, Gellhorn feared, would crush the spirit of these gallant people.

In the 1980s, Gellhorn showed herself to be every bit as engaged with her times as she was in the 1930s. And she still travels, maintains homes in England and in Wales, and is as fiercely outspoken as ever. She has reached a stage where many writers produce memoirs—a rather stodgy form of writing in her view: "I hope I won't become the sort of boring old fart who does reminiscences," she recently told Victoria Glendinning in a published interview. Yet as early as the first edition of *The Face of War,* and in much of her fiction, Gellhorn has fused her personality and her way of reporting. She has wanted to be read not just for events she has witnessed but for herself. Her collections of journalism, *The Face of War* and *The View from the Ground,* give decade-by-decade snapshots of her life and career that are almost coy in their avoidance of the big names in her life, such as Hemingway and Nadezhda Mandelstam.

Having survived so many interesting events, and having led such a colorful life, Gellhorn now finds herself regarded, in her own words, as "an Historic Monument." It has its pleasures, she notes: "I have my gaggle of young chaps." She prefers, however, to be alone. As she recently remarked to Susan Crossland, she is a staunch nonconformist. She can't stand being bored and thinks men find marriage more appealing than do women. Wives have to take care of all the domestic arrangements—a good deal for husbands. Having tried marriage for a total of sixteen years, she favors the freedom of living alone; and loneliness is no problem for her. Everyone's life has some drudgery and most husbands and wives would rather put up with each other than go it alone, yet Gellhorn claims that at least some couples would improve things "if they shot each other." Couples begin to look and to behave like each other; a sameness enters their existence. This is why she likes to see them "separately." Old age, Gellhorn claims, is welcome. It allows you to say whatever you like. When not at home in Wales or in her London flat, she is traveling to places such as the Seychelles for snorkeling.

Gellhorn is still intensely alive. While she is hypercritical of the present, she can be just as withering about the past. She is committed to history, to understanding not only that the times must change but that something useful can be learned from change. As bleak as the prospect of nuclear catastrophe seems to her, she has not given up hope: If "100 million people are employed world-wide in preparing for war," she is also heartened by peace groups all over the world, by the unity of purpose in the Women of Greenham Common, in the "one hundred peace groups in Scandinavia," and in organizations such as Amnesty International. She calls these groups examples of "talented citizenship," which does the hard work of opposing the world's wickedness. In her "relay race theory of history" one generation passes on to the next the spirit of reform.

Gellhorn once thought she might be able to write about her mother, but she could not dwell upon her most intimate feelings. Using the first-person singular in *Travels with Myself and Another* was difficult enough. Even though it was composed in a spirit of fun, it proved to be an ordeal for her. The *I* is a little too naked, a little too center stage, for Gellhorn. She prefers a position a bit off to the side, where she would find her mother, who would certainly approve of her parting image in

The View from the Ground, in which she pictures herself as part of a "global fellowship" of people fighting for the well-being of the earth and of its most vulnerable citizens. In her "remaining highly privileged years," Gellhorn plans to applaud that fellowship, both the young and the old, roaring her encouragement from the fringes: "Good for you, right on, that's the stuff, never give up. Never give up."

EPILOGUE

E very biography has gaps. There are things the biographer suspects but cannot prove, witnesses who will not cooperate, sensitive and sore places that are hard to probe without inflicting pain, and stories that are not legally safe to tell. I wrote T. S. Matthews a blunt, perhaps impertinent letter asking him why his marriage to Gellhorn failed. His reply was to quote Macbeth's dismissal of Banquo's ghost:

> "Hence, horrible shadow!
> Unreal mockery, hence!"

That he would resort to a quotation from Shakespeare in his dismissal of me was about what I expected from such a principled gentleman.

When I asked several of Gellhorn's friends and acquaintances about Sandy, they usually sighed, muttering that they had lost track of him. They remembered his weight problem and how that colored his mother's feelings. I did not look him up.

In a letter to Hemingway's second wife, Pauline, Gellhorn lightly refers to herself as an ambitious woman. It makes me wonder whether her meeting with him in Key West was as accidental as she has always claimed. It seems too good to be true. In retrospect, she suggests she always had her doubts about him, but at the beginning her excitement over their affair was almost uncontrollable—as Max Lerner witnessed when she broke a date with him (sometime in 1937), absolutely thrilled over the prospect of an impending meeting with Hemingway.

If you look at Martha Gellhorn from the point of view of St. Louis, her theatrical, self-made side is apparent. Someone who knew her well from her earliest days remarks:

> She claimed she loved the poor—actually she loved the rich. When she would come back to St. Louis to see her aging mother, she always stayed with people who had swimming pools in their back gardens, and hot and cold running servants—people whom she got to know after her marriage to the famed Hemingway—at least, to know more intimately. She claimed she was a great lover of peace, but wherever there was war she rushed into the fray! She loved her mink coat—and claimed it was her entrée into any office.

Gellhorn fascinates because her contradictions are dramatic, imposing, and comic—as she herself recognizes in *Travels with Myself and Another*. Like Lillian Hellman, though, she loves to exaggerate and then call other people apocryphiars.

Someone else who met Gellhorn very briefly came away with the impression that "her enthusiasms are a vehicle," merely a way of showing off herself in the best light. At least as far back as *A Stricken Field*, Gellhorn scrutinized her egocentrism in the character of Mary Douglas. It often takes a big, self-involved personality to take on subjects such as the Depression and World War II.

The reason why some people have reacted so negatively to Gellhorn is that she has been unable to emulate her mother's selfless concern for others. Edna did not expect that of Martha. Indeed, she knew her daughter was of a different generation and could not be bound by the home rules of St. Louis. Martha was not about to lay herself at the feet of others. As one of Edna's friends has observed, there is an inflexible, ungiving quality about Martha. She can be quite formal, even with members of her own family, and yet redeem herself with a charming, amusing note. Martha can be funny and impulsive, and often the life of the party. Roger Baldwin, an old friend of Edna's, wrote her about a gathering at the Leonard Bernsteins where Martha exploded into the room, looking ravishing and, as usual, overwhelming. He marveled at how she could just pick up and move to Mombasa, set up a household, and go about her business.

Phyllis Rose has suggested that "much biography shares [the] power to inspire comparison. Have I lived this way? Do I want to live this way? Could I make myself live that way if I wanted to?" Martha Gellhorn has always challenged people to make the comparison: Would I have had the nerve to fly over war-torn China in bad weather and in unpressurized airplanes? We want to know more about people who do what we can only imagine having the guts to accomplish. We want to know where such people come from, how they marry, and raise their children. We ask, in other words, personal, biographical questions, knowing—as Phyllis Rose reminds us—that "on the basis of family life, we form our expectations about power and powerlessness, about authority and obedience in other spheres, and in that sense the family is, as has so often been insisted, the building block of society." Certainly Edna Gellhorn thought so, and Martha tried to make it so in her adoption of Sandy and in her marriage to T. S. Matthews.

We pursue our subjects just as surely as Gellhorn pursued Hemingway, craving the intimacy and the touch of great figures, wanting to know them in a family way. Thus the barrier between public and private lives is broken. Gellhorn broke it herself when she permitted Robert Capa to photograph her with Hemingway on one of their Sun Valley vacations. Films of Gellhorn and Hemingway appeared in a Hedda Hopper Hollywood feature on the lives of celebrities.

What makes Gellhorn so angry today about Hemingway is her envelopment in his myth, and yet she helped nurture it. I am reminded of Gellhorn in late 1936—the author of one failed novel and one popular and critical success, struggling to write another novel that was not going well, doubting her talent, knowing she had come nowhere near the genius of her literary hero, and reaching out for his comfort and advice—when I read this passage in *Parallel Lives:*

> We are desperate for information about how other people live because we want to know how to live ourselves, yet we are taught to see this desire as an illegitimate form of prying. If marriage is, as Mill suggested, a political experience, then discussion of it ought to be taken as seriously as talk about national elections. Cultural pressure to avoid such talk as "gossip" ought to be resisted in a spirit of good citizenship.

I wonder what Edna Gellhorn would have made of that last phrase. She would have to agree with Phyllis Rose's argument that "the idea of family life as a school for civic life goes back to the ancient Romans" and still animates our societal dialogue. Indeed, the boundaries between what is personal and what is political have been so violated that there is no standard for a biographer to rely upon, except his own.

While biographies never supply all the answers, they do seem to help us live our lives. When we read biographies, or try to live them as Gellhorn tried to live Hemingway's life, we are looking for a sense of completion. For obvious reasons, a biography of a living figure cannot really conclude, but then the point of this book has been that Gellhorn is living, vibrant, complicated, and incomplete. She has vowed never to write an autobiography, realizing what turmoil it would cost her. She warned Jeffrey Meyers that she could not talk about Hemingway without getting stomach pains, yet she could not stop herself from venting her rage at him. Her journalism and fiction are full of fugitive references to her personal life, but I suspect that if she was to put down the whole story, she would consider herself as good as dead. As someone who knew her from the very beginning said to me:

> She was always restless, hunting for something that she never seemed to find—whether the right husband, or the home in to which to settle. She was continually moving. . . . She built houses in several places . . . some of which she did not finish.

She might have called her autobiography *An Unfinished Woman,* but a rival had already taken that title, a rival who fancied herself a female Hemingway, no less. Another good title: *A Moveable Feast*—taken as well. There is more mystique, perhaps, in the life that dare not speak its name.

A Chronology of Martha Gellhorn's Writing

Articles and Stories

"Rudy Vallee: God's Gift to Us Girls;" *The New Republic,* August 7, 1929, 310–11.

"Toronto Express," *The New Republic,* April 30, 1930, 297–98.

"Geneva Portraits, Glimpses of the Women Delegates to the League of Nations," St. Louis *Post-Dispatch,* November 18, 1930.

"Geneva Portraits, Glimpses of the Women Delegates to the League of Nations," St. Louis *Post-Dispatch,* November 20, 1930.

"Mexico's History in a Film Epic," St. Louis *Post-Dispatch,* August 9, 1931, 2, 6.

"Chez Rockefeller," *La Lutte des jeunes,* May 31, 1933, 831.

"La guerre civile a Vienne," *La Lutte des jeunes,* February 25, 1934, 3.

"La Plume et l'Epee," *La Lutte des jeunes,* June 10, 1934, 9.

"The Federal Theatre," *The Spectator,* July 10, 1936, 51–52.

"Justice at Night," *The Spectator,* August 1936. Reprinted in *Living Age,* November 1936, 155–58, and in *The View from the Ground.*

"Returning Prosperity," *Survey Graphic,* February 26, 1937, 103.

"Only the Shells Whine," *Collier's,* July 17, 1937, 12–13, 64–65. Reprinted as "High Explosive for Everyone" in *The Face of War.*

"Madrid to Morata," *The New Yorker,* July 24, 1937, 31.

"Exile," *Scribner's Magazine,* September 1937, 18–23. Reprinted in *The Honeyed Peace.*

"Visit to the Wounded," *Story Magazine,* October 1937, 58–61.

"Writers Fighting in Spain," in *The Writer in a Changing World,* Henry Hart, ed. (USA: Equinox Cooperative Press, 1937), 67–69.

"Men Without Medals," *Collier's,* January 15, 1938, 9–10, 49.

"City at War," *Collier's,* April 2, 1938, 18–19, 59–60. Reprinted as "The Besieged City" in *The Face of War.*

"Come Ahead, Adolf!," *Collier's,* August 6, 1938, 13, 43–44.

"The Lord Will Provide—for England," *Collier's,* September 17, 1938, 16–17, 35–38. Reprinted in *The View from the Ground.*

"Guns Against France," *Collier's,* October 8, 1938, 14–15, 34–36.

"Obituary for a Democracy," *Collier's,* December 10, 1938, 12–13, 28–29. Reprinted in *The View from the Ground.*

"Slow Boat to War," *Collier's,* January 6, 1940, 10–12.

"Bomb's from a Low Sky," *Collier's,* January 17, 1940, 12–13.

"Blood on the Snow," *Collier's,* January 20, 1940, 9–11.

"Fear Comes to Sweden," *Collier's,* February 3, 1940, 20–22.

"Death in the Present Tense," *Collier's,* February 10, 1940, 14–15, 46.

"Flight into Peril," *Collier's,* May 31, 1941, 21ff.

"Time Bomb in Hong Kong," *Collier's,* June 7, 1941, 13ff.

"These, Our Mountains," *Collier's,* June 28, 1941, 16–17, 38, 40–41, 44. Reprinted in *The Face of War.*

"Fire Guards the Indies," *Collier's,* August 2, 1941, 20–21.

"Singapore Scenario," *Collier's,* August 9, 1941, 20–21, 43–44.

"Her Day," *Collier's,* August 30, 1941, 16, 53.

"The Love Albert L. Guerard Spurns," *The New Republic,* August 10, 1942, 173–75.

"A Little Worse Than Peace," *Collier's,* November 14, 1942, 18–19, 84–86.

"Holland's Last Stand," *Collier's,* December 26, 1942, 25–28.

"Children Are Soldiers, Too," *Collier's,* March 4, 1944, 21, 27.

"Three Poles," *Collier's,* March 18, 1944, 16–17. Reprinted in *The Face of War.*

"Hatchet Day for the Dutch," *Collier's,* March 25, 1944, 27, 59.

"English Sunday," *Collier's,* April 1, 1944, 60–62.

"Visit Italy," *Collier's,* May 6, 1944, 62ff. Reprinted in *The Face of War.*

"Men Made Over," *Collier's,* May 20, 1944, 32, 74–76.

"The Bomber Boys," *Collier's,* June 17, 1944, 58–59. Reprinted in *The Face of War.*

"Postcards from Italy," *Collier's,* July 1, 1944, 41, 56.

"Over and Back," *Collier's,* July 22, 1944, 16.

"Hangdog Herrenvolk," *Collier's,* July 29, 1944, 24, 40–41.

"The Wounded Come Home," *Collier's,* August 5, 1944, 14–15, 73–74.

"Treasure City," *Collier's,* September 30, 1944, 22, 30–31.

"The Wounds of Paris," *Collier's,* November 4, 1944, 72–73.

"Rough and Tumble," *Collier's,* December 2, 1944, 12, 70.

"Death of a Dutch Town," *Collier's,* December 23, 1944, 21, 58–59. Reprinted as "A Little Dutch Town" in *The Face of War.*

"The Undefeated," *Collier's,* March 3, 1945, 42, 44.

"Night Life in the Sky," *Collier's,* March 17, 1945, 18–19, 31. Reprinted as "The Black Widow" in *The Face of War.*

"We Were Never Nazis," *Collier's,* May 26, 1945, 13ff.

"Dachau: Experimental Murder," *Collier's,* June 23, 1945, 16ff. Reprinted in *The Face of War.*

"The Russians' Invisible Wall," *Collier's,* June 30, 1945, 24, 54. Reprinted as "The Russians" in *The Face of War.*

"You're On Your Way Home," *Collier's,* September 22, 1945, 22, 39.

"82nd Airborne: Master of Hot Spots," *The Saturday Evening Post,* February 23, 1946, 22–23ff.

"Java Journey," *The Saturday Evening Post,* June 1, 1946, 11ff. Reprinted in *The Face of War.*

"The Paths of Glory," *Collier's,* November 9, 1946, 21, 74–76. Reprinted in *The Face of War.*

"They Talked of Peace," *Collier's,* December 14, 1946, 19, 83–85. Reprinted in *The Face of War.*

"Miami–New York," *The Atlantic Monthly,* May 1947, 48–56.

"Journey Through a Peaceful Land," *The New Republic,* June 30, 1947, 18–21. Reprinted in *The View from the Ground.*

"An Odd Restless, Beautiful Country," *The New Republic,* August 4, 1947, 26–28. Reprinted as "Journey Through a Peaceful Land" in *The View from the Ground.*

"Cry Shame . . . !," *The New Republic,* October 4, 1947, 20–21. Reprinted in *The View from the Ground.*

"The Honeyed Peace," *The Atlantic Monthly,* August 1948, 48–55. Reprinted in *The Honeyed Peace.*

"Lonely Lady," *The Saturday Evening Post,* November 6, 1948, 18, 70–79.

"Grand Passion," *Woman's Home Companion,* April 1949, 17.

"Alone," *Good Housekeeping,* May 1949, 38–39.

"Children Pay the Price," *The Saturday Evening Post,* August 27, 1949, 17–19ff.

"Everybody's Happy on Capri," *The Saturday Evening Post,* October 8, 1949, 29, 148, 150, 152, 154.

"Party Girl in Paradise," *The Saturday Evening Post,* January 7, 1950, 24–25, 76, 78.

"Little Boy Found," *The Saturday Evening Post,* April 15, 1950, 29, 167–68, 170–72.

"Dream from the Movies," *Good Housekeeping,* August 1950, 52–53.

"The Kids Don't Remember a Thing," *The Saturday Evening Post,* December 23, 1950, 20–21, 56–57.

"There's Nothing Else Like Eton," *The Saturday Evening Post,* March 10, 1951, 33, 114–16.

"Are the British Willing to Fight?" *The Saturday Evening Post,* April 21, 1951, 32–33, 161–63.

"Paco's Donkey," *Good Housekeeping,* April 1951, 60–61.

"Weekend at Grimsby," *The Atlantic Monthly,* May 1951, 391–400. Reprinted in *The Honeyed Peace.*

"The Long Journey," *Good Housekeeping,* June 1952, 53, 120, 123–24, 126, 128–29.

"Strange Daughter," *The Saturday Evening Post,* August 23, 1952, 21, 42, 44, 46, 50, 52.

"A Psychiatrist of One's Own," *The Atlantic Monthly,* March 1953, 30–38. Reprinted in *The Honeyed Peace.*

"Mysterious Lady in Black," *The Saturday Evening Post,* June 13, 1953, 40–41.

"It Takes Two," *McCall's,* August 1953, 26–27.

"The Good Husband," *Collier's,* February 4, 1955, 25, 66–69.

"It Don't Matter Who Gets in, Dear," *The New Republic,* June 6, 1955, 7–10. Reprinted in *The View from the Ground.*

"Kind Hearts vs. Coronets," *The New Republic,* October 31, 1955, 7–8.

"Spies and Starlings," *The New Republic,* November 28, 1955, 14–15.

"The Smell of Lilies," *The Atlantic Monthly,* August 1956, 41–54. Reprinted as "In Sickness and in Health," in *Two by Two.*

"Weekend in Israel," *The New Republic,* October 29, 1956, 14–15; November 5, 1956, 16–17. Reprinted in *The View from the Ground.*

"The Queen's Justice Is Quick," *The Saturday Evening Post,* February 16, 1957, 40–41, 120, 122.

"You Too Can Be a Pundit," *The New Republic,* February 18, 1957, 11–12.

"The Tacopatli Passion Play," *The Atlantic Monthly,* November 1958, 100–106. Later incorporated into *The Lowest Trees Have Tops.*

"Home of the Brave," *The Atlantic Monthly,* March 1959, 33–39. Reprinted in *The View from the Ground.*

"Good Old London," *Harper's Magazine,* October 1959, 78–81.

"Tanganyika: African New Frontier," *The Atlantic Monthly,* September 1963, 40–45.

"Town No Scandal Can Shake," *Vogue,* November 15, 1963, 144–45ff.

"I Have Monkeys on My Roof," *Ladies' Home Journal,* July 1964, 26–31. Reprinted in *The View from the Ground.*

"Animals Running Free, Two Weeks in the Serengeti," *The Atlantic Monthly,* February 1966, 70–76.

"A New Kind of War," *Guardian,* September 12, 1966, 8. Reprinted in *The Face of War.*

"Open Arms for the Vietcong," *Guardian,* September 15, 1966, 10. Reprinted in *The Face of War.*

"Real War and the War of Words," *Guardian,* September 19, 1966, 10. Reprinted in *The Face of War.*

"Orphans of All Ages," *Guardian,* September 23, 1966, 12. Reprinted in *The Face of War.*

"The Uprooted," *Guardian,* September 26, 1966, 8.

"Saigon Conversation Piece," *Guardian,* September 29, 1966, 10. Reprinted in *The Face of War.*

"Casualties and Propaganda," *Guardian,* July 24, 1967, 6. Reprinted in *The Face of War.*

"Why the Refugees Ran," *Guardian,* July 25, 1967, 6. Reprinted in *The Face of War.*

"Thoughts on a Sacred Cow," *Guardian,* July 26, 1967, 8.

"Arab Coffee Break," *The Nation,* October 23, 1967, 395–97.

"The Israeli Secret Weapon," *Vogue,* October 1967, 192–93, 235.

"The Vietcong's Peacemaker," *Times* (London), January 27, 1969, 11. Reprinted in *The Face of War.*

"My Private Anti-Anger War in This Mad, Mad World," *The Times* (London), October 1, 1975, 12a.

"The Indomitable Losers: Spain Revisited," *New York,* February 2, 1976, 42–47. Reprinted in *A View from the Ground.*

"Doomed to the Dole," *The Observer,* January 2, 1977, 9. Reprinted in *A View from the Ground.*

"On Apocryphism," *Paris Review,* Spring 1981, 280–301.

"Testament of Terror," *The New Statesman,* July 1, 1983, 15–17. Reprinted in *A View from the Ground.*

"Frontier Spirit," *The Observer,* February 12, 1985, 8–12.

"We Are Not Little Mice," *The New Statesman,* May 3, 1985, 19–20.

"The Face of War," *The New Statesman,* March 21, 1986, 23–25. Reprinted in *A View from the Ground.*

Collections (Journalism)

The Face of War (New York: Atlantic Monthly Press, 1988).
The View from the Ground (New York: Atlantic Monthly Press, 1988).

Books

What Mad Pursuit (New York: Frederick A. Stokes Company, 1934). [Novel]

The Trouble I've Seen (New York: William Morrow and Company, 1936). [Stories]

A Stricken Field (New York: Charles Scribner's Sons, 1940; and, with a new Afterword by the author, London: Virago Books, paperback, 1986). [Novel]

The Heart of Another (New York: Charles Scribner's Sons, 1941). [Stories]

Liana (New York: Charles Scribner's Sons, 1944; and, with a new Afterword by the author, London: Virago Books, paperback, 1987). [Novel]

The Wine of Astonishment (New York: Charles Scribner's Sons, 1948). Reprinted as *Point of No Return* (New York: New American Library, 1989). [Novel]

The Honeyed Peace (New York: Doubleday, 1953). [Stories]

Two by Two (New York: Simon and Schuster, 1958). [Stories]

His Own Man (New York: Simon and Schuster, 1961). [Novel]

Pretty Tales for Tired People (New York: Simon and Schuster, 1965). [Stories]

The Lowest Trees Have Tops (New York: Dodd, Mead, 1967). [Novel]

The Weather in Africa. (New York: Dodd, Mead, 1978; and Avon Books, paperback, 1981). [Stories]

Travels with Myself and Another (London: Allan Lane, 1978; and Eland Books, paperback, 1983). [Nonfiction]

NOTES

Abbreviations: Books, Articles, and Archives Pertaining to Martha Gellhorn:

BMG   Jacqueline Orsagh, "A Critical Biography of Martha Gellhorn" (Ph.D. dissertation, Michigan State University, 1978).

CM   "Edna Fischel Gellhorn, December 18, 1878–September 24, 1970." Commemorative Meeting, October 11, 1970. Graham Chapel, Washington University Archives, St. Louis, Missouri.

EH   Carlos Baker, *Ernest Hemingway: A Life Story* (New York: Charles Scribner's Sons, 1969).

FDR   Franklin D. Roosevelt Library, Hyde Park, New York.

H   Jeffrey Meyers, *Hemingway: A Biography* (New York: Harper & Row, 1985).

HW   Bernice Kert, *The Hemingway Women* (New York: W.W. Norton and Company, 1983).

HWH   Lloyd Arnold, *High on the Wild with Hemingway* (Caldwell, Idaho: The Caxton Printers, 1968).

JSP   Joseph Stanley Pennell Papers, Special Collections, University of Oregon Library, Eugene, Oregon.

MEF   Martha Ellis Gellhorn, "Martha Ellis Fischel, 1850–1939," records of the Ethical Society, Western Historical Manuscript Collection, Thomas Jefferson Library, University of Missouri, St. Louis, Missouri.

MGRL   Emily Williams interview with Martha Gellhorn, St. Moritz Hotel in New York City, February 20, 1980, on deposit with the Franklin D. Roosevelt Library, Hyde Park, New York.

MHS   Missouri Historical Society, St. Louis, Missouri.

NYPL   New York Public Library, Crowell-Collier Collection.

OA   Martha Gellhorn, "On Apocryphism," *Paris Review,* Spring 1981, 280–301.

OMA   T. S. Matthews, *O My America* (New York: Simon and Schuster, 1962).

PUL   Patrick Hemingway Collection, Hemingway-Lanham Collection, Charles Scribner Collection, Carlos Baker Collection, Firestone Library, Princeton University, Princeton, New Jersey.

SLH   Carlos Baker, ed., *Selected Letters of Ernest Hemingway 1917–1961* (New York: Charles Scribner's Sons, 1981).

SLML   St. Louis Mercantile Library, St. Louis, Missouri.

TG   Denis Brian, *The True Gen: An Intimate Portrait of Hemingway by Those Who Knew Him* (New York: Grove Press, 1988).

TRT   Victoria Glendinning, "The Real Thing," *Vogue,* April 1988, 358–59, 398.

VIT   Bernard Berenson Papers, Villa I Tati, Florence, Italy.

WG   "The Reminiscences of Walter Gellhorn," Part I, April 22, 1955, Columbia Oral History Project, Columbia University Library, New York, New York.

WHMC   Western Historical Manuscript Collection, Thomas Jefferson Library, University of Missouri, St. Louis, Missouri.

WUA   Edna Gellhorn Collection, Washington University Archives, St. Louis, Missouri.

Abbreviations: Books by Martha Gellhorn

ASF   *A Stricken Field*
FW   *The Face of War*
HOA   *The Heart of Another*
HOM   *His Own Man*
HP   *The Honeyed Peace*
L   *Liana*
LTHT   *The Lowest Trees Have Tops*
PTTP   *Pretty Tales for Tired People*
TBT   *Two by Two*
TIS   *The Trouble I've Seen*
TWMA   *Travels with Myself and Another*
VG   *The View from the Ground*
WIA   *The Weather in Africa*
WMP   *What Mad Pursuit*
WOA   *The Wine of Astonishment*

Abbreviations: Author's Interviews (int.)

AF   Mrs. Aaron Fischer, 3/14/88
CD   Carol O. Daniel, 3/17/88
CP   Content Peckham (Mrs. Joseph Cowan), 8/18/88
DM   Delia Mares, 12/2/87; 4/2/88
ELN   Emily Lewis Norcross, 3/19/88
FVF   Frederick Vanderbilt Field, 3/1/88
MK   Martha Kessler, 10/16/88
MLS   Martha Love Symington, 3/19/88
MTH   Mary Taussig Hall, 3/17/88

RS   Randall "Pete" Smith, 8/18/88
RW   Richard Whelan, 12/2/87
SF   Stanley Flink, 12/2/87
TG   Tom Griffith, 7/23/88
VD   Virginia Deutch, 3/18/88
WJP   William Julius Polk, 3/17/88

Prologue

p. xiv   "The truest biography . . .": David Roberts, *Jean Stafford* (New York: St. Martin's Press, 1988), xi.

xiv   "doing her damndest . . .": TRT, 359.

xv   "He did something . . .": Michael VerMeulen, "Bill Buford, *Granta's* Bad Boy," *Vanity Fair,* November 1989, 140.

xvi   "the figure under the carpet . . .": Leon Edel, "The Figure Under the Carpet," in *Telling Lives: The Biographer's Art,* ed. Marc Pachter (Washington, D.C.: New Republic Books, 1979), 24–25.

xvi   "more or less Junior League . . .": *Eleanor Roosevelt's My Day,* introduction by Martha Gellhorn (New York: Pharos Books, 1989), 29.

1. St. Louis: 1860–1923

p. 3   first major projects: Olivia Skinner, "Edna Gellhorn: Long-Time Civic Worker," St. Louis *Post-Dispatch,* undated clipping, MHS.

4   "big game hunt": Clarissa Start, "Edna Gellhorn at 75: 'I Have Infinite Faith in the Future,' " St. Louis *Post-Dispatch,* December 20, 1953; "Mrs Edna Gellhorn Dies at 91; Suffragist Worker, Civic Leader," St. Louis *Post-Dispatch,* September 25, 1970, clippings, MHS.

4   "the spirit of the future": BMG, 5.

4   in yellow . . . sashes: Clarissa Start, "Edna Gellhorn—Still on," St. Louis *Post-Dispatch,* December 15, 1963.

4   VOTES FOR WOMEN: Mary Kimbrough, "Three Decades of Votes for Women," St. Louis *Star-Times,* August 25, 1950, WUA.

4   "The Golden Lane": Start, "Edna Gellhorn—Still on."

4   the men along the route: tape recording of Edna Gellhorn at her eighty-fifth birthday celebration speaking on the beginning of women's suffrage.

4   As she told a reporter: Start, "Edna Gellhorn—Still on."

4   dragging chains: "Mrs Edna Gellhorn Dies at 91; Suffragist Worker, Civic Leader."

4   descended from English settlers: *Notable American Women: The Mod-*

ern Period: A Biographical Dictionary, eds. Barbara Sicherman, Carol Hurd Green, Ilene Kantrov, Harriette Walker (Cambridge: Harvard University Press, 1980), 268.

p. 4   Turner Morehead Ellis: U.S. census records; City of St. Louis Circuit Court File 09101; St. Louis *Republican,* March 3, 1878.

4   Born on May 25, 1850 . . . divided loyalties: "A Sketch of the Life of Mrs. Washington E. Fischel," *Central High School Red and Black,* St. Louis High School yearbook, June 1938.

4   her first act of public protest: MEF.

5   "one of the first of social standing . . .": Marguerite Martyn, "A Defender of the Modern Woman," St. Louis *Post-Dispatch Daily Magazine,* May 30, 1933, in the Ethical Society records, WHMC.

5   teaching English language and customs: printed chronology and handwritten notes in the Ethical Society records, WHMC.

5   Assigned to a school in north St. Louis: "A Sketch of the Life of Mrs. Washington E. Fischel."

5   a native of St. Louis: *Notable American Women,* 268.

5   important internist: BMG, 1.

5   "founder and president . . .": *Notable American Women,* 268.

5   called him "Wash": MEF.

5   self-culture and conscience: "Ethical Society Rites Conducted for Mrs. Fischel," St. Louis *Star-Times,* January 10, 1939, WHMC.

6   "home-making classes . . . her husband and children": "Celebrate 50 Years of Social Service, Mrs. Washington E. Fischel, 88, and Neighborhood House Still Going Strong," St. Louis *Globe-Democrat,* March 27, 1938, WHMC.

6   "fit for discussion in polite society" . . . "My light shines through my daughter": Martyn.

6   memorial tribute: Ethical Society records, WHMC.

7   born in Breslau, Germany: BMG, 2; "George Gellhorn, M.D.," *The History of Missouri, Family and Personal History,* volume III (New York: Lewis Historical Publishing Company, 1967), 187.

7   bright young man . . . antimilitarist: WG, 1.

7   an overwhelming desire to travel: WG, 1; BMG, 2.

7   no plans to stay in St. Louis: WG, 1.

7   studied at the universities of: "Washington Emil Fischel," in *The Book of St. Louisans: A Biographical Dictionary of Leading Living Men of the City of St. Louis,* ed. John W. Leonard (St. Louis: The St Louis Republic, 1906), 192.

7   admired each other: WG, 1.

7   her parents' first meeting: BMG, 400.

7   inherited from her father: Skinner.

8   "nod approvingly": HW, 285.

8   free prenatal clinics . . . study and write at home: WG, 4, 8.

8   well read: BMG, 3.

p. 8 taught himself Portuguese: WG, 6.

8 "loving, merry, stimulating": HW, 285.

8 Herbert Hoover . . . Walter remembers: WG, 4–5.

8 "set icily high standards": TRT, 359.

8 a little taken aback: WG, 8.

8 Germanic precision . . . conjugating Latin verbs: WG, 8.

9 "substitution plan": Martyn.

9 "wonderful": TRT, 359.

9 No typing: BMG, 5.

9 Disputes were resolved: TRT, 359.

9 Martha's great-grandparents: Letter to author from Melvin S. Strassner, Union of American Hebrew Congregations, October 11, 1988.

9 George Gellhorn had concluded: WG, 13.

10 a great-aunt: WG, 12–15.

10 "instituting Sunday School classes": "Sister Miriam, Last Member of Episcopal Order, Dies," St. Louis *Post-Dispatch,* June 18, 1936, 15C.

10 "I have encountered . . .": "In Memoriam: Sister Miriam," *Journal of the Ninety-Eighth Conventions of the Diocese of Missouri,* January 12, 1937.

10 Sunday school . . . Sunday school: WG, 12.

10 He wanted it known: BMG, 8.

11 These trips: BMG, 8.

2. Mother and Daughter: 1894–1924

p. 12 "clear enunciation". . . to the students: Mary Institute catalogue, 1894–1895, 21–22, 24.

12 "development of the whole child": Arthur Newell Chamberlin III, *Mary Institute: The Story of a Hundred and Ten Years in the Pursuit of Excellence* (privately printed, St. Louis: 1959), 19, 26.

12 president of her class: Olivia Skinner, "Edna Gellhorn: Long-Time Civic Worker," St. Louis *Post-Dispatch,* undated clipping, MHS.

12 "But how can women . . .": "Mrs. Gellhorn Subject of Life Sketch in Post," unidentified clipping, WUA; tape recording of Edna Gellhorn at her eighty-fifth birthday celebration speaking on the beginning of women's suffrage.

13 Edna's mother boldly decided: press release, National League of Women Voters, December 1938, WHMC.

13 "the entire class . . .": "Mrs. Gellhorn Subject of Life Sketch in Post."

13 "clear and unstrident . . . natural and unconscious pride": T. S. Matthews, *Angels Unawares: Twentieth-Century Portraits* (New York: Ticknor & Fields, 1985), 266.

13 "trailed": Skinner.

p. 13   "this gorgeous creature . . .": Skinner.

13   "chosen lifetime president . . .": *Notable American Women: The Modern Period: A Biographical Dictionary,* eds. Barbara Sicherman, Carol Hurd Green, Ilene Kantrov, Harriette Walker. (Cambridge: Harvard University Press, 1980), 268.

13   consulted closely by M. Carey Thomas: See, for examples, letters of December 9 and December 22, 1921, from M. Carey Thomas to Edna Gellhorn, WUA.

12   "wasn't the embattled club woman . . .": Matthews, 266.

13   When Edith January Davis: "Mary-ites of Moment," undated issues of Mary Institute alumnae news, WUA.

13   a neighbor: BMG, 4.

14   pretending to knit: *Notable American Women,* 269.

14   "Now I'm being your mother . . .": CM.

14   Avis Carlson remembers . . . "grade A personality clashes": Avis Carlson, "Dame Edna of Saint Louis," *The Greater Saint Louis Magazine,* November 1968, 21.

14   Mr. Hornback: Ethical Culture Society records, WHMC.

14   "Modern woman . . .": "Mrs. Gellhorn Subject of Life Sketch in Post."

15   "Nosey Nellies among the cows": int. VD.

15   "I was very much interested . . ." blanched on one occasion: int. AF.

16   "four inquiring . . .": Matthews, 265.

16   serene, soothing tone: BMG, 5.

16   his or her best: *Notable American Women,* 269.

16   a portrait of Edna: BMG, 5.

16   "human beings of all kinds": OMA, 14.

16   warmth and generosity: BMG, 5.

16   as her son Walter remembered: CM.

16   "She runs as fast to meet me . . .": Skinner.

16   "bickering": CM.

16   "savored": CM.

16   "peels of laughter": CM.

16   "She made it fun . . .": int. AF.

16   "she or he . . .": CM.

17   "doing woman": int. ELN.

17   "Marty's mother . . . governed": int. ELN.

17   "We all grew up . . .": int. MTH.

17   Martha Love Symington . . . "half-Jewish": int. MLS.

17   "but they were accepted in St. Louis as Gentiles": int. MLS.

17   Delia Mares: int. DM.

   Mary Taussig Hall: int. MTH.

17   Another of Martha's friends: int. MLS.

17   "with a little more feeling in those days": int. ELN.

18   "gassy little Friday-night dancing classes": int. MLS.

p. 18   William Julius Polk: int. WJP.
18   "Nice girls . . .": unidentified newspaper column, WUA.
18   eating her lunch alone . . . controversial activities: BMG, 9, 11.
18   Martha Love Symington: int. MLS.
19   "On Saturday . . . certain rules and laws": int. ELN.
19   These people were not professionals: int. MLS.
19   their share of parties . . . "a slight chip . . .": int. MLS.
19   content and comfortable . . . while you danced: BMG, 11.

3. Special: John Burroughs School: 1923–1926

p. 20   "Civics and Social Problems": Mary Institute catalogue, 1918–1919, 52–54.
20   "the new spirit in education": Martin L. Parry, *A Way of Life: The Story of the John Burroughs School, 1923–1973.* (St. Louis: John Burroughs School, 1973), 1.
20   "we came to call it . . .": int. DM.
20   "profit from the best . . . in bleak silence": Parry, 1.
21   "Each time . . .": Parry, 3.
21   "If we teach children . . .": "Educator, in Address, Rejects Theory That School Work Must Be Distasteful to Be of Value, Dr. Otis W. Caldwell of Columbia University Declares Pupils Learn Best when Subjects Are Made Engaging, and Not Unnecessarily Hard," undated clipping in the records of the John Burroughs School.
21   "dividing family against family . . .": Parry, 3.
21   "close to nature . . .": Parry, 3, 5, 6.
21   "He loved personality . . . motive": Parry, 5.
22   "the clang of the elevator gate": Parry, 8.
22   SPECIAL: JOHN BURROUGHS: Parry, 10; int. CD.
22   "the thought that . . .": Parry, 7.
22   "pretty heady living": Parry, 12.
22   "personality . . . influenced by the environment": *John Burroughs Review* (JBR), March 1926, 52.
23   "every joke . . . color and variety": Parry, 12–13.
23   "studying maps . . .": Parry.
24   She assisted: JBR, February 1925, 38.
24   school colors: JBR, June 1926, 12.
24   student solicitors . . . St. Louis shopkeepers: JBR, November 1925, 33.
24   "We had a perfectly . . . talk the birds off a tree": int. ELN.
24   *A Soul in Torment:* JBR, May 1924, 39–40.
24   prose sketch: JBR, November 1924, 7.
24   "Ye Exame": JBR, Christmas 1924, 31–34.
24   "The Sky": JBR, May 1924, 15–16.

p. 24   "Jemima Smyth, Super-Shopper": JBR, May 1924, 22–23.
24   slum housing: JBR, December 1925, 13.
24   travel: JBR, February 1926, 28.
24   sunsets: JBR, May 1925, 24.
25   "Hester, Defiant,": JBR, February 1926, 28.
25   a "character": "Apologia Pro Marta Gellhorna," JBR, May 1924, 24–25.
25   "magnificent Martie": JBR, June 1926, 16.
25   "Wilf": diary, September 30, 1932, JSP.
25   "perfectly cast": JBR, February 1926, 43.
25   She had met Carl Sandburg: Gellhorn's letter to the poet and the poems she enclosed for his inspection are on deposit in the Carl Sandburg Collection, library of the University of Illinois at Urbana-Champaign.
25   if writing is a necessity: BMG, 10.

4. Bryn Mawr: 1926–1929

p. 26   "come out": "Interview with Helen Bell de Freitas '31 by Caroline Smith Rittenhouse '52" (London, May 7, 1985), Oral history transcript, Bryn Mawr College Library, 15.
26   the source for all kinds of news: WMP, 22.
27   "gesture of the brothel" . . . Her friends: "Interview with Helen Bell de Freitas '31 by Caroline Smith Rittenhouse '52," 15–17.
27   "wings had begun to spread a bit . . .": int. ELN.
27   independence . . . adults: *The College News,* October 13, 20, 1926; November 10, 1926; February 23, 1927.
28   published in *The Lantern: The Lantern,* June 1928, 18; November 1928, 20, 36.
28   Most of it she destroyed: BMG, 12.
28   writing dismissively about Wordsworth . . . a pleasure: BMG, 12.
29   chatty letters: Edna Gellhorn Collection, WUA.
31   took to living in a settlement: BMG, 12.
32   the curse of respectability: MGRL.
32   Gellhorn was reading Hemingway: int. ELN.
32   Richmond Barrett . . . As Kenneth Lynn suggests: Kenneth S. Lynn, *Hemingway* (New York: Simon and Schuster, 1987), 336–37.

5. On Her Own: 1929–1930

p. 37   Mary Taussig Hall: int. MTH.
37   "Her father and I . . .": Marguerite Martyn, "St. Louis' Young Woman Novelist," St. Louis *Post-Dispatch,* October 3, 1936, clipping files, SLML.

p. 37   subsisting on doughnuts: VG, 66.
38   "shoestring living": HW, 285.
38   "a penny of support from her father": HW, 285.
38   *disappointed:* HW, 285.
38   liberated life . . . "I paid": TRT, 398.
38   unmanageable garden: MEF.
38   so it seemed: int. DM.
39   Writing to Edna: WUA.
39   These separations: WUA.
39   "She had a certain contempt . . .": int. MTH.
39   "Edna loved St. Louis. . . .": int. AF.
39   "Edna's relationship with Martha . . . rarely came to see her": int. DM.
40   "She had a wonderful guile. . . .": int. VD.
40   "She picked out a few people. . . .": int. AF.
40   "Now, Emily . . . a Viking goddess . . .": int. ELN.
41   like a continuation of her college education: MGRL.
41   *une gamine:* Bertrand de Jouvenel, "Avec Martha Gellhorn, Collaboratrice du President Roosevelt," *Les Nouvelles litteraires,* November 7, 1936, 6.
41   young and delicate: BMG, 12.
41   *lady:* WMP, 27.
41   "The Blonde Peril": BMG, 12–13.
41   Her own memory: MGRL.
41   decidedly ugly: MGRL.
42   star reporter's adventures . . . "stygian bathroom": WMP, 26–29.
42   child psychology: WMP, 27–28.
43   restless: BMG, 13–14.

6. Launched: 1930–1931

p. 44   third class in steerage: VG, 66.
44   "passion for France": HW, 286.
44   sleazy . . . cried: VG, 66.
45   *maison de passe* . . . "White Russian balalaika player": VG, 66–67.
45   low on funds . . . dull copy: BMG, 14–15.
45   "Tall, slim, blonde . . .": Margaret Martyn, "St. Louis' Young Woman Novelist," St. Louis *Post-Dispatch,* October 3, 1936, clipping files, SLML.
45   associating with the gaudy rich and lecturing them: int. MLS; VG, 68.
45   ardently involved in politics: VG, 67.
45   "unemployment . . .": HW, 286.
46   "Real life was . . .": VG, 68.

p. 46   "standing room . . .": VG, 68.

47   militant pacifist: Martha Gellhorn, "Geneva Portraits, Glimpses of the Women Delegates to the League of Nations," St. Louis *Post-Dispatch*, November 18, 1930.

47   smart black dress . . . "pedestal": Ibid.

47   Edna's friends: int. DM, AF, VD.

47   Her second article: "Geneva Portraits, Glimpses of the Women Delegate to the League of Nations," St. Louis *Post-Dispatch*, November 20, 1930.

48   visited striking textile workers: BMG, 16; Bertrand de Jouvenel, *Un Voyageur dans le Siècle* (Paris: Editions Robert Laffont, 1980), 125.

48   to write as many books as possible: Letter to author from John R. Braun, March 17, 1989.

48   Jouvenel had trouble: MG to John R. Braun, January 2, 1979.

48   Lange recalls: MG to JB, January 2, 1979.

49   part of her girlhood: MG to JB, January 2, 1979.

49   traveled in Europe for four months: BMG, 15.

49   rapprochement between France and Germany: FW, 13.

7. Jouvenel: 1876–1930

p. 50   traced its descent: Rudolph Binion, *Defeated Leaders: The Political Fate of Caillaux, Jouvenel, and Tardieu* (New York: Columbia University Press, 1960), 120.

50   "the talent for being loved": Binion, 122; Joanne Richardson, *Colette* (New York: Franklin Watts, 1984), 48.

50   "overwhelm assemblies . . .": Binion, 123.

51   "a broader community": Binion, 136.

51   manufacturing headlights: John R. Braun, *"Une Fidelite Difficile: The Early Life and Ideas of Bertrand de Jouvenel, 1903–1945,"* (Ph.D. dissertation, University of Waterloo, Waterloo, Ontario, Canada, 1985), 22.

51   timid, trembling, awkward boy . . . "mother's spacious apartment": Genevieve Dormann, *Colette: A Passion for Life* (New York: Abbeville Press, 1985), 224.

51   She gave him massages: Richardson, 85.

51   When she stroked his hip . . . If she was doomed: Dormann, 227–28.

52   Uncle Robert had died . . . authority on international affairs: Braun, 28, 49.

52   heavy drinking and womanizing . . . actively involved in politics: Braun, 95, 98–101.

52   divided in feeling: Braun, 130.

53   the epitome of his hedonistic period: Braun, 132.

53   rejuvenation of the non-Marxist left: Braun, 132.

53   he argued that France should: Braun, 146.

p. 53   Europe as a great entity: Braun, 203.

53   earlier enthusiasm for the League of Nations: Braun, 205.

53   reading voraciously: Braun, 260.

53   in his eighties: Dormann, 227, 267; Richardson, 100.

53   He had been ready . . . "love with her": Dormann, 251.

54   *"cet esprit eclectique et curieux"*: Bertrand de Jouvenel, *Un Voyageur dans le Siècle* (Paris: Editions Robert Laffont, 1980), 11.

54   *"la reconciliation franco-allemande"* . . . Bertrand's two grandfathers: Ibid., 17, 25.

54   Buffalo Bill . . . He was scandalized: Ibid., 26–27, 29–30, 41–42, 45.

55   *"A mes yeux . . . la marche future . . ."*: Ibid., 90, 97.

55   "future studies": Pierre Hassner, "Bertrand de Jouvenel," in *International Encyclopedia of the Social Sciences, Biographical Supplement,* ed. David L. Sills (New York: The Free Press, 1979), 360.

56   "politics . . .": Sills.

56   his youthful laugh . . . *"le drame . . ."*: Jouvenel, op. cit., 97–98, 100–101, 112.

56   "the metaphor of the traveler . . .": Hassner, 358.

8. Crossing the Continent: 1931

p. 57   "Spleen, 1931": JSP.

57   come to St. Louis: autobiography, JSP.

57   Desperately trying to write a novel: diary, JSP.

58   On stationery: Edna Gellhorn Collection, WUA.

58   especially Erna Rice . . . as one of her friends remembers: letter to author from Emily Lewis Norcross, May 23, 1988.

58   from California: JSP.

58   Pennell would experience: diary, JSP.

58   From Reno: JSP.

59   By early May . . . On May 14: JSP.

59   On May 19: JSP.

60   it was a relief: JSP.

60   stasis: JSP.

60   to do the washing: JSP.

61   Mexico provided easy living: JSP.

61   going to marry: JSP.

62   a friend of Martha's brother: int. FVF.

62   an interesting, attractive, and entertaining houseguest: int. FVF.

62   reading Communist writers: JSP.

62   "very liberal and observant person": int. FVF.

62   a moment of grave economic crisis: Bertrand de Jouvenel, *Un Voyageur dans le Siècle* (Paris: Editions Robert Laffont, 1980), 126.

62   an outfit: Ibid., 127.

p. 62   Eldorado: Ibid.

62   Waiting: Ibid., 127–28.

62   Gellhorn wanted to show: Ibid., 128.

62   *une immense torpedo:* Ibid.

63   "eight-year-old Dodge . . .": VG, 3.

63   a prized possession: Jouvenel, op. cit., 128.

63   Jouvenel found: Ibid.

63   like a "palette": Ibid.

63   heat and dust: VG, 3.

63   the beauty of nature: Jouvenel, op. cit., 128.

63   ramshackle buildings: VG, 3.

63   the influence of Thomas Wolfe: VG, 132.

63   adventures in Hollywood: int. MLS.

63   figures in society: Jouvenel, op. cit., 132.

63   seven dollars a day . . . looking for gold: Ibid., 133–34.

9. *What Mad Pursuit: 1932–1934*

p. 65   climbed the Pyrenees: int. MLS.

65   written for French newspapers . . . lost her literary journal: BMG, 16.

65   "a certain indisicipline . . . most diverse ones": Pierre Hassner, "Bertrand de Jouvenel," in *International Encyclopedia of the Social Sciences, Biographical Supplement,* ed. David L. Sills. (New York: The Free Press, 1979), 358.

65   "struggle to escape": John Keats, "Ode on a Grecian Urn," line 9.

65   "double standard": WMP, 11.

65   foul corruption of things: WMP, 7.

66   grotesque and destitute-looking . . . "a triumph of living": WMP, 37, 102, 116–17, 131, 202.

66   "one grand person": WMP, 220.

66   Gellhorn had trouble placing . . . "concessions": Olga Clark, "First Novel by Former St. Louis Woman Will Appear During Autumn," St. Louis *Globe-Democrat,* July 11, 1934, 4C.

67   She admits: TRT, 398.

67   He once complained of it: int. ELN.

67   "proud of his wife's first book": int. ELN.

67   married the summer before in Spain . . . an old friend of Colette: undated newspaper clipping, MHC; int. MLS, ELN; Genevieve Dormann, *Colette: A Passion for Life* (New York: Abbeville Press, 1985), 260.

67   a bust of Gellhorn: Clark.

67   "the Franco-American clash . . .": Clark.

67   Bryn Mawr Club meeting: int. DM, ELN.

68   In the summer of 1934 . . . filling stations: int. MLS.

p. 68   Edna was astonished: Clark.
  68   branded as a Fascist: Clark.
  68   "the best way not to fight . . .": Clark.
  68   traveling with a group of French pacifists: FW, 14.
  68   regimented Nazi youths: FW, 14.
  68   An angry Gellhorn: Martha Gellhorn to John Braun, January 2, 1979.
  68   Gellhorn's letters: int. MLS.
  69   equal treatment of each other: John R. Braun, *"Une Fidelite Difficile: The Early Life and Ideas of Bertrand de Jouvenel, 1903–1945,"* (Ph.D. dissertation, University of Waterloo, Waterloo, Ontario, Canada, 1985), 368.
  69   "revive proposals . . .": Braun, 369.
  69   Many years later: Martha Gellhorn to John Braun, January 2, 1979.
  69   analyzing history by generations: Braun, 402–03.
  69   *La Lutte* had begun: Braun, 416.
  70   much could be learned: Hassner, 359.
  70   restrain the more extreme elements: Hassner, 359.
  70   in trouble: VG, 69.
  70   In February 1935 . . . "fear for his safety": Newspaper clipping (February 19, 1935) and United Press Dispatch in JSP.

10. The Trouble I've Seen: 1934–1936

p. 72   pathetic little ship: VG, 69.
  72   Marquis Childs: MGRL.
  72   "young society matron": "Girl Investigator Writes of Experiences in FERA," New York *World-Telegram,* September 19, 1936, 19A.
  72   "distracting" long legs: "Glamour Girl," *Time,* March 18, 1940, 92.
  72   told Hopkins two things . . . by her own estimation: VG, 69.
  72   less than two months: "Girl Investigator," 19A.
  72   thirty-five dollars a week: VG, 69.
  73   "weakness for poker and bowling . . . man of resource and decision": Arthur M. Schlesinger, Jr., *The Age of Roosevelt: The Coming of the New Deal* (Boston: Houghton Mifflin Company, 1959), 265–66, 271.
  73   succumbed to typhoid: VG, 17.
  74   made Gellhorn savage: VG, 18.
  74   Lorena Hickok . . . "like beavers": Schlesinger, 272.
  74   "five families a day" . . . inept: VG, 19–20.
  74   half a dollar a day: Schlesinger, 263.
  74   Catholics who were Democrats: BMG, 32.
  74   "blood and thunder": "Girl Investigator," 19A.
  74   "minimal job" . . . $500 million for the whole country: Schlesinger, 273, 264.
  74   contain his mirth: MGRL.

p. 75   Gellhorn wrote fondly: MGRL.

75   "black sweater and skirt": VG, 70.

75   "talk to that child . . .": MGRL.

75   fascinated: MGRL.

75   to visit him again: VG, 70.

75   result in action: MGRL.

75   off the dole . . . get better: VG, 25.

75   Jouvenel arrived in Washington: John R. Braun, *"Une Fidelite Difficile:* The Early Life and Ideas of Bertrand de Jouvenel, 1903–1945," (Ph.D. dissertation, University of Waterloo, Waterloo, Ontario, Canada, 1985), 492–93.

75   remain close friends: Martha Gellhorn to John Braun, January 2, 1979.

76   writing admiring articles: Bertrand de Jouvenel, "Avec Martha Gellhorn, Collaboratrice du President Roosevelt," *Les Nouvelles litteraires,* November 7, 1936, 6; "La crise a fair surgir en Amerique une nouvelle litterature," *Les Nouvelles litteraires,* August 13, 1938, 6.

76   humiliating means test: VG, 24, 71.

76   questioned their manhood: MGRL.

76   "dangerous Communist": VG, 71.

76   Hopkins regretted it: MGRL.

76   happy to be free of government work: MGRL; VG, 71.

76   Roosevelts were concerned: MGRL.

76   Eleanor wrote to Lorena Hickok: Joseph Lash, *Love, Eleanor: Eleanor Roosevelt and Her Friends* (New York: Doubleday, 1982), 217.

76   near collapse: "Girl Investigator," 19A.

77   she wrote Eleanor: Martha Gellhorn to Eleanor Roosevelt, January 30, 1936, FDR.

77   Later she would admit: MG to ER, September 23, 1941, FDR.

77   fashionable stores: MG to ER, February 7, 1936, FDR.

77   "Shut up and go back to sleep. . . .": TRT, 398.

77   Woollcott had been present: MGRL.

77   The Roosevelts' hospitality: VG, 72–73.

77   little attention was paid to security: TRT, 398.

77   old-fashioned bathrooms . . . bookshelves: *Eleanor Roosevelt's My Day,* introduction by Martha Gellhorn (New York: Pharos Books, 1989), x–xi.

78   She did not like . . . expect help: *Eleanor Roosevelt's My Day,* x–xi.

78   "pathologically modest": *Eleanor Roosevelt's My Day,* x–xi.

78   "lethal Martinis": TRT, 398.

78   "he was a charmer . . .": TRT, 398.

78   "cozy or comforting": MGRL.

78   "a sort of mascot . . . she was love": MGRL.

78   When a friend made available: VG, 72.

p. 78   personal and civic courage: VG, 72.

78   "free and open hospitality . . . quite attractive": David C. Smith, *H. G. Wells: Desperately Moral, A Biography* (New Haven, Yale University Press, 1986), 390, 394.

79   In July: HW, 288.

79   a committed anti-Fascist: VG, 69.

79   Eleanor Roosevelt had received an advance copy: HW, 288.

79   "young, pretty . . .": *Eleanor Roosevelt's My Day,* 29.

79   "She has an understanding . . .": HW, 289.

79   "aristocratic" manners: MGRL.

79   On September 25 . . . thousands of others: Edna Gellhorn–Eleanor Roosevelt correspondence, FDR.

80   In his syndicated column . . . Other reviews: HW, 289.

82   the wind . . . plight: TIS, 11, 86, 92.

83   the wind . . . "the wind yelling": TIS, 221–24.

83   "was based on a waif . . .": HW, 287.

83   Mary Taussig Hall recalls: int. MTH.

84   fictionalizing her journalism: int. ELN.

84   "goddam nigger": VG, 5.

85   reprinted in two magazines . . . confused mind: Martha Gellhorn to Eleanor Roosevelt, November 23, 1936, FDR.

85   persuasive realism: Eleanor Roosevelt to Martha Gellhorn, November 30, 1936, FDR.

85   based on a memory: VG, 68.

85   Gellhorn was now a public figure: BMG, 57; HW, 290.

85   praising her: Eleanor Roosevelt to Martha Gellhorn, November 7, 1936, FDR.

85   talk of dramatizing: HW, 290.

85   spoke at a preview: BMG, 57.

85   Earlier, in April: Martha Gellhorn to Eleanor Roosevelt, April 26, 1936, FDR.

86   "promotional hoopla . . .": HW, 290.

11. Beauty and the Beast: 1936–1937

p. 89   They hated it . . . south of Miami: HW, 290.

89   Edna noticed a bar: HW, 290.

89   "grubby T-shirt": EH, 297.

89   "odoriferous Basque shorts": Kenneth S. Lynn, *Hemingway* (New York: Simon and Schuster, 1987), 464.

89   barefooted: James McLendon, *Papa: Hemingway in Key West* (Miami, Florida: E. A. Seeman Publishing Co., 1972), 164.

89   "large, dirty man": EH, 297.

89   speaking to the Gellhorns first: BMG, 60.

p. 89   her favorite: Martha Gellhorn to Eleanor Roosevelt, February 13, 1942, FDR.

89   Many of Edna's friends: int. AF, MTH, VD.

90   "one-piece black dress and high heels": McLendon, 164.

90   one of her friends remembers: int. ELN.

90   "shoulder-length hair . . .": Lynn, 464.

90   Another friend notes: int. MTH.

90   "Very blond . . .": int. MLS.

90   "low, husky, eastern-seaboard-accented voice": Lynn, 464.

90   shy at their first meeting . . . Bill and Katy Smith: EH, 297.

90   "beauty and the beast": McLendon, 164.

90   "Papa Dobles": McLendon, 164.

90   "literary hero": BMG, 60.

90   Hemingway seemed a little old to her: BMG, 60.

90   a very youthful twenty-eight: HW, 291.

90   "talked older. . . .": HW, 291.

90   "compensated, in part, for the loss of the parent": H, 299.

90   "insinuated herself . . .": H, 298.

91   "inhibited her intimacy with Ernest": HW, 291.

91   "a run of Dobles": McLendon, 165.

91   inside information . . . charming manner: BMG, 407.

91   "He's talking to a beautiful blond . . .": McLendon, 165.

91   Jeffrey Meyers has suggested: H, 299–300.

91   "She was very grumpy": HW, 290.

92   As Lorine Thompson puts it: TG, 102.

92   Leicester Hemingway: Leicester Hemingway, *My Brother, Ernest Hemingway* (Cleveland: World Book Company, 1962), 202–203.

92   admired Hemingway's early work: BMG, 63, 408.

92   "to make the world a better place . . .": L. Hemingway, 203.

92   her favorite Hemingway novel: BMG, 61.

92   "she never saw him in the evening . . .": HW, 291.

92   became an addition there: Martha Gellhorn to Pauline Hemingway, January 14, 1937, PUL.

92   Miriam Williams: McLendon, 166. Gellhorn denies "kissing and carrying on" with Hemingway at this time.

92   sunshine and swimming: HW, 290.

92   "mermaid . . . her writing": H, 300.

92   On January 5: FDR.

93   wrote Pauline: Martha Gellhorn to Pauline Hemingway, January 14, 1937, PUL.

93   to Eleanor Roosevelt: Martha Gellhorn to Eleanor Roosevelt, January 16, 1937, FDR.

94   "history and truth": "Exile," *Scribner's Magazine,* September, 1937, 18.

94   "dirty, messy old German": "Exile," 20.

p. 94 a sense of home: "Exile," 22.

94 "flattered and amazed by his attentions": HW, 293.

94 a book to complete . . . southern Missouri: BMG, 63.

95 "horrors" . . . union: HW, 294.

95 polluted: Martha Gellhorn to Eleanor Roosevelt, February 9, 1937, FDR.

95 Eleanor Roosevelt sent a soothing letter: Eleanor Roosevelt to Martha Gellhorn, January 16, 1937, FDR.

95 put it away: FW, 14.

95 "deluge" . . . Wednesday Club: HW, 294.

95 fellow conspirator . . . doted on him: HW, 294.

95 Hemingway had written Pauline's parents: HW, 294.

95 deeply in love with Pauline: H, 301.

96 "clad in black silk . . . skill as a lover": H, 301. Gellhorn denies having made the statement described.

96 "My beautiful girl friend . . .": H, 311.

96 "going to get Hemingway . . .": TG, 111.

96 "grey flannel trousers . . .": HW, 296.

96 food . . . margins of death: FW, 14–16.

96 lifted his arm: BMG, 67.

97 "I knew you'd get here": EH, 304.

97 The best she could do: HW, 297.

97 knew nothing about war: FW, 16.

97 "made a face . . . giggling and cuddling for warmth": HW, 296.

97 "a sleek woman . . .": EH, 304.

97 snickering at the sound of bombs falling: Herbert Matthews, *Two Wars and More to Come* (New York: Carrick & Evans, 1938), 205.

97 "That's Marty . . .": Peter Wyden, *The Passionate War: The Narrative History of the Spanish Civil War* (New York: Simon and Schuster, 1983), 324; Josephine Herbst, "The Starched Blue Sky of Spain," in *The Noble Savage* (New York: Meridian Books, 1960), 83.

98 "Saks Fifth Avenue slacks . . ." Wyden, 324.

98 "domineering . . . with Ernest": TG, 111.

98 Stephen Spender recalls: TG, 111.

98 "went around Madrid . . .": Virginia Cowles, *Looking for Trouble* (New York: Harper & Brothers, 1941), 31.

98 "seventeen blocks . . .": TG, 321.

98 "filth and vermin . . . fish": Ibid.

98 second night in Madrid . . . "possessiveness": HW, 297.

98 "big, splashy, funny . . . not a grownup": Wyden, 323.

98 "in that pre-historic past . . .": OA, 290.

98 "made the place . . . Ernest and Martha": EH, 309.

99 did not assume her expenses . . . "evil-smelling hospitals": Wyden, 324.

99 dreadful military hospitals: OA, 282.

p. 99   first warm spring day . . . "seam-picking": EH, 304; Martha Gellhorn, "Madrid to Morata," *The New Yorker,* July 24, 1937, 31.

99   "camouflaged . . .": "Madrid to Morata," 31; Cecil Eby, *Between the Bullet and the Lie: American Volunteers in the Spanish Civil War* (New York: Holt, Rinehart and Winston, 1969), 74–75.

99   brightening a soldier's day: BMG, 77.

99   "flimsy ditches" . . . scraping away at each other: Eby, 74–75; "Madrid to Morata," 37–39.

100   "the hub of the world struggle . . .": *Two Wars and More to Come,* 222.

100   "one of the happiest periods of Hemingway's life": Herbert L. Matthews, *A World in Revolution: A Newspaperman's Memoir* (New York: Charles Scribner's Sons, 1971), 23.

100   "the joy in man's tragic struggle . . .": Herbert L. Matthews, *The Education of a Correspondent* (New York: Harcourt, Brace and Co., 1946), 117.

100   much influenced by Matthews's: *A World in Revolution,* 23.

100   "exemplifies . . . a little mad": *The Education of a Correspondent,* 95.

100   saved Matthews's life: *A World in Revolution,* 24–25.

100   "a much-battered apartment house . . .": *The Education of a Correspondent,* 95.

100   grandfather's house: Wyden, 334.

100   "At breakfast . . .": TG, 109–110.

101   Every evening . . . lose his guests: Cowles, 19.

101   "fascist pressure": Wyden, 330.

101   unique and "prophetic": FW, 16.

101   familiar with each other . . . first-name basis: HOA, 154.

101   "Visit to the Wounded": *Story Magazine,* October 1937, 59.

101   "neat round bullet-hole . . .": Cowles, 29.

101   "At the hotel . . .": Cowles, 33.

102   "within a thousand yards . . .": *Two Wars and More to Come,* 282.

102   "shell smashed house . . . dust of it": Ernest Hemingway, *The Fifth Column and Four Stories of the Spanish Civil War* (New York: Charles Scribner's Sons, 1966), 110–11.

102   "It's the nastiest thing . . .": *Two Wars and More to Come,* 34.

102   "idealists and mercenaries . . .": *Two Wars and More to Come, 31.*

102   Franklin was loyal to Pauline: EH, 305.

103   "from the inside" . . . intrigue and luxury: Wyden, 328.

103   "neither a collection . . .": FW, 17.

103   sealed envelope . . . punching Voigt: Phillip Knightley, *The First Casualty: From Crimea to Vietnam: The War Correspondent as Hero, Propagandist, and Myth Maker* (New York: Harcourt Brace Jovanovich, 1975), 198; *Byline: Ernest Hemingway: Selected Articles and Dispatches of Four Decades,* ed. William White (New York: Charles Scribner's Sons, 1967), 294–97.

p. 103   "ten hard days" . . . suffered in World War I: EH, 311; HW, 299.

104   "We were all in it together . . .": Knightley, 215, 192.

12. The Spanish Earth: 1937

p. 105   spirit of fellowship . . . inadequate: FW, 15.

105   Hemingway and Matthews both told her: BMG, 68.

105   To her amazement: FW, 16; HW, 298.

106   "thud" . . . throat: FW, 19.

106   "gently and airily" . . . leg on a chair: FW, 20–21, 23–25.

107   Gellhorn has never made great claims: TRT, 358.

107   "heavy coughing grunt . . . his chin": *By-Line: Ernest Hemingway: Selected Articles and Dispatches of Four Decades,* ed. William White (New York: Charles Scribner's Sons, 1967), 258–59.

108   "two distinct techniques . . . effects on the individual": Phillip Knightley, *The First Casualty: From the Crimea to Vietnam: The War Correspondent as Hero, Propagandist, and Myth Maker* (New York: Harcourt Brace Jovanovich, 1975), 10.

108   "Ernest worked on . . .": Leicester Hemingway, *My Brother, Ernest Hemingway* (Cleveland: World Book Company, 1962) 206.

108   Joris Ivens was sending Hemingway telegrams . . . "the rest of the world": HW, 302.

109   On June 4 . . . clapping had stopped: EH, 313–14.

109   "is a lie told by bullies . . . consider one's own fate": *The Writer in a Changing World,* ed. Henry Hart (USA: Equinox Cooperative Press, 1937), 69, 71.

109   "rushed to the wings": HW, 304.

109   Gellhorn was thrilled: Martha Gellhorn to Eleanor Roosevelt, n.d., FDR.

109   Benson has suggested . . . intelligentsia: Frederick R. Benson, *Writers in Arms: The Literary Impact of the Spanish Civil War* (New York: New York University Press, 1967), 33.

110   "afternoon closed session": HW, 304.

110   how little attention . . . the Republican side of the war: *The Writer in a Changing World,* 63–65, 67.

110   Splitting up . . . her companions died: HW, 304.

110   She implored the Roosevelts: MGRL.

110   mother of a million: Martha Gellhorn to Eleanor Roosevelt, Wednesday, n.d., FDR.

110   an extravagant beauty salon: MG to ER, Wednesday, n.d., FDR.

111   high-strung . . . her experiences: MG to ER, Saturday, n.d., FDR.

111   "was doing most of the courting" . . . another Dreiser: HW, 305.

111   ten days in Hartford, Connecticut: Martha Gellhorn to Eleanor Roosevelt, Sunday, n.d., FDR.

p. 111   White House suppers: EH, 315.

111   As Hemingway later described it: SLH, 460.

112   Gellhorn remained in Manhattan . . . children: Martha Gellhorn to Eleanor Roosevelt, Sunday, n.d., FDR.

112   "cuckoo idealist": HW, 306.

112   her book on Spain . . . the previous winter: Martha Gellhorn to Eleanor Roosevelt, Sunday, n.d., FDR.

112   Archibald MacLeish and John Dos Passos . . . "phoney slob": Roy Hoopes, *Ralph Ingersoll: A Biography* (New York: Atheneum, 1985), 174.

112   "idea of shipboard fun . . .": Marion Meade, *Dorothy Parker: What Fresh Hell is This?* (New York: Villard Books, 1988), 282.

112   sulking company of Lillian Hellman: OA, 289.

112   early September . . . Fascist attack: EH, 318; HW, 306.

113   "gloomily comforted . . .": Herbert Matthews, *Two Wars and More to Come* (New York: Carrick & Evans, 1938), 300.

113   six happily private days . . . "burning stable": OA, 290.

113   she was miffed: Peter Wyden, *The Passionate War: The Narrative History of the Spanish Civil War* (New York: Simon and Schuster, 1983), 404.

113   "steep, rocky trails" . . . Hemingway was impressed: EH, 319.

113   For her *Collier's* readers . . . fellow countrymen: Martha Gellhorn, "Men Without Medals," *Collier's,* January 15, 1938, 9–10.

114   The soldiers enjoyed talking with Gellhorn: BMG, 83–84.

114   blowing over the tailgate: EH, 319.

114   "as quiet and beautiful" . . . leave the Fascists to their shelling: EH, 319.

115   "shut tight . . . to the coast": Matthews, op. cit., 311.

115   quiet October: OA, 292.

115   good weather: HW, 307.

115   wonderful dinner: OA, 292.

115   When it rained: HW, 307.

115   Gellhorn remembers Hemingway . . . broadcasting from Madrid: OA, 295, 301.

115   Tired of war: HOA, 123–24, 127.

116   In one of her *Collier's* articles: "Men Without Medals," 49.

116   a zoo and gun sites . . . artillery fire: HOA, 127.

116   "like a wheat field": Ernest Hemingway, *The Fifth Column and Four Stories of the Spanish Civil War* (New York: Charles Scribner's Sons, 1966), 41.

116   "she's got the longest, smoothest, straightest legs . . .": Ibid., 39.

116   "I want to make . . .": Ibid., 42.

116   "Granted . . .": Ibid., 44.

117   "I'm a sort of . . .": Ibid., 36.

p. 117   "conceited, *conceited* drunkard . . .": Ibid., 84.

117   "fifty years of undeclared wars": Ibid., 80.

117   "impish humor . . .": Wyden, 406; HW, 309.

117   Bridges was a credible character: H, 323.

117   apparent to Stephen Spender . . . Spender has admitted to being as much: TG, 131–34; OA, 281–86.

118   The November weather: HW, 310; FW, 27, 31.

118   As Gellhorn later put it in a story . . . intimate, private matters: HOA, 154, 169.

118   suddenly left: HW, 310.

118   The worst thing: EH, 320.

118   negotiating one's way through dark trenches: FW, 33.

119   Jeffrey Meyers is probably right: H, 317.

119   "Would you like to marry me . . .": quoted in Meyers, 317.

119   Pauline was in Paris: EH, 324.

119   trouble writing . . .: EH, 325.

119   recalling in a letter . . .: SLH, 460.

119   On board the *Normandie:* HW, 311–12.

13. For Whom the Bell Tolls: 1938–1939

p. 120   "single cell . . .": quoted in BMG, 91.

120   exhausting lecture tour: Martha Gellhorn to Eleanor Roosevelt, January 24, 1938, FDR.

120   depleted: MG to ER, January 24, 1938, FDR.

120   interviewed by the press: "Martha Gellhorn Sees Spain as Breeding Place for World War," St. Louis *Globe-Democrat,* January 28, 1938.

120   an enthusiastic Grace Hemingway: HW, 314.

121   no way in an hour to explain . . . a doctor urged her: HW, 314; BMG, 91; Martha Gellhorn to Eleanor Roosevelt, February 1, 1938, FDR.

121   left on February 13: Edna Gellhorn calendar, WUA.

121   "Spain's no place . . . 'the women' might come": Peter Wyden, *The Passionate War: The Narrative History of the Spanish Civil War* (New York: Simon and Schuster, 1983), 450.

121   "military pretensions": Richard Whelan, *Robert Capa: A Biography* (New York: Knopf, 1985), 150.

121   "her legs . . . Ernest's echo": Whelan, 167.

121   "Martha and her companions . . .": HW, 314.

122   Gellhorn wrote Eleanor Roosevelt: April 24, 1938, FDR.

122   "the least important part of their relationship": HW, 315.

122   writing her editor: Martha Gellhorn to Charles Colebaugh, June 1, 1938, NYPL.

p. 122   given some of her earnings away: Ibid.

122   the Republic would fight on: Wyden, 469.

123   "he was sinking . . .": HW, 316.

123   "fine green island": VG, 34.

124   Gellhorn and Cowles interviewed: Virginia Cowles, *Looking for Trouble* (New York: Harper & Brothers, 1941), 126.

124   standard working-class English pub: Cowles, 124.

125   no clear answer . . . Czechoslovakia: Cowles, 126–27.

125   "warmongers" . . . "Yes, m'lord": Ibid., 128.

125   "Just try coming to *my* country . . .": Cowles, 128.

125   "glared ferociously . . . bound to be an Englishman": Cowles, 128–29.

126   the French still made politics: Martha Gellhorn, "Guns Against France," *Collier's,* October 8, 1938, 13.

126   appeasement . . . tragedy of war: Ibid.

127   an ancient baroque clock: Martha Gellhorn, "Come Ahead, Adolf!," *Collier's,* August 6, 1938.

128   a "great race . . .": Ibid, 43.

128   this lovely . . . this period in her novel *A Stricken Field:* ASF, 87, 208.

129   vacation in Corsica: Martha Gellhorn to Eleanor Roosevelt, August 14, 1938, FDR.

129   sending Eleanor Roosevelt: Martha Gellhorn to Eleanor Roosevelt, October 19, 1938 and report, "Anti-Nazi Refugees in Czechoslovakia," FDR.

129   "real life in Paris . . .": HW, 319.

129   From Paris on October 22: Martha Gellhorn to Charles Colebaugh, October 22, 1938, NYPL.

130   "dirty Czechs": VG, 55.

130   Czech women . . . Fascist terror: VG, 56, 58.

131   historic events: ASF, 9.

132   "old John": ASF, 9.

132   panoramic view: ASF, 156, 82.

132   They advanced sluggishly: ASF, 12, 13, 24.

133   an international outcry: ASF, 56.

134   "passport, job, love" . . . repaid: ASF, 57.

134   good spirits: VG, 41.

134   "last ditchers": Whelan, 154.

134   "intense camaraderie . . .": Whelan, 155.

135   agonizing over Spain: Eleanor Roosevelt to Martha Gellhorn, January 26, 1939, FDR.

135   a new granddaughter: Edna Gellhorn to Eleanor Roosevelt, n.d., FDR.

135   failed Spain . . . its own values: Martha Gellhorn to Eleanor Roosevelt, n.d., FDR.

14. *The Heart of Another: 1939–1940*

p. 136   traditional way: Martha Gellhorn to Eleanor Roosevelt, January 1, 1939, FDR.

136   early-morning hours: Edna Gellhorn calendar, WUA.

136   a grieving Edna: Martha Gellhorn to Eleanor Roosevelt, Thursday, n.d., FDR.

136   exchanging news with Eleanor Roosevelt: MG to ER, March 8, 1939, FDR.

137   Americans were no different from others: MG to ER, February 3, 1939, FDR.

137   depressed . . . *A Farewell to Arms:* SLH, 477, 479, 480, 482–83.

137   "I owe him . . .": HW, 325.

137   "funny, wonderful, alive and exciting": H, 353.

137   Hemingway nursed his injured pride: Martha Gellhorn to Gerry Brenner, March 7, 1976, Ernest Hemingway Collection, John Fitzgerald Kennedy Library.

138   "small second-floor room . . .": HW, 325.

138   Hemingway took one look: EH, 340.

138   Using her own money: HW, 326.

138   "Luigi's House": HOA, 1–2.

139   sticking around the house, shopping: Martha Gellhorn to Eleanor Roosevelt, March 8, 1939, FDR.

139   To Jane Armstrong: MG to Jane Armstrong, May 24, 1939, David R. Meeker Collection. Julie Lew, "Hemingway Manuscripts Are Found," *The New York Times,* August 17, 1989, 17.

139   Hemingway saw how attractive . . . wife and mistress: EH, 340–41; HW, 326–27.

139   "jealousy of other women . . .": HW, 328.

139   soothing and stimulating effect: BMG, 105–106.

140   complaining about fatigue: Martha Gellhorn to Jane Armstrong, June 15, 1939, David R. Meeker Collection.

140   she no longer cared: Martha Gellhorn to Eleanor Roosevelt, May 17, 1939, FDR.

140   two-week visit . . . last chapter of her novel: Edna Gellhorn calendar, WUA.

140   glum and frantic . . . excruciating: Martha Gellhorn to Eleanor Roosevelt, May 17, 1939, FDR.

140   joy . . . Poland: MG to ER, August 4, 1939, FDR.

140   idiotic and disloyal: MG to ER, n.d., FDR.

141   "To All American Foreign Service Officers": BMG, 106–107.

141   "melted all through the fabric . . . sobbed uncontrollably": HW, 329.

141   "From Billings . . . fishing: Ibid., 330.

142   smiling at Arnold: HWH, 23.

142   "the Marty": HWH, 25.

p. 142   he had Martha explain: HWH, 28–29.

142   "ecstatic": HW, 330.

142   "responded to [Hemingway's] wishes . . .": HWH, 51.

142   experienced rider: HWH, 52.

142   "a barrel of fun . . .": HW, 331.

142   "paradise": HW, 331.

143   "What old Indian . . . *have* to do it": HWH, 70.

143   hardly contain her excitement: Martha Gellhorn to Charles Colebaugh, September 28, 1940, NYPL.

143   praised Gellhorn's courage: HW, 331.

143   "just get her out . . .": HWH, 70.

143   "this big clown . . . good boy": HWH, 71.

143   not easy finding a ship: Martha Gellhorn to Charles Colebaugh, n.d., NYPL.

143   "Slow Boat to War": FW (1959 edition), 46, 54.

144   On December 2 . . . stirring letters: Edna Gellhorn to Eleanor Roosevelt, n.d.., FDR.

144   reminiscent of Spain: HW, 333.

144   "long emotional letter": HW, 333.

144   It was uncanny . . . told her: FW, 53–66.

144   Hotel Kamp . . . wool stockings: Martha Gellhorn, "Death in the Present Tense," *Collier's,* February 10, 1940, 14–15.

145   One night in December . . . through other evacuations: Virginia Cowles, *Looking for Trouble* (New York: Harper & Brothers, 1941), 321.

145   "Fear Comes to Sweden": Martha Gellhorn, in *Collier's,* February 3, 1940, 20–22.

145   "Good Will to Men": HOA, 186–267.

147   war of survival: FW, 51.

147   terribly upset: HW, 334.

147   To Eleanor Roosevelt . . . "among the finest of the war": BMG, 113; Joseph Lash, *Love, Eleanor* (New York: Doubleday, 1982), 288–89.

147   writing her editor: Martha Gellhorn to Charles Colebaugh, n.d., NYPL.

148   "Mrs. Martha . . . with love": HW, 338–39.

148   Writing to one of her friends: HW, 339.

148   Writing to his editor . . . next day: SLH, 500.

148   "counterforce": EH, 346.

149   "That's my mermaid . . . body of a Circe": Leicester Hemingway, *My Brother, Ernest Hemingway* (Cleveland: World Book Company, 1962), 224.

149   loathe to leave Cuba . . . book writing: Martha Gellhorn to Charles Colebaugh, March 13, 1940, NYPL.

149   took exception: Martha Gellhorn to Eleanor Roosevelt, March 17, 1940, FDR.

p. 149   He was inclined: Charles Colebaugh to Martha Gellhorn, March 21, 1940, NYPL.

149   To Jane Armstrong: Martha Gellhorn to Jane Armstrong, March 15, 1940, David R. Meeker Collection.

149   Gellhorn was gratified: Martha Gellhorn to Charles Colebaugh, March 31, 1940, NYPL.

149   afraid of being typed: MG to CC, April 3, 1940, NYPL.

150   Colebaugh was receptive: Charles Colebaugh to Martha Gellhorn, April 12, 1940, NYPL.

150   "Mango trees . . .": Gregory Hemingway, *Papa: A Personal Memoir* (Boston: Houghton Mifflin, 1976), 47.

150   "a gorgeous blond lady . . . high-born lady": Jack Hemingway, *Misadventures of a Fly Fisherman: My Life with and without Papa* (Dallas, Texas: Taylor Publishing Company, 1986), 30–31.

150   drop Pauline: Ibid, 32.

150   "worst slums" . . . "stand of bamboo" Ibid., 32–39.

151   "beautiful large bedroom" . . . white pouter pigeons: Ibid., 390.

151   "old favorites . . .": Ibid., 39–41.

151   "handsome young people . . .": HW, 341.

151   "more as a friend . . .": H, 349.

151   many talks . . . one of the Hemingways: HW, 341.

151   the next crisis: Martha Gellhorn to Jane Armstrong, February 23, 1942, David R. Meeker Collection.

151   "itch": HW, 343.

152   spoiled . . . house: Martha Gellhorn to Charles Colebaugh, n.d., NYPL.

152   finished a twenty-thousand-word story: BMG, 115.

152   seemed rather eccentric: Martha Gellhorn to Eleanor Roosevelt, June 7, 1940, FDR.

152   caterpillar invasion . . . turn on the Russians: Martha Gellhorn to Charles Colebaugh, June 29, 1940, NYPL.

152   making war . . . govern Europe: Martha Gellhorn to Eleanor Roosevelt, July 7, 1940, FDR.

152   great charm: L. Hemingway, op. cit., 224.

152   so successful: HW, 343.

152   "wondered later . . .": HW, 343.

153   "You can stand me up . . .": EH, 350.

153   The rest of Edna's trip: Edna Gellhorn's calendar, WUA.

153   whale shark . . . local Nazi: Martha Gellhorn to Eleanor Roosevelt, July 20, 1940, FDR.

153   suggested to Colebaugh: Martha Gellhorn to Charles Colebaugh, July 17, 1940, NYPL.

153   Close to two thousand aliens: MG to CC, July 8, 1940, NYPL.

153   The newspaper *PM:* MG to CC, July 17, 1940 (marked *P.M.*), NYPL.

p. 154   Colebaugh was not convinced . . .: Charles Colebaugh to Martha Gellhorn, July 31, 1940, NYPL.

154   She accepted the check . . . November: Martha Gellhorn to Charles Colebaugh, August 8, 1940, NYPL.

154   "absolutely lamentable females": H, 349.

154   written Clara Spiegel: EH, 351–52; HW, 344.

154   advised her not to marry Hemingway: BMG, 116.

154   "war, pestilence . . .": SLH, 511.

154   the off-season . . . United States: Martha Gellhorn to Eleanor Roosevelt, July 20, 1940, FDR.

154   "be careful . . . like an equal": G. Hemingway, op. cit., 41–42.

155   "same goddam face": SLH, 518–19.

155   "well barbered": H, 481.

155   to Alexander Woollcott: Undated letter from Dorothy Parker to Alexander Woollcott, Special Collections, Houghton Library, Harvard University.

156   pack trip . . . flu: SLH, 519.

156   going down the Burma Road: SLH, 519.

156   under the name of Martha Hemingway: EH, 353.

156   Edna Gellhorn's sudden visit: BMG, 117.

156   reading one of Hemingway's letters: int. AF.

156   "We were all . . .": int. MTH.

156   "runaway elevator": HWH, 111.

156   Hemingway and H. G. Wells: HW, 348–49.

157   sixteen: Martha Gellhorn to Eleanor Roosevelt, December 5, 1940, FDR.

157   reveling in nature . . . Mrs. Hemingway: MG to ER, December 27, 1940, FDR.

157   confided to Archibald MacLeish: Ernest Hemingway to Archibald MacLeish, n.d., Archibald Macleish Papers, Library of Congress.

157   she would not have stood for it . . . dutiful wife: Martha Gellhorn to Eleanor Roosevelt, n.d., FDR.

157   telling a reporter: HW, 354.

157   As Bernice Kert has put it: HW, 354.

157   the heart of another . . . "contend with": HW, 347–48.

15. Career and Husband: 1941–1942

p. 158   she wrote Eleanor Roosevelt: Martha Gellhorn to Eleanor Roosevelt, n.d., FDR.

158   "my husband and I . . .": "Martha Gellhorn, Burroughs, '26, Says Youths Must Rebuild World," St. Louis Globe-Democrat, January 16, 1941, SLML; Martha Gellhorn to Eleanor Roosevelt, n.d., FDR.

159   "cool": TWMA, 21.

159   Hemingway got truculent: EH, 360.

p. 159   more pleased . . . shrugged it off: Martha Gellhorn to Charles Colebaugh, March 1, 1941, NYPL.

159   "M. is going off": TWMA, 24.

159   tiny rounded picture: TWMA, 24.

160   coarse blankets: TWMA, 25.

160   healing properties: *Conversations with Ernest Hemingway,* ed. Matthew J. Bruccoli (Jackson: University Press of Mississippi, 1986), 34.

160   "very disappointed": TWMA, 30.

160   China adventure had been her idea: TWMA, 34.

160   "heroic": TWMA, 35.

160   "five foot tall Ali Baba jar": TWMA, 43.

161   dauntless journalist: TWMA, 44.

161   "So far . . .": TWMA, 52.

161   "vegetarian tigers . . . ordinary tree": FW, 78–79.

161   "M. loves humanity . . .": TWMA, 56.

162   "a faint dark eye shadow" . . . ". . . other women": Martha Gellhorn, "Her Day," *Collier's,* August 30, 1941, 16, 53.

163   "upwind": TWMA, 62–63.

163   "mixing concrete . . .": *Conversations with Ernest Hemingway,* 30.

163   "In the long run . . .": FW, 83.

163   writing to Max Perkins: SLH, 523.

163   admitted borrowing: Martha Gellhorn to Charles Colebaugh, n.d., NYPL.

163   A nettled Hemingway: Ernest Hemingway to Charles Colebaugh, June 18, 1941, NYPL.

164   Hemingway told Perkins: SLH, 523.

164   "war of nerves": Martha Gellhorn "Fire Guards the Indies," *Collier's,* August 2, 1941, 51.

164   "as a layman . . .": Martha Gellhorn, "Singapore Scenario," *Collier's,* August 9, 1941, 43.

164   respect for her work: Martha Gellhorn to Charles Colebaugh, n.d., NYPL.

164   cried with "relief and gratitude": HW, 362.

165   a few hours to shop . . . take on another enemy: "Martha Gellhorn, Reporter-Wife of Ernest Hemingway, Clippers into Town," San Francisco *Chronicle,* May 28, 1941, 17.

165   her report: HW, 363.

165   improvised late suppers: HW, 363.

165   genial host: HW, 363.

165   Martha confided to Jane Armstrong: Martha Gellhorn to Jane Armstrong, August 27, 1941, David R. Meeker Collection.

165   "a definite and vigorous reassertion . . .": David C. Smith, *H. G. Wells: Desperately Mortal, A Biography* (New Haven: Yale University Press, 1986), 428.

166   plain homebodies . . . a woman who wrote fiction: Martha Gellhorn to H. G. Wells, August 23, 1941, H. G. Wells Collection, library

of the University of Illinois at Urbana-Champaign, Rare
Book Room.

p. 166   healthy holiday: Martha Gellhorn to Eleanor Roosevelt, November
1 or 2, 1941, FDR.

166   real depth: MG to ER, October 17 and November 1 or 2,
1941, FDR.

166   "Pure Hemingway . . .": quoted in HW, 365.

166   Every writer in America: Martha Gellhorn to Eleanor Roosevelt,
November 1 or 2, 1941, FDR.

166   reminded her of Hemingway: Eleanor Roosevelt to Martha Gellhorn, November 10, 1941, FDR.

167   pleasant, settled life: HOA, 130–34.

167   "driving force or emotional center": Marianne Hauser, "Noise
of Guns," in *The New York Times Books Review,* November 2,
1941, 22.

167   "blond and chic . . . Now you see bead": EH, 370.

168   her contentedness: SLH, 530.

168   Indian country: SLH, 533.

168   poring over . . . college again: Martha Gellhorn to Charles Colebaugh, January 19, 1942, NYPL.

168   report the war: Martha Gellhorn to Eleanor Roosevelt, February 13,
1942, FDR.

168   willing to become a man: MG to ER, February 13, 1942, FDR.

168   old sportsmen: Martha Gellhorn to Charles Colebaugh, February 3,
1942, NYPL.

168   devoted wife: Martha Gellhorn to Eleanor Roosevelt, n.d., FDR.

169   harmlessly dilute . . . Jews: MG to ER, June 22, 1942, FDR.

169   harder than ever: MG to ER, n.d., FDR.

169   more admirable: MG to ER, July 10, 1942, FDR.

169   Gellhorn wrote Patrick Hemingway: Martha Gellhorn to Patrick
Hemingway, April 26, 1942, PUL.

169   Virginia Cowles had visited: Martha Gellhorn to Eleanor Roosevelt,
February 13, 1942, FDR.

169   her belief in human dignity: MG to ER, July 10, 1942, FDR.

169   "Latin, Catholic . . .": H, 327.

170   roaring with laughter: BMG, 128.

170   "She liked everything sanitary . . .": A. E. Hotchner, *Papa Hemingway* (New York: Random House, 1966), 133–34.

170   "I'll show you . . .": HW, 368.

170   Gregory Hemingway: Gregory Hemingway, *Papa: A Personal Memoir* (Boston: Houghton, Mifflin, 1972), 70–71.

171   "I know Martha Gellhorn . . .": TG, 146.

172   "my rival": H, 354.

172   Bernard Berenson: H, 354.

172   "carry her up to the house": H, 354.

p. 172   "*Where* in Cuba . . .": H, 355.

172   "killed him": H, 355.

172   As Jeffrey Meyers has suggested: H, 355.

172   inhibited: HOA, 43.

172   she confessed to Eleanor Roosevelt: HW, 367.

172   came to her . . . travel documents: Martha Gellhorn to Charles Colebaugh, June 10, 1941, NYPL.

173   undid white men: MG to CC, n.d., NYPL.

173   cavorting with joy . . . a book of war writing: Martha Gellhorn to Eleanor Roosevelt, July 10, 1942, FDR.

173   stories about submarines: Martha Gellhorn to Charles Colebaugh, June 28, 1942, NYPL.

174   signed Martha Gellhorn: MG to CC, July 16, 1942, NYPL.

16. *Liana: 1942–1944*

p. 175   "traveling light:" HW, 370.

175   As a journalist . . . pleasure: Martha Gellhorn to Eleanor Roosevelt, August 2, 1942, FDR.

175   "health cure": Martha Gellhorn, "A Little Worse Than Peace," *Collier's,* November 14, 1942, 85.

175   jolly and agile . . . *A Stricken Field:* HW, 370.

176   wrote his first wife: SLH, 535.

176   picking up survivors: TWMA, 66.

176   "chirpy": TWMA, 67.

176   "patchwork quilt": TWMA, 69.

177   "De lady": TWMA, 70.

177   "three hurrycane birds . . .": TWMA, 75.

177   youthful, unencumbered days: TWMA, 82.

177   "boat bum": TWMA, 85.

177   lovely mulatto: TWMA, 86.

178   "good giggle": TWMA, 93.

178   Evan Shipman: SLH, 538.

179   collection: Martha Gellhorn to Eleanor Roosevelt, October 6, 1942, FDR.

179   "back country": SLH, 543.

179   heartbreaking time . . . loneliness: Martha Gellhorn to Charles Colebaugh, October 1 and October 4, 1942, NYPL.

179   "like a dying cow . . .": HW, 373.

179   spoke to Sarah Lawrence students: "Author Speaks to S.L. Students About Writing, Martha Gellhorn Discusses Journalism, War and Literature, *Campus,* Sarah Lawrence College, October 28, 1942, 1, 5.

180   talks with both Eleanor and Franklin Roosevelt: BMG, 133–34.

p. 180   only a divorce: HW, 373.
180   "a spot of domesticity": EH, 378.
180   She wrote Patrick: PUL.
180   Winston Guest: PUL.
180   Durán and his wife: EH, 378–79; HW, 374; H, 369–78.
181   One night in Havana: EH, 380.
181   "feudal": H, 377.
182   "through a ditch . . .": EH, 380.
182   hire a car: EH, 382.
182   "I'll never forget . . .": TG, 144.
182   "rubbish": TG, 144.
182   Gellhorn has admitted: BMG, 130.
182   she wrote Alexander Woollcott: Alexander Woollcott Collection, Houghton Library, Harvard University.
183   "darling, housebroken cobra": HW, 375.
183   home soon: HW, 376.
183   mother's disappointment . . . "real writer": HW, 376.
183   powerfully protective instincts: HW, 376.
183   "like in the good old days . . .": HW, 376.
183   As she wrote in her letters to Patrick: Martha Gellhorn to Patrick Hemingway, July 4, 1943, PUL.
184   terribly drunk: HW, 378.
184   lack of confidence: HW, 378.
184   stomachache: Martha Gellhorn to Patrick Hemingway, July 4, 1943, PUL.
184   longed to be young again: HW, 379–80.
184   "You're the writer . . . deserves one": Gregory Hemingway, *Papa: A Personal Memoir* (Boston: Houghton Mifflin, 1972), 90–91.
185   "strange evenings": int. FVF.
185   "browbeating servants": int. FVF; Frederick Vanderbilt Field, *From Right to Left: An Autobiography* (Westport, Connecticut: Lawrence Hill & Company, 1983), 203–204.
185   Hemingway's son Gregory . . . callous about her feelings: HW, 381–82.
185   "interest in sex . . .": H, 355.
185   confessed to Gregory: G. Hemingway, op. cit., 91.
185   "a symbolic castration . . .": H, 353.
185   "I'm leaving . . .": Norberto Fuentes, *Hemingway in Cuba* (Secaucus, New Jersey: Lyle Stuart, 1984), 22.
185   bided her time in New York: HW, 383.
186   their days along the Loing Canal: HW, 383.
186   "the great unending battle between men and women": EH, 379.
187   "she was something . . .": L, 27.
188   "there is a truth of observation . . .": D. L. Kirkpatrick, *Contemporary Novelists* (New York: St. Martin's Press, 1986), 335.

p. 188   "perfect blending of intellectual and emotional pitch": Diana
          Trilling, "Fiction in Review: 'Liana,'" *The Nation,* January 22,
          1944, 104–105.

188   "come to understand . . .": Mark Schorer, "Exotics," *The New
          Republic,* February 28, 1944, 286, 288.

17. War: 1943–1945

p. 189   "Having a fine, brainless time" . . . phony and foolish: HW, 385.
189   "a piece of cake": FW, 90.
189   no longer on the sidelines: FW, 85–86.
190   her *Collier's* readers: Martha Gellhorn, "Children Are Soldier's,
          Too," *Collier's,* March 14, 1944.
190   "mythical": HW, 386.
191   "German forever": Martha Gellhorn, "Three Poles," *Collier's,*
          March 18, 1944, 16.
191   quite deliberately depriving the Dutch: Martha Gellhorn, "Hatchet
          Day for the Dutch," *Collier's,* March 25, 1944, 27, 59.
191   gruesome consequences of war . . . "joke of disaster": Martha Gell-
          horn, "Men Made Over," *Collier's,* May 20, 1944, 32.
192   profound error . . . eyes: HW, 388.
192   honor her convictions: HW, 389.
192   wrote Archibald MacLeish: Ernest Hemingway to Archibald Mac-
          Leish, December 25, 1943, Archibald MacLeish Papers, Library of
          Congress.
192   "kick her ass good": EH, 386.
192   an English village: Martha Gellhorn, "English Sunday," *Collier's,*
          April 1, 1944, 60–62.
193   "strangled . . .": HW, 390.
193   driving in an army jeep: FW, 102–08.
193   "I ain't had so much fun . . .": Martha Gellhorn, "Postcards from
          Italy," *Collier's,* July 1, 1944, 41.
194   "ARE YOU A WAR CORRESPONDENT . . .": HW, 391.
194   On February 27: William M. Stoneman, "Martha Gellhorn Sets Out
          to See Cassino; Shot At, Dives into Ditch," St. Louis *Post-Dispatch,*
          February 28, 1944, 1, 6.
194   dazzle André Gide: Philip Ziegler, *Diana Cooper* (New York:
          Knopf, 1982), 221.
194   Jack Hemingway: Jack Hemingway, *Misadventures of a Fly Fisher-
          man: My Life With and Without Papa* (Dallas, Texas: Taylor Publish-
          ing Company, 1986), 125.
194   tiring flight from Tangiers . . . ". . . had not": HW, 391.
195   "My father . . .": HW, 390.
195   destroying her love: HW, 392.

p. 195   on May 13: EH, 391; HW, 397.

195   She was angry: EH, 391.

195   At the hospital . . . his "safe angle": EH, 391; HW, 398.

196   got her on the phone: EH, 393.

196   an uncomfortable Leicester Hemingway: Leicester Hemingway, *My Brother, Ernest Hemingway* (Cleveland: World Book Company, 1962), 229, 239–40.

196   "In five seconds . . .": Martha Gellhorn, "Over and Back," *Collier's,* July 22, 1944, 16.

197   "36-foot coffin-shaped" . . . Mr. Hemingway: *By-Line: Ernest Hemingway, Selected Articles and Dispatches of Four Decades,* ed. William White (New York: Charles Scribner's Sons, 1967), 340–55.

197   "painfully white": FW, 109.

197   "floating city . . .": FW, 110.

198   "with his hands on his hips . . . nothing in between": Martha Gellhorn, "Hangdog Herrenvolk," *Collier's,* July 29, 1944, 24, 40–41.

199   She was departing . . . "acidulous marginalia": EH, 395.

199   Gellhorn's plans . . . in Italy: HW, 410.

199   "no papers . . .": HW, 410.

199   "the best written . . .": Harold Acton, *Memoirs of an Aesthete, 1939–1969* (New York: Viking, 1970), 152.

201   "the optimism . . .": FW, 125.

201   the reputation of the Soviet Union: FW, 121.

201   a more difficult and laborious route: Martha Gellhorn, "Treasure City: The Fight to Save Florence," *Collier's,* September 30, 1944, 31.

201   Gellhorn prevailed: HW, 410.

201   unruffled, elegant Florentines: "Treasure City," 31.

202   "neighborly men": FW, 133.

202   "German tank movements . . .": *By-Line: Ernest Hemingway,* 367.

202   "read or write . . . publishable at this time": Ibid., 371.

202   gone to war to see his wife: TG, 149.

202   "whenever he showed up . . .": TG, 152.

202   "When I got to know Marty . . .": TG, 152.

202   "Prima-Donna": SLH, 571.

202   *"insisted* that I have dinner . . .": HW, 411.

203   Gellhorn told Robert Capa . . . more of Hemingway's swearing followed: Richard Whelan, *Robert Capa: A Biography* (New York: Knopf, 1985), 228.

203   visualize the terror: Martha Gellhorn, "The Wounds of Paris," *Collier's,* November 4, 1944, 73.

203   "There will be a damn sight . . .": *My Brother, Ernest* L. Hemingway, op. cit., 256.

203   Nijmegen: Martha Gellhorn, "Death of a Dutch Town," *Collier's,* December 23, 1944, 21, 58–59.

p. 204   without respite or replacements: Martha Gellhorn, "Rough and Tumble," *Collier's,* December 2, 1944, 70.

204   had enlisted in the army: Martha Gellhorn, "82nd Airborne: Master of Hot Spots," *The Saturday Evening Post,* February 23, 1946, 40.

204   "sexual intercourse . . .": James Gavin, *On to Berlin* (New York: Bantam Books, 1985), 5.

204   Gellhorn tried to illustrate: "82nd Airborne," 40.

205   "odor of it in his nostrils": "82nd Airborne," 252.

205   Gavin recalls: BMG, 187.

205   close friends: BMG, 188.

205   On November 3: HW, 411.

205   wrote to his son Patrick: SLH, 576.

205   dived over a sixteen-foot embankment: *The New York Times,* December 14, 1944, 6.

205   anguished letter: Amy Porter, "This Week's Work," *Collier's,* February 3, 1945, 73.

206   straw in frigid cement huts: Martha Gellhorn, "The Undefeated," *Collier's,* March 3, 1945, 42.

206   invited by Colonel John Ruggles: EH, 440.

207   "She was a bitch . . .": TG, 177.

207   "supreme arrogance": EH, 441.

207   other things to demean her: EH, 441; TG, 178.

207   "I'm sure that every word . . .": TG, 177.

208   "Remember this . . .": EH, 441.

208   On New Year's Eve . . . ". . . holy grail": EH, 441; HW, 415–16.

208   dead Germans clumped together: FW, 146.

209   confusing period: FW, 148.

209   "snarling bulldog planes": FW, 153.

210   "girl correspondent . . .": FW, 18.

210   "changed back to Gellhorn. . . .": HW, 417.

18. Point of No Return: 1945–1948

p. 211   On a featureless street: Martha Gellhorn, "82nd Airborne: Master of Hot Spots," *The Saturday Evening Post,* February 23, 1946, 44.

211   "all God's chillun hid Jews: FW, 162.

211   *who* was in charge: FW, 166.

212   "I used to think . . .": FW, 178.

212   awesome fighting force: BMG, 203–04.

212   place of plague: FW, 179.

213   a Polish doctor: FW, 181.

213   once and for all: FW, 185.

213   Back in London: FW, 188; VG, 106–07.

p. 213   resolve things: Norberto Fuentes, *Hemingway in Cuba* (Secaucus, New Jersey: Lyle Stuart, 1984), 376.

214   In an undated reply: Fuentes, 377.

214   jeep mishap: Fuentes, 379.

214   At various times: Ernest Hemingway to Buck Lanham, July 23, 1945; August 25, 1948, PUL.

215   loathed women: Mrs. C. T. Lanham to Carlos Baker, June 1, 1964, PUL; EH, 452; HW, 421.

215   "tactful letter": HW, 423.

215   "those who . . .": HW, 422.

215   "muttered something . . .": Mary Welsh Hemingway, *How It Was* (New York: Knopf, 1976), 177.

215   "I cannot help wondering . . .": Ibid., 178.

215   In late July: Martha Gellhorn, "You're On Your Way Home," *Collier's,* September 22, 1945, 39.

216   On July 24: Clipping file, MHS.

216   "matrimonial plans": "Hemingway-Gellhorn Divorce This Fall," St. Louis *Globe-Democrat,* July 27, 1945, MHS.

216   going door-to-door: FW, 189.

216   newspapers announced "Martha Gellhorn Sued for Divorce," St. Louis *Globe-Dispatch,* November 22, 1945, MHS.

216   In January and February: Ernest Hemingway to Buck Lanham, January 20 and February 21, 1946, PUL.

217   "Asia for Asiatics": FW, 192.

217   "WE WANT TO REIGN . . .": FW, 194.

218   In May: Edna Gellhorn calendar, WUA.

218   "frivolous play": VG, 107.

218   Initial reports: "St. Louisan's Play Given Warm Greeting in London," St. Louis *Globe-Democrat,* June 19, 1946, MHS.

218   loose morals: item 525a, untitled sketch, Ernest Hemingway Collection, John F. Kennedy Library, Boston, Massachusetts.

218   maternal Annabelle: Martha Gellhorn and Virginia Cowles, *Love Goes to Press,* unpublished play, Library of Congress.

219   rare historical event: FW, 205.

219   voice of history: FW, 205.

219   instituted their evil: FW, 207.

219   "mass industry": FW, 208.

219   scrupulously examined: FW, 210.

219   the combined malevolence: FW, 212.

220   In December: FW, 213–20.

220   gypsy: VG, 107.

220   In the banter: VG, 108.

220   *Love Goes to Press:* Edna Gellhorn calendar, WUA.

220   New York reviewers: *The New Yorker,* January 11, 1947, 47; *Theatre Arts,* March 1947, 18; "Martha Gellhorn Co-Author of Play Opening in New York," St. Louis *Post-Dispatch,* January 2, 1947,

MHS; "Martha Gellhorn's Play to Close After Four Days," St. Louis *Post-Dispatch,* January 4, 1947, MHS.

p. 220   an expatriate: VG, 108.

220   James Gavin: Edna Gellhorn calendar, WUA.

220   immutable: VG, 77.

221   fools: VG, 81.

221   After a July break: Edna Gellhorn calendar, WUA.

221   "colored, sweetened horror": VG, 84.

221   big issues: VG, 87.

222   statement: VG, 91.

223   suppressing free speech: VG, 94.

223   an impotent effort: VG, 110.

223   "She is at her best . . . hospitality of the Generals": SLH, 630.

223   "a glamour basis . . . on the Continent": SLH, 630–31.

224   He wrote Lillian Ross: Ibid., 642–43.

224   Hemingway replied on November 17: Ernest Hemingway to Buck Lanham, November 17, 1947, PUL.

224   "To Martha Gellhorn's Vagina": Paul Johnson, *Intellectuals* (New York: Harper & Row, 1988), 164.

224   Hemingway regarded James Gavin: Ernest Hemingway to Buck Lanham, November 27, 1947, PUL.

224   Hemingway had written Charlie Scribner: SLH, 623.

225   Hemingway conducted a campaign: Ernest Hemingway to Buck Lanham, March 2 and November 24, 1948, PUL.

225   Hemingway was pleased . . .: continue to deteriorate: EH to BL, August 25, 1948, PUL.

225   Hemingway got so steamed . . . He was still rankled: EH to BL, November 8, 1948, PUL.

225   As Jeffrey Meyers has suggested: H, 414.

226   When she published a story: Ernest Hemingway to Buck Lanham, November 12, 1948, PUL.

226   "a Jew had to earn being left alone": WA, 12.

227   "Then with a suddenness . . .": WA, 167.

228   not given the war serious attention: WA, 183.

228   retreat: WA, 253.

228   did not take any of it seriously: WA, 289.

228   a right to rule: WA, 292.

229   accepted his Jewishness: WA, 304.

229   Her native land was large: VG, 110.

19. The Honeyed Peace: 1948–1953

p. 233   "private golden age": VG, 111.

233   Riding in jeeps . . . killed: FW, 221–22.

233   "a separate peace": FW, 222; VG, 111.

p. 233   aglow with sun: LTHT, 10.

233   an elemental sense of enchantment: Martha Gellhorn, "Strange Daughter," *The Saturday Evening Post,* August 23, 1952, 21.

234   handsome slim Indians: LTHT, 14.

234   "preserved in amber": LTHT, 14.

234   exotic trees blooming: LTHT, 48.

234   sunning in the afternoons: LTHT, 55–56.

234   the days were unclouded: LTHT, 81.

234   the "sober season": LTHT, 81.

234   she wrote her mother: Martha Gellhorn to Edna Gellhorn, May 28 [1949], Edna Gellhorn Collection, Schlesinger Library, Radcliffe College, Cambridge, Mass.

235   loving letters: MG to EG, May 26 [1949], Edna Gellhorn Collection, Schlesinger Library, Radcliffe College.

235   strategy: MG to EG, May 28 [1949], Edna Gellhorn Collection, Schlesinger Library, Radcliffe College.

235   children: Ibid.

235   Four years after the break with Hemingway: Martha Gellhorn to Edna Gellhorn, May 28 [1949], Edna Gellhorn Collection, Schlesinger Library, Radcliffe College.

235   sequestered from: VG, 97.

235   It was hot . . . not give him up: Martha Gellhorn to Eleanor Roosevelt, July 14 and 16, 1949, FDR.

236   "Miss Pauline . . . pumping them for material": SLH, 669.

236   "turn in my suit . . .": SLH, 669.

236   major writers: Ernest Hemingway to Charles Scribner, October 4, 1949, PUL.

236   "She had more ambition . . . conceited": Ernest Hemingway, *Across the River and into the Trees* (New York: Charles Scribner's Sons, 1950), 212.

236   "I'd look straight through her . . .": Ibid., 213.

236   Other passages: Ibid., 251, 273.

236   "There's no need . . .": H, 356. Gellhorn denies having made the statement quoted.

236   Hemingway admitted: Ernest Hemingway to Buck Lanham, April 14, 1950, PUL.

237   the facts: Anna Lord Straus to Edna Gellhorn, December 15, 1949, WUA.

237   Better to have one parent . . . he had adopted her: Martha Gellhorn, "Little Boy Found," *The Saturday Evening Post,* April 15, 1950, 168.

238   Hearing everyone speak English . . . adaptable child: Martha Gellhorn to Eleanor Roosevelt, December 14, 1949, FDR.

239   She left the publisher: HW, 458.

239   told Bernice Kert: HW, 458.

239   cutting remarks about Mary Hemingway: confidential source. Gellhorn denies having made such remarks.

p. 239   maintained his right . . . crystal and china: HW, 423, 458–59.

239   comical progress . . . working: Martha Gellhorn to Eleanor Roosevelt, February 12 and February 28, 1950, FDR.

239   Dorothy Parker and others: Martha Gellhorn to Eleanor Roosevelt, March 29, 1950, FDR.

239   Bernard Berenson . . . next meal: Martha Gellhorn to Bernard Berenson, March 7, April 2, 23, May 9, 19, 31, June 18, 1950, VIT.

240   not forsaking men: Martha Gellhorn to Eleanor Roosevelt, May 28, 1949, Edna Gellhorn Collection, Schlesinger Library, Radcliffe College.

240   "slim, elegant, and smiled shyly": Joseph Lash, *A World of Love: Eleanor Roosevelt and Her Friends, 1943–62* (New York: Doubleday, 1984), 239.

240   "psychic healing gifts": Ibid., 248.

240   "Gentlemen . . .": Ibid., 249.

241   spend all her concern . . . throttle: MGRL, 29.

241   psychological insights: Lash, op. cit., 283.

241   "I would be broken hearted . . .": Ibid., 241.

241   "not really far away . . .": Ibid., 242.

241   "could almost see . . . joy": Ibid., 243.

241   "beyond . . . look out on": Ibid., 246.

241   jealous of him: Ibid., 303.

241   "constant thought and love": Ibid., 247.

241   intimate scenes between them: Ibid., 248.

241   "vibrated with the delighted discovery . . .": Ibid., 250.

241   "You have done nothing but . . .": Ibid., 259.

242   "over the rough spots . . .": Ibid., 254.

242   "lean" . . . "cling": Ibid., 263.

242   "a state not altogether unpleasant . . .": Ibid., 337.

242   always knew: Ibid., 259.

242   "I feel a little shy . . .": Ibid., 341.

242   Roosevelt wanted him to confide: Ibid., 342–43.

242   "worthy . . . seems to me": Ibid., 346.

243   "I realize . . .": Ibid., 347.

243   "Perhaps one basic thing . . .": Ibid.

243   "spoiled by pursuit . . .": Ibid.

243   "when the man . . .": Ibid.

243   "underestimated the strength . . .": Ibid.

243   "Even at your age . . .": Ibid.

243   "How do you sleep with . . .": Ibid., 348.

243   "an old hand . . .": Ibid., 349

244   "David dearest . . .": Ibid.

244   "an undercurrent of desperation . . .": Ibid.

244   confided to a close friend: confidential int.

245   "hurt . . . marriages are two way streets . . .": Lash, op. cit., 356.

245   "Marty will be alright . . .": Ibid.

p. 245   "wonderful rest from tension": Ibid., 357.

245   "I'm trying not to think . . .": Ibid.

245   "Cannot commit myself . . .": Ibid., 363.

245   "Martha understands . . .": Ibid.

245   "I'm glad Martha . . .": Ibid., 364.

245   "starting life here": Ibid.

245   "no hurry": Ibid.

245   "a willfulness . . .": Ibid., 370.

246   "I wrote Marty . . .": Ibid., 373.

246   writing Buck Lanham: Ernest Hemingway to Buck Lanham, April 14, 1950, PUL.

247   "if any man . . .": HP, 31.

247   "female Flying Dutchman . . . solitary life in a cellar": HP, 60–62, 65, 75–76.

248   correspondence with Berenson: SLH, 789; H, 414–15; HW 468–69; Ernest Hemingway to Bernard Berenson, May 27, 1953, VIT.

248   "There's my beautiful Martha . . .": H, 415.

249   "discipline and skill": HP, 93.

250   As Jacqueline Orsagh has suggested: BMG, 267.

20. Open Marriage: 1952–1962

p. 251   On a trip to Italy . . . Rome: Martha Gellhorn to Eleanor Roosevelt, September 8 and March 1, 1952, FDR.

251   Edna arrived in Rome: Edna Gellhorn calendar, WUA.

252   "correctness": HP, 195.

252   "train and explore . . .": HP, 197.

252   since good Italian: HP, 204.

252   wife, profession: HP, 235.

252   "Frightfully bad luck . . .": HP, 253.

253   hiding their heartlessness: Martha Gellhorn to Bernard Berenson, September 11, 1953, VIT.

253   "You know what got me . . .": int. MLS.

253   "A big cheat" . . .: int. MLS.

253   tied down to New York: Martha Gellhorn to Bernard Berenson, July 27, 1953, VIT.

253   partly responsible: Martha Gellhorn to Bernard Berenson, August 9, 1953, VIT.

253   awkwardness: Martha Gellhorn to Eleanor Roosevelt, June 28, no year, FDR.

254   "roam freely . . .": VG, 157.

254   He was a poet: Martha Gellhorn to Bernard Berenson, December 31, 1953, VIT.

254   fiercely determined . . . day to day: MG to BB, n.d., VIT.

p. 254   Content Peckham: int. CP.

254   "We were all sitting on the floor . . .": int. CP.

255   "presence" . . . ploy: int. CP; I. S. Matthews, *Jacks or Better: A Narrative* (New York: Harper & Row, 1977), 71.

255   equal parts male and female: Martha Gellhorn to Bernard Berenson, September 17, 1953, VIT.

255   early months of the marriage: MG to BB, n.d., VIT.

255   "we all got the general impression . . .": confidential source.

255   disgusted by his social connections: Martha Gellhorn to Bernard Berenson, December 27, 1953, VIT.

255   her husband took a sympathetic view: MG to BB, March 30, 1954.

255   his inept writing: MG to BB, April 14, 1954, VIT.

256   grandiose and snide: MG to BB, April 26, 1954, VIT.

256   "hot jungle breath" . . . how he took to Hemingway: MG to BB, March 30 and April 26, 1954, VIT.

256   "extremely nice": Ernest Hemingway to Bernard Berenson, August 18, 1956, VIT.

256   Filling in the margins: EH to BB, July 9, 1955, VIT.

256   Establishing a pattern: Edna Gellhorn calendar, WUA.

256   "She didn't suffer fools . . . you wouldn't even see her": confidential source.

257   urbane, attractive pair: int. SF.

257   to be "afraid . . . dearest hope": T. S. Matthews, *Name and Address* (New York: Simon and Schuster, 1960), 3.

257   "We loved my mother . . .": T. S. Matthews, *The Worst Unsaid* (London: Anthony Blond, 1962), 98.

257   "shy and pious misfit": Matthews, *Jacks or Better,* 16.

258   "the essence . . .": Ibid., 17.

258   did not regard himself: T. S. Matthews to Allen Tate, January 16, 1942, Allen Tate Papers, Princeton University Library.

258   by his own account . . . "morbid": Matthews, *Name and Address,* 166; *Jacks or Better,* 20.

258   "Worst poet": *Jacks or Better,* 22.

258   A "slow developer . . .": Ibid., 26–27.

258   Max Gissen: "The Reminiscences of Max Gissen. Elisabeth Freidel interview with Max Gissen in New York City, 1962–1963, for the Oral History Research Office," Columbia University Library, Transcript, 155.

258   "respectable journalism . . . dirtier": Matthews, *Name and Address,* 202–03; Gissen, 200.

258   "great writing": *Name and Address,* 204.

258   company man: Ibid., 260–61.

258   told an interviewer: T. S. Matthews interview with Joan Pring in London, 20 Chester Square, 1958–59, Columbia University Library, transcript, 24.

p. 258   air of self-importance: Ibid., 46.

258   "servitude": Matthews, *Jacks or Better,* 124.

259   "respectable . . . serious": T. S. Matthews interview with Joan Pring in London, 20 Chester Square, 1958–59, Columbia University Library, Transcript, 75.

259   tough on clichés: "The Reminiscences of Max Gissen. Elizabeth Freidel interview with Max Gissen in New York City, 1962–63, for the Oral History Research Office," Columbia University Library, Transcript, 155.

259   "There are only two or three points": Ibid.

259   quite rigid: Ibid., 161.

259   compromised his integrity: Ibid., 155.

259   "higher authorities . . . unloving": Ibid., 161.

259   a devout Matthews: Ibid., 163.

259   the type of man: Ibid., 164.

259   the hero of a Graham Greene novel: Ibid., 164.

259   a compassionate, sincere man: Ibid., 160.

259   unfaithful to her: Matthews, *Jacks or Better,* 234.

259   "Love God": Ibid., 269.

259   "I am fifty-four years old" . . . totally dominated: "The Reminiscences of Max Gissen. Elizabeth Freidel interview with Max Gissen in New York City, 1962–63, for the Oral History Office," Columbia University Library, Transcript, 165.

260   "I think you should declare war on Ohio": Adlai Stevenson Oral History Project, Columbia University Library, tape recording.

260   "vulture in human form . . .": Ibid.

260   "This is not my day . . .": Matthews, *Name and Address,* 297.

260   "Communist threat . . .": Ibid., 299.

260   "fancied moral superiority . . .": Ibid., 300.

260   He liked women: "The Reminiscences of Max Gissen. Elizabeth Freidel interview with Max Gissen in New York City, 1962–63, for the Oral History Office," Columbia University Library, Transcript, 162.

261   "doom": Matthews, *The Worst Unsaid,* 68.

261   As one of Gellhorn's friends put it: unidentified letter to Edna, March 18, 1955, WUA.

261   on a treadmill: Matthews, op. cit., 93.

261   "put my best foot forward . . .": Ibid., 97.

261   censure McCarthyism itself: VG, 119.

261   access to Adlai Stevenson: Adlai Stevenson Oral History Project, Columbia University Library, tape recording; Martha Gellhorn to Eleanor Roosevelt, September 7, 1954, FDR.

262   "The Good Husband": *Collier's,* February 4, 1955, 25, 66–69.

262   sensible English electoral system: VG, 120–28.

262   no McCarthyism in England: VG, 131.

p. 262   burdensome house: Martha Gellhorn to Bernard Berenson, January 14, 27, and March 14, 1956, VIT.

262   missed him terribly: MG to BB, n.d., VIT.

262   an article in *The New Republic:* VG, 134–41.

263   "lion-hearted gaiety": VG, 150.

263   "fear neurosis": VG, 158.

263   "four years running": Martha Gellhorn, "Good Old London," *Harper's Magazine,* October 1959, 79.

263   "the hang of central heating": Ibid.

263   "So he's getting married again . . .": Ibid., 81.

263   "If I hadn't . . .": Philip Ziegler, *Diana Cooper* (New York: Knopf, 1982), 15.

264   The "background music . . .": Martha Gellhorn, "Good Old London," 81.

265   "I quit my job . . .": Matthews, *Jacks or Better,* 331.

265   "beauty was a public service": TBT, 72.

265   "elegant, serene . . .": TBT, 65.

265   "I thought Chloe . . .": TBT, 72.

266   "the exquisite curve of her mouth": TBT 61.

267   "angry to pop": TBT, 210.

267   "sister *and* brother": TBT, 211.

267   "major tic": TBT, 222.

267   Marushka loved humanity . . .": TBT, 222.

268   "nothing": TBT, 224.

268   "home": TBT, 239.

268   "everyone was poor . . .": TBT, 239.

268   "perfectibility of man" . . .": FW, 1.

268   "a special type of war profiteer": FW, 2.

268   "form of honorable behavior": FW, 3.

269   "brilliant anti-war book . . .": Herbert Mitgang, "A Message for Today," *The New York Times,* March 22, 1959, Section 7, 10.

269   "one of the best correspondents . . .": Nigel Nicolson, "A Woman at the Wars," *The New Statesman,* October 17, 1959, 517.

269   "Martha was always talking pacifism . . ." " . . . *very dramatic*": int. MTH, ELN, MLS.

269   torture for her: Martha Gellhorn to Bernard Berenson, January 8, 1959, VIT.

269   nomads: MG to BB, n.d., VIT.

269   "rentable castle": OMA, 15.

270   Edna had read: Edna Gellhorn calendar, WUA.

270   Edna was agreeable: OMA, 15.

270   "kill an ox . . . a thing": OMA, 17.

270   a bother for Martha: OMA, 19–25.

270   such a sensible person: int. MLS.

271   "terrific . . .": int. ELN.

p. 271   Each year after Edna's death: int. MTH.

271   Martha called Polk: int. WJP.

271   "overprivileged poops . . .": OMA, 36.

271   "What about all the overworked psychiatrists . . .": OMA, 40–41.

272   "forthright and funny . . .": OMA, 45.

272   a sign of her Germanic blood: Martha Gellhorn to Bernard Berenson, n.d., VIT.

272   hardly better than "Arab females": OMA, 70–71.

273   "pea-brained talkative South": OMA, 143.

273   "explosive": OMA, 143.

273   "screened-in balcony": OMA, 145.

273   reminded her of Henry James: Martha Gellhorn to Bernard Berenson, n.d., VIT.

273   "the essence of Paris": Ned Calmer, "A Nice World He Never Made," *The Saturday Review,* September 2, 1961, 19.

273   "Half my friends . . .": quoted in BMG, 318.

273   "I never thought of . . .": BMG, 356.

274   "a traveler in life": HOM, 54, 128.

274   "I had a perfectly okay time . . .": HOM, 93.

274   The truth was . . . constant and loyal friend: confidential int.

274   When Mary Hall visited her: int. MIH.

275   "the hope of the world": Matthews, *Jacks or Better,* 331.

275   "collapsing civilization": Ibid.

275   lauding the importance of the private conscience: VG, 226–43.

275   the Poles: VG, 167–82.

275   Kennedy administration: Martha Gellhorn to John Fitzgerald Kennedy, April 8, November 6, 1961., John Fitzgerald Kennedy Library, Boston, Massachusetts.

21. Africa and a New Kind of War: 1960–1966

p. 276   hideous Silesian mining town: VG, 169.

276   "the Polish Fun Fellowship": VG, 291.

277   "rules of evidence": VG, 230.

277   "the greatest organization man . . .": VG, 240.

277   deferring the consideration of all moral issues: VG, 242.

278   "Arab women of the West": VG, 254.

278   a letter to President Kennedy: Martha Gellhorn to John Fitzgerald Kennedy, April 8, 1961, John Fitzgerald Kennedy Library, Boston, Massachusetts.

278   confided to James Gavin: BMG, 325, 433.

278   "adores America . . . admit Italians": "Miss Gellhorn's Adopted Son May Become Citizen," St. Louis *Post-Dispatch,* March 28, 1961, Vertical File, MHS.

p. 278   cultivated background: Ibid.

279   wrote the President: Martha Gellhorn to John Fitzgerald Kennedy, November 6, 1961, John Fitzgerald Kennedy Library, Boston, Massachusetts.

279   hot-water bottle: TWMA, 111.

280   composedly: TWMA, 114.

280   "literally nauseated . . .": TWMA, 118.

280   an odor . . .: TWMA, 118.

281   morning bath: TWMA, 137.

281   where it was: TWMA, 138.

282   "Oh, *nice*": TWMA, 185.

282   sweated "dirty": TWMA, 197.

282   "offended damsel": TWMA, 210.

283   "mechanism . . . heart's desire": TWMA, 232.

283   In late May 1962 . . . several days in New York: Edna Gellhorn calendar, WUA.

283   on April 30, 1963: BMG, 325.

283   "terrible mistakes": H, 546, 560.

283   thank her . . . Baker described Gellhorn: BMG, 325.

284   In Chapter 41: PUL.

285   pioneering: VG, 294.

285   the noise monkeys made: VG, 260–68.

286   "an irreplaceable art museum of creation": Martha Gellhorn, "Animals Running Free, Two Weeks in the Serengeti," *The Atlantic Monthly,* February 1966, 76.

286   "time sense": Martha Gellhorn, "Tanganyika: African New Frontier," *The Atlantic Monthly,* September 1963, 42.

286   Martha's apprehensions: Reverend Langton to Edna Gellhorn, June 23 and November 10, 1964, WUA.

286   napalming poor villagers: VG, 295.

287   "Buster": VG, 270.

287   people whose lives: VG, 277.

287   admirable virtues: VG, 275.

288   lovely black woman: VG, 275.

288   Flanner's encouraging letter: Martha Gellhorn to Janet Flanner, May 18, 1966, Janet Flanner–Solita Solano Papers, Library of Congress, Manuscript Division.

288   Earlier: MG to JF, April 5, 1966, Janet Flanner–Solita Solano Papers, Library of Congress, Manuscript Division.

289   immerse himself: LTHT, 163.

289   not exactly stay-at-homes: LTHT, 164.

290   "good Americans": BMG, 336.

290   contacts . . . too old: VG, 296.

290   censored herself: FW, 262.

290   unrecorded: FW, 230.

290   no conscience: FW, 233.

p. 291   overstaffed war commands: FW, 242.
 291   Gellhorn reminded her readers: FW, 262.
 291   South Vietnamese blacklist: VG, 296.
 291   "grossly careless": FW, 270.
 291   Nuremberg: FW, 274.
 292   *"single"*: VG, 281.
 292   deficient in insight and mercy: VG, 284.
 292   "all theaters of war . . .": FW, 279.
 292   Americans suffered most: FW, 280.
 292   "we are overweight . . .": FW, 238.
 292   "joined the Vietcong": VG, 298.

22. Hope Against Hope: 1967–1972

p. 293   "bombed by poverty": FW, 250.
 293   she asked him in disgust: FW, 250.
 293   "Negro" looks: FW, 250.
 294   fortitude and wisdom . . . "safe for the world": FW, 250.
 294   Nasser had vowed: FW, 283–84.
 294   "Slaughter . . .": FW, 284.
 294   Israel had . . . Israeli Arabs: Ibid.
 294   "unparalleled military achievement": FW, 287.
 294   bunches of rags: FW, 285.
 294   Men wore beards: Martha Gellhorn, "The Israeli Secret Weapon," *Vogue,* October 1967, 192.
 295   "soft black ballet slippers": FW, 286.
 295   dribbling lips: FW, 287.
 295   Bethlehem: FW, 291.
 295   a battle of armies: FW, 295.
 295   murder all Jews: FW, 298.
 295   35 million refugees: FW, 302.
 296   encyclopedic letters: Martha Gellhorn to Edna Gellhorn, n.d., WUA.
 296   outwitting pessimistic physicians: T. S. Matthews to Edna Gellhorn, n.d., WUA.
 296   heard from Diana Cooper: TSM to EG, June 17, 1968, WUA.
 296   unpredictable: TSM to EG, June 3, 1968, WUA.
 296   gas-fueled icebox: Martha Gellhorn to Edna Gellhorn, June 12, 1968, WUA.
 296   lumbered along: MG to EG, June 15, 1968, WUA.
 297   sad notes: MG to EG, June 20, 1968, WUA.
 297   to watch inane television: Martha Gellhorn to Edna Gellhorn, June 29, 1968, WUA.
 297   sunny: Ibid.

p. 297   disorderly and incompetent: MG to EG, July 12, 1968, WUA.
297   Ten days later: MG to EG, July 24, 1968, WUA.
297   the most serious: MG to EG, August 9, 1968, WUA.
297   Felicia Bernstein: MG to EG, August 24, 1968, WUA.
297   indomitable woman: VG, 286.
298   "Fuck Nixon": VG, 308.
298   on her smile: VG, 309.
298   "I'm here to see my mother": int. MLS.
298   Edna was far more giving: int. MTH.
298   "The reason I talk so much . . .": int. MTH.
299   "My mother is definitely going to die . . .": int. MLS. Gellhorn questions the accuracy of the first full paragraph on this page.
299   Walter's wife, Kitty: int. MTH, AF.
299   family tensions: Martha Gellhorn to Edna Gellhorn, July 24, 1968, WUA.
299   "paralysis . . . gripped": VG, 328.
300   disorganized group . . . wandering: TWMA, 277–79.
300   Knowles was seeking: A. S. Knowles to Martha Gellhorn, February 29, 1972, courtesy of A. S. Knowles.
301   On May 3: Martha Gellhorn to A. S. Knowles, May 3, 1972, courtesy of A. S. Knowles.
301   Knowles visited Gellhorn: letter to author from A. S. Knowles, August 25, 1988.
302   quick, sharp style: TWMA, 236.
302   "Thank you, my blossom": TWMA, 272.
303   other people's anguish: TWMA, 263.
303   the most appalling event: TWMA, 263.
303   "Stalin-Gothic": TWMA, 243.
303   the landscape: TWMA, 239.
303   "Squalor Society": TWMA, 244.
303   "claustrophobic prison-land": TWMA, 272.
303   one of the gods: VG, 329.
303   she rang doorbells: BMG, 380.
303   Martha Kessler: int. MK.
304   "last hurrah": BMG, 380–81.

23. Never Give Up: 1972–1988

p. 305   James Gavin was sure: BMG, 381.
305   attacking Nixon's "peace with honor": BMG, 381.
305   precedent for succeeding generations: BMG, 381.
305   expansive world: VG, 329.
306   large, bright, austere . . . wastebasket: BMG, 384.
306   never getting close enough: TWMA, 235.

p. 306   Markham's sturdy "settler" furnishings: quoted in Mary Lovell, *Straight On Till Morning: A Biography of Beryl Markham* (New York: St. Martin's Press, 1987), 312.

306   condescending and contemptuous: WIA, 15.

307   heavy depression: WIA, 23.

307   "inner and outer weather . . .": Victoria Glendinning, "Colonials," *The New York Times Book Review,* March 30, 1980, 9.

308   quiet immensity of the view: TWMA, 233.

308   incredibly fresh and clear: WIA, 87–88.

309   never did entirely please her: BMG, 387.

309   to contact protestors in the Soviet Union: VG, 323.

309   "She tells the people . . .": VG, 332.

309   It was a different country . . . reviewed: MGRL, 1–2, 33–34.

310   immobilizing rage attacks: Martha Gellhorn, "My Private Anti-Anger War in This Mad, Mad World, *Times* [London] October 1, 1975, 12a.

310   "apocryphiars": OA, 281.

311   "banter between Hemingway and her . . .": OA, 304.

311   "Built-in falsehood . . .": OA, 281.

312   "firsthand" description of an air raid: OA, 292.

312   "slowly floated . . .": OA, 293.

312   mentally unstable: Martha Gellhorn to Marion Meade, April 6, 1983, courtesy of Marion Meade.

312   cruel and false: Martha Gellhorn to the author, May 23, 1986.

313   Richard Whelan: int. RW.

313   Danish Modern: int. BK.

313   "pacts": int. BK.

313   "Not quite so angry . . . today": "Interview with Helen Bell de Freitas '31 by Caroline Smith Rittenhouse '52," London, May 7, 1985, 12.

314   "went round . . . abusive behavior": Jeffrey Meyers, "The Quest for Hemingway," *Virginia Quarterly Review,* Autumn 1985, 592–93.

314   "nobody would send" her: Julia Edwards, *Women of the World: The Great Foreign Correspondents* (Boston: Houghton Mifflin, 1988), 133.

315   moral distinction: FW, 326.

316   intimate form of address in Spanish: VG, 384.

317   choices and the liberty: VG, 349.

317   thrilled Gellhorn: VG, 351.

317   "fact of history": VG, 353.

317   "I hope I won't . . .": TRT, 398.

318   "an Historic Monument . . . chaps": TRT, 398.

318   a staunch noncomformist . . . snorkeling: Susan Crossland, "Messages from Martha," *Times* magazine (London), March 30, 1986, 36–38.

318   "100 million people" . . . "theory of history": FW, 333.:

p. 318   write about her mother: MGRL, 62–63.

319   "global fellowship " . . . "Never give up": VG, 419.

Epilogue

p. 321   His reply: T. S. Matthews to author, April 26, 1988.

322   as Max Lerner witnessed: int. ML.

322   "She claimed . . .": confidential int.

322   "her enthusiasms . . .": confidential int.

322   As one of Edna's friends has observed: WUA.

322   Martha exploded into the room: Roger Baldwin to Edna Gellhorn, May 21, 1964, WUA.

323   "much biography . . .": Phyllis Rose, *Parallel Lives: Five Victorian Marriages* (New York: Vintage Books, 1984), 5.

323   "on the basis of . . .": Rose, 7.

323   "We are desperate . . .": Rose, 9.

323   "the idea of family life . . . ": Rose, 7.

324   "She was always restless . . .": confidential int.

ACKNOWLEDGMENTS

I began the research for this biography in the summer of 1987 as I was completing a draft of *Lillian Hellman: Her Legend and Her Legacy*. Martha Gellhorn figures in that biography in a very small way, having met Hellman a few times and having attacked her veracity in a savagely amusing article in the *Paris Review*. Eighteen months earlier, an editor had suggested a Gellhorn biography when my work on Hellman was still in the proposal stage. My time spent on Hellman was also a time of mulling over the possibilities of writing about Gellhorn's life.

Biographers depend on sources, so I made a quick survey of what I could draw upon. There was Gellhorn's work itself, some of it clearly autobiographical. While the Hemingway biographies concentrated on her years with him, they contained evidence of her earlier and later life. I had the good fortune to have at hand Bernice Kert's excellent book on Hemingway's women and Jacqueline Orsagh's informative Ph.D. dissertation on Gellhorn's life and work. Members of the Gellhorn family, particularly her mother, Edna, were well-known in St. Louis. Surely there would be valuable information there to examine. Judging from my experience on the Hellman book, I knew that by diligent research and interviewing I would obtain the essential materials for a biography. I decided to proceed.

By the fall of 1987, I was corresponding with several libraries in search of manuscripts, documents, and correspondence, and with several people who might be willing to be interviewed. Not surprisingly, there were some who did not wish to speak while Martha Gellhorn was still alive; others spoke with the understanding that they would not be identified. Still getting my bearings, I wrote to St. Mary's High School in St. Louis (at the recommendation of a librarian) to ask about Martha Gellhorn's school records. In a cordial reply, the school's principal, Eleanore Berra Marfisi, noted that had Gellhorn attended St. Mary's she would have been in "deep trouble! Our school is an all-male student body and has been for over half a century." In reply to my letter addressed to James Gavin, I received another cheerful correction: "I am sorry to disappoint you, but

I am afraid you have got the wrong General Gavin! I have never known Martha Gellhorn so I imagine that you want my American namesake— General James Gavin, wartime commander of the U.S. 82nd Airborne Division (hero of the battle for the Nijmegen bridge)." Kyle Crichton wrote me to say, "I'd like to help you with your research, but I'm afraid I can't. I'm not the Kyle Crichton you want. He was my grandfather, who died in 1960. He'd be 91 if alive today."

I got help at just the right time from a friend and fellow biographer, Ann Waldron, who gave me the address of Delia Mares, one of Edna Gellhorn's close associates. Mrs. Mares, in turn, provided me with the names, addresses, and phone numbers of several people in St. Louis whom I was able to visit and interview: Mrs. Virginia Deutch, Mrs. Aaron Fischer, Mary Taussig Hall, and Emily Lewis Norcross. Mrs. Hall suggested I see William Julius Polk and Martha Love Symington, both of whom were very helpful on Martha Gellhorn's St. Louis years. Mrs. Deutch provided an invaluable tape recording of Edna Gellhorn and helped me to secure an important early photograph of Martha.

My trip to St. Louis in April 1988 yielded an enormous amount of information. Carol O. Daniel, director of the library of the John Burroughs School, took me on a tour of the school, provided me with Gellhorn's publications in *The John Burroughs Review,* and assisted me in obtaining several photographs, and a recording of Edna Gellhorn speaking at the school. Patricia Adams, Associate Director of the Western Historical Manuscript Collection, University of Missouri-St. Louis, was especially helpful in locating information on the Gellhorn and Fischel families. Charles Brown, reference librarian of the St. Louis Mercantile Library, retrieved from clipping files a number of significant items. Noel C. Holobeck in the History and Genealogy Department of the St. Louis Public Library patiently dealt with my inquiries about the Fischels and Gellhorns and recommended Mrs. Coralee Paull, who did some of the genealogical investigation for me and turned up several items that proved useful. Beryl Manne and Kevin Ray of the Washington University Archives, John M. Olin Library, made available files from the Edna Gellhorn Collection, and Katherine Burg sent materials from the Mary Institute.

Outside of St. Louis, several librarians and archivists have supplied me with invaluable information: Fred Bauma, Manuscripts Reading Room, Library of Congress, Washington, D.C.; Denison Beach, Houghton Reading Room, Houghton Library, Harvard University, Cambridge,

Massachusetts; Norman B. Brown and Anne E. Champagne, Special Collections, University Library, University of Illinois, Urbana-Champaign; Ned Comstock, Archives of Performing Arts, University Library, University of Southern California, Los Angeles, California; Megan Floyd Desnoyers, John Fitzgerald Kennedy Library, Boston, Massachusetts; Ken Duckett, University of Oregon Library, Eugene, Oregon; Fiorella Superbi Gioffredi, Villa I Tati, Florence, Italy; Alan Goodrich, John Fitzgerald Kennedy Library, Boston, Massachusetts; Cathy Henderson, Harry Ransom Humanities Research Center, University of Texas, Austin, Texas; James R. Hobin, Albany Public Library, Albany, New York; John Hoffman, University of Illinois Library, Urbana-Champaign, Illinois; Patrick Lawler, Rare Books and Manuscripts, Columbia University Library, New York City; Jane Moreton and Jean Preston, Firestone Library, Princeton University, Princeton, New Jersey; Caroline Rittenhouse, Bryn Mawr College Library, Bryn Mawr, Pennsylvania; Elizabeth Shenton, The Arthur and Elizabeth Schlesinger Library on the History of Women in America, Radcliffe College, Cambridge, Massachusetts; Andar Skotnes, Biographical Oral History Collection, Columbia University Library, New York City; Audrey J. Smith, Humanities Reference Services, New York State Library, Albany, New York; Raymond Teichman, Franklin D. Roosevelt Library, Hyde Park, New York; Ann Van Arsdale, Firestone Library, Princeton University, Princeton, New Jersey; Patricia C. Willis, Beinecke Rare Book and Manuscript Library, Yale University, New Haven, Connecticut.

Lisa Middents at the John Fitzgerald Kennedy Library in Boston, Massachusetts, assiduously sought out items that might be of interest to me in the Ernest Hemingway Collection. Similarly, Hilary Cummings in Special Collections, University of Oregon Library, Eugene, Oregon, not only did a thorough search of the Joseph Stanley Pennell Papers, she also put me in touch with two researchers, Mary Anteaux and Sally Hague, who found more material. It was my good fortune that Sally Hague, having returned to New York City, was able to do further research in Special Collections at the New York Public Library, where the *Collier's* magazine archive—which had been under my nose—had been located by Rutherford Witthus, a librarian at Auraria Library in Denver, Colorado, contacted by my old friend Joan Fiscella. Eric Neubacher, who is known as the genius of interlibrary loan at Baruch College, saved me many hours of time and trouble in securing hard-to-find books and articles. Similarly, Diane DiMartino went out of her way to conduct successful searches for information that I could define only in the vaguest terms.

An American Council of Learned Societies grant-in-aid provided the assistance and the recognition that made it possible for me to complete my research more quickly than I had anticipated.

I have often found it profitable to call upon my fellow biographers for information and advice. Bernice Kert was very generous in giving me background information about *The Hemingway Women*. Jeffrey Meyers suggested several avenues of research, gave me a quick sketch of Gellhorn, and directed my attention to a stimulating article he had written about researching his Hemingway biography. Michael Reynolds wrote me a very thoughtful letter. One of his suggestions led me to the discovery of a cache of new material at the New York Public Library. Similarly, Kenneth S. Lynn suggested an archival source that was of immense help to my biography. When I wrote to Genevieve Dormann inquiring about the life of Bertrand de Jouvenel, she recommended that I consult his associate Jeannie Malige, who, in turn, gave me the address of John R. Braun, who sent me a detailed letter about his biography of Jouvenel and several articles Gellhorn published in France. Marion Meade shared her Gellhorn correspondence with me and alerted me to an important item in the Houghton Library at Harvard. Richard Whelan answered a letter of mine with a friendly phone call about his impressions of interviewing Gellhorn for his biography of Robert Capa. Other biographers, Blanche Cooke, Eric Gordon, Robert Newman, Joan Peyser, and Frances Saunders have been great sources of information, inspiration, encouragement, and advice.

Frederick Vanderbilt Field patiently went over for me his reminiscences of Gellhorn and Hemingway, which are included in his autobiography—as did Stanley Flink, who had a passing but vivid recollection of Martha Gellhorn and T. S. Matthews. Sydney Knowles shared his Gellhorn correspondence and his sharp memory of their meeting. Frances Saunders alerted me to the existence of David R. Meeker's fine Hemingway collection. I am indebted to Mr. Meeker (Nick Adams & Co., Rare Books) for allowing me to examine the superb materials he has collected.

Minnie Magazine of the Time-Life Alumni Association tracked down several of T. S. Matthews's *Time* colleagues for me, including Mrs. Joseph Cowan (Content Peckham), who treated me to a rare glimpse of the inner workings of the magazine. Randall "Pete" Smith provided what he called a "worm's-eye view" of what it was like in Spain during Hemingway's and Gellhorn's sojourn there. Pauline Gadd put me in touch with her uncle and aunt, Ron and Beryl Gadd, whose hospitality and helpfullness made my trip to Wales such a success.

Several people should be acknowledged for responding to my requests for information: Cornell Capa, Norman Cousins, Max Lerner, and Roger W. Straus.

In the fall of 1987, shortly after I arrived at Baruch College and assumed my position as Associate Dean, I found several colleagues eager to hear about my work and to help in a variety of ways. I am indebted to Martin Stevens for his recollections of Germany in the 1930s and to Martha Kessler for the glimpse she gave me of Gellhorn working on the McGovern campaign. In the busy office of the Dean of Liberal Arts and Sciences, a cheerful staff helped with the countless tasks involved in producing a biography. I thank them all: Denise Cascini, Connie Conway-Terrero, Marcia Laguer, Eileen Leary, Ken Liebowitz, Joyce Marrotta, Violet Parnass, Carmen Pedrogo, David Thomas, and Marlene Thompson. Dean Norman Fainstein, my colleague and good friend, provided the strong support that is needed when a scholar is trying to balance the demands of administration and research.

Midway through the writing of this biography, I assumed the position of Acting Associate Provost of Baruch College, a position I could not have taken on without the full confidence of President Joel Segall, Provost Paul LeClerc, Acting Provost John McGarraghy, and Associate Provost Louanne Kennedy. My secretary, Lenora Rock, has performed more services for this book than she knows—as have Miriam Allen, Evelyn Bargas, Katherine Curtis, Jacqueline Gathers, and Tessa Rougier. For last-minute assistance I thank Debra Dorry and Yat Wong.

My agent, Elizabeth Knappman of New England Publishing Associates, has been a joy to work with in the shaping of this book. Toni Lopopolo, my editor, has been a believer in my work for a long time and has worked hard to make it a success. In the day-to-day existence of the writer—when I have needed the right word—I have always turned to my wife, Dr. Lisa Paddock. I have never felt the need of another muse.

INDEX

385